IN SEARCH OF THE CLASSIC

STEVEN SHANKMAN

IN SEARCH
OF THE CLASSIC

RECONSIDERING THE
GRECO-ROMAN TRADITION,
HOMER TO VALÉRY
AND BEYOND

THE PENNSYLVANIA STATE UNIVERSITY PRESS
UNIVERSITY PARK, PENNSYLVANIA

Library of Congress Cataloging-in-Publication Data

Shankman, Steven, 1947–
    In search of the classic / Steven Shankman.

        p.   cm.
    Includes bibliographical references and index.
    ISBN 0-271-01322-2 (cloth). —ISBN 0-271-01323-0 (paper)
    1. Canon (Literature)   2. Literature—History and criticism.
I. Title.
PN81.S375   1994
809—dc20   93-35008
                                                                      CIP

Published by The Pennsylvania State University Press,
University Park, PA 16802-1003

For my mother and to the memory of my father

CONTENTS

PREFACE

What is a classic? This question provided the title of two well-known essays, the first by Charles Augustin Sainte-Beuve in 1850 and the second by T. S. Eliot in 1944. As Eliot began, so must I by stating what I do not mean by the word *classic*. I do not mean a work by a canonical author. I do not mean a work that says "what oft was thought but ne'er so well express'd" and therefore elicits from us the response, "This is a classic." I do not use the term in opposition to *romantic*. Nor do I necessarily mean by it the "classical" literatures of Greece and Rome, although I do discuss works from those literatures and suggest that my understanding of the classic was in fact first articulated in Greek and Roman literature and literary theory.

In today's climate of critical opinion one answer to the question "What is a classic?" comes readily to mind: a classic work of literature is a work that for political reasons those in power have decided to call a classic. There is some merit to this definition, for there are classics that have indeed created, or have attempted to create, a political order, and their status is in part derived from their relation to that political order. Homer's poems, for example, were probably composed, in part, in order to create a Hellenic identity after the disastrous end of the Mycenaean age. Virgil's *Aeneid* was an attempt to create a mythological paradigm for the Rome of Augustus. It is thus perhaps no coincidence that Eliot—twenty years before he addressed the Virgil Society on the topic of the classic—could say "I am all for empires."[1]

---

1. Quoted in Frank Kermode, *The Classic* (London: Faber & Faber, 1975), 15. Eliot's remark appeared in the *Transatlantic Review*, January 1924.

There is, then, a relation between the notion of the classic and politics, even the notion of the classic and imperialism.[2]

"A classic, according to the usual definition," Sainte-Beuve writes—in "Qu'est-ce qu'un classique?"—"is an author of past times, already hallowed by general admiration, who is an authority in his own style." Sainte-Beuve continues:

> The word *classic,* taken in this sense, begins to appear among the Romans. With them the *classici,* properly so called, were not all the citizens of the different classes, but only those of the highest class, who possessed, at least, an income of a certain fixed figure. All those who had a lower income were known by the appellation of *infra classem,* below *the* class, properly so called. For example, we find the word *classicus* used by Aulus Gellius and applied to writers: a writer of worth and mark is *classicus assiduusque scriptor,* a writer who counts, who has some possessions under the sun, and who is not confounded with the proletariat crowd.[3]

As Frank Kermode informs us, it was Aulus Gellius, a second-century author who was himself something of a snob, who first applied the term *classic* to an author. And the *classicus scriptor,* according to Gellius, is specifically *non proletarius.*[4] The word *classic,* then, has clear social implications, if we trace it back to its philological origin, with the very kind of elitism that many critics find offensive today.[5] For Aulus Gellius, a classic author was a classy thing to be.[6]

2. As Kermode explains, Eliot in 1924 approved of empires as opposed to competing, petty nationalisms (ibid.). Given the bloody history of the competing nations of Europe, Eliot's remarks gain some substance.

3. "Qu'est-ce qu'un classique?" trans. A. J. Butler, under the title "What Is a Classic?" in *Critical Theory Since Plato,* ed. Hazard Adams, rev. ed. (New York: Harcourt Brace Jovanovich, 1992), 568.

4. Kermode, *The Classic,* 15.

5. As E. R. Curtius anticipates in his important chapter on classicism in *European Literature and the Latin Middle Ages,* trans. Willard Trask (New York: Harper & Row, 1963), 249–50. There Curtius quotes Sainte-Beuve's paraphrase of Gellius's description of the classic author in the following, "un écrivain de valeur et de marque, un écrivain qui comte, qui a du bien au soleil, et qui n'est pas confondu dans la foule des prolétaires." The great scholar then goes on to remark, "What a tidbit for a Marxist sociology of literature!"

6. This seemingly political meaning of "classic" has a less politically charged precedent in those Alexandrian scholars who, as Gregory Nagy informs us, considered "the Classical authors" those "who were 'judged worthy of inclusion' within the canon" and hence "were called the

The classic may thus legitimately be viewed as a work that confers prestige on its reader, its worth conveyed by its status as a classic. To adapt a remark of Samuel Johnson (*Rambler,* no. 156), however, the task in the evaluation of literature is to distinguish that which is right only because it is established from that which is established because it is right. The classic must continually re-earn and, in a sense, overcome the prestige of its own canonicity. There indeed exists a continual tension between the classic as intrinsically valuable and essential, and the classic as a work the institutionalized mastery of which brings social and political prestige to its approved explicator. Although the works I discuss in this book are drawn from the Western tradition, it is worth observing here that we see this tension in the very word *ching* (classic) in the Chinese tradition. According to one plausible etymology of the word *classic* in Chinese, the Chinese written character (糹巠) is compounded of ideographs depicting the vertical threads of silk (糹) on a loom (巠). The warp, which consists of these vertical threads, is the heart of the loom and is twisted harder than the woof, with which these threads are crossed in the process of weaving. The ideographs in the word *ching* therefore suggest that the classic, by analogy to the warp of a loom, is something enduring and essential.[7] On the other hand, the mastery of the classics in traditional Chinese society brought political power and prestige to those who excelled in the notoriously arduous civil service examinations, which were based on the Confucian understanding of the classics. The conservatism associated with the institutionalization of the Chinese classic has often eclipsed the value that can be seen in the classic as a work that is essential, which creates a tension in Chinese culture that continues to be felt.

In reductionist ideological or political criticism, this tension collapses. The question of value is often ignored, and in some cases the possibility of the existence of rational critical evaluation is dismissed as trivial or even denied. In this book I argue the following, currently unorthodox positions: first, there is a conception of literature that can be called "classical" in the

---

enkrithentes, a term that corresponds to the Roman concept of the *classici,* who are authors of the 'first class,' *primae classis."* From his "Early Greek Views of Poets and Poetry," in *The Cambridge History of Literary Criticism,* vol. 1, *Classical Criticism* (Cambridge: Cambridge University Press, 1989), 1. Nagy is referring here to Rudolf Pfeiffer, *History of Classical Scholarship from the Beginnings to the End of the Hellenistic Age* (London: Oxford University Press, 1968), 206–7.

7. I am indebted to Stephen Durrant for this etymology.

normative rather than in the vulgarly political sense; and second, that interpretation is always evaluative, whether or not we are conscious of the
principles that inform our acts of evaluation and however imperfect those
acts of evaluation might be. It is, in part, in the awareness that our attempts
at critical evaluation and inquiry—specifically an inquiry into the nature of
literature—are always subject to revision that I have titled this book *In
Search of the Classic* and not, for instance, *The Discovery of the Classic.* The
very word classic may imply, for some, an absolutist conception of truth
memorialized and sealed forever in marble. It is this view of the classic that
Heinrich Wölfflin had in mind when he remarked, "The word 'classic' has a
somewhat chilly sound."[8] I am obviously thinking of something very different and more fluid.

Hans-Georg Gadamer comes close to my meaning of the word as it will
emerge in this book. The classical, for Gadamer, exists in the tension between the historical moment and what is enduring. "The classical," Gadamer
writes, "is what resists historical criticism because its historical dominion,
that binding power of its validity that is preserved and handed down, precedes all historical reflection and continues through it."[9] Gadamer here
articulates my own view, especially if we understand the word "precedes" in
the Aristotelian sense that the very apprehension of any particular necessi-
tates our simultaneous awareness of the general or universal in which that
particular participates. "What we call classical," Gadamer continues, "is
something retrieved from the vicissitudes of changing time and its changing
taste. . . . [It] is a consciousness of something enduring, of significance that
cannot be lost and is independent of all the circumstances of time, in which
we call something 'classical'—a kind of timeless present that is contemporaneous with every other age."[10]

Thus the "classical" should not be confused with a particular historical
period of Western antiquity, even if it owes its original emergence to the
literary and philosophical explorations of Greek authors from the eighth
through the fourth centuries B.C. This book is constructed as a series of
related essays that search for and attempt to formulate the shape of the
continuing presence—as embodied in particular literary works mainly from
Western antiquity and from the neoclassical and modern periods—of what I
am positing as a "classical" understanding of literature. The theme of this

8. Quoted as one of the epigraphs to Kermode, *The Classic,* 15.
9. *Truth and Method* (New York: Crossroad, 1986), 255.
10. Ibid., 256.

study, then, runs counter to the tendency of the newer historicisms to consider literature as just one semiotic system or set of discursive practices among many. I explicitly "privilege" literature, not arbitrarily, but because the classical view that I shall be defending argues that literature offers one of the fullest ways of understanding and representing human experience.

I should state, at the outset and as explicitly and concisely as possible, what I mean by a classic: in terms of what I call the classical position, a work of literature is a compelling, formally coherent, and rationally defensible representation that resists being reduced either to the mere recording of material reality, on the one hand, or to the bare exemplification of an abstract philosophical precept, on the other.[11] I have drawn this definition largely from my own reading of Greek literature from Homer through Plato, from the history of literary criticism, and from the Greco-Roman tradition in English, American, and French literature. It is essentially an Aristotelian—or for reasons that will become clear in the course of this book, a *Platonic/ Aristotelian*—defense of poetry. I am wary of definitions, and am in sympathy with Samuel Johnson's belief that "to circumscribe poetry by a definition will only shew the narrowness of the definer,"[12] but in teaching the history of criticism over a number of years I have found that any literary theory that slights any one of the components of this paradigm to that extent leaves out a crucial element of what literature uniquely has to offer.

The book is divided into four sections. Part 1 ("Classic Rationality") is addressed to what I understand by "reason" as implied in the phrase "rationally defensible." After the Enlightenment narrowed the very concept of reason and in the wake of the contemporary attacks against "logocentrism," it seems necessary to devote the first three chapters to the recovery of the meaning of rationality in the classic sense before we even begin to discuss literature or poetry per se. In the three parts that follow I describe how authors resist the reduction of their works to formalism for its own sake (Part 2: "The Limits of Formalism"); to the bare exemplification of abstract philosophical precepts, that is, to didacticism or ideology (Part 3, "Resisting

11. One can find this position articulated even today. In defense of poetry, Timothy Steele has recently written: "Neither abstracted to philosophical precept nor confined to the literalness of history, poetry can speak with special vividness and comprehensiveness" (*Missing Measures: Modern Poetry and the Revolt Against Meter* [Fayetteville: University of Arkansas Press, 1990], 293). In this analysis of why modern poetry abandoned meter, Steele argues for a return to form to complement the resistance to didacticism and to mimetic literalism.

12. *Life of Pope*, in *Lives of the English Poets*, ed. G. B. Hill, 3 vols. (Oxford: Clarendon Press, 1905), 3:251.

the Didactic Heresy"); or to the mere recording of material reality (Part 4, "Resisting Mimetic Literalism").[13]

If we want to know what literature is, we must go back to its sources and follow the original articulations of literary forms through their various re-statements. We must go back to the source, for as Eric Voegelin puts it, that is where the water is clearest.[14] To be as specific as possible, we cannot evaluate Derrida's critique of "logocentrism" without returning to the Platonic texts that allegedly gave rise to this concept; for, as I shall suggest, Derrida's real target is not what Plato means by reason but rather the rationalist tradition from Descartes through Hegel. We cannot understand what Jonathan Swift means—in his critique of what was the new concept of rationality in his day—by the phrase *animal rationis capax* unless we return to the classical understanding of reason in Plato. We cannot appreciate what a poet like William Collins is trying to achieve in the Pindaric "Ode on the Poetical Character" unless we go back to Pindar. We cannot understand J. V. Cunningham's poem "Montana Pastoral" unless we know something about the pastoral tradition. And, on a more general level, we cannot evaluate a particular poem without making assumptions about what poetry or literature is.

It is not only the notion of the classic that has come under attack in recent discussions about literature and the curriculum; the category of the "literary" itself has been scrutinized by recent criticism. Much of contemporary theory places itself in opposition to New Critical formalism, and with that stance believes itself to be thereby questioning the ontological status of literature. Jacques Derrida, for example, in his essay "Le Parergon,"[15] points out the logical inconsistencies in Kant's analysis of "disinterestedness" and of "purposiveness without purpose" in those sections of *The Critique of Judgment* that are the source of New Critical modern aestheticism. Derrida's analysis is typically subtle and relentless, and he does convincingly call into question the logical coherence of the Kantian analysis. Terry Eagleton, in *The Ideology of the Aesthetic,* attempts to uncover the hidden ideological assumptions that make their way into the allegedly apolitical aestheticism of

13. In its overall conception of the nature of literature and of the kinds of reductive theories to which literature is subject, this book is indebted to Wesley Trimpi's landmark study of the history of literary theory, *Muses of One Mind: The Literary Analysis of Experience and Its Continuity* (Princeton: Princeton University Press, 1983).

14. Voegelin's remark to Gregor Sebba is recorded in Sebba's "Prelude and Variations on the Theme of Eric Voegelin," *The Southern Review* 13 (Autumn 1977): 658n.

15. "Le Parergon" is chapter 2 of *La Vérité en peinture* (Paris: Flammarion, 1978).

Kant.[16] But even if both of these influential thinkers are correct in their critiques of aestheticism, have they thereby called into question the onto- logical status of literature? They have done so only if we accept the equation of literature with the formalism—derived most immediately from Kant— that we associate with the New Criticism. One of the purposes of this book is to present an alternative to the eighteenth-century aestheticism of which much of postmodernism is a critique. But I also wish to pose an alternative to ideological criticism, for I argue that literature, in the classic sense, has traditionally resisted being deformed into an ideological tool.

I discuss authors mainly from antiquity and the neoclassical period of the late seventeenth through the eighteenth centuries, but I shall also be discuss- ing three twentieth-century poets: Paul Valéry, Yvor Winters, and J. V. Cun- ningham. There is an important rationale for including these writers. T. S. Eliot is the poet who most readily comes to mind in discussions of the classic or of classicism. After all, it was Eliot who wrote the famous essay "What Is a Classic?" where he made his case for the quintessential classicism of the *Aeneid.* And Eliot, toward the end of his career, declared his allegiance to classicism, along with Anglicanism and royalism, three allegiances not necessarily linked. But what make Eliot and his stylistic maestro, Ezra Pound, less classical in my view than the three poets I have just mentioned is that they both abandoned traditional meter in favor of a vers libre that ranges from the gorgeous to the banal. Even the freest-seeming verse of Greek lyric poetry—the odes of Pindar or the choruses of Euripides' plays—scan pre- cisely. If, in terms of my own definition, formal coherence is one of the requirements of the classic, then the classical status of any poem that es- chews the three-thousand-year-old tradition of formal meter is cast into serious doubt. The three modern poets I discuss write as rigorously and regularly metrical a poetic line as Homer or Horace.

The historical emergence of philosophy, and in particular the philosophi- cal speculations of Plato, may be viewed as a concrete response to the

---

16. *The Ideology of the Aesthetic* (London: Basil Blackwell, 1990). Eagleton distances himself from those reductive ideological critics who associate the aesthetic only with "the dread phrase 'liberal humanist' " (8) and thereby disavow the importance of Enlightenment thought, which made possible true revolutionary, Marxist thought. Although Eagleton there- fore distinguishes himself from extreme reductionism, he nevertheless views literature/ literary theory as important only insofar as it promotes revolutionary social change. Eagleton and the reductionists from which he wishes to distance himself thus share the view that serious criticism is didactic. Eagleton's critical position—when viewed from the perspective of the present study—therefore represents a deformation of the classic as articulated in this book.

existential and spiritual disorder of the late fifth and early fourth centuries B.C. The articulation of philosophical experience was thus a way to analyze and resist the pressures of the prevailing climate of opinion. Philosophizing does not happen in a vacuum. *In Search of the Classic* thus attempts both to illuminate and enact the classical philosophical stance by questioning the current climate of critical discourse in literary studies.

There is no doubt that "the politics of interpretation" has to a considerable extent dictated to the academy what texts are taught and who gets to teach them. These issues need to be raised. Any accepted canon of authors must be challenged on rational grounds and that canon—that is, our curriculum—adapted and expanded. As someone who studied at Stanford with some of the students of the deeply classical and therefore allegedly iconoclastic Yvor Winters, I experienced personally how the power of received opinion and academic prestige can make it almost impossible for a marginalized voice—in this case, the voice of Winters, or the voices of his students—to be heard. The appearance of new works or the serious consideration of previously unnoticed or undervalued works is an opportunity for us to examine our own assumptions about the nature of literature.

Since our experience of literature is structured by our assumptions about it, whether or not we are conscious of those assumptions, it would seem useful to try to discover and to formulate quite explicitly what we might take to be a normative understanding of the distinctive nature of literature. I believe the time is ripe for such an endeavor. For when a famous critic like Terry Eagleton says that literature does not exist, and that we may discover tomorrow that Shakespeare is worthless;[17] when Paul de Man says that there is essentially no difference between literature and criticism,[18] then perhaps it is time to begin thinking again about what distinguishes literature from other efforts of the human mind, to search for the classic. And if we find it, or if we even begin to sense that we may be on its trail, then perhaps there is a chance that those of us who have devoted our lives to the study of literature may not, after all, have simply made a naive and clumsy mistake.

17. *Literary Theory: An Introduction* (Minneapolis: University of Minnesota Press, 1983), 10: "We can drop once and for all the illusion that the category 'literature' is 'objective,' in the sense of being eternally given and immutable. Anything can be literature, and anything which is regarded as unalterably and unquestionably literature—Shakespeare, for example—can cease to be literature."

18. "Semiology and Rhetoric," in *Allegories of Reading: Figural Language in Rousseau, Nietzsche, Rilke, and Proust* (New Haven: Yale University Press, 1979), 19: The "difference between . . . literature" and "criticism" is "delusive." De Man's essay was originally published in *Diacritics* in 1975.

ACKNOWLEDGMENTS

The early stages of this project were generously supported by an Andrew W. Mellon Faculty Fellowship at Harvard University in 1984–85 and a John Simon Guggenheim Memorial Foundation Fellowship in 1985–86. I wish to thank, as well, the Oregon Humanities Center for its timely support in awarding me a research fellowship for the spring term of 1990 and the University of Oregon for granting me a summer research award in 1991.

To those who have taken the time from their busy schedules to read and comment on individual chapters or sections and, in some cases, the whole manuscript, I owe my thanks: Paul B. Armstrong, James L. Boren, Louise Bishop, Lou Caton, James Crosswhite, Stephen Durrant, James W. Earl, William Edinger, Thomas D'Evelyn, Robert Fagles, Thelma N. Greenfield, Michaela Grudin, Robert Grudin, Nathaniel Kernell, Andrew Miller, Pamela Plimpton, William H. Race, George Rowe, Richard L. Stein, Richard C. Stevenson, John J. Stuhr, Donald S. Taylor, Helen Pinkerton Trimpi, and Wesley Trimpi. The late William Arrowsmith, who did so much to invigorate the contemporary study and appreciation of Greek and Roman literature, read and astutely criticized an earlier version of Chapter 2. I am especially grateful to Louis Orsini, who read the entire manuscript in an earlier draft and offered very helpful criticisms. I wish also to thank the readers selected by Penn State Press for their encouraging responses to the book and for their excellent suggestions on how to improve it. Since one of these readers, James Engell, has identified himself, I can take this opportunity to thank him for his careful reading of my manuscript and for his thoughtful suggestions for revision. I am grateful to Philip Winsor, the senior humanities editor at Penn State Press, for his warm response to my project and for encouraging me to submit my manuscript to Penn State. My wife, Marsha Maverick Wells Shankman, has been a constant source of encouragement and prudent counsel. I am grateful to Andrew Lewis for his skillful copyediting and judicious suggestions for stylistic revision. My thanks go also to Steven Shurtleff for his invaluable research assistance and to the University of Oregon for funding that assistance.

Earlier versions of parts of this book have appeared: Chapter 2 in *The Southern Review* 11, no. 4 (1981): 972–84; Chapter 3 in *Religion and Literature* 16, no. 2 (1984): 1–24; Chapter 4 in *Classical Antiquity* 2, no. 1 (1983): 108–16; Chapter 5 in *Comparative Literature* 40, no. 3 (1988): 219–44; Chapter 7 in *Classical and Modern Literature: A Quarterly* 14, no. 2 (1994): 167–81; Chapter 9 in *Classical and Modern Literature: A Quarterly* 5, no. 4 (1985): 293–300; Chapter 14 in *Modern Philology* 90, no. 1 (1992): 80–83. I am grateful to these journals for granting me permission to draw from those materials here.

The text of Pindar's third Pythian ode printed in the appendix is quoted from *Pindari Carmina cum Fragmentis,* ed. C. M. Bowra (Oxford: Clarendon Press, 1968). I wish to thank New Directions Publishing Corporation for allowing me to quote from the *Collected Poems* of Yvor Winters.

Unless otherwise noted, translations from foreign languages are my own.

PART I

CLASSIC RATIONALITY

1

PLATO AND POSTMODERNISM

Much of the critical theory that we associate with postmodernism, most especially deconstruction, explicitly questions the assumptions of Western metaphysics. In his well-known essay "La Pharmacie de Platon," for example, Jacques Derrida refers to "Platonisme" as "la structure dominante de l'histoire de la métaphysique"[1] and then attempts to expose what he considers to be the rickety foundations of this Platonism. I wish to rescue Plato from what Derrida calls Platonism; to allow Plato's texts to speak for them-

---

1. In *La Dissémination* (Paris: Éditions du Seuil, 1972), 172. "Platonism," as Barbara Johnson translates, is "the dominant structure of the history of metaphysics" ("Plato's Pharmacy," in *Dissemination* [Chicago: University of Chicago Press, 1982], 149).

selves, unencumbered by the "tradition," so often lamented in today's critical climate, that they have initiated; and then to measure some of contemporary criticism's hallowed presuppositions against what Plato actually says. I
shall argue that Plato in fact shares some of the concerns of "postmodern"
theory and that Plato anticipated,[2] and attempted to protect his work
against, many of the kinds of criticisms made by later thinkers, including
some of today's literary theorists.

"Postmodernism" is admittedly a slippery and unsatisfying term.[3] Nonetheless, the concerns that Plato anticipates *and goes well beyond* can usefully
be grouped under its general rubric, or under the rubric of "poststructural-
ism." The specific currents I place under the heading of postmodernism are
Derridean and de Manian deconstruction; Foucauldian social construc-
tionism and the New Historicism that it ushered in; and that side of feminist
thought, following Derrida and Lacan, represented by Luce Irigaray.

In the course of my thinking about how Plato and postmodernism relate
to certain issues raised by some recent feminist theory, I felt compelled to
coin a critical term that I introduce here, with no small degree of Socratic
irony, as a specific example of what I take to be a general Platonic strategy:
prophylactic phallocentrism. I shall explain in more detail what I mean by
this term when I discuss the *Symposium.* For now suffice it to say that Plato,
although certainly no feminist in the postmodern or even modern sense,
virtually anticipates the charge of "phallocentrism" and protects himself in
advance against it. Perhaps "protection" is the wrong word, for it connotes a

2. David L. Roochnik argues that "Plato comprehends, and then criticizes, the thoughts that
underlie what we would now call postmodernism" ("Plato's Critique of Postmodernism," *Philosophy and Literature* 11, no. 2 [1987]: 282). Although Roochnik and I agree on what
constitutes a quintessentially "postmodern" set of attitudes, our analyses are quite different.

3. *Modernism,* with its apocalyptic sense that it is the final and culminating stage of historical progress, makes the term *postmodernism* both necessary and absurd. On the historical
emergence and philosophical connotations of the term *modern,* see Tilo Schabert, "Modernity
and History," *Diogenes,* no. 123 (Fall 1983): 110–24, and "Modernity and History I: What Is
Modernity?" in *The Promise of History: Essays in Political Philosophy,* ed. Athanasios Moulakis
(New York: Walter de Gruyter, 1986). For a useful definition of postmodernism, see Jean-
François Lyotard, *The Postmodern Condition* (Minneapolis: University of Minnesota Press,
1984). "I will use the term *modern,*" Lyotard writes, "to designate any science that legitimates
itself with reference to a metadiscourse ... making an appeal to some grand narrative, such as
the dialectics of Spirit, ... the emancipation of the rational or working subject, or the creation
of wealth.... [S]implifying to the extreme, I define *postmodernism* as incredulity towards
metanarratives" (xxiii–xxiv). See also Lyotard's "Answering the Question: What Is Postmodernism?" in *Innovation/Renovation* (Madison: University of Wisconsin Press, 1983), 329–41, and,
more recently, John McGowan, *Postmodernism and Its Critics* (Ithaca, N.Y.: Cornell University
Press, 1991).

defensiveness that tends to be absent from the Socratic stance. That defensiveness is more accurately associated with a sophist such as Thrasymachus in the *Republic,* whose emotional investment in his opinions often makes him an edgy and aggressive opponent whom Plato contrasts with the gentleness of the philosopher. Plato cannot be easily convicted of phallocentrism because he attempted to articulate a notion of language and truth that resists being deformed into an ideologically airtight or absolutist "position." I hope to point out sufficient similarities between the concerns of Platonic thought and postmodern criticism to call into question the insidious and ideologically motivated opposition between the conservatives who wish to enlist Plato as a traditionalist and the radicals for whom Plato is a repressive reactionary.

Problems of Language

Probably the most striking resemblance to Jacques Derrida in the Platonic corpus can be found in the person of Cratylus, in the dialogue of the same name. Before I elaborate on this resemblance in the section that follows, I feel it necessary to remark on what makes the *Cratylus* so relevant to postmodernism. The dialogue speaks to the question whose answer has decided to a large degree the direction contemporary critical theory has taken since the days of structuralism: Are names—and by implication linguistic signs—natural or conventional? We have long since decided that signs are merely conventional, that there is no necessary relation between signs and what they signify. Plato asks us to reconsider.

The antagonists of the dialogue are Cratylus and Hermogenes. Cratylus believes in the natural sign, Hermogenes in the conventional, that reality is completely "constructed," in Foucauldian and New Historicist terms. It is the role of Socrates in this dialogue to question these ideological positions and to suggest a solution to the problem articulated from a philosophical perspective. In Cratylus we find a paradox that may strike us as strange, but which I find remarkably postmodern. Cratylus believes in the reality of the natural sign and yet follows the Heraclitean doctrine that all is flux. One might think that these attitudes are incompatible, that the believer in the natural sign would be an absolutist rather than a relativist. What the dialogue reveals, however, is that it is precisely the relentless demand for identity between signified and signifier that results in the kind of radical skepticism indulged in by Cratylus. As M. H. Abrams has said of Derrida, Cratylus is "an absolutist without absolutes."[4]

Socrates begins his investigation—or mediation—by having Hermogenes concede that a completely arbitrary relation between names and things implies a Protagorean relativism that would be unacceptable even to Hermogenes. Names cannot simply fluctuate according to our fancy (386d); some hint of the essence of a thing is surely suggested by its name. The elaborate etymologies indulged in by Socrates have two functions in the dialogue. On the one hand, these etymologies suggest that one can indeed argue for a natural relation between things and their names. On the other hand, the intricacy of the arguments and their sometimes questionable veracity undercut the very point Socrates is attempting to make about the completely natural relations between names and things. Hermogenes, at any rate, appears to be convinced by Socrates' arguments to abandon his radically nominalist position. But then Cratylus's ideological certainty that there must be a purely natural relation between names and things must also be shaken.

Plato begins by showing the incompatibility of ideological fervor with common sense. Socrates asks, "Well, what do you say to the name of our friend Hermogenes, which was mentioned before—assuming that he has nothing of the nature of Hermes in him, shall we say that this is a wrong name, or not his name at all?"[5] To which Cratylus answers: "I should reply that Hermogenes is not his name at all, but only appears to be his, and is really the name of somebody else, who has the nature which corresponds to it" (429c). Hermogenes clearly believes that his name is Hermogenes. But if Hermogenes has in him nothing of the nature of Hermes, Cratylus would rather deny the fact of Hermogenes' name than give up his theory that only natural names are truly names. According to Cratylus, Hermogenes must be wrong about his own name. Derrida appears to share Cratylus's insistent skepticism on this very point, for as Vicki Hearne informs us, "the French philosopher Jacques Derrida, in a lecture on memory and mourning, remarked that we never know, that we die without ever being sure, what our proper names are."[6]

4. "How to Do Things with Texts," in *Critical Theory Since 1965*, ed. Hazard Adams and Leroy Searle (Gainesville: University of Florida Press, 1986), 438.

5. *Cratylus*, trans. Benjamin Jowett, in *The Collected Dialogues of Plato*, ed. Edith Hamilton and Huntington Cairns (Princeton: Princeton University Press, 1961), 463. All translations of Plato's dialogues are from this edition, unless otherwise stated. The Greek will be cited from the *Oxford Classical Texts*. I have occasionally made slight variations in the translations cited.

6. *Adam's Task: Calling Aminals by Name* (New York: Knopf, 1986), 192.

Socrates then attempts to articulate a notion of language based on likeness rather than identity. Although Plato has been taken—wrongly, in my view—as an enemy of the notion of imitation (μίμησις), in this dialogue it is clear that he values imitation as a necessary mediator between words and things, especially when we are dealing with qualitatively rather than quantitatively describable experience. It is here that Socrates puts forth his argument for the necessity of the distinction between resemblance (which works through imitation) and identity. That a thing and what nominally represents it must be identical, Socrates says,

> may be true about numbers, which must be just what they are, or not be at all. For example, the number ten at once becomes other than ten if a unit be added or subtracted, and so of any other number, but this does not apply to what is qualitative [τοῦ δὲ ποιοῦ τινος] or to anything which is represented under an image [καὶ συμπάσης εἰκόνος]. I should say rather than the image, if expressing in every point the entire reality, would no longer be an image. Let us suppose the existence of two objects. One of them shall be Cratylus, and the other an image [εἰκών] of Cratylus, and we will suppose, further, that some god makes not only a representation [ἀπεικάσειεν] such as a painter would make of your outward form and color, but also creates an inward organization like yours, having the same warmth and softness, and into this infuses motion, and soul, and mind, such as you have, and in a word copies all your qualities and places them by you in another form. Would you say that this was Cratylus and the image of Cratylus, or that there were two Cratyluses? (432b–c)

Names, therefore, cannot be exactly identical with things, or they would be copies of the things themselves. What is important in names is that "the general character [of the thing named] be preserved" (433a), even if there is not correspondence at every point, for the thing will nevertheless be signified (λέξεταί γε τὸ πρᾶγμα) through resemblance.

The word σκληρός (hard) contains the letter lambda (λ), which is a liquid and thus, because of its softness, contradicts the meaning of the word it helps to constitute. Cratylus suggests to Socrates that perhaps the letter should indeed be changed to one more appropriate to the meaning of the word, but Socrates gets Cratylus to admit that the word is nonetheless intelligible as it is conventionally spelled. Socrates thus persuades Cratylus that custom or convention does in fact contribute to our understanding of language.

In "La Pharmacie de Platon," Jacques Derrida appears to have mistaken Cratylus's view of language, which seeks a consistent and transparent identity between signifier and signified, for Plato's own. Derrida's strategy in that essay is concisely stated by Charles L. Griswold Jr.:

> Derrida deconstructs the *Phaedrus* by concentrating on the ambiguity of the pivotal word "pharmakon," a word which can mean both "cure" and "poison." He grants that Plato has led himself to the brink of a *topos* in which metaphysical distinctions cannot be sustained. Plato reveals this difficulty even as he attempts to distinguish between spoken and written discourse, for he uses the latter to articulate the former: true spoken dialectic will, Socrates suggests, be "written" in the soul of the learner.[7]

The more rigorously one wants to define distinctions, the more quickly one becomes entangled within those distinctions' actual denials of their own validity. Derrida, in his own words, wishes "appeler la suspicion sur le droit à poser de telle limites" [to put in doubt the right to posit such (definitional) limits in the first place]. He continues:

> En un mot, nous ne croyons pas qu'il existe en toute rigeur une texte platonicien, clos sur lui-même, avec son dedans et son dehors.

> [In a word, we do not believe there exists, in all rigor, a Platonic text, closed upon itself, complete with its inside and its outside.]

Definitional limits in Plato's texts, for Derrida, are always blurring, turning into their opposites, despite the author's efforts to distinguish them from each other. How, then, are we to understand what Plato is saying? Is the text then simply a kaleidoscope of free-playing signifiers? Derrida is careful to guard against this conclusion:

> Non qu'il faille dès lors considérer qu'il fait eau de toute part et qu'on puisse le noyer confusément dans la généralité indifférencié de son élément.

7. *Self-Knowledge in Plato's Phaedrus* (New Haven: Yale University Press, 1986), 234.

[Not that one must then consider that it is leaking on all sides and can be drowned confusedly in the undifferentiated generality of its elements.]

But what, precisely, is the alternative to free play? One need not resort to the extreme view that the text is leaking on all sides. Derrida states and offers the mediating solution to the either/or predicament:

> Simplement, pourvu que les articulations soient rigoureusement et prudemment reconnues, on doit pouvoir dégager des force d'attraction cachées reliant un mot présent et un mot absent dans le texte de Platon. Une telle force, étant donné le *système* de la langue, n'a pas pu ne pas peser sur l'écriture et sur la lecture de ce texte.

> [Rather, provided the articulations are rigorously and prudently recognized, one should simply be able to untangle the hidden forces of attraction linking a present word with an absent word in the text of Plato. Some such force, given the *system* of the language, cannot *not* have acted upon the writing and the reading of this text.][8]

This "simplement" confuses me. It seems that somehow, independent of the author Plato, a "System of Language Itself" is establishing the meaning of Plato's text. But what is this system, and how can one gain access to it? Despite Derrida's claim to the contrary, it appears that we are indeed left with an either/or situation. Either Plato must define precisely what he means, in a noncontradictory way, each time he uses the word *pharmakon;* or, if he does not, then the text is perceived to be "leaking on all sides" [il fait eau de toute part] and drowning in its own internal contradictions. I realize that Derrida suggests a middle ground introduced by that "simplement," but the alternative that follows the "simplement" is articulated in prose itself so leaky that a serious attempt at grasping its meaning is frustrated.

If Plato really knew what he was doing, if he was in control rather than under the control of his language, Derrida implies, he would have made sure that the word *pharmakon* everywhere and unambiguously referred to the same specific thing: he could not have allowed it to mean both poison *and* remedy at the same time. Derrida's impressively learned, agile, but overly long and meandering essay then consists—to a large degree—of a relentless

8. "La Pharmacie de Platon," 149; trans. Johnson, "Plato's Pharmacy," 130.

scholasticism that points out the often contradictory nature of the various things referred to chiefly by the word *pharmakon* and its cognates as Derrida ultimately argues that "la pharmacie n'a pas de fond" [the pharmacy has no foundation].[9] Derrida, however, appears to be confusing the views about language of the philosopher Plato with those of the ideologist Cratylus. The philosopher knows that words need not always mean the same thing, that ambiguity is intrinsic to the linguistic process.[10] It is not Plato's pharmacy that has no foundation. It is rather Derrida's reading of Plato's pharmacy that has no foundation, because Derrida has made the fundamental mistake of assuming that for Plato being a philosopher means, above all, achieving systematic terminological consistency.[11] Plato, however, was profoundly aware of the capacity of language both to reveal and to conceal reality. In the *Cratylus,* Socrates—half jokingly—explains to Hermogenes the etymology of his near namesake, the god Hermes who, he says, is both an "interpreter [ἑρμενεύς], or messenger" as well as a "thief." Similarly, Pan, who is the son of Hermes, is "smooth in his upper part, and rough and goatlike in his lower regions." And this kind of powerful ambivalence, he adds, "has a great deal to do with language" (408a). Derrida's mistake is that

---

9. "La Pharmacie de Platon," 170; trans. Johnson, "Plato's Pharmacy," 148.

10. As David Bromwich has noted in his discussion of Derrida's assumptions about language: "The chapters on Rousseau in *Of Grammatology* and on Plato in *Dissemination* proceed by translating such distinctions as that between voice and writing, or cure and poison, into the undistinguishable doubles they become when the concepts of philosophy are read with the ambivalences language can never exclude" ("Literature and Theory," in *A Choice of Inheritance: Self and Community from Edmund Burke to Robert Frost* [Cambridge: Harvard University Press, 1989], 270). What Bromwich refers to as "the all-or-nothing propensities of literary theorists" is central to Roger Kimball's critique of Geoffrey Hartman's defense of Paul de Man: Hartman, Kimball writes, "assumes that if one has not abandoned the belief in the intelligibility of language and adopted the skepticism that deconstruction preaches, one must be a kind of cartoon Cartesian, holding that language is a perfectly transparent medium that renders our thoughts about the world without loss or ambiguity. The possibility of a middle ground between nihilistic skepticism and naive belief never seems to occur to him" (*Tenured Radicals: How Politics Has Corrupted Our Higher Education* [New York: Harper & Row, 1990], 108). See, also, Jasper Neel, who suggests that "Derrida suffers from a radically oversimplified, even nostalgic, conception of what Plato, and other thinkers since his time, considered truth to be" (*Plato, Derrida, and Writing* [Carbondale: Southern Illinois University Press, 1988], 197).

11. As Jasper Neel acutely observes: "The possibility that Plato *may* be playing, may in fact be toying with the play of meaning himself, never seems to cross Derrida's mind. Derrida reads *Phaedrus* the way he reads Saussure" (*Plato, Derrida, and Writing,* 187). That "Plato" never speaks to us directly in his dialogues in order to deliver The Absolute Truth in its unmediated purity further confirms the view that Plato was open, tentative, undogmatic; in brief, Plato was not Saussure [i.e., so sure].

he assumes that Plato cannot tolerate the inherently ambiguous and analogical nature of language; that in the *Phaedrus* the philosopher intended that there be a consistent identity between *pharmakon* and all the signifieds to which this word refers; and that if there is no identity, then there is only difference.

The preceding analysis was not meant as a point-by-point critique of Derrida. My aim has been rather to suggest not only that Plato anticipates some of Derrida's concerns, but that Plato abandons Derrida's nominalist deconstructions as impediments to true philosophical enquiry. In response to Derrida's essay, I therefore cannot resist recalling what Plato has to say about difference in the *Sophist:*

> Merely to show that in some unspecified way the same is different or the different is the same, the tall short, the like unlike, and to take pleasure in perpetually parading such contradictions in argument [χαίρειν οὕτω τἀναντία ἀεὶ προφέροντα ἐν τοῖς λόγοις]—that is not genuine criticism, but may be recognized as the callow offspring of a too recent contact with reality.... Yes, my friend, and the attempt to separate everything from every other thing not only strikes a discordant note but amounts to a crude defiance of the philosophical muse.... *The isolation of everything from everything else means a complete abolition of all discourse* [Τελεωτάτη πάντων λόγων ἐστὶν ἀφάνισις τὸ διαλύειν ἕκαστον ἀπὸ πάντων]. (259d–e)[12]

The perpetual parading of contradictions in argument—in which Derrida often indulges in "Plato's Pharmacy"—is, from Plato's perspective, just so much nominalist nitpicking that finally renders all speech meaningless and all philosophical inquiry impossible.

Derrida's linguistic inheritance appears to be Lockean/Enlightenment nominalism, against which he is rebelling. As in the nominalist view of language, there is an unstated expectation in Derrida's assumptions about the Platonic use of language that technical philosophical terms should, optimally, always and unambiguously refer to discrete particulars. Derrida's rebellion, however—by implicitly rejecting an ambiguous or analogical view of language—implicitly accepts the assumptions of the very nominalism it allegedly rejects. But as Erich Frank has argued, analogy "is the ultimate

---

12. *The Sophist,* trans. F. M. Cornford, in Hamilton and Cairns, eds., *Collected Dialogues of Plato,* 1006.

foundation upon which logic and philosophy must be built. This is an axiom which modern philosophers," in their quest for a certainty that is characteristic of mathematics, "seem to have forgotten." Frank continues:

> Plato and Aristotle were careful to distinguish the truth of philosophy from that of mathematics and understood even their ultimate metaphysical principles as mere analogies of absolute being. Philosophy is not science, nor can it attain to the exactitude of mathematics. The truth of philosophy is superior and at the same time inferior to that of science. It is inferior in so far as it cannot be proved cogently and always retain the character of human analogy; it is superior in so far as it is aware of its own analogical nature.[13]

It is worth contrasting Derrida's assumptions about Plato's use of language with those of another contemporary thinker whose view of language came to have much in common with Plato's own. I refer here to Eric Voegelin, and particularly to the slender but majestic final volume of *Order and History*. In that final posthumous volume, *In Search of Order,* Voegelin, whose work was deeply influenced by Plato, discusses what he calls "the paradox of consciousness" and "the complex of consciousness-reality-language."

The paradox of consciousness consists in the awareness that consciousness be understood in both its intentionalist and participatory modes. We say that we are conscious of something, that we remember something, that we think about something. "By its position as an object intended by a consciousness that is bodily located," Voegelin writes, "reality itself acquires a metaphorical touch of external thingness." For those not familiar with Voegelin's work, it might be useful to explain this sentence before we proceed. We often think of reality as being "out there," as having an objective existence, Voegelin is saying, especially since this reality can be seen as a projection of a consciousness that itself has an objective and concrete locus in the physical body. Hence, the term *reality* is often equated with *objective reality*. Indeed, it might be added at this point that many contemporary critiques of allegedly "classical" objective truth exclusively (and wrongly) equate classical philosophizing with precisely this one meaning of "reality." But this is hardly the

---

13. *Philosophical Understanding and Religious Truth* (New York: Oxford University Press, 1966), 163. Eugene Webb discusses how the language of participation was gradually eclipsed by nominalism—and the nominalism of Ockham in particular—in *Eric Voegelin: Philosopher of History* (Seattle: University of Washington Press, 1981), 68–88.

whole story; indeed, it is a distortion of the classical paradigm. Voegelin continues: "On the other hand, we know the bodily located consciousness also to be real." The language in this posthumous work, which was not polished by its author for publication, is sometimes rather terse and in need of explication. What Voegelin is saying is that the consciousness is "real" in more than the sense that it is an objective fact, an externally verifiable "thing." For there is a "second sense" in which "reality is not an object of consciousness but *the something in which consciousness occurs as an event of participation* in the community of being" (emphasis mine).[14]

The word *reality,* then, is equivocal. And given the nature of reality, we should not expect anything else. We should not expect—as Derrida implicitly does of Plato's use of *pharmakon,* as Cratylus explicitly does of the name Hermogenes—an uncomplicated, one-to-one relation between name and thing. For "reality" covers the experiences both of objects intended by subjects (what we generally mean by the phrase "objective reality" or what Voegelin calls thing-reality) as well as the comprehending reality in which the consciousness participates (what Voegelin calls the It-reality, the "It" being the structure referred to "in everyday language in such phrases as 'it rains' "). Hence, "there is no autonomous, nonparadoxic language, ready to be used by man as a system of signs when he wants to refer to the paradoxic structures of reality and consciousness. Words and their meanings are just as much a part of the reality to which they refer as the being things are partners in the comprehending reality; *language participates in... [this] paradox*"[15] (emphasis mine). Language that is truly philosophical, such as Plato's in the *Phaedrus,* must openly acknowledge its own paradoxical nature if it is to be true to the paradoxical nature of reality.

Voegelin then goes on to relate this last statement to the very issue that lies at the heart of the *Cratylus:* Is language "conventional" or "natural"?

> The conventionalist opinion, today the more fashionable one, is moved by the intentionality of consciousness and the corresponding thing-reality to regard words as phonic signs, more or less arbitrarily chosen to refer to things. The naturalists are moved by a sense that signs must have some sort of reality in common with the things to

---

14. *Order and History,* 5 vols. (Baton Rouge: Louisiana State University Press, 1956–87), 5:15. For Voegelin, the "luminosity" of consciousness consists specifically in one's awareness of reality as reality becomes luminous for its own apprehension.

15. Ibid., 17.

which they refer, or they would not be intelligible as signs with certain meanings. Both of the opinions are precariously founded because their adherents were not present when language originated, while the men who were present left no record of the event but language itself. As I understand the issue, both groups are right in their motivations, as well as in their attempts to explore the conditions incidental to the origin of language and its meaning; and yet both are wrong inasmuch as they disregard the fact that the epiphany of structures in reality . . . is a mystery inaccessible to explanation.[16]

Like Socrates in the *Cratylus,* Voegelin wishes to mediate between conventionalists and naturalists. That "the epiphany of structures in reality is [ultimately] a mystery inaccessible to explanation" should not result in a skepticism about knowing, *unless we think of knowing only in the intentionalist mode.*

This brings us to a few speculative questions, all pointing in a similar direction. Is Derrida's skepticism the result, first, of an entirely understandable disenchantment with an intentionalist view of language, a view he wrongly ascribes—by implication—to the Plato of the *Phaedrus?* And does Derrida, the critic of Saussure's conventionalist linguistic system,[17] having first deconstructed this intentionalist view, then, in response to the results of his deconstruction, perhaps go on to desire—like Cratylus—the natural sign, only to react once again with an equally understandable skepticism to this unrealizable desire? Aristotle, in the *Metaphysics* (1010a), attempts to refute the extreme relativism of those Protagoreans who, observing that all of "nature is in motion, and thinking that nothing is true of that which changes, . . . came to the belief that nothing indeed may be truly said of that which changes altogether and in every way." From this belief, Aristotle continues, issued the most extreme forms of skepticism, such as that "held by Cratylus, who finally thought that nothing should be spoken but only moved his finger."[18] Would it be too reductive to suggest that Derrida's

---

16. Ibid.

17. As Derrida writes in *Of Grammatology,* "Beyond the scruples formulated by Saussure himself, an entire system of intralinguistic criticism can be opposed to the thesis of the 'arbitrariness of the sign' " (trans. Gayatri Spivak [Baltimore: Johns Hopkins University Press, 1974], 326).

18. *Aristotle's Metaphysics,* trans. Hippocrates G. Apostle (Bloomington: Indiana University Press, 1968), 66–67. Aristotle goes on to say that Cratylus "criticized even Heraclitus for saying that one cannot step into the same river twice, for he himself thought that one could not do so even once" (67). As Apostle explains in his commentary, "while speaking about a thing, the

writings, which so often appear to teeter on the brink of meaning, are our (post)modern equivalent to Cratylus's finger-wagging?

Rhetoric and Truth

The word *rhetoric* has undergone a remarkable change in our critical vocabulary. When a critic talks of "rhetoricity" today, what is usually meant is the figural nature of language. This is what Paul de Man means by "rhetoric" in his essay "Semiology and Rhetoric": "Rhetoric radically suspends logic and opens up vertiginous possibilities of referential aberration. And although it would perhaps be somewhat more remote from common usage, I would not hesitate to equate the rhetorical, figural potentiality of language with literature itself."[19] Tropes and figures, however, are only a small part of what the ancients considered the art of rhetoric. Rhetoric was the art of persuasion. When the history of rhetoric is written, Plato is usually portrayed as its enemy, Aristotle as its champion; we shall note this same pattern in the history of literary criticism. Plato's *Gorgias* is thus traditionally seen as an attack against rhetoric on behalf of dialectic. In part this is what it is, but—as de Man constantly points out—"rhetoricity" can never be abandoned. Plato knew this; indeed, that is what the *Gorgias* is in large part about.

Socrates argued against rhetoric, but he should not be taken as believing that one must abandon rhetoric.[20] What he is criticizing in this dialogue, as well as in the *Phaedrus,* is a notion of rhetoric that is divorced from dialectic. Indeed Socrates is himself a master rhetorician, as Plato himself acknowledges at one point in the *Gorgias.* After Socrates gives an imaginative and moving account of his love affair with *philosophia,* thus personifying philosophy as a lover, Callicles responds by saying, "Socrates, it seems to me that you run wild in your talk like a true mob orator" [ὡς ἀληθῶς

---

thing has changed; but in pointing a finger, one indicates the continuous change which really takes place." Of the reference to Heraclitus he remarks, "It takes time to step into the river once; but, according to Cratylus, during this time it is not the same river" (291).

19. *Allegories of Reading* (New Haven: Yale University Press, 1979), 10.

20. For a recent account that emphasizes Plato's positive contributions to the history of rhetoric, see James L. Kastely, "In Defense of Plato's *Gorgias,*" *PMLA* 106 (January 1991): 96–109.

δημηγόρος ὤν] (482c).[21] Again and again as the dialogue proceeds, Socrates uses allegories, fictions, and images in order to try to persuade Callicles of his point. Persuasion, however, is different from coercion. It is Socrates' contention that most rhetoricians enslave their audiences and keep them from engaging in reasoned argument. Socrates is aware that the same charge can be made against his own impassioned arguments, and so Plato therefore has Socrates' interlocutor, Callicles, make such a charge on two occasions (482c, as mentioned above, and 494d), thus anticipating that such charges can and will be made. One notes in Socrates' use of myth in this dialogue a movement from allegory, to image, to a grand myth at the conclusion of the work that presents itself as "true," thus questioning the very notion of what "truth" means.

In his essay "The Rhetoric of Temporality," de Man questions the romantic preference for symbol over allegory. "Whereas the symbol postulates the possibility of an identity or identification, allegory designates primarily a distance in relation to its own origin, and, renouncing the nostalgia and the desire to coincide, it establishes its language in the void of this temporal difference."[22] Allegory may, however, be viewed—in a nonromantic context—as a heuristic device that blends rhetoric (pleasing fiction) and truth (what the allegory means); rhetorical *exempla* offer provisional fictions that may be discarded as one proceeds toward greater dialectical precision.[23] Allegory is no longer for de Man, as it was for Plato, such a heuristic device, a way of moving along a scale of relative degrees from nontruth to truth. In this context, Paul de Man's remark quoted earlier ("Rhetoric radically suspends logic . . .") can be taken as that of a sophist who is profoundly aware of the separation between rhetoric and truth, but whose skepticism about knowing discourages him from taking the next step. And this skepticism derives from a nominalist/intentionalist view of language that refers to provisional fictions as "mystifications."[24]

21. *Gorgias,* trans. W. D. Woodhead, in Hamilton and Cairns, eds., *Collected Dialogues of Plato,* 265.

22. *Blindness and Insight: Essays in the Rhetoric of Contemporary Criticism* (Minneapolis: University of Minnesota Press, 1983), 207.

23. Cf. Wayne Booth, *The Company We Keep: An Ethics of Fiction* (Berkeley and Los Angeles: University of California Press, 1988), 357: "To me the greatest of all metaphoric critics is Plato. Both in his largest views and in the minutest details of each dialogue, he questions our temptation to see the world (and our place in it) *under* any one reductive metaphor."

24. Cf. Fredric Jameson's view of de Man as nominalist in "Deconstruction as Nominalism," in *Postmodernism, or the Cultural Logic of Late Capitalism* (Durham, N.C.: Duke University Press, 1991), 217–59. "De Man was an eighteenth-century mechanical materialist, and much

De Man's intentionalism is implied in his attempt to reverse, in "The Rhetoric of Temporality," Coleridge's preference for symbol over allegory. Coleridge, in preferring the symbol, argued for a return to a participationist, analogical way of thinking about language. As W. J. Bate has written, in a succinct and readable description of Coleridge's relation to the participationist tradition: "With his back firmly braced upon the entire classical tradition, and the Hebraic and Christian thinking with which it had combined, he [Coleridge] affirmed at every opportunity that reason—as in the Platonic conception of it (*nous*)—is able, as it transcends the experience and judgments drawn from the concrete world, to touch directly a reality to which it is itself the mental analogue or counterpart."[25] De Man wishes to discredit (or as he might say, "demystify") participationist thinking—which assumes that "creatures are not Being as such but are 'participations,' that is, finite analogues of Being as such"[26]—and the result is a return to pre-Coleridgean, Enlightenment intentionalism. De Man differs from Enlightenment intentionalism in that he is fully aware of its reductiveness and wishes to unmask its naive claims to transparent referentiality. He appears to wish, therefore, to demystify both intentionalism and participationism. But participationist thinking assumes that mystery—in large part because of what Voegelin calls the paradox of consciousness—cannot on principle be overcome. Plato (and Voegelin) accept the necessary relation between mystery and rationality. In Paul Ricoeur's terms, understanding for them involves a hermeneutic of

---

that strikes the postcontemporary reader as peculiar and idiosyncratic about his work will be clarified by juxtaposition with the cultural politics of the great Enlightenment philosophes: their horror of religion, their campaign against superstition and error (or 'metaphysics'). In that sense, deconstruction itself . . . can be seen to be an essentially eighteenth-century philosophical strategy. . . . What De Man clearly was was not a nihilist but a *nominalist,* and the scandalized reception that greeted his views on language is comparable to nothing quite so much as the agitation of Thomist clerks confronted unexpectedly with the nominalist enormity" (246, 250). De Man's work, Jameson writes, can be seen "as the place in which a certain experience of nominalism, in the specialized realm of linguistic production itself, was, as it were, lived to the absolute and theorized with a forbidding and rigorous purity" (251). The purity sought by de Man is the state of total demystification. For a critique of de Man's reading of the Coleridgean symbol that is similar to my own, see Thomas McFarland, "Involute and Symbol," in *Coleridge, Keats, and the Imagination,* ed. J. Robert Barth, S. J., and John L. Mahoney (Columbia: University of Missouri Press, 1990), 29–57.

25. *Coleridge* (New York: Collier Books, 1968), 185.

26. Webb, *Eric Voegelin,* 72–73. In order for Webb's phrase to make sense, one must resist hypostatizing—in nominalist fashion—the phrase "Being as such" into merely one entity among others.

faith; for de Man, understanding involves "demystifying" such a hermeneutic in favor of what Ricoeur calls a hermeneutic of suspicion.[27]

Plato's "Attack" on Poetry Reconsidered

In histories of literary criticism Aristotle is usually cast as the hero, Plato as the villain. It cannot be denied, of course, that Plato explicitly censures poetry in the *Republic* and that Aristotle, in the *Poetics,* appears to be responding to Plato's critique. Yet what has not received adequate attention is that Plato answers his own objections in the *Republic* itself. Even so subtle and aware a critic as Harold Bloom literalizes Plato in this regard, for in the preface to the first volume of *The Art of the Critic* he writes, "It is true that Socrates, in *Republic* 10, rejects poetry that is an *imitation,* but nowhere does Plato discourse explicitly as to what the nature of a nonmimetic or visionary poetry might be."[28] Perhaps the key word here is "explicitly," for Plato does articulate what a nonmimetic or visionary poetry might be, but he does so not through the kind of explicit statement we associate with Aristotle, but through poetic exemplification, through the "rhetoricity" of his own discourse.

The famous critique of poetry in *Republic* 10, for example, must be read in the context of the work as a whole, and this means reading the *Republic* as itself a work of carefully crafted and symbolically evocative *poēsis* that culminates in the myth of Er, in which Plato explicitly evokes in his reader many of the emotions—such as pity, fear, laughter, and astonishment—that he earlier has associated with Homer (the first and greatest of the tragic poets, according to Plato, *Republic* 595b and 607a and *Theaetetus* 152e) and had considered as worthy more of being extirpated than elicited. These are those specifically tragic emotions the stirring up of which Aristotle felt compelled to defend in the *Poetics.* Plato's alleged attack on poetry should be viewed, to a large degree, as a critique of flatly naturalistic literature and of those contemporary habits of interpretation that would read even the great mythic poems such as Homer's epics as exciting stories sapped of their philosophical intentions. Plato's critique of Homer is more a critique of how

27. See Ricoeur's *Freud and Philosophy: An Essay in Interpretation,* trans. Denis Savage (New Haven: Yale University Press, 1970), 9.

28. *The Art of the Critic* (New York: Chelsea House, 1985), 1:xx.

Homeric poetry was being understood than of the poetry itself. It is no wonder, then, that the hero of the myth of Er is Odysseus and that in the tale Plato evokes precisely those tragic emotions that he had only just moments earlier castigated. The myth of Er must be read, Plato suggests, not as a naturalistic and exciting adventure story—that is, not literally—but as a symbolically evocative *mythos* that provides an artistically fitting conclusion to the poem that is the *Republic.*[29]

What characterizes Plato's use of myth, in the *Republic* and elsewhere, is his awareness, on the one hand, of myth's shadowy ontological status and, on the other, of his belief that myth can point us in a profitable direction. If there is, in Derrida's terms, a "transcendental signified" to which a particular myth may correspond, Plato—even as early as the *Republic*—is very cautious about stating myth's ability to evoke it. After narrating the famous allegory—Plato actually describes it as an εἰκών, an "image" or "semblance" (517b)—of the cave, for example, Socrates tells Glaucon, "Maybe God knows whether or not it happens to be true; but this, at any rate, is how these appearances appear to me" [θεὸς δέ που οἶδεν εἰ ἀληθὴς οὖσα τυγχάνει. τὰ δ' οὖν ἐμοὶ φαινόμενα οὕτω φαίνεται] (517b). There is to be sure in Plato a desire for the center, but even the earlier Plato recognizes that fictions—while provisional—are necessary, that one never gets quite beyond the realm of "play," albeit (in Paul Friedländer's words) "serious play."[30] Derrida himself questions the assumption "that Plato simply condemned play."[31] Indeed, Plato refers favorably to play throughout his works and, as Derrida notes, in his sixth letter he referred to play as "the sister of seriousness" [τῇ τῆς σπουδῆς ἀδελφῇ παιδιᾷ].[32] I do not want, however, to leave the reader with the impression—as Derrida does—that the Platonic dialogues reflect merely the free play of floating signifiers. For Plato, the

29. In *Republic* 367a Adeimantus laments, what justice is "in itself, by its own inherent force, when it is within the soul of the possessor and escapes the eyes of both gods and men, no one has ever adequately set forth in poetry or prose" [οὐδεὶς πώποτε οὔτ' ἐν ποιήσει οὔτ' ἐν ἰδίοις λόγοις] (367a, trans. Paul Shorey, in Hamilton and Cairns, eds., *Collected Dialogues of Plato*). One implication of this passage is that this theme will find its poet in the Plato of the prose poem known as the *Republic.* See the final chapter for further discussion of this issue. In *Plato's Defence of Poetry* (Albany: State University of New York Press, 1984), Julius A. Elias similarly argues that throughout his works Plato offers a defense of poetry that answers his own objections.

30. *Plato: An Introduction,* trans. Hans Meyerhoff (Princeton: Princeton University Press, 1973), 123.

31. "Plato's Pharmacy," trans. Johnson, 156.

32. Letter VI 323d; quoted by Derrida as part of the epigraph to chapter 9 of "Plato's Pharmacy," 156.

intuition of the form of a thing (whether it be rhetoric or justice) is what guides the seriously playful intellective process.

I shall say something later about the relation of some examples of feminist criticism to Platonic thought, but I should mention here Luce Irigaray's speculations on Plato's imagery of the cave. In "L'ύστέρα de Platon," in *Speculum de l'autre femme*, Irigaray suggests that Plato depicts his cave (*antre*) as a womb (*ventre*),[33] and that the prisoners by trying to escape to the light are in fact attempting to leave behind imagery associated with the mother and enter the more abstract and "truthful" realm of the phallus/father. The prisoners must negotiate the distance

> Entre . . . Entre . . . Entre l'intelligible et le sensible. Entre le bien et le mal. L'Un et le multiple. Entre tout ce que l'on voudra. Oppositions qui supposent toujours le *saut* d'un pire à un mieux. Une ascension, un déplacement (?) vers le haut, une progression le long d'une ligne. Verticale. Phallique?

> [Between . . . Between . . . Between the intelligible and the sensible. Between good and evil. The One and the many. Between anything you like. All oppositions that assume the *leap* from a worse to a better. An ascent, a displacement (?). Vertical. Phallic even?][34]

There is something to be said for the associations of the cave with the world of becoming and hence of generation and femininity, on the one hand, and the world of Being with light and the father, on the other. Part of the problem with Irigaray's critique, however, is what one might call the generative fallacy, the reduction of the symbolic meaning of mythic images to their (speculative) historical genesis. Symbolic language, it is true, always retains the traces of its own origins. But Plato knows that there is no uncontaminated language lying around somewhere to be applied unambiguously to transcendental signifieds. Plato is not Cratylus. He is aware of what Voegelin refers to as the paradox of consciousness and the complex of consciousness-reality-language. Plato did not assume that his own myths were unproblematic. In composing his para-

33. "Des hommes donc—sans spécification de sexe—demeuraient dans un même lieu. Temps même, dans un même lieu. Lieu qui aurait la forme d'un antre, ou ventre" [As the story goes, then, men—with no specification of sex—are living in one, same, place. A place shaped like a cave or womb] (*Speculum de l'autre femme* [Paris: Éditions de Minuit], 301; trans. Gillian C. Gill under the title *Speculum of the Other Woman* [Ithaca, N.Y.: Cornell University Press, 1985], 243).

34. *Speculum de l'autre femme*, 306; trans. Gill, *Speculum of the Other Woman*, 246–47.

ble of the cave, he used the language symbols that were available to him in order to explore and illuminate (the metaphor seems irresistible) his own experiences of what it means to be enslaved to opinion as opposed to being open to truth. As Jürgen Gebhardt beautifully remarks in his fine epilogue to Voegelin's *In Search of Order:* "The philosopher's reflective acts of cognition—as Voegelin states . . . , referring once more to the first philosopher Plato—are distinguished by the precarious balance they strike between the finality of the language of truth experienced and articulated historically and the nonfinality determined by the language's position in an ongoing, open-ended process."[35] Irigaray appears to wish to restrict Plato's mythopoesis to the finality of the language of truth experienced and articulated historically.

Even if Irigaray were right about the genesis of Plato's metaphorical language, and if she had then gone on to articulate the consequences of her position for a reevaluation of Platonic thought, her argument—in trying to deconstruct Plato from a radically feminist perspective—would have paradoxically been reenacting the very process of illumination that Plato intended the parable of the cave to represent. For the assumptions of the philosopher—as opposed to what Plato calls the philodoxer ("the lover of opinion," *Republic* 480) and what today we might refer to as the ideologue—are on principle always open to question. One presumes that Plato would have been open to such a critique, that he would have wished to be led out of the shadows. For Plato was aware that, however much one wishes to ascend to the light, it is precisely in the In-Between—Irigaray's *entre,* which she punningly rhymes with *antre* (cave) and *ventre* (womb)—that one resides. The point of Irigaray's punning on the words *antre, ventre,* and *entre* indeed has its parallel in *Symposium,* in which Plato articulates his notion of the *metaxy* (In-Between), symbolized through a mythic representation that self-consciously combines masculine and feminine qualities.

The Metaxy *("In-Between"), Philosophy, and the Question of Gender*

The Symposium is one of Plato's great literary efforts. It is hard to believe that critics can still write about Plato's alleged hostility to art when he has

35. *In Search of Order,* 116.

left us so striking a literary masterpiece. The literary quality of the work, moreover, cannot be separated from its philosophical meaning. Indeed, one of Plato's intentions is—as in the *Republic*—to question the very distinction between poetry and philosophy.

Recent critical theory often emphasizes the historicizing of all "discourse" and sets this historicizing against allegedly Platonic transcendentalizing tendencies. We see this in recent reflections on "subject positions"; the disinterested subject is, according to this view, a chimera and the subject is "constructed." Such a view tends to be contrasted with the "transcendentalizing" nature of classical "metaphysics." It may come as something of a surprise to be reminded that Plato, at the beginning of that allegedly otherworldly and transcendentalizing work, *The Symposium,* goes out of his way to cast doubt—with his characteristically subtle irony—on philosophical absolutism. The dialogue that, through Diotima's speech, argues for the ontological primacy of the unitary Beautiful itself, begins by framing that speech with narrators of questionable reliability and a fanatical Socratism that Plato portrays as being rather ludicrous.

Let us look at the beginning of the dialogue, a masterpiece of Platonic narrative art. The dialogue opens with a question from an unidentified enquirer who wants to know what transpired that evening when Socrates and others, at a by now famous banquet, gave speeches on love. Apollodorus responds to this unidentified inquirer: Δοκῶ μοι περὶ ὧν πυνθάνεσθε οὐκ ἀμελέτητος εἶναι [I believe I am not exactly unpracticed concerning the things you are asking about] (172a). The dialogue that suggests that the spirit of existential inquiry defines human nature in its essence itself begins with a question from an inquirer with whom the reader naturally identifies; for is it not the reader's own curiosity that causes him (or her; in the *Republic* Plato argues that women as well as men have the capacity to be philosophical rulers) to learn about the famous symposium at which Socrates and others gave their views on the meaning of love? The inquirer has a question: what happened that day? The only way that we can truly find out is through an eyewitness. Apollodorus tells this inquirer not what happened directly, but of a conversation he had with Glaucon, who had asked the very same question. The dialogue consists of Apollodorus telling this unidentified inquirer what Apollodorus had told Glaucon (who had asked Apollodorus to tell him what someone said that a certain Phoenix, the son of Phillip, had said that he, Apollodorus, knew) that Aristodemus had told him (Apollodorus). To describe a very complicated narrative frame in a somewhat more streamlined manner: the dialogue consists of Apollodorus telling an unidentified inquirer what he (Apollodorus) had told Glaucon that Aristodemus, who was actually at the banquet, had told him (Apollodorus). Do we ever find out with certainty what happened at that banquet at which "Plato" makes explicit his "metaphysics" of love and being? Who can tell? Our chief narrator, Apollodorus, it turns out, was not even there. He heard the story from Aristodemus.

Both our eyewitness Aristodemus and our narrator Apollodorus are, moreover, depicted by Plato as rather foolish, and the nature of their foolishness casts real doubt on the allegedly "absolutist" cast of Platonic thought. They are both disciples of Socrates, or perhaps Socrates "groupies" would be a more appropriate way to put it. Plato describes Aristodemus, "the little guy who's always barefoot" [σμικρός, ἀνυπόδητος ἀεί] (173b), as a caricature of Socrates. Our narrator Apollodorus is self-righteous and has the (questionable) conviction of a recent convert to Socratism, as we see in his remarks to Glaucon as he reports them to the unidentified inquirer. Since he met Socrates, Apollodorus says, he has "made it my business to know everything he says and does every day [ἑκάστης ἡμέρας εἰδέναι ὅτι ἂν λέγῃ ἢ πράττῃ]. Before that I was running in circles, acting at random, thinking I was accomplishing something though I was unhappier than anyone, no less than you are now, imagining that anything was more necessary than philosophy" (173a).[36] Apollodorus similarly describes himself to the companion who asked about the banquet. In a priggishly self-righteous manner, Apollodorus says,

> As far as I'm concerned, any sort of philosophical discussion I have or listen to is immensely enjoyable, apart from its practical benefit. It's when I hear other kinds of talk, particularly the sort you have with the rich and with businessmen that I get angry, and pity you and your friends for thinking you're accomplishing something when, in fact, you're not doing a thing! I suppose, in turn, you think I'm unhappy, and I suppose you're right; but for my part it's not that I think it of you, I know it for a certainty [ἐγὼ μέντοι ὑμᾶς οὐκ οἴομαι ἀλλ' εὖ οἶδα]. (173c–d)

As do so many disciples, Apollodorus here is distorting the master's message. The philosopher is the lover of knowledge, not the one who possesses

---

36. *The Symposium of Plato*, trans. Suzy Q. Groden (Amherst: University of Massachusetts Press, 1970), 37–38. English quotations from the *Symposium* will be cited from the Groden translation.

knowledge; his knowledge is tentative, not certain and beyond argument. Whereas Socrates is depicted in this dialogue as physically the toughest of Athenian soldiers, his disciple Apollodorus is known as a "softy" (τὸ μαλακός, 173d5). Is it not difficult to imagine a committed ideologist, of whatever persuasion, beginning a serious ideological tract with a comic depiction of a ridiculous young convert to that particular ideology? Herein lies one important difference between ideology and philosophy.

Thus Plato believes, with much postmodern theory, that the disinterested subject is a chimera, for Diotima's "metaphysical" account of the ladder of knowledge is purposely presented to us through the eyes of a self-interested disciple of Socrates who is depicted as somewhat ridiculous. Plato is as aware as any deconstructionist of the virtual necessity of subjective distortion, although he believes we can move beyond mere impressions toward greater understanding.[37]

I come now once again to the controversial issue of Plato's relation to feminism. Women are indeed excluded from the banquet, and they make their appearance either as lowly flute girls or in the disembodied presence of the lofty priestess Diotima. Plato was a brilliant narrative artist with the flair of a novelist, and it should be remarked that one does not recall any female character depicted by Plato with the lively particularity of an Alcibiades. However "essentialist" Plato was in his basic understanding of the differences between the sexes, it could nonetheless be argued that in his depiction, via Diotima, of the philosopher, he wishes to criticize the excesses of "male" rationalism in favor of a blend of male and female qualities.

Diotima has just told Socrates—in what I take to be the philosophical core of the *Symposium*—that love (Ἔρως) exists in between (μεταξύ) the mortal and the immortal (202e). Love's character was determined by the qualities of his mother and father. His father was Resource (Πόρος) and his mother was Need or Poverty (Πενία). She continues:

> Therefore, as the son of Resource and Poverty, Love finds himself in this situation: first of all, he is always impoverished [πένης ἀεί]. . . . Possessing his mother's nature, he is always in need. But, then again, through his father he turns out a schemer [ἐπίβουλος] for beautiful things and good things, is courageous, bold, and intense, an awesome

37. Cf. Martha C. Nussbaum, who makes some interesting comments on the "Chinese box"–like quality of the *Symposium*'s narrative frame in *The Fragility of Goodness: Luck and Ethics in Greek Tragedy and Philosophy* (Cambridge: Cambridge University Press, 1986), 168.

hunter always devising some machination or other [ἀεί τινας πλέκων μηχανάς], eager for understanding and inventive [πόριμος]; he is a lover of wisdom [φιλοσοφῶν] all of his life and an intellectual virtuoso [σοφιστής]. . . . Love is never utterly at a loss nor completely wealthy. He exists in the middle, between ignorance and wisdom [σοφίας τε αὖ καὶ ἀμαθίας ἐν μέσῳ εστίν]. (203d–e)

Plato does indeed appear to be here anticipating Freudian associations of the feminine with lack and the masculine with fullness. A few observations should be made about this passage, however, before we jump to the conclusion that Plato's articulation of the philosophical experience is marred by the stereotypically "gendered" nature of his symbolic language. For one thing, the scheming quality of the father (ἐπίβουλος, 203c4) is not quite absent in the mother, whom Diotima says schemed (ἐπιβουλεύσουσα) to seduce the father of love. For another, Plato is rejecting the uninhibitedly "male" quality of aggressive self-assertion (embodied in Alcibiades)[38] and desire for mastery by depicting need as essential to the philosophical experience. Most important, the participants in the dialogue reverse (one is tempted to say "deconstruct") the gender roles of the allegory. Plato does not see need or lack as the lesser or dependent "term" in a hierarchical arrangement that would grant greater importance to the experience of fullness. In the allegory, it is the female who is lacking and needs the resourcefulness of the male. *In the narrative itself, however, it is the male Socrates who is in need and the female Diotima who is full.* One way to read this reversal of gender roles is to infer that Plato wishes the listener to understand that the philosophical experience he is describing is a universal one, not limited to men alone, that it is not necessarily gender-specific. It is after all Plato who in book 5 of the *Republic* maintains, in a stunningly revolutionary passage, that women as well as men have the capacity to be philosophical rulers and should be trained as such, since "the only difference" between men and women is "that the male begets and the female brings forth" (454e).[39] Plato, thus, I would suggest, is (prophetically) protecting himself against the charge of phallocentrism, for even if his lan-

---

38. Who, as Plutarch tells us, dreamed that he was dressed in women's clothes the night before he died (*Alcibiades* 39). "In the soul of this proudly aggressive man," Martha Nussbaum interestingly speculates, Alcibiades' dream "expresses the wish for unmixed passivity" (*Fragility of Goodness,* 199). Plato symbolizes philosophical *eros*—of which Alcibiades is finally incapable—as partaking of both activity and passivity. What Alcibiades could not achieve in reality thus expresses its repressed self, with a vengeance, in a dream.

39. *The Republic of Plato,* trans. F. M. Cornford (London: Oxford University Press, 1945).

guage does generally tend to subordinate the female to the male, by having
the narrative reverse the gender roles of the myth of the conception of Eros,
Plato is engaging, in brief, in what I described at the beginning of this chapter
as *prophylactic phallocentrism.*[40]

I do not wish to make the argument that Plato is any more of a feminist—
in the modern sense—than he truly was. Even in book 5 of the *Republic,* he
refers to women as generally the "weaker" sex (456a), although as Gregory
Vlastos has argued, Plato's estimate of women's characters could be viewed
as the result of empirical observations of contemporary Athenian women
whose very disadvantaged status would be reversed under Plato's own educational program.[41] Even if Plato's language does generally tend to subordinate the female to the male, it must be said that Platonic philosophy in
principle welcomes the critique of all assumptions, including Plato's own,
on all issues, including the issue of gender. This very openness is itself
symbolized, in the *Symposium,* in the myth of the conception of Eros and
the subsequent in-between nature of Eros as the symbol of the philosopher.
It is of course possible that the language symbols of the philosopher, after
they have been articulated historically, may eventually carry so much connotative baggage that the philosopher will need a new vocabulary, a situation
we are experiencing today. But does not this very acknowledgment of the
need for a new philosophical vocabulary itself confirm the intent of Plato's
symbolism of the essentially needy philospher?

Difference, Sameness, and the In-Between

We have found several of Plato's dialogues, apart from the usual ones taught
in courses in critical theory, crucial to an understanding of some postmod-

40. It would not be quite correct to translate this, into common parlance, as "safe sexism."
"Prophylactic phallocentrism" might be taken as metonomy for a general Platonic strategy. Cf.
Plato's use of the word *politeia* in the myth of Er, which I discuss in Chapter 14.

41. "Was Plato a Feminist?" *Times Literary Supplement,* March 17–23, 1989, 276–89. For a
less positive assessment of Plato's attitude toward women, see Julia Annas, "Plato's *Republic*
and Feminism," *Philosophy* 51 (1976): 307–21. On the Platonic "appropriation" of the repro-
ductive images associated with the female body, see the last chapter of Page duBois's *Sowing
the Body: Psychoanalysis and Ancient Representations of Women* (Chicago: University of
Chicago Press, 1988). DuBois's reading of Plato is marred by the very tendency we noted in
Irigaray's reading of the cave analogy: duBois's reading, like Irigaray's, tips the balance—in
Gebhardt's words—on the side of "the finality of truth experienced and articulated historically"
rather than on "the language's position in an ongoing, open-ended process."

ern assumptions. I have already argued for the importance of the *Cratylus* and the *Symposium*. It is time to attend as well to the *Parmenides* and the *Sophist*. These dialogues are central for gaining a perspective on one of the most famous of Derrida's essays, "Différance."

Let us begin by examining Derrida's assertion that "*différance is not*."[42] One cannot, truly, speak "différance," according to Derrida, because the "word"—coined by Derrida—describes precisely what constantly differs from itself and defers presence. One should recall in this context the goal of the Athenian stranger in Plato's *Sophist*. His goal is to hunt down the sophist, who claims that "what is not" (τὸ μὴ ὄν, 258b) has no existence. Here, paradoxically, the consequences of the positions of the relativistic sophist and the absolutist Parmenides come to the same thing. Parmenides, like Derrida, believes that difference is not. Since only the One (and not the many) has being, and since difference is never in what is the same, then "difference can never be in anything that is" (146e). The sophist in Plato's dialogue of that name can take refuge in the view that falsehoods have no real existence, for if a lie does not exist, then it cannot be refuted. If "*différance* is not," then how can we enter a discussion with Jacques Derrida on this point? Taking the Athenian stranger as our model, let us try.

We must, first of all, do what Derrida says is taboo, that is, attempt to break "différance" down into its constituent parts. These two parts are "différance" in the sense (1) of "difference" and (2) of the deferring of presence.

We must, with the Athenian stranger (1) suggest that difference can only exist if it differs from something other than itself. That something is sameness. If we do not admit the existence of sameness as well as difference, then all discourse is impossible. This is precisely the view of the Athenian stranger, who suggests that "difference [τὸ ἕτερον], by partaking of existence, *is* by virtue of that participation [μέθεξιν], but on the other hand *is not* that existence of which it partakes, but is different, and since it is different from existence, quite clearly it must be possible that it should *be* a thing that *is not*" (259b).[43] As if he had been reading Derrida's analysis of Plato's sometimes contradictory uses of the word *pharmakon*, the Athenian stranger, in a passage I quoted earlier, goes on to say:

---

42. "*Différance*," trans. Alan Bass, in Adams and Searle, eds., *Critical Theory Since 1965*, 122. The essay was first published in 1968.

43. *The Sophist*, trans. F. M. Cornford, in Hamilton and Cairns, eds., *Collected Dialogues of Plato*, 1006.

Merely to show that in some unspecified way the same is different or the different is the same, the tall short, the like unlike, and to take pleasure in perpetually parading such contradictions in argument [χαίρειν οὕτω τἀναντία ἀεὶ προφέροντα ἐν τοῖς λόγοις]—that is not genuine criticism, but may be recognized as the callow offspring of a too recent contact with reality.... Yes, my friend, and the attempt to separate everything from every other thing not only strikes a discordant note but amounts to a crude defiance of the philosophical muse.... *The isolation of everything from everything else means a complete abolition of all discourse* [Τελεωτάτη πάντων λόγων ἐστὶν ἀφάνισις τὸ διαλύειν ἕκαστον ἀπὸ πάντων]. (259b–e)

If one accepts the notion that only difference exists, then discourse (λόγος) becomes impossible.[44]

We must now analyze critically what Derrida means by (2) the deferral of presence. What does Derrida mean by the term *presence?* Here Derrida draws on Heidegger's equating "the difference between Being and beings" with "the difference between presence and the present," and he gives a quotation from "The Anaximander Fragment" of Heidegger: "Oblivion of Being belongs to the self-veiling essence of Being. It belongs so essentially to the destiny of Being that the dawn of this destiny rises as the unveiling of what is present in its presencing. This means that the history of Being begins with the oblivion of Being, since Being—together with its essence, its distinction from beings—keeps to itself."[45] This proposition provokes the following comment from Derrida:

44. It is precisely Derrida's emphasis, in his reflections on genre theory in "The Law of Genre," on difference rather than sameness (and participation in a common "form") that Ralph Cohen critiques in "History and Genre," *New Literary History* 17 (1985–86): 203–18. Cohen remarks, as I have, on Derrida's extreme nominalism. "The reasons for identifying texts differently do not interest Derrida; the identifications themselves do. He wishes to demonstrate that generic traits cannot *belong* to genres: [As Derrida writes,] 'This supplementary and distinctive trait, a mark of belonging, of inclusion, does not properly pertain to any genre or class' " (Cohen is quoting Derrida, "The Law of Genre," *Critical Inquiry* 7 [Autumn 1980]: 56). And once again that hair-splitting nominalism appears to be a skeptical reaction to the Cratylus-like desire for perfect identity between signifiers (in this case, particular works that bear generic traits) and signifieds (the genres themselves). Cohen remarks: "Derrida does not pursue the historical inquiry of the types of 'participation' involved in specific works; he assumes that all such participations are to be distinguished from 'belonging.' Indeed, for him, the individual text has so many contrary markings that participations undo belonging" ("History and Genre," 205).

45. "The Law of Genre," 134.

> Since the trace is not a presence but the simulacrum of a presence
> that dislocates itself, displaces itself, refers itself, it properly has no
> site—erasure belongs to its structure. . . . [T]he present becomes the
> sign of the sign, the trace of the trace. It is no longer what every
> reference refers to in the last analysis. It becomes a function in a
> structure of generalized reference. It is a trace, and a trace of the
> erasure of the trace.[46]

Both Heidegger and Derrida, in these passages, are more Platonic than it
might first appear—as long as we do not think of Plato as an absolutist who
ascribes reality only to immutable Being.[47] We should remember that the
Plato of the *Parmenides* and the *Sophist* rejects the association of reality
exclusively with Being rather than—in Heidegger's terms—with "beings."
"Being," Heidegger says, "keeps to itself." It is precisely the Parmenidean
assertion that essential reality is unknowable that provokes the Platonic/
Socratic critique—in favor of the notion of "participation"—of the Eleatic
belief that only the One is real.

For Heidegger and Derrida, then, the present is not to be equated with
presence. Here Plato, the prepostmodernist Heidegger, and the postmodernist Derrida are at one. Despite Derrida's assertions to the contrary, one
often feels that his skepticism is a defensive reaction against a frustrated
(and from a Platonic perspective, unrealistic) expectation of full presence.[48]
One recalls here, once again, Abrams's remark that Derrida is an "absolutist
without absolutes." Indeed the philosopher who most resembles Derrida in

46. Ibid.
47. The passage in his oeuvre that should forever discourage the association of Plato with
idealist absolutism is his description, in the *Sophist,* of the battle between the materialist giants
and the idealist gods, who maintain "with all their force that true reality consists in certain
intelligible and bodiless forms" (246c). Real being, the Athenian stranger goes on to argue,
exists in the "intercourse" (248b) between becoming and absolute being. The importance of
this Platonic passage for the history of literary theory is well discussed by Wesley Trimpi in
Muses of One Mind: The Literary Analysis of Experience and Its Continuity (Princeton:
Princeton University Press, 1983), 106–16.
48. Cf. Martha Nussbaum, who criticizes the tendency in some recent literary theory "to
respond to the putative collapse of unqualified metaphysical realism (the view that we have
truth only when we have a completely unmediated and noninterpretative access to the structure of reality as it is in itself) by espousing some form of radical subjectivism, relativism, or
skepticism. . . . The literary world's lack of interest in . . . alternatives [to radical subjectivism,
relativism, and skepticism] seems to betray an excessive attachment to metaphysical realism
itself" (*Love's Knowledge: Essays on Philosophy and Literature* [New York: Oxford University
Press, 1990], 229).

the passage quoted from "Différance" is the great theorizer of the One, Plotinus. Both Plotinus and Derrida state that human beings experience only a "trace" of pure presence, but there is a world of difference between these respective traces of Plotinus ("trace" = ἴχνος, as in, for example, *Enneads* 3.8.20) and Derrida. For Plotinus, the trace in the necessarily material world of the divine and immaterial One, regardless of how remote from the One that particular emanation might be, still beckons the seeker to continue the quest for more complete participation in divine being. Pure presence is experienced—as in much traditional classical and Christian thought—only as an intense desire, as a movement of the soul toward what has been experienced and then symbolized as the divine source of being. This existential movement is articulated brilliantly by Plotinus, who is consistently on his guard against hypostatizing the One into a proposition, or into what Eric Voegelin refers to as "thing-reality." For Derrida, the trace hints at a pseudodivinity that tantalizes the consciousness with the phantom reality of pure presence, although such presence is in fact consistently retreating from consciousness. Derrida's problem, I believe, is that he—unlike Plotinus and unlike Plato—"hypostatizes" the One into a thing and then consistently refutes its existence. It is perhaps more accurate, however, to relate the One to what Voegelin calls "It-reality," the comprehending reality in which the consciousness participates. In a real sense, then, what Derrida critiques throughout his work is not true Platonic philosophy, which argues for the In-Between nature of existence, but the Parmenidean association of truth with Being rather than beings.

Postmodernism is indeed a critique of Western "metaphysics." The word "metaphysics" itself, however, is a philological mistake. It was originally merely the translation, from the Arabic, of the treatise that appears after the *Physics* in a medieval edition of Aristotle's works and came to refer to a purely propositional exposition of what was originally genuine philosophical experience and its articulation.[49] "Metaphysics" itself, then is a reduction of philosophy to "thing-reality." Thus we cannot properly speak of Plato as a

49. In his *Autobiographical Reflections* (Baton Rouge: Louisiana State University Press, 1989), Voegelin suggests that the science of "metaphysics" is an example of the deformation of philosophical experiences and their symbolization into doctrines, and he reflects as follows on the philological origin of the word: "The term *metaphysics* is not a Greek term but an Arabic deformation of the Greek title of Aristotle's *meta ta physica*. . . . [I]t had been taken over from the Arabs by Thomas and for the first time used in a Western language in the introduction to his commentary on Aristotle's *Metaphysics*; and . . . ever since there existed an odd science that was called metaphysics. . . . [T]he cliché 'metaphysics' has become the magic word by which one can cast a shadow on all philosophical analysis in the Classic sense" (79–80).

"metaphysician," since the term *metaphysics* is foreign to his philosophical vocabulary. Plato was interested in exploring reality, not in building metaphysical systems; nor was it his highest priority to achieve terminological consistency. In "Plato's Pharmacy" Derrida offers a critique—in terms largely of "thing-reality" philosophizing—of a thinker who had articulated his experience of reality in a language that is necessarily paradoxic. I have spent much of this chapter discussing similarities between Platonic and postmodern philosophical concerns, but this fundamental disagreement about the nature of language is a point of perhaps irreconcilable difference.

2

RATIONALISM ANCIENT
AND MODERN

As I suggested in Chapter 1, the Plato deconstructed by Derrida is largely the rationalist Plato, the Plato who wants above all to keep his terms clean and consistent, the Plato who founded the alleged science of "metaphysics," the "logocentric" Plato.[1] Logocentric in the sense, first, that this is the Plato

---

1. No one—not even many of Derrida's admirers—seems quite to know exactly what "logocentrism" is, as John M. Ellis argues in chapter 2 of *Against Deconstruction* (Princeton: Princeton University Press, 1989). By "logocentrism" Derrida appears to mean the "privileging" of the spoken over the written word, but the term has acquired a life of its own and for many people "logocentricism" is the rough equivalent of a blind faith in so-called absolute truth that on closer examination is revealed to have been a "mystified" form of parochial prejudice mistakenly elevated to an absolute. The meaning of the word *deconstruction* is likewise extraor-

who, although explicitly expressing a preference for the spoken word (*lo-gos*) over the written (*gramma*), nevertheless *writes* the dialogue in which this preference is enunciated and, shortly after enunciating it, goes on to use a metaphor that implicitly contradicts his explicit preference (*Phaedrus* 278b). And logocentric, more importantly, in the vulgar sense of what we might better render as "rationalistic," that is, having a penchant for meta-physical systems that promise a totalizing purchase of truth.

But this is not the Plato I wish to argue for, the Plato I see as the culmina-tion of a literary and protophilosophical tradition that eschews rationalism in favor of what I would like to call rationality.[2] I treat the rationality of Plato more explicitly in Chapter 3. In the present chapter I wish to discuss how this notion of rationality, which I associate with the repudiation of narrow rationalism in the history of ancient Greek literature, is articulated in a relatively modern poem by Yvor Winters, who has written some of the most solidly classical poems of our century and many of whose theoretical writ-ings on the art of poetry[3] are vital restatements of the classical view of poetry I articulate in this book.

It is in one sense unfortunate that Winters titled what was to become his most famous critical book *In Defense of Reason,* for he has often been mistak-enly regarded as a "rationalist." But if *rationalist* is taken to mean a believer in the virtually unlimited power of the utilitarian, purely quantitative, calculat-ing reason, then Winters surely is no rationalist. In fact, one of his most moving and prophetic poems is an indictment of precisely this Enlighten-ment and post-Enlightenment understanding of reason, which has its distant roots in the Greece of the fifth century B.C. What I would like to point out in this chapter are the extraordinary similarities between Winters's critique of modern rationalism in the poem "An Elegy (for the U.S.N. Dirigible, *Macon*)"

---

dinarily elusive, and not only because of the view of the slipperiness of language espoused by its proponents; on this phenomenon, see the opening chapter of David Lehman's *Signs of the Times: Deconstruction and the Fall of Paul de Man* (New York: Poseidon Press, 1991).

2. By opposing "rationality" to "rationalism," I am using "rationalism" in a nontechnical and perhaps unconventional sense. "Rationalism," as I am using it here, is not necessarily to be equated with a specific school or movement in the history of either theological thought (in which "reason" is given primacy over "supernatural revelation") or seventeenth- and eighteenth-century philosophical thought (in which "rationalism" will later be opposed by "empiricism").

3. *In Defense of Reason* (New York: Swallow Press and William Morrow, 1947); *The Func-tion of Criticism: Problems and Exercises* (Denver: Alan Swallow, 1957); *Forms of Discovery: Critical and Historical Essays on the Short Poem in English* (Chicago: Alan Swallow, 1967); and *Uncollected Essays and Reviews,* ed. Frances Murphy (Chicago: Swallow Press, 1973).

and the powerful analysis of Athenian rationalism made by Sophocles and Thucydides, an analysis that culminates in the articulation by Plato and Aristotle of the classical experience of reason.[4] Although Winters's own view of reason derives, in part, from Thomistic thought, which was itself greatly influenced by Aristotle, I shall not in this chapter try to demonstrate that Winters was influenced, directly or indirectly, by fifth- or fourth-century Greek thought. I wish only to point out some striking parallels between the articulation of rationality in the Platonic-Aristotelian sense and as embodied in two of Yvor Winters's later poems. I wish to point out, in other words, the continuity between two instances of rationality ancient and modern.

It will be helpful, first of all, to distinguish between rationality and rationalism. The distinction is central, since I wish to associate the classical view of reason not with rationalism but with what I shall define in this chapter as rationality. I have suggested that literature, in the classical articulation, may be described as a compelling, formally coherent, and *rationally defensible* representation that resists being reduced either to the mere recording of material reality, on the one hand, or to the bare exemplification of an abstract philosophical precept, on the other. The phrase "rationally defensible" has no doubt given pause to those who feel that I have thereby severely restricted the field of poetic content to the empirically verifiable, to the positivist world of the Enlightenment. What I need to stress and clarify here and in the following chapter, therefore, is the meaning of reason—the Platonic/Aristotelian voῦς—assumed in the phrase "rationally defensible."

Truth, Eric Voegelin writes in "Wisdom and the Magic of the Extreme,"

> is a perspective of reality, arising from man's participation, with his conscious existence, in the reality of which he is a part. Hence, the consciousness of a reality intended as its object of consciousness is accompanied by the consciousness of the quest as an event within the reality intended: the human intentionality of the quest is surrounded by the divine mystery of the reality in which it occurs. The mystery is the horizon that draws us to advance toward it but withdraws as we advance; it can give direction to the quest of truth but it cannot be reached; and the beyond of the horizon can fascinate as

---

4. For an illuminating discussion of the historical emergence of reason in the Platonic and Aristotelian sense, see Eric Voegelin's "Reason: The Classic Experience," *The Southern Review* 10, no. 2 (Spring 1974): 237–64; reprinted in *Anamnesis* (Notre Dame, Ind.: University of Notre Dame Press, 1978), 89–115, and to be discussed in Chapter 3.

the "extreme" of truth but it cannot be possessed as truth face-to-face within this life.[5]

Intentionality and mystery—what Plato refers to as the experiences of seeking (ζήτησις) and being drawn (ἑλκεῖν)—may be seen as the structures of consciousness, and these must be kept in a state of constant balance if the life of reason, in the classical sense, is to be maintained. "Neither must the desire to know reality as the intended object of consciousness," Voegelin continues, "degenerate into an intentionalist desire to know the mystery of the horizon and its beyond as if it were an object this side of the horizon; nor must the consciousness of the omnipresent mystery thwart the desire to know by assuming objects this side of the horizon to belong to the sphere of the mystery."[6]

Rationality, then, can be described as the constant attempt by the consciousness to achieve a balance between intentionality and mystery. I equate this notion of rationality with reason in the classic sense. Rationalism, on the other hand, is the "intentionalist desire to know the mystery of the horizon and its beyond as if it were an object this side of the horizon." The rationalist does not have the patience to achieve, in the moment-by-moment reality of existence, an at best precariously balanced consciousness, but will attempt to escape from the tension of this balancing act by trying to bring "the beyond," once and for all, into total clarity. The rationalist enterprise can take such forms as the construction of a systematic ideology, the pursuit of world empire, or the moral myopia that will result from focusing the mind too exclusively on the tangible results of technological progress.

Modern Rationalism: Yvor Winters's Symbol of the U.S.N. Dirigible Macon

Winters's poem, first published in 1941, describes the demise of the *Macon,* a huge, lighter-than-air craft, 785 feet long, with the capacity to house five

5. "Wisdom and the Magic of Extreme," in *The Collected Works of Eric Voegelin, Published Essays, 1966–1985* vol. 12, edited with an introduction by Ellis Sandoz (Baton Rouge: Louisiana State University Press, 1990), 326. The essay first appeared in *The Southern Review,* n.s., 17 (1983): 235–87.
   6. Ibid., 327.

fighter planes in its hull. "The pride of the Navy's air forces," as the *New York Times* called the *Macon* in the front-page obituary that appeared on the day following the disaster, plunged 2,500 feet into the Pacific and sank just off the coast of California on February 12, 1935:

> The noon is beautiful: the perfect wheel
> Now glides on perfect surface with a sound
> Earth has not heard before; the polished ground
> Trembles and whispers under rushing steel.
>
> The polished ground, and prehistoric air!
> Metal now plummets upward and there sways,
> A loosened pendulum for summer days,
> Fixing the eyeball in a limpid stare.
>
> There was one symbol in especial, one
> Great form of thoughtless beauty that arose
> Above the mountains, to foretell the close
> Of this deception, at meridian.
>
> Steel-gray the shadow, than a storm more vast!
> Its crowding engines, rapid, disciplined,
> Shook the great valley like a rising wind.
> This image, now, is conjured from the past.
>
> Wind in the wind! O form more light than cloud!
> Storm amid storms! And by the storms dispersed!
> The brain-drawn metal rose until accursed
> By its extension and the sky was loud!
>
> Who will believe this thing in time to come?
> I was a witness. I beheld the age
> That seized upon a planet's heritage
> Of steel and oil, the mind's viaticum:
>
> Crowded the world with strong ingenious things,
> Used the provision it could not replace,
> To leave but Cretan myths, a sandy trace
> Through the last stone age, for the pastoral kings.[7]

7. *Collected Poems* (Chicago: Swallow Press, 1960), 119. All quotations of Winters's poetry are taken from this edition.

The opening stanza is a good example of Winters's postsymbolist method. The *Macon* lifts off at high noon, but the poet invests the particulars with broader significance. To return to our classical paradigm: the *Macon* and the other particulars of the poem are not reducible to discrete or literally mimetic particulars. Nor is the *Macon* as symbol reducible to an abstract moral truth: the poem is not precisely equivalent to its paraphrasable content. Winters's postsymbolist method requires that particulars be rendered with perceptual freshness, and that these perceptions have, as well, an intellective dimension. Although the *Macon* cannot be reduced simply to an allegorical representation of a particular moral truth, its construction nonetheless can be taken as a symbol of the rationalist desire—as it manifests itself in the mind's obsession with technological ingenuity—"to know the mystery of the horizon (of consciousness) and its beyond as if it were an object this side of the horizon." That such a desire is inherently unrealizable is subtly suggested by the poet in his choice of the words *beautiful, perfect,* and *polished,* which carry idealist connotations. There are other ominous signs: the ground beneath the great ship "trembles" and the pristine clarity of high noon seems almost to invite disaster. These are only hints, however, that the poet's attitude toward the building of the flawless technological machine is ambivalent.

The ambivalence becomes more explicit in the second stanza, in which the poet ominously contrasts the artificially "polished ground" (the pavement) over which the man-made *Macon* glides with the "prehistoric air" into which it is now ascending. The *Macon* "plummets upwards," a bold phrase that conveys a sense both of tragic foreboding and of the poet's intuition that the ascent of the *Macon* may be seen as a perverse assault on the forces of nature. The poet then compares the *Macon* to "a loosened pendulum for summer days, / Fixing the eyeball in a limpid stare." The suggestion here is that the machine, although a technological wonder, is in effect a useless diversion. If an ordinary pendulum were loosened from the rod to which it is attached, gravity would cause it to plummet to the ground; but the *Macon,* which like a pendulum is built of "metal," defies the laws of gravity and "plummets upward." The reason for the existence of this "loosened pendulum" appears to be chiefly to astound those who have the leisure, on listless "summer days," to observe it suspended in the air.

The *Macon,* the poet says in the next stanza, is a "great form of thoughtless beauty." It is beautiful because it was intended as a grandiose display of the human mind at the "meridian" of its powers; but it is essentially "thoughtless" because it becomes, instead, in the course of the poem, a symbol of the mind's rationalist tendency to deceive itself into believing in the reality of its beautiful but insubstantial projections.

In the fourth stanza the poet describes the "shadow, than a storm more vast" that the *Macon* in the brightness of high noon casts on the ground, a portent of the storm that will eventually bring the great ship down. Its engines, he says in another portentous phrase, "shook the great valley like a rising wind." The last line of the stanza brings us from a vision of the *Macon* at the acme of her powers at high noon to a sudden awareness of what is now seen as the insubstantial quality of the vision. All that now remains of the reality that was the huge and magnificent *Macon* is a mere "image . . . conjured from the past."

The opening lines of the fifth stanza make explicit, with subtle irony, how the flight of the *Macon* can be viewed as an impossible and doomed attempt on the part of humankind to rival nature: in an allusion to the "engines" that "shook the great valley like a rising wind" mentioned in the previous stanza, the airship is now seen as "wind in the wind"; because it is, for the moment, a lighter-than-air craft, the *Macon* is described as a "form more light than cloud"; and the poet refers to it as a "Storm amid storms! And by the storms dispersed," an allusion again to the previous stanza in which the "shadow" cast by the *Macon* was seen as vaster than a storm.

In the final stanzas the poet suggests that modern man, by crowding "the world with strong ingenious things," such as the *Macon,* has managed to gut the earth of "the provision it could not replace." What we have left our descendants are "but Cretan myths," myths, that is, similar to that of the fatal flight from Crete of Icarus, who, wearing the wings designed by his father, the great craftsman Daedalus, flew too close to the sun, thus causing the wax that fastened the wings to his body to melt; the boy, like the *Macon,* fell into the sea and met disaster. I shall give a fuller interpretation of these difficult stanzas at the conclusion of the following section on the analysis, by Sophocles and Thucydides, of Greek rationalism, an analysis that bears remarkable similarities to Winters's twentieth-century critique.

Ancient Rationalism as Critiqued by Sophocles and Thucydides

The inheritor of the extraordinary inventive skills of the Athenian Daedalus was fifth-century Athens, which saw an enormous rise in the interest of specialized, technical skills—of τέχναι—considered more and more in isolation from the ethical implications and consequences of these skills. In a famous chorus in the *Antigone* (442 or 441 B.C.), Sophocles expresses an ambivalent attitude toward the astounding inventive capacity that had enabled humanity to master the external world:

> Many the wonders [τὰ δεινά] but nothing is stranger [or
>   more wonderful, δεινότερον] than man.
> This thing crosses the sea in the the winter's storm,
> making his path through the roaring waves.
> And she, the greatest of gods, the earth—
> ageless she is, and unwearied—he wears her away
> as the ploughs go up and down from year to year
> and his mules turn up the soil.
>
> Gay nations of birds he snares and leads,
> wild beast tribes and the salty brood of the sea,
> with the twisted mesh of his nets, this clever man.
> He controls with craft [κρατεῖ δὲ μηχαναῖς] the beasts of
>   the open air,
> walkers on hills. The horse with his shaggy mane
> he holds and harnesses, yoked about the neck,
> and the strong bull of the mountain.
>
> Language, and thought like the wind
> and such dispositions as regulate cities
> he has taught himself, and shelter against the cold,
> refuge from rain. He can always help himself.
> He faces no future helpless. There is only death
> that he cannot escape from. He has contrived
> refuge from illnesses once beyond all cure [νόσων δ'
>   ἀμηχάνων].
>
> Clever beyond belief
> the inventive craft [μηχανόεν τέχνας] that he has
> which may drive him one time or another to well
>   [ἐσθλόν] or ill [κακόν].
> When he honors the laws of the land and the gods' sworn
>   right
> high indeed is his city; but stateless [ἄπολις] the man

who dares do that which is not good. Not by my fire,
never to share my thoughts, who does these things.[8]

(332–75)

"Many the wonders [δεῖνα], but nothing is stranger [or more wonderful,
δεινότερον] than man." The Greek word δεῖνος is ambiguous, for that which
is δεῖνος is startling to behold, but is also fearful, potentially very dangerous.
Man's "inventive craft (μηχανόεν τέχνας) is "clever beyond belief," and although such cleverness may bring about good or even noble results, it can
also, Sophocles warns, be a source of evil (κακόν). Humanity has, in Winters's
words, "crowded the world with strong ingenious things," such as the *Macon,*
but as a result of such progress we may well have turned ourselves, paradoxically, into inhabitants of "the last [that is, the final] stone age."

The chorus from the *Antigone* suggests, as does Winters in the last two
stanzas of "An Elegy," that by attempting to master the external world humanity may well be wearing the earth away. But apart from this suggestion,
the Greek poet does not explain how specifically the exploitation of technical skills may "drive him . . . to ill." In the *Philoctetes* (produced 409 B.C.), by
having the bow represent—in part—the inherent amorality of τέχνη, Sophocles is much more explicit. By saying that the bow represents the inherent
amorality of τέχνη, I do not wish to claim that it is not, as well, the great
symbol of heroic virtue. But I believe that Sophocles wishes to suggest that
the proper use of the powerful weapon demands that the hero act in accordance with divine will. The bow is δεῖνος, and a thing of wonder will turn to
a thing of terror in the wrong hands.

Philoctetes, abandoned by Odysseus and his fellow Greeks nine years
before on the desolate island of Lemnos because his comrades could not
bear the stench of his wound, survives only because he has with him the
bow of Heracles, which he uses to hunt for food. Philoctetes' skill with the
bow is the τέχνη that permits his survival. The Greeks receive a prophecy
that Troy can be taken only with Heracles' bow, and so a thoroughly unscru-
pulous and pragmatic Odysseus comes to Lemnos to secure the bow, by any
means possible, from Philoctetes. Odysseus orders Neoptolemus to bring
Philoctetes to him, even if this means deceiving the wounded hero as to why

8. *Antigone,* trans. Elizabeth Wyckoff, in *The Complete Greek Tragedies,* ed. David Grene
and Richmond Lattimore (Chicago: University of Chicago Press, 1959), 2:170–71. I have made
slight alterations in the translation. The Greek is cited from *Sophocles: The Text of the Seven
Plays,* ed. Sir Richard Jebb (Cambridge: Cambridge University Press, 1957).

he has been sought out and where he is to be taken. Lying will be necessary, for, as Odysseus rightly suspects, Philoctetes is by now so overcome with hatred of the Greeks who abandoned him that he will never agree to help them take Troy, even if he is told that the gods have so decreed. The naturally noble Neoptolemus—the son of Achilles—is troubled about having to be dishonest, but he goes through with the deception until he hears Philoctetes cry out in pain. The pain he suffers because of his wound is so severe that he asks Neoptolemus to relieve him of his bow.

Neoptolemus then experiences a crisis of conscience. He has the bow and can leave with it at once, but he suddenly realizes the significance of the divine command—that if the bow is to be secured, Philoctetes must sail with it to Troy. Just at this moment Philoctetes gratefully remarks upon Neoptolemus's tolerance of "the offense of my cries and the smell" (876)[9] and I believe what Sophocles is suggesting is that the mature and responsible use of the powerful bow, the symbol (like Winters's *Macon*) of the terrifying capacities of τέχνη, requires that its practitioners recognize its potential—to evoke the chorus from the *Antigone*—for both good and evil. The instrument must not be separated from the offensive cries and smells of the suffering Philoctetes: one must be profoundly aware, that is, of the narrowness of vision induced by the pursuit of τέχνη for its own sake. To reformulate the problem in our modern context: could those who originally fashioned the atomic bomb have followed through with their coolly rationalistic scheme had they personally experienced, with all five of their senses, the horrors of Hiroshima and Nagasaki? The horror evoked by such an abstraction when it suddenly receives its perverse material embodiment is hauntingly suggested by Winters in the moving lines that conclude the fifth stanza of "An Elegy": "The brain-drawn metal rose until accursed / By its extension and the sky was loud!"

Sophocles' most powerful attack on fifth-century rationalism occurs in the *Oedipus Tyrannus*. To ask whether Oedipus "deserves" the terrible consequences that befall him is to read the play too literally: it is to read it in that very spirit of flattened rationalism which, for Sophocles, specifically characterizes the mind of Oedipus. Oedipus is largely a symbol, a type, and what he represents, to a great degree, is the Athenian mind of the fifth century.[10] The

9. *Philoctetes*, trans. David Grene, in *The Complete Greek Tragedies*, 2:435.
10. On Oedipus as a symbol of Greek rationalism, see Bernard Knox, *Oedipus at Thebes* (New Haven: Yale University Press, 1957). The comic counterpart to the tragic Oedipus is Pisthetairos in Aristophanes' brilliant satire of Greek rationalism, *The Birds*.

Athenians, as the Corinthians portray them during the congress of the Peloponnesian confederacy at Lacedaemon, are, according to Thucydides,

> addicted to innovation, and their designs are characterised by swift-
> ness alike in conception and execution. . . . The deficiency created by
> the miscarriage of an undertaking is soon filled up by fresh hopes;
> they alone are enabled to call a thing hoped for a thing got, by the
> speed with which they act upon their resolutions. (1.70)[11]

It is this same addiction to innovation that, in Winters's view, encouraged
those who designed the *Macon* to try to invent "the perfect wheel," which
would glide "on perfect surface with a sound / Earth has not heard before."
And it was this same Athenian impatience, this same compulsion "to call a
thing hoped for a thing got" that would drive those who supported the
project to persist, even though more than half the dirigibles ever built met
with disastrous ends. One of these dirigibles was the *Akron,* the sister ship of
the *Macon,* which crashed into the Atlantic during an electrical storm,
killing seventy-six of the seventy-nine people on board less than two weeks
before the *Macon* was launched on her maiden flight.

The Athenian addiction to innovation evolved, in the words of the prudent
and balanced general Nicias, into "that mad passion [δυσέρωτας] to possess
that which is out of reach" (6.13)[12] which would culminate in the paradigmatic Sicilian disaster. With a deep sense of tragic foreboding, Thucydides
describes the Athenian display of splendorous pomp as the soldiers prepare
to depart from the Piraeus. The sight was, he says, "surpassing all belief" (here
one recalls Winters's line, "Who will believe this thing in time to come?").
"Indeed this armament that first sailed out," the historian continues, "was by
far the most costly and splended Hellenic force that had ever been sent out by
a single city up to that time." The Athenians spent "lavishly upon figureheads
and equipments," and the expedition itself seemed "more of a display of
power and resources than an armament against an enemy" (6.32).

11. *The Complete Writings of Thucydides: The Peloponnesian War,* trans. Richard Crawley
(New York: The Modern Library, 1951), 40. The Crawley translation will be cited throughout
this chapter, unless otherwise stated. Although the work of Thucydides can be viewed as a
critique of what I call Athenian rationalism, there is a sense in which Thucydides' own work
participates in the very rationalist *ethos* that it implicitly criticizes. Note, for example, Thucydides' tone of condescension toward the allegedly too fanciful Homer and Herodotus in book 1 of
his history.

12. My own translation.

The mission ends in disaster. The rationalist dream of possessing that which is out of reach becomes a nightmare, a tragic *peripeteia* in the fortunes of Athens and her armed forces. Thucydides goes on to describe the "lamentable [δεινόν] scene" of the physically and morally crushed Athenian forces who, he says, felt the disgrace of their defeat even more overwhelmingly

> when they contrasted the splendor and glory of their setting out with the humiliation in which it ended. For this was by far the greatest reverse that ever befell an Hellenic army. They had come to enslave others, and were departing in fear of being enslaved themselves: they had sailed with prayer and paeans, and now started to go back with omens directly contrary; travelling by land instead of by sea, and trusting not in their fleet but in their heavy infantry. (7.44–45)

The tragic pathos of these passages from Thucydides is remarkably similar to that of Winters's elegy. "A loosened pendulum for summer days / Fixing the eyeball in a limpid stare" describes precisely the fatal attractiveness to the Athenians of the idea of the Sicilian expedition and of the splendor that accompanied its inception. The expedition was a "great form of thoughtless beauty" and turned out to be an example of the self-deception of the Athenian mind at the "meridian" of its power and status in the world. The problem with the expedition was that it was merely "brain-drawn," a rationalist projection doomed to explosive failure once it entered the reality of time.

The *Oedipus Tyrannus* was produced in 428 B.C. The Sicilian disaster did not occur until 413, but it can almost be said that Sophocles predicted it. What *had* occurred just two years before the play was produced was the great plague of Athens in the second year of the war. In his alarmingly graphic depiction of the symptoms experienced by those struck down by the plague—one of whom was the historian himself—Thucydides remarks on how some of the victims lost their fingers and toes, how others lost their eyes. As the *Oedipus* begins, the *polis* of Thebes is beset by a terrible plague, and it is hard to imagine that the audience, many of whom had suffered from the plague, would interpret the Theban plague as a mere literary symbol. It is, rather, a symbol dense with experiential content, for what Sophocles may well be suggesting is that the Athenian plague of 430 B.C. can be seen in retrospect as divine punishment for the excesses of Athenian rationalism. Just as Thebes in Sophocles' play will not be delivered from destruction until Oedipus, the symbol of rationalism—and, like some of the victims of the plague, left ultimately blinded—is exiled, so Athens, Sophocles is saying, will not be delivered from internal disorder until the rationalist ethos is exiled.

As a supposed foreigner, Oedipus achieves success by virtue of his quick-witted intelligence, his cleverness. He becomes king of Thebes by solving the riddle of the Sphinx: "What is it," the riddle asks, "that walks on four legs in the morning, on two at noon, on three in the evening?" Oedipus gets the right answer, which is "man," but it is an answer that he understands only on the level of a proto-positivist notion of truth or falsity, only on the level of what Voegelin refers to as "thing-reality." For what the play tells us is that it is precisely the nature of man that Oedipus does *not* understand. His conception of himself, it turns out, is, like the Athenian dream of world conquest, a rationalist projection. Oedipus's rise to the top was—to borrow a phrase from Winters's elegy—a kind of perverse and unnatural plummeting upward. His understanding of who he is is seen, in the reality of time, to have been a vast "deception, at meridian," as the chorus comes to recognize at the end of the play:

> O generations of man, how I
> count you as equal with those who live
> not at all!
> What man, what man on earth wins more
> of happiness than a seeming [δοκεῖν]
> and after that a falling away?
> Oedipus, you are my pattern [παράδειγμα] of this,
> Oedipus, you and your luck [τὸν σὸν δαίμονα]!
> Miserable Oedipus, whom of all men I count the least
> happy.[13]
>
> (1186–96)

All that remains of the reality that was the esteemed King Oedipus of Thebes is, in the words of "An Elegy," an "image . . . conjured from the past." "Do not seek to be master in everything," Creon tells the fallen Oedipus as the play

---

13. *Oedipus Tyrannus,* trans. David Grene, in *The Complete Greek Tragedies: Sophocles I* (1954; reprint, Chicago: University of Chicago Press, 1976). I have altered the translation. In his poetic rendering of the lines, Robert Fagles translates the word ἀποκλῖναι ("falling away," 1192) in a manner that describes precisely the kind of paradigmatic catastrophe of which I find the demise of the *Macon* to be a late example. Man's vision of his own happiness, Fagles translates, "no sooner dawns that dies / blazing into oblivion" (Sophocles, *The Three Theban Plays* [London: Penguin, 1984], 233).

concludes, "for the things you mastered did not follow you through your life" (1522–23). Oedipus is a symbol of the intentionalist desire to master reality, to know it from the outside rather than patiently to participate in it; he is a symbol, that is, of rationalism rather than of rationality.[14]

The final stanzas of Winters's poem are a powerful indictment of rationalism in its modern guise:

> Who will believe this thing in time to come?
> I was a witness. I beheld the age
> That seized upon a planet's heritage
> Of steel and oil, the mind's viaticum:
>
> Crowded the world with strong ingenious things,
> Used the provision it could not replace,
> To leave but Cretan myths, a sandy trace
> Through the last stone age, for the pastoral kings.

Modern man has "crowded the world with strong ingenious things"; he has pursued technological ingenuity for its own sake. But since our supply of precious elements—such as the steel of which the *Macon* was built and the oil which served as its fuel—is limited, such supplies should be used for more intelligent ends: we have "seized upon a planet's heritage / Of steel and oil" and thereby used "the provision" the world cannot "replace." As a result of this shortsightedness, man will have left himself a provisionless "viaticum" for the remainder of his journey through history. Supposed technological advances will, paradoxically, end in a return to a primitive and final "stone age" ruled by "pastoral kings."

But the conclusion of the poem goes beyond these remarkably topical warnings about the purely pragmatic consequences of the modern obsession with technological progress, for Winters suggests that "steel and oil" have, to our peril, become the modern sacraments. The modern mind, the poet is saying, by substituting the materialistic entities of "steel and oil" for the bread and wine that symbolize the spiritual communion with the body

14. If Oedipus represents rationalism, Plato depicts Socrates as the embodiment of rationality. The two figures are opposites in many ways. One seems to be a social success; the other a social misfit. Oedipus does everything in his power to evade the oracle; Socrates does everything in his to understand it. Oedipus is a foreigner to Thebes (or thinks he is); Socrates is an Athenian. Oedipus is quick to anger when reality blocks his preconceptions; Socrates patiently uses such apparent blocks as keys to greater understanding.

and blood of Christ, has administered to itself its own peculiarly modern "viaticum," a term for the Eucharist given to one whose death is imminent. Winters was not a Christian, and he is not here advocating a return to a ritual observance of Christianity. What he is saying is that in place of a profound awareness of the need for spiritual salvation, modern man has substituted the rationalist dream of mastering the material world, an enterprise that can lead only to suicide both spiritual and material. If the poem is a defense of reason, then, it is so chiefly by implication. "An Elegy" is a moving analysis of what rationality is not.

I would like to conclude this chapter by discussing another poem by Winters, written at roughly the same time as the "Elegy," and which is also a critique of what I am calling rationalism. The poem "An October Nocturne" poses, by implication, a notion of rationality that is in line with what Plato refers to in the *Symposium* as the "In-Between" (*metaxy*), which I shall elucidate further in the next chapter. Here is the poem:

> The night was faint and sheer;
> Immobile, road and dune.
> Then, for a moment, clear,
> A plane moved past the moon.
>
> O spirit cool and frail,
> Hung in the lunar fire!
> Spun wire and brittle veil!
> And trembling slowly higher!
>
> Pure in each proven line!
> The balance and the aim,
> Half empty, half divine!
> I saw how true you came.
>
> Dissevered from your cause,
> Your function was your goal.
> Oblivious to my laws,
> You made your calm patrol.

The plane here is, like the *Macon,* a symbol of the rationalist ethos, of a notion of reason that leaves no room for the human. It exists in the cool and inhuman—yet seductively pure—environment of a moonlit evening. It is a rationalist invention ("Spun wire and brittle veil!"), perfect in its conception

("Pure in each proven line!"). Plato in the *Symposium* referred to human existence as taking place between the extremes of ignorance and knowledge, of mortality and immortality. There is no room for the human in this vision, for the plane appears to be a symbol—like Sophocles' Oedipus or like the Alcibiades of Thucydides and Plato[15]—of that which attempts to take its place outside the In-Between; the plane is not "half human, half divine" but is rather "half empty, half divine." The plane, "dissevered from" its "cause," and like Oedipus until the end of the play, "oblivious" of the "laws" of human nature, becomes a symbol of that which bizarrely exists outside what Eric Voegelin calls the "tension of existence."

In Sophocles' play Oedipus becomes a symbol of the rationalist desire to master reality, to know it from the outside—thereby attempting to turn it into a thing—rather than patiently participating in it. The analysis of Athenian rationalism made by Sophocles and Thucydides culminates in the articulation by Plato and Aristotle of the classical experience of reason. And it is to this experience, so fundamental to any understanding of the classical and hence of the classic, that I shall turn in the following chapter.

15. In the *Symposium,* the dialogue in which (as I discussed in the previous chapter) Plato explicitly articulates his notion of the In-Between (202e), the drunken Alcibiades represents the kind of soul that, through a "lust for massively possessive experience," cannot live in the tension of this In-Between. Alcibiades' response to the Socratic invitation to live in this tension is to desire to possess, carnally, the bearer of the invitation. Nothing less possessive will do. The phrase "lust for massively possessive experience" is from Eric Voegelin, *The New Science of Politics* (Chicago: University of Chicago Press, 1952), 122.

3

ANIMAL RATIONIS CAPAX

GULLIVER'S TRAVELS AND THE CLASSICAL EXPERIENCE OF REASON

I now wish to discuss in more detail the meaning of the word *reason,* which is crucial to any understanding of the classic. This is necessary because this word is much misunderstood today, particularly in the wake of several phenomena: the Enlightenment reduction of reason to the purely intentional consciousness; the association of the term with specific philosophical systems such as Hegel's; and Derrida's attack on what he has named "logocentrism."

When we use the term *reason,* then, it is reasonable to ask: do we mean the divinely sanctioned reason of Plato and Aristotle, a notion of reason that was transmitted to the Middle Ages and the Renaissance? Or do we mean the quantitative or humanly autonomous reason of the French philosophes of the eighteenth century, an understanding of reason that found itself—as it still finds itself today—at odds with religious revelation? And where are we to place, in this continuum, the views toward reason articulated by Jonathan Swift, the eighteenth-century classicist and divine who devoted much of his life to the hopeless task of plugging up that rapidly gaping hole in the wall that separated the world he wished to preserve from the floodwaters of the Enlightenment?

What I would like to point out in this chapter are the similarities between the Platonic and Aristotelian understanding of reason and Swift's view of what constitutes reason as this is implied—largely by its very conspicuous absence—in *Gulliver's Travels,* particularly in book 4 of that work. In my discussion of the Platonic and Aristotelian view of reason I shall take the liberty of drawing at some length on the important essay "Reason: The Classic Experience" by Eric Voegelin, which first appeared in *The Southern Review* in 1974.[1] Voegelin's essay is a succinct and very useful analysis of the classical position. The striking similarities between Voegelin's explication of the Platonic and Aristotelian understanding of reason and Swift's are not merely coincidental, for Voegelin's explication, which he derives from the texts of the classical philosophers, is at the same time an attempt to recover an understanding of a rationality whose passing Swift was already lamenting two hundred and fifty years earlier. There is a perceptible historical continuity between the two figures. Swift's writing constitutes an act of resistance against the rationalism of early Enlightenment thought, with its penchant for systems-building, on the one hand, and its fixation on a purely empirical science, on the other.[2] Voegelin attempts to recover the experience of classic rationality that had been eclipsed by many Enlightenment and post-Enlightenment thinkers.[3] Swift, moreover, knew something about classical philosophy. He had read a good deal of Aristotle while a student at Trinity College, Dublin, and he knew and admired Plato. In *A Letter to a Gentleman, Lately Entered into Holy Orders,* for example, he recommends that

1. The present chapter is not the first attempt to suggest the relevance of Voegelin's work for understanding Swift and the English eighteenth century. See, for example, Martin Price, *Swift's Rhetorical Art* (New Haven: Yale University Press, 1953), 89; Ronald Paulson, *Theme and Structure in Swift's "A Tale of a Tub"* (New Haven: Yale University Press, 1960); and G. Douglas Atkins, "The Ancients, the Moderns, and Gnosticism," *Studies in Voltaire and the Eighteenth Century* 151, no. 1 (1976): 149–66.

2. See Samuel Holt Monk's fine essay, "The Pride of Lemuel Gulliver," *The Southern Review* 63 (1955): 48–71.

3. Voegelin's most direct critique of Enlightenment thought can be found in *From Enlightenment to Revolution* (Durham, N.C.: Duke University Press, 1975).

the young man read "the Heathen Philosophers" and "make their Works a considerable Part of [his] Study." He remarks in the same treatise, "I am deceived, if a better Comment could be anywhere collected upon the Moral Part of the Gospel, than from the Writings of these excellent men."[4]

For Voegelin, the Greek philosophers discovered reason—the Platonic and Aristotelian νοῦς—"as the source of order in the *psyche* of man."[5] The discovery of reason was "the process in reality in which concrete human beings, the 'lovers of wisdom,' the philosophers as they styled themselves, were engaged in an act of resistance against the personal and social disorder of their age. From this act there emerged the *nous* as the cognitively luminous force that inspired the philosophers to resist and, at the same time, enabled them to recognize the phenomena of disorder in the light of a humanity ordered by the *nous.*"[6] Plato, thus, articulated the nature of reason as an act of resistance against the sophistic climate of opinion. Swift's articulation of reason in *Gulliver's Travels* is an analogous act of resistance against the increasingly popular view of the self-sufficiency of human reason, which would reach its fulfillment in the Enlightenment.

"In their acts of resistance to the disorder of the age, Socrates, Plato, and Aristotle," Voegelin writes, "experienced and explored the movements of a force that structures the *psyche* of man and enabled it to resist disorder. To this force, its movements, and the resulting structure, they gave the name *nous.*"[7] Aristotle therefore specifically "characterized man as the *zoon noun echon,* as 'the living being that possesses *nous.*' "[8] This conception of a human being as the ζῷον νοῦν ἔχων was abbreviated into ζῷον νοητικόν, the Latin translation of which became the well-known and influential *animal rationale.* From the Aristotelian exploration and its resulting definition, therefore, humans came to be known in the Western tradition as "rational animals." Jonathan Swift confronted this definition in the twilight years of that tradition, and he was not very impressed by it. In a famous letter to Alexander Pope written just before *Gulliver's Travels* was about to be published, Swift remarked, "I have gotten Materials Towards a Treatis proving

4. *Irish Tracts 1720–1723 and Sermons,* with introductory essay and notes on sermons by Louis Landa, in *The Prose Works of Jonathan Swift,* ed. Herbert Davis, 14 vols. (Oxford: Basil Blackwell, 1939–68), 9:73–74.

5. "Reason: The Classic Experience," in *Anamnesis* (Notre Dame, Ind.: University of Notre Dame Press, 1978), 26.

6. Ibid.

7. Ibid., 91.

8. Ibid.

the falsity of that Definition *animal rationale;* and to show it should be only *rationis capax.*"[9] Swift was correct in objecting to this definition, for it is mere shorthand and can be misconstrued when the particular experiences from which the definition long ago emerged are forgotten. Once we clarify the classical experience of reaason, we will see that Swift's description of a human being as *animal rationis capax* is congenial with the Aristotelian characterization ζῷον νοητικόν (or *animal rationale*).

What Plato and Aristotle articulate is what Voegelin calls the tension of existence. The philosopher experiences reality in a state of unrest. "Man, when he experiences himself as existent," Voegelin writes, "discovers his specific humanity as that of the questioner for the where-from and the where-to, for the ground and the sense of his existence."[10] Human beings, of course, have always been questioners,[11] but what the philosophers realized was that it was precisely this questioning consciousness that constituted humanity. Hence, the vocabulary of wondering and searching permeates the writings of Plato and Aristotle. In the *Theaetetus,* for example, Socrates says that wonder (τὸ θαυμάζειν) is the only beginning of philosophy, that humans are moved to the study of philosophy by wonder (155d). And Aristotle opens the *Metaphysics* by stating that "all men by nature desire to know." The awareness of one's own ignorance is the starting point of the quest for knowledge. The insight is the source, as it is well known, of the meaning of the Delphic oracle as revealed to Socrates: he was the wisest of all men because he was, more than anyone else, profoundly aware of his own ignorance. As Aristotle later puts it, "A man in confusion or wonder [θαυμάζων] is conscious of being ignorant" (*Metaphysics* 928b18).

For both Plato and Aristotle, then, humans exist in a state of tension between ignorance and knowledge. For Plato, the philosopher is the spiritual man (δαιμόνιος ἀνήρ) who is conscious of his existence between (μεταξύ)

9. *The Correspondence of Jonathan Swift,* ed. Harold Williams, 5 vols. (Oxford: Clarendon Press, 1963–65), 3:103.

10. "Reason," 92–93.

11. Odysseus's journey home in the *Odyssey,* for example, although of course a literal journey, may also be viewed as a pretheoretical (I do not mean "allegorical") symbolization of "the tension of existence." Homer even expresses, with precision, the Platonic articulation of what Voegelin calls the poles of existential tension. In order to continue his journey home, Odysseus must overcome the temptations of the obliteration of consciousness through (1) a hedonistic immersion in undifferentiated particulars (Calypso) and (2) the promise of perfect knowledge offered by the Sirens (12.184–91), the acceptance of which has resulted in the death of the spirit in those who have succumbed (12.39–46). Odysseus is tempted, that is, with hypostatizations of both of the poles of existential tension.

the states of ignorance and full knowledge (*Symposium* 203a). In the process of philosophizing, humans nourish the immortal part of themselves, and it is this which enables them to participate, so far as it is humanly possible, in the divine (cf. Plato's *Timaeus* 90a–b). "We must follow those who advise us, being men, to think of human things," Aristotle says in the *Nicomachean Ethics* (1177b32–1178a), "and being mortal, of mortal things, but must, so far as we can, make ourselves immortal [ἀθανατίζειν], and strain every nerve to live in accordance with the best thing in us,"[12] in accordance, that is, with reason (νοῦς).

If human beings exist in the *metaxy*, in the tension between mortality and immortality, "any attempt to define man as a world-immanent [i.e. wholly 'mortal'] entity will destroy the meaning of his existence, because it deprives man of his specific humanity."[13] To be human, that is, is to seek answers to fundamental questions about existence and, thereby, to immortalize our psyches in the process of asking the questions. God, as Aristotle says in the *Metaphysics* (1073a3), is "eternal, unmovable, and separate from sensible things"; he is transcendent reality in its purity, the divine mover. If humans conceive of themselves as having a purely immanent existence, they will have blocked their capacity to participate, so far as they are able, in the noetic process. They will remain in a state of complacent ignorance. Crucial to Voegelin's articulation of the noetic process is his constant warning that "the poles of the tension must not be hypostatized [i.e., reified] into objects independent of the tension in which they are experienced as its poles."[14] The poles of the divine and the human, that is, or of the one (τὸ ἕν) and the unlimited (τὸ ἄπειρον, *Philebus* 16d–e), or (in the language of medieval scholasticism) of transcendence and immanence, are not objects in the world, nor are they even objects of cognition; they are symbolic representations of the poles of existential tension as this tensional process was experienced and articulated by Plato and Aristotle. Any attempt to consider these poles as reified objects independent of an experiencing consciousness is to destroy the reality of existence in the *metaxy*.

In the *Philebus* Socrates compares the noetic process with the kind of

---

12. *Nicomachean Ethics*, trans. W. D. Ross, in *The Basic Works of Aristotle*, ed. Richard McKeon (New York: Random House, 1941), 1105. The passages from the *Metaphysics*, quoted in the preceding paragraph of the text, are also translated by W. D. Ross in *Basic Works*, 689, 692.

13. Voegelin, "Reason," 104.

14. Ibid. The preceding passage from the *Metaphysics* is translated by W. D. Ross in *Basic Works*, 881.

mental activity practiced by "the man who is considered wise these days."
Such a man, Socrates says,

> while making his one [ἕν]—or his many, as the case may be—more
> quickly or more slowly than is proper, when he has got his one [ἕν]
> proceeds to his unlimited [ἄπειρα] straightaway, allowing the inter-
> mediates to escape [ἐκφεύγει] him, whereas it is the recognition of
> those intermediates that makes all the difference in discussing prob-
> lems in a philosophical manner [διαλεκτικῶς] rather than conten-
> tiously [ἐριστικῶς]. (17a)[15]

Since humans exist in the *metaxy,* moreover, the questions that they ask and
which define their humanity cannot be reduced to questions of objective
fact, to questions, that is, which admit of only quantitative answers. This may
be an adequate definition of the questioning consciousness of Lemuel Gulliver, but in the classical experience of reason the questioning consciousness
is supremely conscious of its participation in the reality that it is attempting
to understand. "In the Greek conception," as Eugene Webb has remarked,
"*nous* is never, as the modern conception of mind would have it, a detached,
neutral contemplation or a dispassionate calculative process."[16]

Let us now recall how Lemuel Gulliver, having returned from his enlightening voyage to the land of the Houyhnhnms, reacts to his reunion with his
family:

> My wife received me with great Surprise and Joy, because they con-
> cluded me certainly dead; but I must freely confess, the Sight of them
> filled me only with Hatred, Disgust and Contempt; and the more, by
> reflecting of the near Alliance I had to them. For, although since my
> unfortunate Exile from the *Houyhnhnm* Country, I had compelled
> myself to tolerate the Sight of *Yahoos,* and to converse with *Don
> Pedro de Mendez* [the benevolent sea captain who rescued Gulliver];
> yet my Memory and Imaginations were perpetually filled with the
> Virtues and Ideas of those exalted *Houyhnhms.* And when I began to
> consider, that by copulating with one of the *Yahoo-* species, I had

15. Trans. R. Reginald Hackforth, *The Collected Dialogues of Plato,* ed. Edith Hamilton and
Huntington Cairns (Princeton: Princeton University Press, 1961), 1093. I have slightly adapted
the translation.

16. *Eric Voegelin: Philosopher of History* (Seattle: University of Washington Press, 1981),
96–97.

become a Parent of more; it struck me with the utmost Shame, Confusion and Horror.

As soon as I entered the House, my Wife took me in her Arms, and kissed me; at which, having not been used to the Touch of that odious Animal for so many Years, I fell into a Swoon for almost an Hour. At the Time I am writing, it is five Years since my last Return to *England:* during the first year I could not endure my Wife or Children in my Presence, the very smell of them was intolerable; much less could I suffer them to eat in the same Room. To this Hour they dare not presume to touch my Bread, or drink out of the same Cup; neither was I ever able to let one of them take me by the Hand.[17]

What is the source of Gulliver's profound sense of alienation and what might be its relationship to the classical experience of reason?

When a person, Voegelin writes, "experiences himself as existent, he discovers himself as the questioner for the where-from and the where-to, for the ground and the sense of his existence."[18] Now Gulliver, at the beginning of his travels, can be described as anything but a questioner: he is a decent and rather unimaginative—indeed an obtuse and literal-minded—middle-class conformist. As a student he pursues those subjects—medicine and navigation, for example—which he feels will be "useful" for one who, like himself, intends to travel, as he believed "it would some time or other" be his "Fortune to do." Theology and philosophy are absent from the syllabus. Marriage, for Gulliver, is no sacred rite; it is merely respectable and financially prudent: "Being advised to alter my Condition," he tells us, "I married Mrs. *Mary Burton,* second daughter of Mr. *Edmond Burton,* Hosier, in *Newgate-Street,* with whom I received four Hundred Pounds for a Portion."[19] Such are the epithets that describe the Penelope to whom Gulliver, after his long and arduous journeys, finally returns. Gulliver does, of course, experience himself as existing in a state of unrest. Such an experience is inescapable since it defines the human condition, but Gulliver would rather ignore the reality of the experience; he tells us that he has "been condemned by Nature and Fortune to an active and restless Life."[20] But the

17. *The Prose Works of Jonathan Swift,* ed. Harold Williams, 14 vols. (Oxford: Shakespeare Head Press, 1939–68), 11:273–74.
18. "Reason," 92–93.
19. *Prose Works,* 11:3–4.
20. Ibid., 67.

restlessness has no direction and, specifically, has no transcendental direction. The *Travels* is conspicuously *not* a *Pilgrim's Progress.*[21]

Gulliver leaves home not in search of salvation or even of knowledge or wisdom, but "to get Riches, whereby I might entertain myself and my Family when I should return."[22] And somehow the itch to travel—the expression of his experience of unrest—will not go away, despite his better judgment. "I continued home with my Wife and Children about five months in a very happy Condition," Gulliver confesses at the beginning of book 4, "if I could have learned the Lesson of knowing when I was well."[23] Swift has presented Gulliver as a man defined largely as a "world-immanent" entity. He is not accustomed to experiencing reality in its transcendental dimension, as Swift suggests in his description of the Lilliputians' bewilderment at discovering that strange machine we moderns immediately recognize as Gulliver's watch. "He put this Engine to our Ears," one of the Lilliputians reports, "which made an incessant Noise like that of a Water-Mill. And we conjecture it is either some unknown Animal, or the God that he worships: But we are more inclined to the latter Opinion, because he assured us . . . that he seldom did any Thing without consulting it. He called it his Oracle, and said it pointed out the Time for every Action of his Life."[24] A being so totally immersed in the world of time would not be a likely candidate for experiencing reality in its transcendental dimension.

The experience that shakes Gulliver out of his complacency is his voyage to the land of the Houyhnhnms. The gestures of these marvelous creatures impress Gulliver as being "not unlike those of a Philosopher," and it is precisely the achievement of the philosophical ideal that the Houyhnhnms embody. Their "grand Maxim," Gulliver tells us, is

21. The implicit comparison with *Pilgrim's Progress* was not lost on the eighteenth-century reader. Shortly after *Gulliver's Travels* was published, John Arbuthnot wrote to Swift on November 6, 1726, that he believed the work "will have as great a Run as John Bunian" (*Correspondence*, 3:179). Swift admired Bunyan. "I have been better entertained, and more informed by a Chapter in the *Pilgrim's Progress*," he wrote in *A Letter to a Gentleman, Lately Entered into Holy Orders*, "than by a long discourse upon the *Will* and the *Intellect*, and *Simple* or *Complex Ideas*" (*Prose Works*, 9:77). The insight that *Gulliver's Travels* is a secularized version of Christian's spiritual pilgrimage provides the title of L. J. Morrisey's book, *Gulliver's Progress* (Hamden, Conn.: Archon Books, 1978), which illuminates the biblical references in Swift's satire.

22. *Prose Works*, 11:227.

23. Ibid., 205.

24. Ibid., 19.

to cultivate *Reason,* and to be wholly governed by it. Neither is *Reason* among them a Point problematical as with us, where Men can argue with Plausibility on both Sides of a Question; but it strikes you with immediate Conviction; as it must needs do where it is not mingled, obscured, or discoloured by Passion and Interest. I remember with extreme Difficulty that I could bring my Master to understand the Meaning of the Word *Opinion,* or how a Point could be disputable; because *Reason* taught us to affirm or deny only where we are certain; and beyond our Knowledge we cannot do either. So that Controversies, Wranglings, Disputes, and Positiveness in false or dubious Propositions, are Evils unknown among the *Houyhnhnms.*[25]

Truth may indeed strike the Houyhnhnms with "immediate Conviction," but in mere mortals such immediate conviction is a sure sign of intellectual arrogance and wrongheadedness. It is a sign, in short, of the spiritual pride that alienates Gulliver—whose "Memory and Imaginations were perpetually filled with the Virtues and Ideas of those exalted *Houyhnhnms*"—from his fellow humans when he returns home.

The reader must not repeat Gulliver's mistake and hypostatize the poles of existential tension into the extremes of ignorance and knowledge, the human and the divine, Yahoo and Houyhnhnm. And Swift presents the Houyhnhnms as precisely the hypostatization of pure rationality. They have achieved the impossible. They intuit absolute truth, their minds unclouded by passion or interest. And since they intuit absolute truth, the notion of lying is inconceivable to them; they refer to what, for human beings, is a lie,

25. Cf. the remarkable similarities between this passage and Plotinus's description of dialectic as that process which operates in the ethereal regions of the second hypostasis (the νοῦς). As truth "strikes" the Houyhnhnms with "immediate conviction," so whatever is submitted to dialectic "it perceives by . . . intuition, as sense perception also does, but it hands over pretty precisions of speech to another discipline which finds satisfaction in them" (*Enneads* 1.3.5, trans. A. H. Armstrong, 6 vols., Loeb Classical Library [1966–88], 1:161). The Houyhnhnms perceive truth, then, by direct intuition; and they do not descend to using "pretty precisions of speech": "It put me to the Pains of many Circumlocutions," Gulliver discovers, "to give my [Houyhnhnm] Master a right Idea of what I spoke; for their Language doth not abound in Variety of Words, because their Wants and Passions are fewer than among us" (*Prose Works,* 11:226). That the Houyhnhnms "have no Letters" is reminiscent of Plotinus's description of the dialectical process when it arrives at the One: "It leaves what is called logical activity, about propositions and syllogisms, to another art, as it might leave learning how to write" (*Enneads* 1.3.4, trans. Armstrong, 1:159).

as "the thing which is not."[26] They feel a general benevolence toward all their fellow creatures, since "*Nature* teaches them to love the whole Species," a love which Swift felt himself incapable of experiencing. For in a letter to Pope, Swift says that he

> has ever hated all Nations and Communityes and all my love is to-ward individualls for instance I hate the tribe of Lawyers, but I love Councellor such a one, Judge such a one for so with Physicians (I will not speak of my own Trade) Soldiers, English, Scotch, French, and the rest but principally I hate and detest that animal called man, although I hartily love John, Peter, Thomas and so forth.[27]

In so far that the Houyhnhnms "love the whole Species" they have achieved a godlike state of pure rationality, for as Pope writes in the *Essay on Man*, "God loves from Whole to Parts: but human soul / Must rise from Individual to the Whole" (4:361–62). To return to the language of Plato's *Philebus:* Gulliver had for so long been living in a world of undifferentiated particulars—of the unlimited—that once he feels he has apprehended the One he is unable to return to the reality of life in the In-Between (Plato's *metaxy*). "The many Virtues of those excellent *Quadrapeds,*" Gulliver says of the Houyhnhnms after his conversion, "had so far opened my Eyes, and enlarged my Understanding, that I began to view the Actions and Passions of Man in a very different Light; and to think the Honour of my kind not worth managing." My Houyhnhnm master, Gulliver goes on to say, "daily convinced me of a thousand Faults in my self, whereof I had not the least Perception before . . . and *Truth* appeared so amiable to me, that I determined upon sacrificing every thing to it. . . . I had not been a Year in this Country, before I contracted such a Love and Veneration for the Inhabitants, that I entered on a firm Resolution never to return to human Kind."[28]

The analogies between the Platonic analysis and that of Swift may be more than fortuitous. R. S. Crane intuited Platonic undertones in book 4 of the

---

26. The phrase seems almost a direct translation of the Greek τò μὴ τὰ ὄντα (*Cratylus* 429d).

27. From a letter of September 29, 1725, in *Correspondence,* 3:103. Cf. Dostoevsky on atheism in the notebooks for "A Raw Youth": "Atheism—I have felt universal love, but I don't love Mother" and "I am destined to love *everybody,* and so no one" (Ellis Sandoz, *Political Apocalypse: A Study of Dostoevsky's Grand Inquisitor* [Baton Rouge: Louisiana State University Press, 1971], 160).

28. *Prose Works,* 11:242.

Travels when he compared Gulliver's extreme reluctance to reenter the human race to the experience of the prisoner in the cave described by Plato in the seventh book of the *Republic.*[29] The prisoners in the cave have had their necks chained from childhood so that they are unable to turn their heads and see that what they had taken for reality all their lives are in fact mere shadows. There is a fire shining behind the prisoners and along a parapet just in front of the fire those who control the world of opinion parade objects that cast their reflections on the wall. Once a prisoner turns around, sees this shadow-reality for what it truly is and ascends to the light, Socrates says, it will be difficult for him—as it was for Gulliver—to return to life in the cave. John F. Richert, following Crane's suggestion, gives convincing evidence that the *Republic,* included in the edition of Plato's works printed in Geneva in 1578 which Swift owned, was, more than any other work, very much on Swift's mind when he composed book 4 of *Gulliver's Travels.*

And more parallels can be found in other parts of the *Travels.* There is, for example, the striking resemblance between the absurd games in which the Lilliputian minister has his lackeys compete in hope of preferment and those similar contests alluded to in the seventh book of the *Republic* (516d). "If there had been honors and commendations among them which they bestowed on one another and prizes for the man who is quickest to make out the shadows as they pass and best able to remember their customary precedences, sequences, and coexistences, and so most successful at guessing at what was to come," Socrates asks Glaucon, "do you think he [the prisoner who has ascended out of the cave and into the light] would be very keen about such rewards, and that he would envy and emulate them?"[30] This passage might be compared with Swift's analogous description from book 1:

> The Emperor holds a Stick in his Hands, both Ends parallel to the Horizon, while the Candidates advancing one by one, sometimes leap over the Stick, sometimes creep under it backwards and forwards several times, according as the Stick is advanced and depressed. Sometimes the Emperor holds one End of the Stick, and his first Minister the other; sometimes the Minister has it entirely to himself. Whoever performs this Part with the most Agility, and holds out the longest in

29. "The Rationale of the Fourth Voyage," in *Swift: Gulliver's Travels, A Casebook,* ed. Richard Gravil (London: Macmillan, 1974).

30. Trans. Paul Shorey in *The Collected Dialogues of Plato,* ed. Edith Hamilton and Huntington Cairns (Princeton: Princeton University Press, 1961), 749.

> *leaping* and *creeping,* is rewarded with the Blue-coloured Silk; the
> Red is given to the next, and the Green to the third, which they all
> wear girt twice round about the Middle; and you see few great Persons
> around the Court, who are not adorned with one of these Girdles.[31]

Thus we have a depiction of one aspect of Lilliputian society as it was
uncritically described by Gulliver in the days before his precipitous ascent
out of the cave and into the blinding light of book 4.

Gulliver, then, has fled from the reality of life in the In-Between, from what
Swift's friend Pope referred to, in the *Essay on Man,* as "this isthmus of a
middle state" (2:3), and in so doing he has joined ranks with other similar
types in the *Travels,* such as the abstrusely speculative and physically inert
Laputans, of whom Allan Bloom has perceptively written: "On the flying
island men have one eye turned inward, the other toward the zenith; they are
perfect Cartesians—one egotistical eye contemplating the self, one cosmological eye surveying the most distant things. The intermediate range, which
previously was the center of concentration and which defined both the ego
and the pattern for the study of the stars, is not within the Laputan purview."[32]
Just so was the eye of Thucydides' Alcibiades, to recall our discussion of fifth-
century Athenian rationalism in the previous chapter, preoccupied with "surveying the most distant things." What Gulliver had said of the Lilliputians in
book 1 is equally true of himself before his fanatical conversion to true belief
in the hypostatization of the philosophical ideal: "They see with great Exactness, but at no great Distance."[33] By the end of book 4, Gulliver—his "Memory and Imaginations . . . perpetually filled with the Virtues and Ideas of those
exalted *Houyhnhnms*"—is repelled by those very particulars in which he had
for so long been unconsciously immersed. In his rapid flight from immersion
in the unlimited to true belief in the One, he willfully renders himself incapable of participating in the classical experience of reason.

Swift, then, by showing in *Gulliver's Travels* that a human being was
better defined as *rationis capax* rather than as *animal rationale,* may be

31. *Prose Works,* 11:41.
32. "An Outline of *Gulliver's Travels,*" in *Ancients and Moderns,* ed. Joseph Cropsey (New
York: Basic Books, 1964), 79. It might be relevant here to remark on the similarities between
Swift's critique of the Laputans and the fifth-century (B.C.) critique of rationalism, discussed in
the previous chapter. What Bloom says of the Laputans is precisely what Swift's kindred spirit,
Aristophanes, says about the Athenian character as embodied in his view of Socrates in *The
Clouds.*
33. *Prose Works,* 11:41.

viewed as advocating a return from the fossilized popular definition, which had been torn from its experiential roots, to the classical experience of reason—of νόησις or *ratio*—as articulated by Plato and Aristotle. In *A Tale of a Tub* Swift had defined moral sanity by presenting a detailed picture of what he conceived to have been its opposite, the endlessly digressive and self-important madness of the paradigmatic Modern. So, in *Gulliver's Travels,* although Swift does not explain what Plato's *metaxy* is, he does depict, with considerable analytic insight, precisely what it is not.

My purpose in this chapter has been to describe the historical emergence of the experience of reason in Plato that is central to any understanding of the classic, as well as to describe the eclipse of rationality that Swift, in *Gulliver's Travels,* tried to prevent. In conclusion, I cannot help observing how Swift himself appears to have had difficulties living in the In-Between. It is perhaps the cardinal sin in the interpretation of *Gulliver's Travels* to equate Lemuel Gulliver with Jonathan Swift. Swift is not Gulliver. Nor is Gulliver even represented as a living and developing personality, such as we increasingly find in the literary form of the novel,[34] and *Gulliver's Travels* certainly is not a novel. Although it is clear that Swift is not Gulliver, it would nevertheless be a mistake to overlook how Swift, like Gulliver, was often drawn to the extreme poles of what Voegelin calls existential tension.

Like Gulliver, Swift was drawn to the pole of pure immanence, to inert, self-opaque thinghood, to an unconscious immersion in the world of time. We might here recall Swift's description, in Lilliput, of Gulliver's watch. Having discovered this strange "Engine," the Lilliputians conjecture as to whether it is "some unknown Animal, or the God that he worships" but decide in favor of "the latter Opinion, because [Gulliver] assured us . . . that he seldom did anything without consulting it. He called it his Oracle, and said it pointed out the Time for every action of his life." Samuel Johnson, that most judicious and shrewd observer of human nature, remarks, in his *Life of Swift,* on what he considers to be one of the idiosyncrasies of Swift's behavior: "Of time, on all occasions," Johnson writes, "he was an exact computer, and knew the minutes required to every common operation."[35]

And, like Gulliver, Swift was also drawn to the opposite pole of pure transcendence. His rage for perfection, it is true, was held in check by his healthy Christian belief in the imperfectibility of human nature, but his nagging impa-

---

34. I discuss the relation of the principle of gradual psychological development to the very definition of the novel in Chapter 12.

35. In *Lives of the English Poets,* ed. G. B. Hill, 3 vols. (Oxford: Clarendon Press, 1905), 1:60.

tience with human imperfection remained nevertheless. Once again Samuel Johnson, who appears to have been more successful in adapting his powerful and often resistant frame to life in the In-Between, makes some pertinent observations about Swift's character. Johnson, in showing considerable leniency toward what he felt was Swift's error in permitting himself to toy with Vanessa's affections, remarks: "If it be said that Swift should have checked a passion which he never meant to gratify, recourse must be had to that extenuation which he so much despised, *men are but men.*"[36]

Johnson elsewhere speaks of Swift's "severe and punctilious temper" and in a well-known passage observes that "to his domesticks he was naturally rough; and a man of a rigorous temper, with that vigilance of minute attention which his works discover, must have been a master that few could bear."[37] Swift's impatience with imperfection is beautifully expressed in J. V. Cunningham's poem "With a Copy of Swift's Works":

> Underneath this pretty cover
> Lies Vanessa's, Stella's lover.
> You that undertake this story
> For his life nor death be sorry
> Who the Absolute so loved
> Motion to its zero moved,
> Till immobile in that chill
> Fury hardened in the will,
> And the trivial, bestial flesh
> In its jacket ceased to thresh,
> And the soul none dare forgive
> Quiet lay, and ceased to live.[38]

Swift, the advocate in book 4 of *Gulliver's Travels* of classical rationality, appears to have experienced considerable difficulties living in accordance with the results of his own analysis. Perhaps it was Swift's personal experience of the tension between the poles of immanence and transcendence in an age when many had abandoned themselves to one or the other that lends to Swift's works their peculiarly relentless and abiding philosophical power.

36. Ibid., 32.
37. Ibid., 56.
38. In *The Exclusions of a Rhyme* (Chicago: Swallow, 1960), 85.

4

LED BY THE LIGHT OF THE MAEONIAN STAR

Aristotle on Tragedy and Some Passages in the *Odyssey*

In the first chapter I described how Plato can be read as addressing many of the concerns we associate with contemporary literary theory and discussed certain fundamental philosophical assumptions that must underlie any understanding of the classic. I also suggested that if Plato's work is truly classic, then it will be perpetually relevant and that it would therefore be profitable to test recent formulations in the light of Platonic thought. In Chapters 2 and 3 I elucidated the experience of reason often implicit in the classic. Now I wish to focus on more specifically literary matters. The critic most quintessentially associated with the classic is Aristotle; the poet, Homer. Here I wish to point out how many of Aristotle's most enduring critical insights are implied in Homer.

Aristotle's *Poetics* is not an exciting work to read. It is dry. And since it is the quintessential document in the soundest tradition of the classical defenses of poetry, the *Poetics* has through its method of presentation not thereby helped to dispel preconceptions about the alleged aridity of classicism. In Chapter 2 I discussed the concerns that, in my judgment, make Sophocles' *Oedipus Tyrannus* so powerful a work. Aristotle mentions none of these concerns in his discussion of the play; for him in the *Poetics* only the structure of the play is of interest. Is this so because—if one can interpret Sophocles' play, as I have, as a plea for a participationist notion of reason, for a view of rationality that Plato makes explicit throughout his work—Aristotle assumed that his readers were themselves convinced Platonists, that the philosophical revolution had been victorious, and that he could therefore attend to more technical matters? Perhaps. But there is a sense in which the "rationalism" of Aristotle's analysis manifests the very same bent of mind that Sophocles so profoundly excoriates. We might call this the tragic irony of the *Poetics*. As a scholar of the *Poetics* has recently remarked, Aristotle deprives tragedy "of the scope to move to the edge of, and even outside, the realm of rational understanding, or to dramatise events whose meaning cannot be encompassed by the logic of probability or necessity."[1] It is at any rate truly ironic that Plato, who is known as the great enemy of poetry, is so much more poetic than poetry's defender, Aristotle, although there is evidence that Aristotle's early works were written in dialogue form and were delightful to read. There are those who say that the *Poetics* is nothing more than lecture notes compiled by Aristotle's students, although we must observe that compared to the rest of the Aristotelian corpus, the *Poetics* does not stand out as particularly aberrant. Still, it is for the pithy and businesslike expression of many of the most enduring principles of literary theory we associate with the classic—such as the primacy of plot, the distinction between poetry and history, the importance of *katharsis*—that we go to the *Poetics*. The genius of the work resides in how much truth there is in so many of its seemingly dispassionate formulations.

There was a time in literary history when critics and even major poets considered the ancient critics to have been appropriate commentators on the ancient poets themselves. That time was coming to an end by the middle of the eighteenth century, but in 1711 Alexander Pope, when reviewing the

---

1. Stephen Halliwell, from his chapter on Aristotle's *Poetics,* in *The Cambridge History of Literary Criticism,* vol. 1, *Classical Criticism,* ed. George A. Kennedy (Cambridge: Cambridge University Press, 1989), 175.

achievements of the great critics of antiquity, could still praise Aristotle as the pioneer of ancient criticism:

> The mighty *Stagyrite* first left the Shore,
> Spread all his Sails, and durst the Deeps explore;
> He steer'd securely, and discover'd far,
> *Led* by the Light of the *Maeonian* Star.
> *(Essay on Criticism,* 645–48)

Pope, of course, believed that

> Those RULES of old *discover'd,* not *devis'd,*
> Are *Nature* still, but *Nature Methodiz'd.*
> (88–89)

And he was convinced that *"Nature* and *Homer* were ... the *same"* (135).[2] Homer, the *"Maeonian Star,"*[3] is a prime example of *"Nature Methodiz'd"*— which is to say, the Aristotelian treatise attempts to elucidate, in explicitly analytical terms, the principles of order that are implicit in the perfectly executed Homeric poems. This idea was not new in neoclassical criticism. John Dryden, in the preface to his translation of the *Aeneid* (1697), spoke of "those many rules of imitating nature which Aristotle drew from Homer's *Iliads* and *Odysseys,* and which he fitted to the drama."[4] The tradition of viewing Homer as the first and greatest of the tragic poets begins at least as far back as Plato (*Republic* 595b and 607a; *Theaetetus* 152e). Plato's view, recalled in the second century A.D. by the Greek rhetorician Hermogenes

2. The lines from *An Essay on Criticism* are cited from *Pastoral Poetry and An Essay on Criticism,* ed. E Audra and A. Williams, in vol. 1 of *The Twickenham Edition of the Poems of Alexander Pope,* ed. John Butt et al., 11 vols. (New Haven: Yale University Press, 1938–68), 311–12, 249, 255. For the phrase *"Nature Methodiz'd"* (89), as the Twickenham editors suggest (249), Pope appears to be indebted, perhaps via Dryden, to Thomas Rymer's translation of René Rapin's *Reflections on Aristotle's Treatise of Poesie* (1674), 16: "If the Rules be well considered one shall find them to be made only to reduce Nature into method." Dryden quotes this passage at the conclusion of his preface to *Troilus and Cressida* (1679). Cf. the remark of John Dennis, also cited by Audra and Williams, that "the rules of *Aristotle* are nothing but Nature and Good Sence reduc'd to a method."

3. Maeonia, where Homer was supposed by some to have been born, was the name often given to Lydia.

4. *Of Dramatic Poesy and Other Critical Essays,* ed. George Watson, 2 vols. (London: Everyman's Library, 1962), 2:226. Aristotle himself explicitly states that tragedy descends from the *Iliad* and *Odyssey* (*Poetics* 1449).

(*On the Means of Forcefulness,* 36), survives well into the eighteenth century in, for instance, Fielding's *Joseph Andrews* (1742).[5]

Modern Homeric scholarship, with its emphasis on the preliterate nature of the ancient epics, has tended to downplay their relationship to the later literate tradition and, as a consequence, to discourage use of the *Poetics* as a guide to their interpretation. But let us for the moment step back more than two hundred years and sympathize with the convictions of Pope. Let us assume that although Homer obviously did not compose the *Iliad* or the *Odyssey* according to Aristotle's "rules," he nevertheless embodied in those poems very definite principles of order which Aristotle was later to recognize and explicate. The following analysis is not an attempt to "apply" the terminology of the *Poetics* to the *Iliad* and the *Odyssey.* My assumption is rather that the literary theory proposed by Aristotle emerged directly from his reading not only of Greek tragedy but of Homer, his admiration for whom, as Gerald F. Else has remarked, "approaches nearer to idolatry than any other attitude we can discern in him towards a mortal."[6] Pope wisely believed that the "Just *Precepts*" offered by Greek literary criticism were drawn from the "great *Examples*" (*Essay on Criticism,* 97) provided by the literary works themselves. Theorizing in the classic sense is drawn from empirical observation, as Quintilian remarked in his discussion of the use of arguments in rhetoric: "The discovery of arguments was not the result of the publication of text-books, but every kind of argument was put forward before any rules were laid down, and it was only later that writers of rhetoric noted them and collected them for publication."[7]

In the thirteenth chapter of the *Poetics,* Aristotle describes what he believes to be (1) the most effective kind of tragic plot, and (2) the emotions that such a plot should evoke in the audience (1452b30–53a12). These explicit theoretical formulations are implicit in a passage of the *Odyssey.*

The *Odyssey* is an epic in which quality of character is tested again and

---

5. *Joseph Andrews,* part 3, chapter 2.

6. *Aristotle's Poetics: The Argument* (Cambridge: Harvard University Press, 1967), 499. As Stephen Halliwell reminds us, it is very likely that Aristotle discussed Homer at length in the "three books of *On Poets,* and the six or more books of *Homeric Problems*"; both of these works are lost.

7. "Neque enim artibus editis factum est, ut argumenta inveniremus, sed dicta sunt omnia, antequam praeciperentur, mox ea scriptores observata et collecta ediderunt" (*De institutione oratoria* 5.10.120, trans. H. E. Butler, Loeb Classical Library [1921], 4 vols., 2:269). Pope cites this passage from Quintilian in the notes (first included in the edition of 1717) to lines 98–99 of his *Essay on Criticism:* "Just *Precepts* thus from great *Examples* giv'n, / She ["learn'd *Greece*," 92] drew from *them* [the Greek poets] what they deriv'd from *Heav'n.*"

again. In the first half of the poem Odysseus must endure a formidable set of trials, and in the second half the hero tests the character of those around him. In book 17 Odysseus, disguised as a beggar, tests the character of the suitors by asking them for alms. He singles out Antinoös and relates to him the following tale of misfortune:

> Give, dear friend. You seem to me, of all the Achaians,
> not the worst, but the best. You look like a king.
>   Therefore,
> you ought to give me a better present of food than the
>   others
> have done, and I will sing your fame all over the endless
> earth, for I too once lived in my house among people,
> blessed with great wealth, and often I gave to a wanderer
> according to what he was and wanted when he came to
>   me;
> and I had countless serving men, and many other
> good things by which men live and gain a reputation for
>   prosperity.
> But Zeus, son of Kronos, spoiled it all—somehow he
>   wished to—
> when he put it into my head to go with the roving pirates
> to Egypt, a long voyage, so that I must be ruined.
> I stayed my oarswept ships inside the Aigyptos River.
> Then I urged my eager companions to stay where they
>   were, there
> close to the fleet, and to guard the ships, and was urgent
>   with them
> to send lookouts to the watching places, but they,
>   following
> their own impulse, and giving way to marauding violence,
> suddenly began plundering the Egyptians' beautiful
>   fields, and carried off the women and innocent children,
> and killed the men, and soon the outcry came to the city.
> They heard the shouting, and at the time when dawn
>   shows, they came
> on us, and all the plain was filled with horses and infantry
> and the glare of bronze; and Zeus who delights in the
>   thunder flung down

foul panic among my companions, and none was so hardy
as to stand and fight, for the evils stood in a circle around
   them.
There they killed many of us with the sharp bronze, and
   others
they led away alive, to work for them in forced labor;
but they gave me away, into Cyprus, to a stranger arriving,
Dmetor, Iasos' son, who was the strong king in Cyprus.
From there I came here, where I am now, suffering
   hardships.

$$(415-44)^8$$

What is the possible relevance of these Homeric lines to Aristotle's
Poetics? Let us look at the passage from chapter 13. Since tragedy, Aristotle
says, is

an imitation of fearful [φοβερῶν] and pitiable [ἐλεεινῶν] events, this
being the mark of tragic imitation, it follows plainly, in the first place,
that the change of fortune presented must not be the spectacle of a
virtuous man, brought from prosperity to adversity; for this moves
neither pity nor fear; it merely shocks us. Nor, again, that of a bad man
passing from adversity to prosperity: for nothing can be more alien to
the spirit of Tragedy; it possesses no single tragic quality; it neither
satisfies the moral sense nor calls forth pity or fear. Nor, again, should
the downfall of the utter villain be exhibited. A plot of this kind
would, doubtless, satisfy the moral sense, but it would inspire neither
pity nor fear; for pity [ἔλεος] is aroused by unmerited misfortune,
fear [φόβος] by the misfortune of men like ourselves. Such an event,
therefore, will be neither pitiful nor terrible. There remains, then, the
character between these two extremes—that of a man who is not
eminently good and just, yet whose misfortune is brought about not
by vice or depravity [μήτε διὰ κακίαν], but by some error [ἀλλὰ διὰ
ἁμαρτίαν τινά]. (1452b31–53a10)[9]

---

8. The translation is that of Richmond Lattimore (New York: Harper and Row, 1965), 265. I
have made some slight alterations in Lattimore's version.

9. The translation, with slight alterations, is that of S. H. Butcher, *Aristotle's Theory of Poetry
and Fine Art* (New York: Dover, 1951), 45.

The most effective kind of tragic plot, Aristotle says, will feature a protagonist who (1) moves from a state of prosperity to adversity and (2) is of a
moral stature that places him between the extremes of goodness and depravity, since he brings about his misfortune through an action which is the
result not of a settled disposition to wrongdoing but of some error.[10]

The plot of the "tragedy" narrated by Odysseus for his "audience," Antinoös, anticipates these formulations. Its protagonist was at first "blessed
with great wealth" (ὄλβιος ἀφνειόν, 420) and possessed "countless serving
men, along with many other things by which men live well and gain a
reputation for prosperity" (422–23), but he was then sold into slavery and
is now a penniless beggar. As for his moral stature, his character is not
flawless, for he joined a group of pirates who tried to sack an Egyptian city.[11]
(The disclaimer that it was Zeus who put the idea into his head and that he
himself therefore is not to blame for the decision must be seen in the light of
the crucial speech on the relation between human choice and responsibility
which Zeus makes at the very beginning of the poem: men are always
blaming the gods for evils that they in fact bring upon themselves, Zeus says,
because of their own recklessness [1.23–34]). But he is certainly not villain-
ous, for he often demonstrated his compassion by giving alms to poor
vagabonds when he was living as a prosperous landholder, and when he
joined the group of pirates he tried desperately to discourage them from
devastating the Egyptians' beautiful fields and from recklessly carrying off
their women and young children (432–33).

The best plot, according to Aristotle, is that which imitates an action that
will most effectively evoke the distinctively tragic emotions of pity and of
fear. Is there any indication that these are the specific emotions Odysseus is
attempting to evoke in Antinoös?

As one of the two leaders of the suitors, Antinoös may be taken as exempli-
fying the qualities of their characters as a whole, characters that are de-

10. For the definition of "error" (ἁμαρτία or ἁμάρτημα) as opposed to "mere misfortune"
(ἀτύχημα) on the one hand and "intentional wrongdoing" (ἀδίκημα) on the other, see
Nicomachean Ethics 5.8.6–8. An enlightening discussion of the meaning of ἁμαρτία may be
found in D. Armstrong and C. W. Peterson, "Rhetorical Balance in Aristotle's Definition of the
Tragic Agent," *Classical Quarterly* 30, no. 1 (1980): 62–71.

11. Piracy, it is true, was accepted behavior in the Homeric world (see, for example, W. W.
Hyde, *Ancient Greek Mariners* [New York: Oxford University Press, 1947], 45), but that the
activity could be viewed less than sympathetically by some of the morally sensitive members of
the society Homer depicts is suggested by the remarks made by Eumaeus (*Odyssey* 14.83–88),
which I shall discuss later in this chapter.

scribed as follows by the just and balanced Eumaeus. The suitors, the swine-
herd says,

> have no regard for anyone in their minds, no pity
>   [ἐλεητύν].
> The blessed gods have no love for callous actions
> but, rather, they reward justice and actions that are lawful.
> And though those are hateful and lawless men who land
>   on a foreign
> shore, and Zeus grants them spoil and plunder; and they
>   load
> their ships with these goods and set sail for home—even
> in the minds of these men there is a strong fear [δέος] of
>   the vengeance that will be meted out by the gods.
> But these suitors have heard some god-sent rumor, and
>   they know
> about the dismal death of my master, and they will not
>   decently
> make their suit, nor go home to their own houses, but at
>   their
> leisure with wanton violence [ὑπέρβιον] they eat up his
>   property, and spare nothing.
> For as many as are the nights and the days from Zeus, on
>   not one
> of these do they offer even one or two animals for
>   sacrifice
> and they wantonly [ὑπέρβιον] drink up the wine and
>   exhaust the supply.
>
> (14.82–95)[12]

The suitors act in a manner that is wantonly violent (ὑπέρβιον, 92 and 95);
Telemachus in 1.368 angrily addresses the suitors as "you whose hubris is
overweening" (ὑπέρβιον ὕβριν ἔχοντες). They reveal their insolence
through both their blatant disregard for the rules of just and civilized behavior toward the household of Odysseus and their contempt for the gods by
refusing them even the most meager sacrifice. And two specific emotions

---

12. Lattimore's translation, 212. Alterations have been made in the translation, as they have
in the passage from Lattimore's version of *Odyssey* 1.346–55, yet to be discussed.

which their souls are shown to be hardened against experiencing are pity (ἐλεητύν, 82) and fear (δέος, 88).

But is there a relationship between one's insolent behavior and his or her capacity or incapacity to experience pity and fear? Indeed there is, and Aristotle discusses the precise nature of the relationship in the *Rhetoric.* Pity may be defined, Aristotle says,

> as a feeling of pain caused by the sight of some evil, destructive or painful, which befalls one who does not deserve it, and which we might expect to befall ourselves or some friend of ours, and, more-over, to befall us soon. In order to feel pity, we must obviously be capable of supposing that some evil may happen to us or some friend of ours.... It is therefore not felt by those who imagine them-selves ... immensely fortunate—they are, rather, presumptuously in-solent [ὑβρίζουσιν]. (2.8.1385b11–23)

And if fear

> is associated with the expectation that something destructive will happen to us, plainly nobody will be afraid who believes nothing can happen to him; we shall not fear things that we believe cannot hap-pen to us, nor people who we believe cannot inflict them upon us; nor shall we be afraid at times when we think ourselves safe from them. It follows therefore that fear is felt by those who believe some-thing is likely to happen to them.... People do not believe this when they are ... in the midst of great prosperity, and are in consequence insolent [ὑβρισταί], contemptuous, and reckless [θρασεῖς]—the kind of character produced by wealth, physical strength, abundance of friends, power. (2.5.1382b30–83a2)[13]

These two passages suggest that the ability to experience the emotions of pity and fear is essential to the proper functioning of a person's moral being, for those who are incapable of experiencing these emotions are described by Aristotle as "presumptuous" and "insolent" (ὑβρισταί, 2.5.1383; ὑβρίζουσιν, 2.8.1385b).

Exactly what Aristotle means when he says in the *Poetics* that tragedy

---

13. The translation of the two passages from the *Rhetoric,* which I have adapted slightly, is by W. R. Roberts, *Rhetoric and Poetics* (New York: The Modern Library, 1954), 113, 105.

"through pity and fear effects a proper purgation [κάθαρσις] of such emotions" (1449b27–28) is one of the most variously debated subjects in classical philology, largely because we simply do not know enough about Aristotle's conception of κάθαρσις, which he does not make explicit here and which he discusses only briefly in the *Politics* (8.7.1341b33–42a18). And it is not likely that our knowledge of these problems will improve very considerably.[14] But we do know that Aristotle believed that it was and should be the intention of tragic poets to evoke the emotions of pity and fear, and we can reasonably suppose that in espousing such a view he was responding to the objections of Plato. For Plato, also, pity and fear are the emotions evoked by tragedy (see, for example, *Phaedrus* 268c). But it was precisely because tragic poetry appealed to such emotions rather than to the rational faculty that Plato believed such poetry should be censored from the curriculum of the future guardians of the state. "Passages that evoke terror and fear [τὰ δεινὰ τε καὶ φοβερά]," Plato says in the *Republic*, "should be censored because *we* are in fear [φοβούμεθα] for our guardians lest the habit of such thrills make them more sensitive and soft than we would have them" (3.387b). And if impressionable minds develop the habit of pitying (ἐλεεῖν) the heroes of "Homer or some of the other makers of tragedy" (10.605d),[15] they will not easily restrain their pity (τὸ ἐλεεινόν) when they themselves suffer hardships (606b).

To this Platonic disapproval of the appeal to the emotions of pity and of fear, Aristotle responds not only in the *Poetics* and the *Rhetoric*, but in the *Nicomachean Ethics* (2.5) as well. Moral virtue, according to Aristotle, may

14. The κάθαρσις passage reads as follows in the original Greeek: "Tragedy is an imitation of an action that is serious, complete, and of a certain magnitude" [δι' ἐλέου καὶ φόβου περαίνουσα τὴν τῶν τοιούτων παθημάτων κάθαρσιν]. On the problems of interpretation of this passage and for relevant bibliography, see particularly Else, *Aristotle's Poetics*, 224–32. On the improbability of advancing our knowledge of the meaning of the passage, see D. W. Robertson Jr., "Sidney's Metaphor of the Ulcer," in *Essays in Medieval Culture* (Princeton: Princeton University Press, 1980), 381 n.3. The reader might also consult the various essays of Leon Golden in *Transactions of the American Philological Association* 93 (1962): 51–60; *Classical Philology* 64 (1969): 143–53; *Classical Quarterly* 23 (1973): 45–46; *Journal of Aesthetics and Art Criticism* 21 (1973): 473–79; *Classical Journal* 72 (1976): 21–33; and *Classical Philology* 71 (1976): 77–85. See also the D. W. Lucas edition of the *Poetics* (Oxford: Clarendon Press, 1968), Appendix 2, 273–90, and Stephen Halliwell, *Aristotle's Poetics* (Chapel Hill: University of North Carolina Press, 1986), esp. 184–201 and 350–56.

15. The passages from *The Republic* are translated by Paul Shorey, in *The Collected Dialogues of Plato*, ed. Edith Hamilton and Huntington Cairns (Princeton: Princeton University Press, 1961), 632 and 831. For a qualification of this Platonic critique, see the final chapter of this book.

be defined as a habit or fixed disposition (ἕξις). Such dispositions are formed not by extirpating the emotions, but rather by learning to modulate emotional response according to the situation. We may be said to have a bad disposition with regard to the emotion of anger, for example, "if we are disposed to get angry too violently or not violently enough, a good disposition if we habitually feel a moderate amount of anger; and similarly in respect of the other emotions."[16] Two of these other emotions, Aristotle says, are fear (φόβος) and pity (ἔλεος). And these are two of the emotions that Odysseus, the "tragic actor," attempts to evoke, unsuccessfully, in the hardened soul of his "audience," Antinoös.

What I am suggesting, then, is that Odysseus is attempting to get Antinoös to experience a tragic *katharsis* of the emotions of pity and of fear. M. E. Hubbard writes in the introduction to her translation of the *Poetics* that Aristotle's reference to *katharsis* is a response to Plato's contention that poetry "stimulates emotions that a good man tries to suppress."[17] Hubbard goes on to mention with approval the suggestion of Humphrey House, who, she says, "takes *catharsis* in the . . . sense of the production of a 'mean' in Aristotle's own sense. When we consider what degree of emotion is 'undue,' we take into account not merely the quantity of emotion but its object and circumstances" (*Nicomachean Ethics* 1106b18ff.: "One can feel fear, confidence, desire, anger, pity . . . both too much and too little, and in both cases wrongly; but the mean is attained when we feel them at the right time, at the right objects, towards the right people, for the right reason, in the right way").[18] "A tragedy," House writes,

> rouses the emotions from potentiality to activity by worthy and adequate stimuli; it controls them by directing them to the right objects in the right way; and exercises them within the limits of the play, as the emotions of the good man would be exercised. When they subside to potentiality again after the play is over, it is a more "trained" potentiality than before. This is what Aristotle calls κάθαρσις. Our responses are brought nearer to that of the good and wise man.[19]

16. *The Nicomachean Ethics,* trans. Harris Rackham, Loeb Classical Library (1934), 87.

17. *Ancient Literary Criticism: The Principal Texts in New Translations,* ed. D. A. Russell and Michael Winterbottom (Oxford: Clarendon Press, 1972), 87–88.

18. Ibid., 88.

19. *Aristotle's Poetics: A Course of Eight Lectures,* revised, with a preface, by Colin Hardie (London: Rupert Hart-Davis, 1967), 109–10.

We are informed in the *Problems*—a work, as Humphrey House tells us, "of Aristotle's school rather than of Aristotle himself, but not much later than Aristotle and reasonably good evidence of his teaching"[20]—that a state of physical and emotional health can be achieved not through evacuating the substance of black bile from the body but, rather, through restoring the proper equilibrium of the elements of heat and cold within the black bile (*Problems* 30). This, according to House, is "a medical form of catharsis."[21] Hence, the implication is that when an audience undergoes a catharsis of pity and fear, such emotions are not eliminated from the psyche but are brought back to a balanced state and experienced as a wise man would experience them. This is essentially what Aristotle means, in the *Politics,* by the cathartic effect of certain melodies: "Take pity and fear, for example, or again enthusiasm. Some people are liable to become possessed by the latter emotion, but we see that, when they have made use of the melodies which fill the soul with orgiastic feeling, they are brought back by these sacred melodies to a normal condition as if they had been medically treated and undergone a catharsis [ὥσπερ ἰατρείας τυχόντας καὶ καθάρσεως]" (1342a).[22]

In order to sympathize emotionally with the representation of pitiable and fearful events, then, Aristotle assumes that the audience must—and, it is implied, *should*—be capable of experiencing the emotions of pity and fear. The kind of person who is incapable of experiencing these emotions—the person who by implication cannot experience a tragic *katharsis*—he characterizes in the *Rhetoric* as hubristic.

And then there is the other side of the coin. This is the person whose preoccupation with the pitiable and fearful events that have befallen or shall befall him or her equally render this person a less than ideal tragic spectator. In the first book of the *Odyssey,* Penelope reveals herself to be such a "spectator." Phemios has been singing the "pitiable" or "sad" song (νόστον λυγρόν, 326–27; ἀοιδῆς λυγρῆς, 340–41) of the return of the heroes from Troy. Penelope hears the song and asks Phemios to stop because, she says, it "always afflicts the deep heart inside me, / since the unforgettable sorrow comes to me, beyond others, / so dear a one do I long for whenever I am reminded / of my husband" (340–44). Telemachus had just been told by Athena that, if he wants a change for the better in the sorry state of affairs on

20. Ibid., 106.
21. Ibid.
22. The translation is that of J. Burnet as adapted by House, *Aristotle's Poetics,* 107.

Ithaca, he should try to find out for himself where Odysseus is and when he might return and restore order to his kingdom.

As the first and remarkably immediate demonstration that Telemachus is beginning to take on the responsibility that befits his position, he responds to Penelope's request with the following words: "Why, my mother, do you begrudge this excellent singer / his pleasing himself as the thought drives him? . . . There is nothing wrong in his singing the sorry fate [κακὸν οἶτον] of the Danaans. . . . So let your heart and spirit stand firm and endure to listen. / Odysseus is not the only one who lost his homecoming day / at Troy. There were many others who perished, besides him" (346–55).[23] This passage suggests that a spectator's overindulgence in emotions such as pity and fear, when such emotions are reflections of one's merely private suffering—however grievous and justified that suffering may be—renders one incapable of responding appropriately to the representation of pitiable and fearful events that would reveal these events to be a universal condition.

A person has a faulty disposition in regard to pity and fear, according to Aristotle, if these emotions are not felt sufficiently in a situation that requires their response or if they are felt to excess in a situation that invites their measured response. An inability to experience these emotions at all suggests that a person has an insolent character. One of the moral functions of tragedy is to teach an audience the proper circumstances under which they should feel pity and fear.[24] And these emotions will be most effectively evoked by a tragic plot that depicts a protagonist whose moral character is neither impeccable nor base and who, through some mistake, precipitates a stark reversal of his fortunes.

In *Odyssey* 17.415–44 Odysseus, that supreme teller of tales, performs just such a tragedy for Antinoös, whose emotional response is somewhat less than that to be expected from the ideal spectator. The ideal is more closely approximated by the humble Eumaeus, who, in response to a longer and slightly different version of the same tale, responded by telling the disguised Odysseus, "I will entertain you and befriend you because I fear [δείσας] Zeus, the protector of guests, and because I have pity [ἐλεαίρων] for you"

23. Lattimore's translation, which I have again adapted.

24. Cf. the Renaissance gloss of G. B. Casalio (d. 1590), who writes in his *De tragoedia et comoedia lucubratio:* "cum in Tragoediis proponuntur res commiseratione, ac terrore dignissimae, apprehendunt homines quid et quo tempore dolendum et commiserandum sit" (because tragedy portrays events that excite pity and fear, men learn what kinds of things and on what occasions they should feel grief and compassion). This passage is quoted from Jacobus Gronovius, *Thesaurus graecarum antiquitatum* (Leyden, 1697–1702), vol. 8, col. 1600.

(14.388–89). The response of the arrogant Antinoös is, in contrast, to hurl a footstool at a man whose feigned condition as a beggar he should pity, both because this is the proper response and for fear of the vengeance of Zeus, whose duty it is to protect such strangers or guests (ξεῖνοι) in a foreign land. Homer therefore suggests in *Odyssey* 17.415–44 that it is precisely Antinoös's incapacity to experience the tragic emotions of pity and fear that makes him, very fittingly, the first victim of Odysseus's massacre of the insolent suitors at the conclusion of the poem. And when Aristotle set out on the search for his classic formulations about the distinctive nature of literature, "the mighty *Stagyrite*" found them fully embodied in Homer: "He steer'd securely, and discover'd far, / *Led* by the Light of the *Maeonian* Star."

PART II

THE LIMITS OF FORMALISM

5

THE PINDARIC TRADITION AND THE QUEST FOR PURE POETRY

In part 1, I presented some of the fundamental characteristics of classical rationality. In the first chapter, I felt it necessary to clarify misconceptions about Platonic "metaphysics" that are often assumed by postmodern critiques of Plato and to show how Plato—when not read literally—may be said to share many of the concerns of postmodern theory. I also suggested that Platonic thought attempts to avoid the extremes of skepticism, on the one hand, and of ideological absolutism, on the other, that characterize much of contemporary criticism. Since the meaning of reason is badly misunderstood in contemporary theory, which so often laments our inheritance of "logocentrism," it was necessary to devote Chapters 2 and 3 to a discussion of the historical emergence of reason in Greek literature and philosophy and its relevance for understanding two more modern but classically oriented authors, Yvor Winters and Jonathan Swift.

In Chapter 4 I suggested how certain key concepts of Aristotelian critical theory were implicit in some passages in the *Odyssey*. Any attempt to understand the classic must confront the *Poetics*, for despite its dryness, it is the soundest presentation of many of the principles of literary theory associated with the classic. It was necessary to read the *Poetics*, however, within the context of the entire Aristotelian corpus. One cannot understand what Aristotle means by catharsis, for example, without looking at the *Rhetoric*, the *Nicomachean Ethics*, and the *Politics*. As a literary critic, therefore, Aristotle is not a formalist in the Kantian sense. He does not discuss "aesthetic" pleasure purified of cognitive and prudential concerns in the manner of Kant in *The Critique of Judgment*. In the *Philebus*, Plato addresses the question of whether there is such a thing as pure aesthetic pleasure, divorced from the cognitive, and his answer was that there is not (see especially 1113–14). Gadamer restates this classical view when he says, in *Truth and Method*, that "in order to do justice to art, aesthetics must go beyond itself and surrender the 'purity' of the aesthetic."[1] In the classical position as I am trying to define it, purely formal, "aesthetic" pleasure is not an end in itself. Indeed, literature often resists such a reduction to the "aesthetic," to pure formalism.

In this chapter I trace the aestheticizing of the Pindaric ode from its origins through its eighteenth-century transformation into the "purified" Pindarics of Collins and Gray. These later Pindarics become "purified," that is, of Pindar's circumstantial details and of any subject matter extrinsic to the writing of poetry itself. We associate the doctrine of pure poetry with Mallarmé, but such a doctrine was already implicit in eighteenth-century notions of the Pindaric lyric. As I analyze selected odes of the Age of Sensibility, I shall stress the less positive consequences of this preoccupation with the purely connotative powers of language.

In Chapter 6 I supplement what may have seemed a one-sidedly critical view of these poets' achievements by gratefully acknowledging the contribution they tried to make in recovering the capacity of language to be suggestive of a reality beyond what Eric Voegelin calls "thing-reality." I go on to discuss how Paul Valéry, by retreating from the extreme aestheticism associated with Mallarmé, brought poetry more in line with the classical view in *Le Cimetière marin*, which begins with an epigraph from Pindar's third Pythian

---

1. *Truth and Method* (New York: Crossroad, 1986), 83.

ode—a poem that shares many of the concerns of Valéry's meditation. In Chapter 7 I argue that the principle of order that structures Pope's *Epistle to a Lady* is not chiefly aesthetic, but rather encomiastic in the manner of Pindar. In Chapter 8 I show how the divorce of the ethical from the aesthetic makes itself felt in Diderot's *Le Neveu de Rameau.* And in Chapter 9 I suggest how writers of the pastoral must always contend with the legacy of formal preciosity bequeathed by Alexandrian Greece.

"I have been asked why I call the poem an ode," Allen Tate has said of his "Ode to the Confederate Dead." "I suppose in so calling it," Tate continues, "I intended an irony: the scene of the poem is not a public celebration, it is a lone man by a gate."[2] The classically educated Tate recognizes that the ode is traditionally a public celebration, as is true, for example, of the victory odes of Pindar. A contemporary critic, in a fairly recent book on the ode, is not so sure. "I think that what Tate says here about his own ode," Paul Fry writes, "can and should be said about all important odes."[3] And in the course of his book this is what Fry says about the many English odes he discusses from the Renaissance through the Romantic period.

Let us dwell on Tate's phrase "a lone man by a gate." The phrase suggests, first of all, that the poetic utterance of the modern lyric poet is a private one. And it further suggests that this private poetic utterance is not, finally, communicable, for the man who utters it is standing alone in front of a gate, which in Tate's poem remains shut. The subject of every ode, then, according to Fry's deconstructive argument is its inability to communicate. "Not only is the ode from its first appearance a vehicle for ontological and vocational doubt, but it also raises questions more steadily than any other poetic mode about the aesthetic shibboleth of the unified whole. Not one of the odes I shall discuss," he continues, "is hopeful . . . about the resources of its own artistry."[4]

The ode from its first appearance was not, however, a vehicle for ontological and vocational doubt, nor was the achievement of formal unity beyond its reach, at least if we take the not exactly unexemplary Pindaric ode as our prototype.[5] But there is a solid grain of truth in Fry's argument, for there do

2. "Narcissus as Narcissus," in *Essays of Four Decades* (Chicago: Swallow Press, 1968), 602.

3. *The Poet's Calling in the English Ode* (New Haven: Yale University Press, 1980), 1.

4. Ibid., 1–2.

5. For George N. Shuster, the able historian of *The English Ode from Milton to Keats* (New York: Columbia University Press, 1980), an ode is "taken to mean a lyric poem derived, either directly or indirectly, from Pindaric models" (12).

empirically exist the very kind of odes of which he speaks, odes that appear to be vehicles of vocational, and perhaps even of ontological, doubt. I am thinking of certain odes written in the middle of the eighteenth century in England—such as Collins's "Ode on the Poetical Character" and Gray's "Progress of Poesy," to which I shall return—odes that have as their subject their inability to get themselves written, or to get themselves written as impressively as their authors had hoped they might have been written. But is this true of all odes? Or perhaps we should ask a less ambitious question: is this true of Pindar?

I would like first of all, then, to look at one of Pindar's odes in order to suggest that notions about these poems' lack of unity arise chiefly from the failure to attend to the rhetorical structure of the odes, a structure that has as its primary intention the praise of the athletic victor.

Unity and Encomiastic Intention

All of Pindar's complete poems that have come down to us are *epinikia*, poems in praise of the victor following his victory in the games held at Olympia, Nemea, Delphi, and at the Isthmus of Corinth, each of these the site of a Panhellenic festival. The ode itself, however, was usually sung and danced, not at the site of the games themselves, but in the victor's home town, at the time of the victor's return. Pindar was commissioned by a member of the victor's family; he was a professional poet, paid by a patron, and virtually every word of each ode was spoken in order to praise the victor and his family. A lesser poet than Pindar would have turned such an ode into an occasion for mere flattery, always a danger in writing encomia. It was Pindar's extraordinary genius that enabled him to celebrate the occasion by placing the particular victory within the broadest context of analogous experience.

The moment of victory is celebrated by Pindar as an epiphany. The poet lauds the victor for achieving success largely through his own efforts, but, Pindar insists, the victory could never have been achieved had the moment not been prepared for by the victor's heritage—both immediate and remote—and by the gods themselves. Quintessentially Pindaric is how the poet reminds the audience, at the time of an individual's greatest achievement, of the true insignificance of all individuals in comparison with divinity, and of the fleeting quality of human achievement. As the poet says in a famous—perhaps *the* most famous passage in all of the odes:

ὁ δὲ καλόν τι νέον λαχών
ἁβρότατος ἔπι μεγάλας
ἐξ ἐλπίδος πέταται
ὑποπτέροις ἀνορέαις, ἔχων
κρέσσονα πλούτου μέριμναν. ἐν δ' ὀλίγῳ βροτῶν
τὸ τερπνόν αὔξεται. οὕτω δὲ καὶ πίτνει χαμαί,
ἀποτρόπῳ γνώμᾳ σεσεισμένον.

ἐπάμεροι. τί δέ τις; τί δ' οὔτις; σκιᾶς ὄναρ
ἄνθρωπος. ἀλλ' ὅταν αἴγλα διόσδοτος ἔλθῃ,
λαμπρὸν φέγγος ἔπεστιν ἀνδρῶν
καὶ μείλιχος αἰών.

[He who has achieved a new success
basks in the light,
            soaring from hope to hope.
His deeds of prowess
let him pace the air,
            while he conceives
plans sweeter to him than wealth.
But the delight of mortal men
            flowers,
                        then flutters to the ground,
                                    shaken by a mere
                                                shift of thought.

Creatures of a day!
What is a man?
                        What is he not?
Man: a shadow's dream.
                        But when the Godsent brightness comes
a brilliant light shines upon men and our life is sweet.][6]

6. The Greek text is that of Alexander Turyn in *Pindari Epinicia* (New York: Herald Square Press, 1944), 126–27. The translation, which I have adapted slightly, is by Frank J. Nisetich, *Pindar's Victory Songs* (Baltimore: Johns Hopkins University Press, 1980), 205.

Pindar's odes celebrate that privileged moment when—as D. S. Carne-Ross is fond of observing[7]—the "Godsent brightness" (αἴγλα διόσδοτος) shines on mortals.

But Pindar's odes have not received universal acclaim among modern readers, and the debate that has raged most fiercely is over the problem of the unity of the individual odes. Pindar's detractors and even many of Pindar's admirers have despaired at finding unity in the odes. Pindar's admirers have rhapsodized about the brilliant metaphors, the extraordinary wrenching of words from their normal usage, the furious pressure to which Pindar subjects his language, the pure poetry of the odes. Even so famous a classical scholar as Gilbert Murray can say of Pindar that he "is nothing but a poet. There is little rhetoric, no philosophy, little human interest, only that fine bloom . . . which comes when the most sensitive language meets the most exquisite thought."[8] Pindar's detractors have, at least since the Renaissance, associated the name Pindar rather with pure bombast[9] than with pure poetry: they are impatient with what they take to be the constant and pointless digressions, the numerous epithets, the hollowness of the poet's sincerity. Neither group has found a principle of unity in the odes. It was Elroy L. Bundy who, in a seminal monograph published in 1962, decisively demonstrated that the unity of the poems must be sought in their encomiastic intention, even if this means abandoning our modern notion, derived from the aestheticism of Kantian formalism, that such a principle of order is inherently unpoetic.[10]

I would like now to look at *Olympian* 11 for Hagesidámos of Western Lokroi, the winner of the boys' boxing contest in 476 B.C. This is not one of the greatest of the odes, but it is a lovely one, and because it is uncharac-

---

7. See his *Pindar* (New Haven: Yale University Press, 1985), 24.

8. *The Literature of Ancient Greece* (Oxford: Clarendon Press, 1897), 112.

9. In 1915 Ezra Pound, for example, wrote of Pindar as follows to Harriet Monroe: " 'Theban Eagle' be blowed. A damn'd rhetorician half the time." In a letter to Iris Barry the following year Pound calls Pindar "the prize wind-bag of all ages" (*The Letters of Ezra Pound, 1907–1941*, ed. D. Paige [New York: Harcourt, Brace, 1950], 55, 87). Such characterizations of Pindar's poetry did not, however, prevent Pound from inserting passages from the odes of the Theban Eagle into his own verse; see *Hugh Selwyn Mauberley*, section 3, and the third line of *Canto* 4.

10. See *Studia Pindarica I and II, University of California Studies in Classical Philology* 18, no. 1 (1962): 1–92. For a good survey of the history of Pindaric scholarship, particularly on the problem of the unity of the poems, see David C. Young, "Pindaric Criticism," *The Minnesota Review* 4 (Summer 1964): 584–641. A revised version of Young's essay can be found in *Wege der Forschung: Pindaros und Bakchylides*, ed. William Musgrave Calder III and Jacob Stern (Darmstadt: Wissenschaftlichegesellschaft, 1970), 1–95.

teristically brief, it will give us a clear and concentrated idea of how, in a Pindaric ode, every element that may appear at first to be superfluous or perhaps even an expression of "vocational doubt" is in fact designed to accomplish the task of praising the victor. *Olympian* 11, which Bundy treats in his monograph, consists of a single triad of strophe, antistrophe, and epode:

Ἔστιν ἀνθρώποις ἀνέμων ὅτε πλεῖστα
χρῆσις, ἔστιν δ' οὐρανίων ὑδάτων,
ὀμβρίων παίδων νεφέλας.
εἰ δὲ σὺν πόνῳ τις εὖ πράσσοι, μελιγάρυες ὕμνοι
ὑστέρων ἀρχὰ λόγων
τέλλεται καὶ πιστὸν ὅρκιον μεγάλαις ἀρεταῖς.

ἀφθόνητος δ' αἶνος Ὀλυμπιονίκαις
οὗτος ἄγκειται. τὰ μὲν ἁμετέρα
γλῶσσα ποιμαίνειν ἐθέλει.
ἐκ θεοῦ δ' ἀνὴρ σοφαῖς ἀνθεῖ πραπίδεσσιν ὁμοίως.
ἴσθι νῦν, Ἀρχεστράτου
παῖ, τεᾶς, Ἁγησίδαμε, πυγμαχίας ἕνεκεν

κόσμον ἐπὶ στεφάνῳ χρυσέας ἐλαίας
ἁδυμελῆ κελαδήσω,
Ζεφυρίων Λοκρῶν γενεὰν ἀλέγων.
ἔνθα συγκωμάξατ'· ἐγγυάσσομαι
ὕμμιν, ὦ Μοῖσαι, φυγόξεινον στρατὸν
μήτ' ἀπείρατον καλῶν,
ἀκρόσοφόν τε καὶ αἰχματὰν ἀφίξεσθαι. τὸ γὰρ
ἐμφυὲς οὔτ' αἴθων ἀλώπηξ
οὔτ' ἐρίβρομοι λέοντες διαλλαξαίατ' ἦθος.

[There is a time when men need most
The winds; there is a time when water from the sky,
Rain, child of darkened cloud, best serves their needs;
And, when a man, striving, has won success,
Then honeyed hymns are due,
First taste of later fame, to be,
On oath, the trusted seal of great achievements.

>Full praise lies up in readiness,
>Abundance due Olympic victors; and my tongue
>Longs eagerly to shepherd all the story.
>But God prompts in me bolder, more direct
>Blossoming of my praise.
>Son of Arkhéstratos, know now,
>In tribute to your boxing victory,
>
>Hagesidámos, I shall sing
>Sweet strains—adorning thus your crown
>Of golden olive, including, too, your race
>Of the Zephyrian Lokrians. O Muses,
>There join the revels, and I make
>My bond with you that there you will encounter
>No thoughts that turn from welcome,
>No people strangers to fair acts and arts,
>But great in wisdom and in warfare. So,
>Whether of ruddy fox or bolder lion,
>The nature native to a man cannot
>Change its expression.][11]

The great pitfall for the writer of an encomium is that the praise may easily shade into flattery, with the result that what is said will not be believed. The problem remains even if we recognize that the athletic prowess to which Pindar gave tribute was a more serious and spiritually significant quality than its modern-day counterpart. The praise will be believed by an audience—a sense of verisimilitude, that is, will be lent to it—if it is placed within the broadest context of analogous experience.

The strophe begins with a *priamel,* which is a selecting or focusing device:

>There is a time when men need most
>The winds; there is a time when water from the sky,
>Rain, child of darkened cloud, best serves their needs;

---

11. *Pindari Epinicia,* 59. The interpretation that follows is essentially that put forward by E. L. Bundy in *Studia Pindarica I.* The translation is Bundy's with revisions by Helen Pinkerton, and appeared in *The Southern Review* 15, no. 4 (1979), 1019; I have made some slight alterations. For further bibliography on this ode, see Douglas E. Gerber, *A Bibliography of Pindar, 1513–1966, Philological Monographs of the American Philological Association,* no. 28 (1969): 37–38.

And, when a man, striving, has won success,
Then honeyed hymns are due,
First taste of later fame, to be,
On oath, the trusted seal of great achievements.

Pindar speaks here about the needs (χρῆσις, 2) that people feel at different times. Two such needs are (1) for wind, required—it is implied—by sailors, who bring needed goods back to their homeland, and (2) for rain, required—it is again implied—by farmers, who provide needed food. Another such need of the community is for song, "honeyed hymns" (μελιγάρυες ὕμνοι, 3) that will commemorate great prowess (μεγάλαις ἀρεταῖς, 6).

The focus is then narrowed, in the first line of the antistrophe, to excellence achieved in the Olympic games:

Full praise lies up in readiness,
Abundance due Olympic victors.

Pindar, thus, has established a general context for his praise of the particular achievement of an Olympic victor, although we must wait before the victor is formally identified and therefore more narrowly particularized. "My tongue / Longs eagerly [ἐθέλει, 9] to shepherd all the story," Pindar goes on to say, "But God prompts in me bolder, more direct / Blossoming of my praise." The poet eagerly desires to shepherd all the story—to recount in full, that is, all the elements that contributed to the greatness of this Olympic victory—but his longing remains unfulfilled. Or *frustrated,* shall we say?

Probably not. In these compressed lines Pindar rather efficiently accomplishes several aims that would be consonant with his public role as epinician poet. He is enhancing the glory of the victor by suggesting that the things that could possibly be said about him are many. He is implying to his audience that, because this is a brief ode, the praise will necessarily be brief and they should not therefore infer that brevity of praise suggests a paucity in the victor of qualities that could be praised. Quite to the contrary, in this instance, Pindar suggests, because he is inspired by God (ἐκ θεοῦ, 10), the poet will dispense with elaborate and diffuse mechanical praise and will come to the point briefly and with full force.

Having established a persuasive context for his praise, the poet finally mentions the victor by name, addressing him first as "Son of Arkhéstratos" and then, as the focus finally narrows to its most sharply defined particular, as "Hagesidámos":

> Son of Arkhéstratos, know now,
> In tribute to your boxing victory,
> Hagesidámos, I shall sing
> Sweet strains—adorning thus your crown
> Of golden olive, . . .

The focus begins to broaden again as Pindar goes on to praise the countrymen of Hagesidámos:

> including, too, your race
> Of the Zephyrian Lokrians. O Muses,
> There join the revels, and I make
> My bond with you that there you will encounter
> No people strangers to fair acts and arts,
> No thoughts that turn from welcome,
> But great in wisdom and in warfare. So,
> Whether of ruddy fox or bolder lion,
> The nature native to a man cannot
> Change its expression.

The Zephyrian Lokrians are well-rounded human beings, great both "in
wisdom and in warfare" [ἀκρόσοφόν τε καὶ αἰχματάν]. And these considerable virtues—the first characteristic of the "ruddy fox," the second of the
"bolder lion"—are fully ingrained (ἐμφυές); they are there for everyone to
see, and do not require—it is implied—a honey-tongued poet to bring them
to light. The praise of the countrymen of Hagesidámos is, indirectly, a praise
of Hagesidámos himself, who it is assumed has inherited these virtues. Since
"the encomium deals with achievements," as Aristotle says in the *Rhetoric*
(1.9.33), "all attendant circumstances [τὰ δὲ κύκλῳ], such as noble birth
and education, merely conduce to persuasion; for it is probable [εἰκὸς γάϱ]
that virtuous parents will have virtuous offspring and that a man will turn
out as he has been brought up."[12] And by praising the Zephyrian Lokrians in

---

12. *The Art of Rhetoric,* trans. John Henry Freese, Loeb Classical Library (1926), 101.
Aristotle's word for the probable (εἰκός) in this passage is precisely that which he uses in the
Poetics (1451b4) to describe mimetic probability: τὸ εἰκός. "It is the function of the poet,"
Aristotle says, "to relate . . . what is possible according to the law of probability [τὸ εἰκός] or
necessity." For Irving Babbit, Pindar is "superbly imaginative," but his is an "imagination . . . not
in the service of sensibility." It is largely Pindar's sober sense of probability that renders him,
from Babbit's point of view, "in the Aristotelian sense, an imitator" ("Romantic Melancholy," in

this way Pindar implicitly conveys, as well, his respect for the moral integrity of his audience who will clearly not be content with a poet who does not express what is just and truthful.

It is worth observing that the opening lines of this ode are imitated by Abraham Cowley at the beginning of what is probably the best known and most influential of his Pindaric odes, "The Resurrection" (1668):

> Not *Winds* to *Voyagers* at Sea,
>   Nor *Showers* to *Earth* more necessary be,
> (*Heav'ns* vital *Seed* cast on the *Womb* of *Earth,*
>   To give the *fruitful Year* a *Birth*)
>   Than *Verse* to *Virtue,* which can do
> The *Midwife's* Office, and the *Nurse's* too;
> It *feeds* it strongly, and it *cloathes* it gay,
>   And when it dies, with comely Pride
> *Embalms* it, and erects a *Pyramid*
>   That never will decay
> Till *Heaven* it self shall melt away,
> And nought behind it stay.[13]

In the Pindaric original the references to wind and rain are devices used, as I have argued, for focusing on the achievement of the Olympic victor. In Cowley these same references are used to illustrate the power of poetry. The object of praise, then, in Cowley's ode, is poetry rather than the Olympic victor. In terms of poetic "self-referentiality," we have not, however, come as far as Kantian and post-Kantian formalism, for Cowley praises poetry because it has an end—a *telos*—apart from the assertion of its own autonomy: "*Verse,*" for Cowley, can teach "*Virtue*" because poetry can graphically and powerfully depict, in this case, the just deserts awaiting men and women at the end of time, which Cowley describes in the third stanza. Thus poems such as Cowley's own "Resurrection" can serve to incite their readers to virtuous conduct.

Critical Theory Since Plato, ed. Hazard Adams, rev. ed. [New York: Harcourt Brace Jovanovich, 1992], 769).

13. *Pindarique Odes, Written in Imitation of the Stile and Manner of Pindar* (London, 1668). All quotations from Cowley's Pindaric odes will be from this edition.

Implicit Principles of Literary Theory

In his odes Pindar places the praise of a particular athlete on a particular occasion within the broadest context of analogous experience, both human and divine. Pindar's poems, in this sense, are good examples of the Aristotelian view of poetry, for, to adapt one scholar's succinct paraphrase of the Aristotelian position, poetry seeks to articulate an appropriate "relation of given particular events, real or imaginary, to a principle by means of which they may gain significance."[14] So the Pindaric ode begins with a particular instance: an athlete has won a victory in the games, and the poem explains the general significance of this particular instance and of how it might have come about in terms of the victor's previous athletic experience, his noble heritage, the will of the gods, and so on. Lest it be objected that the starting point of Aristotle's preferred genre of tragedy is "myth," but of the Pindaric ode it is verifiable fact, it should be noted that, for Aristotle, there is nothing to prevent the poet, like the historian, from representing what has happened, provided that it is represented as having happened according to probability (*Poetics* 1451b9).

Some of the fullest and soundest "Aristotelian" defenses of fiction in antiquity can be found in the works of rhetoricians such as Cicero and Quintilian, and their articulation of the structure and aims of fiction bears striking similarities to some of the central principles of poetry exemplified by the Pindaric ode. The orator most resembles the poet—and will often make use of fictional argument—when he places the particular case he is treating within the most general philosophical context. Each ode of Pindar's, like each case the orator argues, is deeply implicated in place, time, and circumstance; but the poet places the praise of a particular athlete on a particular occasion within the broadest context of analogous experience. The poem, like the orator's argument, exists as a means of relating the particular (Aristotle's καθ᾽ ἕκαστον, *Poetics* 1451b4) to the universal (Aristotle's καθόλου).[15]

---

14. Wesley Trimpi, *Muses of One Mind: The Literary Analysis of Experience and Its Continuity* (Princeton: Princeton University Press, 1983), 271.

15. In this section I am much indebted to Wesley Trimpi's *Muses of One Mind,* which contains a meticulous analysis of the relation of philosophical and rhetorical to literary discourse. For Cicero's defense of a rhetorical analysis of experience that must turn "from the particular occasion and individual to general conceptions of circumstances and kinds," see *De oratore* 2.133–36 (trans. H. Rackham, *Cicero in Twenty-Eight Volumes,* Loeb Classical Library [1942], 3:294–97). For Quintilian's discussion of the relation between definite (i.e., "specific") and indefinite ("general") questions, see *De institutione oratoria* 3.5.5–18. Trimpi discusses these passages in *Muses of One Mind,* chap. 10. For Pindar's ability—which he shares with

Literary discourse was often described in antiquity as that method of analysis which drew on the most liberal uses of the ancient—and often competing—disciplines of rhetoric, on the one hand, and of philosophy, on the other. The orator deals with particular cases, the philosopher with general principles. But the orator must persuade a jury to understand and judge the facts of a particular case, and he does this best by removing the question to the more general or philosophical level. The philosopher, on the other hand, is concerned with arriving at a definition of the just or the good, and he does this best by locating the definition within a particular set of circumstances. Although literature draws on the resources of both rhetoric and philosophy, it also, as Wesley Trimpi has elucidated, resolves the antithetical aims of these efforts of the mind at their most conservative extremes.[16] Rhetorical discourse, when reduced to its most conservative articulation, deals with discrete particulars; philosophical discourse, when reduced to *its* most conservative articulation, deals with general truths drained of circumstantial detail. The most liberal articulation of rhetoric and philosophy is expressed in fiction or poetry, which—in the Aristotelian tradition—mediates between the particular and the universal.

I should remind the reader here of the "classical" definition of literature I offered in the preface and suggest how well the Pindaric ode exemplifies this definition. Having just discussed the relationship of rhetoric to philosophy in the constitution of literature, I can slightly amplify that paradigm: a work of literature is a coherent, compelling, and rationally defensible representation that draws on the resources of both rhetoric and philosophy, but at the same time resists being reduced either to the mere recording of material reality, on the one hand, or to the bare exemplification of an abstract philosophical precept, on the other. It is the function of poetry, then, to mediate between the particular and the universal. So, in the Pindaric ode, the poem is that which illuminates the general principles the poet finds to be implicit in a particular occasion. It is in this sense that Pindar's odes embody the finest principles of classical art and even antici-

---

Homer—to "see the general behind the particular," see the fine remarks of Frank J. Nisetich, *Pindar's Victory Songs,* 23. See also S. H. Butcher: "The poet, starting from the individual victor in the games, raises the interest above the personal level and beyond the special occasion, by giving historical perspective and background to the event. . . . Thus the ode is more than an occasional poem, and the theme as it is unfolded acquires a larger meaning. . . . The ode rises by clear ascents from the individual to the universal" (*Aristotle's Theory of Poetry and Fine Art* [4th ed. 1932; reprint, New York: Dover Publications, 1951], 406–7).

16. See *Muses of One Mind,* 1–79.

pate a central tenet of classical philosophy. This central tenet I take to be the ability to find a principle of order—an ἀρχή, which Pindar often finds in legend or myth—that will illuminate particular impressions, experiences, events, or occasions that would otherwise remain discrete and therefore unintelligible.

The Horatian Inheritance

But the question must be asked: how did the misunderstandings of Pindar arise? How did it happen that the rational, classical Pindar I have tried to present came to be seen as a fiery and often undisciplined genius who "rises to gorgeous irrelevance in avoiding his unpromising subject"?[17] I would like to point to two sources of this misunderstanding, one remote and the other more immediate.

The more remote source is to be found in the characterizations of Pindaric poetry offered by Horace in his extraordinarily influential *Odes* 4.2 (*Pindarum quisquis studet aemulari*). The ode is a typical *recusatio* (a "refusal"): Horace, that is, allegedly refuses to write in the Pindaric high style and in refusing to do so he describes Pindar's style in a manner that is designed to reflect favorably on his own. This immensely influential ode warrants the most careful analysis if we are to distinguish the subtle realization of Horace's actual intentions from the kind of literal-minded reading that has, to a large degree, resulted in the widespread misunderstanding of Pindar.

Horace was asked by Iulus to write a triumphal ode for the return of Augustus Caesar from Gaul. He refuses because, he says, any lofty Pindaric effort he attempts is doomed, as Icarus was, to fail:

> Pindarum quisquis studet aemulari,
> Iule ceratis ope Daedalea
> nititur pennis vitreo daturus
> nomina ponto.
>
> (1–4)

---

17. Bundy, *Studia Pindarica I,* 4. Bundy is here ironically characterizing those critics who found it embarrassing that Pindar's pursuit of pure poetry should have been constrained by his given encomiastic task.

[Whoever strives, Iullus, to rival Pindar, relies on wings fastened with wax by Daedalean craft, and is doomed to give his name to some crystal sea.][18]

Horace then describes the Pindaric style, which he is, so he claims, incapable of imitating; and he specifically mentions, along the way, four Pindaric genres—dithyrambs (stanza 3), hymns in honor of the gods and heroes (stanza 4), epinikia (stanza 5), and dirges (stanza 6)—which he claims are beyond his poetic powers:

> monte decurrens velut amnis, imbres
> quem super notas aluere ripas,
> fervet immensusque ruit profundo
>   Pindarus ore,
>
> laurea donandus Apollinari,
> seu per audaces nova dithyrambos
> verba devolvit numerisque fertur
>   lege solutis;
>
> seu deos regesve canit, deorum
> sanguinem, per quos cecidere justa
> morte Centauri, cecedit tremendae
>   flamma Chimaerae;
>
> sive quos Elea domum reducit
> palma caelestes pugilemve equumve
> dicit et centum potiore signis
>   munere donat,
>
> flebili sponsae iuvenemve raptum
> plorat et vires animumque moresque
> aureos educit in astra nigroque
>   invidet Orco.
>
>   (5–24)

[Like a river from the mountain rushing down, which the rains have swollen above its accustomed banks, so does Pindar seethe and,

18. *Q. Horati Flacci Opera,* ed. Edward C. Wickham (London: Oxford University Press, 1967); the English translation, which I have adapted slightly, is by C. E. Bennett, Loeb Classical Library (1929).

brooking no restraint, rush on with deep-toned voice, worthy to be
honored with Apollo's bays, whether he rolls new words through daring dithyrambs and is borne along in measures freed from rule, or sings
of gods and kings, the progeny of gods, at whose hands the Centaurs
fell in death deserved and by whom was quenched the fire of dread
Chimaera; or when he sings of those whom the Elean palm leads home
exalted to the skies, of boxer, or of steed, and endows them with a tribute more glorious than a hundred statues; or laments the young hero
snatched from his tearful bride, and to the stars extols his prowess, his
courage, and his golden virtue, begrudging them to gloomy Orcus.]

These lines perhaps are, as Steele Commager has suggested, an example of
"tribute through imitation";[19] but the imitation is so extreme that it borders
on parody. Horace's lines in imitation of Pindar themselves swell above and
beyond the banks of the Sapphic stanza, and rush so impetuously—notice,
for example, the initial and very purposeful enjambment "imbres / quem
super notas aluere ripas" [which the rains have swollen above its accustomed banks] (5–6), an enjambment that imitates the action it describes by
spilling over from stanzas 2 through 6.

   Horace, then, has shown that he certainly can write in the lofty Pindaric
style, even though he claims that such a style is beyond his powers. He goes
on in the following famous stanzas to contrast the lofty Pindaric style with
his own more homespun and labored style:

> multa Dircaeum levat aura cycnum,
> tendit, Antoni, quotiens in altos
> nubium tractus. ego apis Matinae
>   more modoque
>
> grata carpentis thyma per laborem
> plurimum circa nemus uvidique
> Tiburis ripas operosa parvus
>   carmina fingo.
>
>   (25–32)

[A mighty breeze uplifts the Dircaean swan, Antonius, as often he
attempts a flight to the lofty regions of the clouds. I, after the way and

   19. *The Odes of Horace: A Critical Study* (Bloomington: Indiana University Press, 1962),
60 n.10.

manner of the Matinian bee, that gathers the pleasant thyme labori-
ously around many a grove and the banks of well-watered Tibur, I, a
humble bard, fashion my verses with incessant toil.]

Pindar depicts himself as the poet of "nature" rather than of the laborious
and technical preciosities of "art." Here Horace claims, in his habitually self-
deprecating style, that he is the poet of "art" rather than of "nature":
"operosa parvus / carmina fingo" [I, a humble bard, fashion my verses with
incessant toil] (31–32). Horace continues:

> concines maiore poeta plectro
> Caesarem, quandoque trahet feroces
> per sacrum clivum merita decorus
>   fronde Sygambros,
>
> (33–36)

[You, a poet of loftier strain, shall sing of Caesar, when, honored with
the well-earned garland, he shall lead in his train along the sacred hill
the savage Sygambri]

"It is for you to sing aloud [*concines*]"), Horace writes, "[the praise of]
Caesar, since you are a poet of a loftier strain." Note the artful—thus demonstrating the very quality of poetry which Horace contends is his hallmark—
juxtaposition of *fingo*,[20] the last word of the preceding stanza, and *concines*,
the first word of this stanza, a juxtaposition through which Horace further
"denigrates" his own allegedly merely feigned and playfully artful—but not,
so he pretends, ultimately serious—poems by contrasting them to Iullus's
grander compositions. The self-denigration, of course, can hardly be taken at
face value.

Just as Horace in stanzas 2 through 5 claims to be incapable of imitating
Pindar and then goes on to imitate him brilliantly, so here Horace claims he
is incapable of praising Augustus in the lofty strains of a poet such as Iullus,
but he then goes on to praise Augustus, both in the high style and in his own

---

20. "The word *fingo*," Gregson Davis observes, "is evocative" of the kind of "finesse" Horace
would have associated with the Callimachean stress on the poet's craft (*Polyhymnia: The
Rhetoric of Horatian Lyric Discourse* [Berkeley and Los Angeles: University of California Press,
1991], 138). Davis's excellent analysis (133–43) of *Carmina* 4.2 is very much in sympathy
with my own.

more intimate style—and leaves the reader to decide which of these is the more effective. Caesar, Horace writes, is a ruler

> quo nihil maius meliusve terris
> fata donavere bonique divi,
> nec dabunt, quamvis redeant in aurum
>   tempora priscum.
>
> concines laetosque dies et urbis
> publicum ludum super impetrato
> fortis Augusti reditu forumque
>   litibus orbum.
>
> (37–44)

[than whom nothing greater, nothing better, have the Fates and gracious gods bestowed upon the world, nor shall bestow, even though the centuries roll backward to the ancient age of gold. You shall sing of the festal days, of the city's public games to celebrate the return of brave Augustus in answer to our prayers, and of the Forum free from strife.]

The tone of self-deprecation resumes:

> tum meae, siquid loquar audiendum,
> vocis accedet bona pars, et "O sol
> pulcher, o laudande!" canam recepto
>   Caesare felix.
>
> tuque dum procedis, io Triumphe!
> non semel dicemus, "io Triumphe!"
> civitas omnis dabimusque divis
>   tura benignis.
>
> (45–52)

[If I have anything deserving to be heard, the best powers of my voice shall swell the acclaim, and happy at Caesar's coming home, I'll sing: "O glorious day, with honor to be mentioned!" And as you take the lead along the ways, "Io triumphe!" we shout all of us together, and not only once: "Io triumphe!" and incense we will offer to the kindly gods.]

"If, when Caesar returns victoriously, I have anything worth saying [*si quid loquar audiendum*], I will sing *o sol / pulcher! O laudande!*" The simplicity of Horace's praise—"The form is simple, almost rustic," Eduard Fraenkel notes, "but what a depth of affection is expressed in the words *o sol pulcher, o laudande!*"[21]—thus contrasts sharply with the insincere ornateness to be expected, it is implied, from the formal praises of a poet such as Iullus. And this point is elaborated in the final stanzas:

> te decem tauri totidemque vaccae,
> me tener solvet vitulus, relicta
> matre qui largis iuvenescit herbis
>   in mea vota,
>
> fronte curvatos imitatus ignis
> tertium lunae referentis ortum,
> qua notam duxit, niveus videri,
>   cetera fulvus.
>
>   (53–60)

[Your promises, ten bulls and as many cows shall satisfy; mine a tender calf, which, having left its dam, is growing on the generous pasturage to fulfill my vows, imitating with its brow the curving crescent of the moon at its third rising, snow-white where it bears a mark, but elsewhere tawny.][22]

Steele Commager's paraphrase of these stanzas succinctly addresses the significance of the metaphor of the sacrifice to Horace's definition of his own style and its relation to Pindar:

Aristotle insisted that proportion was the basis of metaphor, and the last stanzas here are best taken as metaphors of a sort, the sacrifices being proportionate to the styles of the donors. Iullus' grand gesture incarnates his grandiloquence, while Horace's slender talent is implicit in the tiny calf he offers, the detailed description being itself calculated to prove the humble industry of the Matine bee.... In his contrast of victims Horace may glance as well at a familiar literary distinction, the *tener vitulus* insinuating his own *tenuis spiritus,* and Iullus' herd suggesting an almost *pinguis* mode.... The exaggerated modesty of the comparison recalls the terms of the contrast between

---

21. *Horace* (Oxford: Clarendon Press, 1962), 439.
22. Translation and original from *Horace: The Odes and Epodes,* trans. C. E. Bennett, Loeb Classical Library (1929). I have altered the translation slightly.

Pindar's style and Horace's own, and that between Iullus' *maius plectrum* and Horace's *parvos* talent. The Ode progresses through these antithetical similes and metaphors, and its logic lies in the terms of the various tensions it so maintains.[23]

In the famous second stanza of the ode, Horace describes Pindar's style as unrestrained, "like a river rushing down from the mountain, which the rains have swollen above its accustomed banks" [monte decurrens velut amnes, imbres / quem super notas aluere ripas] (5–6). This is not a sincere and straightforward description of Pindar's style, although Thomas Gray, for instance, appears to have so understood it, as his adaptation of this passage in his Pindaric ode "The Progress of Poesy" suggests; here Gray likens the power of ancient poetry to a "rich stream of music" (7), which he describes as

Now rolling down the steep amain,
Headlong, impetuous, see it pour:
The rocks and nodding groves rebellow to the roar.
                                                    (10–12)[24]

Horace's characterization of Pindar is, rather, a lightly ironic description that subtly suggests that such wild—and, it is implied, perhaps even irresponsible—flights of Pindaric impetuosity will not be found in the more carefully crafted, rationally responsible, and sincere, if more modest, odes of Horace himself. Thus Horace's famous description of Pindar's style should not be taken at face value: Pindar's style is described by Horace as antithetical to his own, which is itself exaggerated in the opposite extreme. Neither is Pindar's poetry as impetuous as Horace claims, nor is Horace's own poetry as trifling.

The important point to be noted is that Horace's description of the allegedly impetuous flow of Pindaric verse—with the sense of irony missed, of course—did much to spread the popular misconception about Pindar, as did the example of the irregular verse with which Cowley in his freewheeling Pindarics imitated the ancient poet. Cowley's imitations of Pindar, furthermore, loosened the association of the Pindaric ode with its original encomiastic intention, since many of these seventeenth-century odes are not about individuals at all but rather have such subjects as the resurrection, destiny, or fame.

23. *The Odes of Horace*, 64–65.
24. All quotations from the poetry of Gray and Collins are from *The Poems of Gray, Collins, and Goldsmith*, ed. Roger Lonsdale (New York: Longman, 1969).

The Quest for Pure Poetry

Both the encomiastic intention and occasional nature of Pindar's victory odes are preserved in that most public of poets, John Dryden, and not only in his more obviously Pindaric odes such as "To the Pious Memory of . . . Mrs. Anne Killegrew" (1686) and "Threnodia Augustalis: A Funeral-Pindarique" (1685). Dryden, in the dedicatory preface to his poem "Eleanora" (1692), refers to his panegyric as being "of the Pindarique nature," although written in "Heroique Verse."[25] Here occasionality and elevation of thought and style are not seen to be mutually exclusive, as becomes increasingly the case in the eighteenth century, but are seen rather as intimately and inextricably connected. "On all occasions of Praise," continues Dryden in the dedication,

> if we take the Ancients for our Patterns, we are bound by Prescription to employ magnificence of Words, and the Force of Figures, to adorn the sublimity of Thoughts. *Isocrates* among the Grecian Orators; and *Cicero,* and the younger *Pliny,* amongst the *Romans,* have left us their Precedents for our security: For I think I need not mention the inimitable *Pindar,* who stretches on these Pinnions out of sight, and is carried upward, as it were, into another World.[26]

Pindar is here directly associated with the rhetorical tradition of encomiastic oratory.[27] In Dryden as in Pindar, the poem is that which relates the particular to the universal. As James D. Garrison has noted, Dryden's "elaboration" of the "analogies" he develops in "Eleanora" "typically involve a pattern of elevation from local to universal."[28]

25. *The Works of John Dryden,* ed. Edward Niles Hooker, H. T. Swedenberg, Jr., et al. (Berkeley and Los Angeles: University of California Press, 1956–), 3:232.

26. Ibid.

27. As Penelope Burke Wilson observes in "The Knowledge and Appreciation of Pindar in English Literature in the Seventeenth and Eighteenth Centuries" (Ph.D. diss., Oxford University, 1974).

28. *Dryden and the Tradition of Panegyric* (Berkeley and Los Angeles: University of California Press, 1975), 193. Norman Maclean, in his excellent and well-known essay "From Action to Image: Theories of the Lyric in the Eighteenth Century," in *Critics and Criticism Ancient and Modern,* ed. R. S. Crane (Chicago: University of Chicago Press, 1952), notes the encomiastic intention of Dryden's "Alexander's Feast" (433ff.). The poem is greatly elucidated by the interpretive method Bundy employed in his treatment of Pindar. Virtually the entire poem, in a grandly baroque gesture, can thus be seen to be "foil"—to borrow Bundy's terminology—for the last two lines of the last stanza, lines that are repeated in the Grand Chorus that concludes the poem: "He [Timotheus, the ancient musician who is representative of the classical world, to

What ultimately loosened the conception of the Pindaric ode from its original encomiastic intention was the rise of formalist or aestheticist attitudes toward poetry. I have suggested, following Wesley Trimpi, that to the specifically literary analysis of experience rhetorical discourse contributes particularity and philosophical discourse contributes generality; that it is the function of *poēsis* to mediate between the particular and the universal; and that, for Pindar, the poem is that which illuminates the general principles implicit in a particular occasion. The aestheticist view of Pindar is perfectly stated by Gilbert Murray, for whom poetry, we can infer, has no relation either to rhetoric or to philosophy; it was Murray who stated, it will be recalled, that Pindar "is nothing but a poet. There is [in his odes] little rhetoric, no philosophy, little human interest, only that fine bloom . . . which comes when the most sensitive language meets the most exquisite thought." Thus Pindar is transformed by Murray into the ancient Greek version of Stéphane Mallarmé.

But the pursuit of "la poésie pure"—a notion of poetry that stresses the connotative powers of language to the virtual exclusion of its denotative qualities—precedes Mallarmé, for it is an active concern of many critics and poets of the eighteenth century.[29] In 1756 Joseph Warton, in his well-known dedication to *An Essay on the Genius and Writings of Pope,* for example,

---

which the entire poem has thus far been devoted] raised a Mortal to the Skies; / She [St. Cecelia, the representative of the Christian world, and the subject of the poem's praise] drew an Angel down" (*The Poems of John Dryden,* ed. James Kinsley, 4 vols. [Oxford: Clarendon Press, 1958], 3:1443). Dryden's poem is 180 lines long; this means that, in a grand baroque gesture, the first 168 lines of the poem have been foil for the direct praise of Divine Cecelia. David Young, *Three Odes of Pindar: A Literary Study of Pythian 11, Pythian 3, and Olympian 7* (Leiden: E. J. Brill, 1968), argues that Pindar, in *Pythian 3* (a poem I discuss at length in the next chapter), constructed the first 76 lines of the 115-line poem as a *recusatio* for the remainder of the poem. In the words of W. J. Slater, Pindar takes the "structure of a utopian wish" and uses it "as a foil for a realistic hope, wish, or assertion." This pattern is "common enough" in Greek rhetoric and poetry, "even though no one had ever dared to use it on such a grand scale before. . . . Pindar has taken a common formal structure and exaggerated it in his baroque manner to form the basis for a whole poem" ("Pindar's *Pythian 3:* Structure and Purpose," *Quaderni Urbinati di Cultura Classica,* n.s., 29 [1988]: 51). Dryden was certainly thinking of Pindar when he composed the Pindaric "Alexander's Feast"; and it is possible that the kind of baroque gesture alluded to by Slater provided the model for the daring rhetorical construction of Dryden's grand ode.

29. Two significant studies of the doctrine of pure poetry are Sister Clarice de Sainte Marie Dion, *The Idea of 'Pure Poetry' in English Criticism, 1900–1945* (Washington, D.C.: The Catholic University of America Press, 1948), and D. J. Mossop, *Pure Poetry: Studies in French Poetic Theory and Practice 1746–1945* (Oxford: Clarendon Press, 1971). In *Muses of One Mind,* Wesley Trimpi traces the nondiscursive practices of "la poésie pure" back to Plotinus. See especially 164–228.

cites Gray's Pindaric ode "The Bard" as an example of "*PURE POETRY*"[30] but denies this elevated status to the poetry of Pope, which, he claims, is "MO-RALITY, and not POETRY."[31]

In articulating his view of the "true poet" as opposed to the "man of wit" and the "man of sense," Warton in his dedication quotes in his defense some lines from Horace's *Sermones* 1.4: "Had you written only . . . Satires," Warton says to Dr. Young,

> you would have indeed gained the title of wit, and a man of sense; but, I am confident, would not insist on being denominated a POET MERELY on their account.
>
> NON SATIS EST PURIS VERSUM PERSCRIBERE VERBIS.
>
> It is amazing that this matter should ever have been mistaken, when Horace has taken particular and repeated pains, to settle and adjust the opinion in question. He has more than once disclaimed all right and title to the name of POET, on the score of his ethic and satiric pieces.
>
> —NEQUE ENIM CONCLUDERE VERSUM DIXERIS ESSE SATIS—
>
> are lines, often repeated, but whose meaning is not extended and weighed as it ought to be.[32]

Just as in the case of Horace's description of Pindar's style in *Odes* 4.2, so here it would be a naive mistake to take the wily Horace at his literal word. The whole of the *sermo* is a defense of Horace's urbane and witty style, and the satire is a critique, by sinuous but clear implication, of the very notion of "pure poetry" that Warton has set out to defend in his essay.

We can better understand Horace's aims once we differentiate between Horace the artist and the more disingenuous *persona* of Horace as he is cunningly portrayed in the satire itself. The claim of the plain stylist is, of course, precisely that there *is* no distinction between the poet and how that poet portrays himself in his poem, and if the plain stylist in question happens to be Thomas Wyatt or Ben Jonson then there is much to this claim. But with Horace and that most craftily Horatian of poets, Alexander Pope, the case is

---

30. *An Essay on the Genius and Writings of Pope,* 5th ed., 22 vols. (London, 1806), 1:ii.
31. Ibid.
32. Ibid., 1:iii–iv.

otherwise; the reader must at all times stay on his or her toes. Warton, I believe, was taken in by this Horatian pose of artless innocence.

"You would not call it enough to round off a verse [*neque, enim concludere versum / dixeris esse satis,* 40–41], nor would you count anyone a poet who writes, as I do, lines more akin to prose [*sermoni propiora,* 42]." By the same token, Horace suggests, there are those who "have questioned whether comedy is or is not poetry; for neither in diction [*verbis*] nor in matter [*rebus*] does it possess heightened spirit [*acer spiritus*] and force [*vis*], and save that it differs from prose-talk [*sermoni*] in its regular beat, it is mere prose [*sermo merus*]." But, Horace imagines his interlocutor objecting, are not the following typical lines from comedy full of heightened spirit and force?

> "at pater ardens
> saevit, quod meretrice nepos insanus amica
> filius uxorem grandi cum dote recuset,
> ebrius et, magnum quod dedecus, ambulet ante
> noctem cum facibus." (48–52)

["There is a father storming in passion because his spendthrift son, madly in love with a wanton mistress, rejects a wife with large dower, and in drunken fit reels abroad—sad scandal—with torches in broad daylight."][33]

Horace is here conceding, to some extent, half of his interlocutor's point: with regard to diction (*verbis,* 47), yes, perhaps these lines might be considered elevated, Horace appears to be saying. For strong emotion does undeniably characterize this passage, the style of which is heightened with a charged vocabulary reminiscent of the more traditionally weighty genres of epic and tragedy: the father is storming (*ardens*),[34] the son is not merely foolhardy but "mad" (*insanus*), the disgrace he is bringing upon himself is

---

33. Latin text and translation quoted from *Horace: Satires, Epistles, Ars Poetica,* trans. H. Rushton Fairclough, Loeb Classical Library (1926).

34. The adjective *ardens* appears to respond specifically to the half-ironic acknowledgment, made just two lines earlier (46), that Horace's satires do not possess *acer spiritus.* For *acer* as an adjective associated with the high style, see G. C. Fiske, "Lucilius and Horace: A Study in the Classical Theory of Imitation," *University of Wisconsin Studies in Language and Literature* 7 (1920): 117, and Kirk Freudenburg, "Horace's Satiric Program and the Language of Contemporary Theory in *Satires* 2.1," *American Journal of Philology* 3 (1990): 187–203, in which Freudenburg cites Cicero, *De oratore* 2.42.180, 22.58.236, and 22.49.236.

great (*magnum*), and the dowry he is refusing is very considerable (*grandi*).

With regard to subject matter (*rebus,* 47), however, Horace—as he portrays his self-effacing and guileless *persona* in the *sermo*—will not accept these lines as being truly elevated. Viewed from the standpoint of the traditional levels of style and their corresponding literary genres, the subject matter of this passage, it is true, is not elevated, for here we have no emperors, no affairs of state, but rather a private, domestic conflict.[35] And this is precisely the point of Horace the magisterial artist and subtle ironist as distinguished from Horace as he portrays himself as the more ingenuous and straightforward character in the satire itself. "Would Pomponius," Horace continues, "hear a lecture with a less weighty import [*leviora*], were his father still alive?" To make explicit, through paraphrase, the delicate irony here: "How can you *really* call this poetry," Horace is saying, "which, as we know, is lofty and elevated beyond the mundane concerns of everyday life, if this is the kind of homely (although perhaps profitable) advice a father might give to his son?" "And so," Horace goes on—and here we come to the lines quoted by Warton—"It is not enough to write out a line of simple words [*non satis est puris versum perscribere verbis*] such that, if you were to break it up, any father whatever would rage in the same fashion as the father in the play." The style and import of this speech, however, cannot, as I have suggested, be described as unelevated and unadorned idiomatic speech. Horace's witty point has escaped Warton in his pursuit of a classical authority who would sanction his own notion of "pure poetry."

So much for the style (*verbum*). Now, as to the subject matter: is the representation of a father warning his son about the perils he must avoid in life an elevated subject (*res*)? Perhaps not, in terms of the traditional levels of style, but Horace obviously feels sufficient passion for this subject such that he ends this very poem by evoking his own beloved father (*pater optimus,* 105) as the source of his (Horace's) method of depicting ethical examples in his satires. As Horace's father molded his son's character by pointing out to him examples to follow or to avoid (115–28), so this is the

---

35. That this passage is an exception to the rule of generic decorum is suggested by the fact that Horace cites just such an example from New Comedy in the *Ars Poetica.* Although each style, Horace says, should keep "the place alloted to it [*locum ... decentem*], ... yet at times even Comedy raises her voice, and an angry Chremes storms in swelling tones [*interdum tamen et vocem Comoedia tollit, / iratusque Chremes tumido delitigat ore*]" (92–94, Loeb Classical Library). "The angry father Chremes," as B. L. Ulman informs us, "appears in four plays of Terence" ("Horace on Satire and Comedy," *Classical Philology* 9 [January 1914], 188).

method, and with the same high moral aim, of Horace's satires. Perhaps the central intention of Horace's plain style—which has its origins in Plato's critique, in the name of philosophy, of sophistic rhetoric—is to reclaim for poetry the ability to deal with ethical questions. Such ethical questions, for Warton, belong to "morality" and not to poetry.[36] Warton's notion of "pure poetry," for Horace, would be simply another name for bombast, for rhetoric divorced from philosophy. Warton wishes to *exclude* ethical and satiric authors from the rank of "pure" poets; Horace wishes to revamp the notion of poetry so that it will include just such poets—such as Horace himself—who will make ethical statements, but who will make them with exquisite poetic tact.[37] Much of what earns Horace's *sermo* its status as poetry in the supremely classical sense is its attempts to bring together—as had the Pindaric ode as it was originally intended—the competing claims of rhetoric and philosophy.

More radical than Warton's conception of "pure poetry" is that put forward—apparently with some hesitation—by Anna Laetitia Barbauld who, in the preface to her edition of *The Poetical Works of Mr. William Collins* (London, 1797), distinguishes "pure Poetry, or Poetry in the abstract," from "didactic and dramatic compositions." Pure poetry, she continues,

> is conversant with an imaginary world, peopled with beings of its own creation. It deals in splendid imagery, bold fiction, and allegorical personages. It is necessarily obscure to a certain degree; because, having to do with ideas generated within the mind, it cannot be at all

36. As William K. Wimsatt and Cleanth Brooks pertinently observe, "in Warton's satire, *Ranelagh House,* 1744, Pope in the Elysian fields is found not among the poets but among the philosophers" (*Literary Criticism: A Short History,* 2 vols. [Chicago: University of Chicago Press, 1957], 1:298 n. 8).

37. Because Horace wishes to reconcile philosophy (or ethics) and rhetoric in his satires does not mean that such poetry is *merely* didactic. In fact, it is highly artful, although it of course pretends precisely *not* to be artful. Notice, for instance, the very clever ending of the poem. In order to establish his *ethos* as poet, Horace states that his own poetic practice of choosing examples of virtue and vice—in order to recommend to his readers what kinds of behavior are to be sought after or avoided—was suggested to him by his venerable father, who may not have been philosophically sophisticated, but who had been brought up with sound traditional values: "Your philosopher," he would tell his son, "will give you theories for shunning or seeking this or that: enough for me, if I can uphold the rule that our fathers have handed down" [*sapiens, vitatu quidque petitu / sit melius, causas reddet tibi; mi satis est, si / traditum ab antiquis morem servare*] (*Sermones* 1.4.115–17). Thus the solid though unsophisticated paternal traditionalist is invoked by Horace in order to sanction this most innovative and sophisticated poetic genre, the Horatian *sermo.*

comprehended by any whose intellect has not been exercised in similar contemplations; while the conceptions of the Poet (often highly metaphysical) are rendered still more remote from common apprehension by the figurative phrases in which they are clothed. All that is properly Lyric Poetry is of this kind.... The *substratum*, if I may so express myself, or subject matter, which every composition must have, is, in a poem of this kind, so extremely slender, that it requires not only art, but a certain artifice of construction, to work it up into a beautiful piece.[38]

It would seem that Pindar, who Quinitilian believed was the prince of lyric poets (*De institutione oratoria* 8.6.71), would now be clearly out of the running, since in the light of this definition, Pindar—as the odes were originally intended to be understood—would not be considered a true lyric poet at all.

Nor would Pindar's odes exemplify the highest kind of poetry if judged by the formalist standards of Immanuel Kant. In the *Critique of Judgment* (1790) Kant makes the important distinction between free beauty (*pulchritudo vaga*) and dependent beauty (*pulchritudo adhaerens*). The highest kind of beauty, according to Kant, is found in a work of art in which "there is presupposed no concept of any purpose" [es ist kein Begriff von irgend einem Zwecke].[39] It follows, according to this distinction, that Pindar's odes—as they were originally intended to be understood—would be representative, for Kant, of merely dependent beauty, having as their chief purpose the praise of the victor. That true lyric poetry may have no subject other than itself, which is strongly suggested in Barbauld's definition of the lyric, is explicitly stated by Kant's disciple Friedrich Schiller, when he says that "subject matter, however sublime and all-embracing it may be, always has a limiting effect upon the spirit."[40]

38. Quoted from the 1802 edition, iv–v.

39. From section 16, "The Judgement of Taste, by Which an Object is Declared to be Beautiful Under the Condition of a Definite Concept, Is Not Pure," trans. J. H. Bernard, in Adams, ed., *Critical Theory Since Plato*, 383. The German is cited from *Kritik der Urtheilskraft*, ed. J. H. v. Kirchman (Berlin: L. Heimann, 1869), 74.

40. "Twenty-Second Letter," in *Letters on the Aesthetic Education of Man*, trans. E. M. Wilkinson and L. A. Willoughby, in Adams, ed., *Critical Theory Since Plato*, 425. Hans-Georg Gadamer discusses the limitations of Schiller's views in *Truth and Method*, 76, and the limitations in general of the quest for poetic purity. See, especially, *Truth and Method*, 508 n.173.

Collins and Gray: The Purified Pindaric

It is probably no coincidence that Joseph Warton and Anna Barbauld cite the odes of Gray and Collins as their examples of "pure poetry." I would like now to look at Collins's "Ode on the Poetical Character" (published in 1746) and to suggest how it may be seen as a transformation of the Pindaric ode into "pure poetry."

Collins gives his reader not a few indications that one is to think of Pindar when reading this ode. The poem—which Oliver F. Sigworth describes as embodying the quintessence of the eighteenth-century Pindaric[41]—is written in a Pindaric triad, although the epode appears here between the strophe and antistrophe, which, as in Pindar, correspond metrically. The poem is marked by the obscurity so often associated with Pindar; the syntax does not disintegrate quite so completely as it does in, for example, the "Ode to Evening," but it is very difficult to follow. The transitions are sudden,[42] as in the popular conception of Pindar influenced by Horace's ode. As in Pindar, we are presented (in the second stanza) with a myth, specifically with a myth about origins, such as we often find in Pindar. We have a contest, as in Pindar, but this is a contest to decide who will win the "magic Girdle" that symbolizes the poetic imagination:

> One, only One unrival'd Fair
> Might hope the magic Girdle wear,
> At solemn Turney hung on high,
> The Wish of each love-darting Eye.
>   (5–8)

The victor is not an athlete, however, nor is it even one of these rival nymphs. The ultimate victor is, rather, the unsurpassable John Milton, whose "guiding Steps" the poet's "trembling Feet . . . pursue," but pursue

> In vain—Such Bliss to One alone
> Of all the Sons of Soul was known,
> And Heav'n, and *Fancy,* kindred Pow'rs,

41. *William Collins* (New York: Twayne Publishers, 1965), 106.

42. A.S.P. Woodhouse remarks on one such "sudden transition"—that in line 40—"characteristic of the Pindaric ode," in "The Poetry of Collins Reconsidered," in *From Sensibility to Romanticism: Essays Presented to Frederick A. Pottle,* ed. Frederick W. Hilles and Harold Bloom (New York: Oxford University Press, 1965), 102.

> Have now o'erturned th'inspiring Bow'rs,
> Or curtain'd close such Scene from ev'ry future view.
>   (72–76)

The poem was published in Collins's *Odes on Several Descriptive and Allegoric Subjects* (1746) and the epigraph that appears on the title page—part of which reappears, in translation, in our poem—is from Pindar:

> Might I now be a poet of bold invention [εὑρησιεπής], might I be worthy of being lifted in the chariot of the Muses—and might daring [τόλμα] and all-embracing power [ἀμφιλαφὴς δύναμις] attend me!

This epigraph from *Olympian* 9 (86–89) is meant to associate Pindar with the poetic imagination: with inspiration, bold inventiveness, poetic power. And these are precisely the poetic qualities Collins longs—in vain, as it turns out—to achieve in his "Ode on the Poetical Character." These may be the qualities of a Spenser or a Milton, Collins's poem suggests, and although the modern poet can attempt to achieve these qualities, the most he realistically can hope for is to write a poem that acknowledges and even enacts this failed attempt—a poem that expresses, in other words, the poet's profound "vocational doubts."

Only one "unrival'd Fair," the poet writes in the first stanza, will inherit the desired "magic Girdle." The remaining nymphs will feel "loath'd and "dishonour'd" in their "vain Endeavor" to possess it. It would even have been better had each "nymph" never learned of the existence of this great prize. The poet compares this scene, which is derived from Spenser's *Faerie Queene*—and Spenser is important because, as a poet associated with the imagination, he provides a link to what immediately follows—to his own frustrating situation as a poet:

> Young *Fancy* thus, to me Divinest Name,
> > To whom, prepar'd and bath'd in Heav'n,
> > The Cest of amplest Pow'r is giv'n:
> > To few the God-like Gift assigns,
> > To gird their blest prophetic Loins,
> And gaze her Visions wild, and feel unmix'd her Flame!

In like manner, Collins is saying, is the heaven-descended faculty of imagination—"The Cest of amplest Pow'r"—frustratingly denied poets including, one must infer, the poet writing the present poem. "Amplest Pow'r" is a direct translation of the phrase ἀμφιλαφὴς δύναμις from the Pindaric epigraph on the title page of Collins's *Odes.*[43] Collins as poet has tried to be, as Pindar in fact was, εὑρησιεπής, "boldly inventive in verse," but all he can manage here is a feeble pun on "Loins" / "lines" (21), a quality of style more closely associated with the "Myrtle Shades" of Edmund Waller—the proto-typical neoclassical poet—from which the aspiring modern poet wishes to retreat than with the sublimity of Milton.

It could of course be argued that Collins has, in Horatian fashion, himself written a *recusatio,* that his admission of failure in his attempt to write imaginative verse worthy of Pindar, Spenser, and Milton is itself a rhetorical ploy, and that he has in fact written a sublime and imaginative poem in the very act of saying that he cannot write one. After all, that second stanza—difficult as it is to paraphrase—is boldly imaginative, or is at least very fanciful. Here Collins describes how God created the world through sexual union with imagination or fancy ("the loved Enthusiast," 29). The band of poetry, Collins appears to be saying, was woven on the day God created the universe. This act of divine creation—which is analogous to poetic creation (this analogy seems to be the point of Collins's remarking that the band "was wove on that creating Day," 24)—is the result of a sexual union between God and Fancy, the "loved Enthusiast" who had long "wooed" God. From this union (described in 30–38) was born the sun ("the rich-haired youth of morn," 39) and all things under the sun ("and all thy subject life," 39), including the band of poetry, "the sainted [i.e. sacred] growing woof" (42). Near this "woof" (the "it" of line 43, "But near it sat ecstatic Wonder") sat, along with "Wonder," also "Truth," "All the shadowy tribes of Mind," "And all the bright uncounted powers, / Who feed on heaven's ambrosial flowers." It is often hard to ascertain the referents of Collins's pronouns, but in the four concluding lines (51–54) of this stanza ("Where is the bard whose soul can now / Its high presuming hopes avow? / Where he who thinks, with rapture

---

43. No one has, to my knowledge, pointed out that Collins's phrase "amplest Pow'r" is a translation of Pindar's ἀμφιλαφὴς δύναμις. Roger Lonsdale, in his commentary in *The Poems of Gray, Collins, and Goldsmith,* suggests that Collins's "Ode to Liberty," 133–36, and "Ode to Mercy," 4–6, recall the beginning of *Pythian* 1. Perhaps the strongest influence on Collins's "Ode on the Poetical Character" was the poet Mark Akenside, who was familiar with Pindar; see Penelope Wilson, "The Knowledge and Appreciation of Pindar," 232ff. M. H. Abrams, in *The Mirror and the Lamp* (New York: Oxford University Press, 1953), 64, points out the Plotinian influence on Akenside's "Pleasures of the Imagination," a poem that is frequently echoed in Collins's ode. Abrams also observes that Warton cites, in his *Essay on Pope,* an ode of Akenside as an example of pure poetry.

blind, / This hallowed work for him designed?") "Its" (52) appears to refer, once again, to the sacred band of imaginative poetry, "the hallowed work" designed for the truly worthy bard.

This stanza is indeed very fanciful, but as the difficulties of even the most basic paraphrase suggest, the quality of imaginative vision achieved here is won through considerable and even crippling strain. The "steep" (57) on which the oak associated with Milton—who is the paradigm of the sublime poet—sits is indeed, Collins appears to feel, "jealous" of modern-day intruders. Very often in his odes Pindar locates the origins of the present victory in myth; for Pindar it is myth that prepares the way for the present moment of victory. Collins's evocation of myth—in this case the myth of the creation of the world through the union of God with Fancy—serves rather to stress how this myth which records the divine favor accorded to the imagination *fails* to illuminate the present, for Milton, Collins is saying, was the last truly imaginative poet.

Collins expresses a similar sense of despair at the conclusion of "The Passions. An Ode for Music," when he asks the female personification of Music,

> Why, Goddess, why to us deny'd?
> Lay'st Thou thy antient Lyre aside?
> (97–98)

Why, Collins asks, does the "Warm, Energic, Chaste, Sublime" art of ancient Greece elude "this laggard Age"?[44] Horace remarks about his own limitations as a poet with more than a little irony; Collins is deadly serious.

Thomas Gray, in the conclusion to the first of his Pindaric efforts, "The Progress of Poesy. A Pindaric Ode" (1757), also sees himself as incapable of reaching Miltonic and Pindaric heights, although he appears somewhat more confident than does Collins. Gray was a superb Latinist, and he is in this Pindaric ode often reading his Pindar through Horace, as David Garrick believed Gray had done in his second Pindaric ode, "The Bard." Gray wrote to Thomas Warton on October 7, 1757, that he had read Garrick's review of the poem and professed to "admire it, particularly that observation, that the 'Bard' is taken from *Pastor, cum traheret*"—taken, that is, from Horace's *Odes* 1.15.[45]

---

44. Lonsdale, ed., *Poems of Gray, Collins, and Goldsmith*, 485.

45. So Gray states in a letter to Thomas Warton dated October 7, 1757 (*Correspondence of Thomas Gray*, ed. P. Toynbee and L. Whibley, 3 vols. [Oxford: Clarendon Press, 1971], 2:532). In a letter written in December 1758, however, Gray appears to disclaim this particular Horatian influence.

It was Horace, as I mentioned earlier, who compared the flow of Pindaric verse to a river "rushing down from a mountain, which the rains have swollen above its accustomed banks" (*Odes* 4.2, 5–6). Gray, likewise, in the first stanza of his poem recalls Horace's portrait when he says of the "rich stream of music" (7) that is winding its way down the slopes of Mt. Helicon:

> Now rolling down the steep amain,
> Headlong, impetuous, see it pour:
> The rocks and nodding groves rebellow to the roar.
>   (10–12)

As the poem begins with a reference to Horace's *Odes* 4.2, so it ends with one. Gray traces the progress of poetry from Greece to Italy to England, and, in England, from Shakespeare to Milton to Dryden. The poet, then, in an apostrophe to the lyre, asks who will continue this lofty poetic tradition:

> Oh! lyre divine, what daring spirit
> Wakes thee now? Though he inherit
> Nor the pride nor ample pinion,
> That the Theban eagle bear
> Sailing with supreme dominion
> Through the azure deep of air:
> Yet oft before his infant eyes would run
> Such forms as glitter in the Muses' ray
> With orient hues, unborrowed of the sun:
> Yet shall he mount and keep his distant way
> Beyond the limits of a vulgar fate,
> Beneath the Good how far—but far above the Great.
>   (112–23)

The crescent-shaped spot ("fronte curvatos imitatus ignes / tertium lunae referentis ortum," 57–58) on the forehead of the calf that Horace, in the concluding stanzas of *Odes* 4.2, is about to sacrifice to Augustus is a metaphor for the kind of poetry he wishes to write. Pindaric verse is associated with the mighty and glaring sun, and the poet who wishes to emulate Pindar, Horace suggests, is inviting the very same fate that overcame the unfortunate Icarus. Horace associates his own, less ambitious verse with the reflected light of the moon. Here Gray says that Pindar—"the Theban eagle"

(115)—sails "with supreme dominion / Through the azure deep of air";
Gray's own poetry, in contrast, may not be as magnificent as Pindar's, whose
verse Horace had associated with the sun, but it has its own peculiar kind of
visionary power, since "oft before" the poet Thomas Gray's "infant eyes
would run / Such forms as glitter in the Muse's ray / With orient hues,
unborrowed of the sun."

The concluding line of the poem ("Beneath the Good how far—but far
above the Great") is difficult. Gray may well have been thinking of his
Pindaric predecessor Cowley's poem "A Vote,"[46] in which the earlier poet
writes:

> This only grant me: that my meanes may ly
> Too low for envy, for contempt too high.
> Some honour I would have
> Not from great deeds, but good alone.
>
> (65–68)

Gray seems to be referring to the kind of distinction between "good" and
"great" that the Restoration poet Katherine Philips makes in the line "Still
shew how much the Good outshine the Great."[47] The apparent meaning of
Gray's concluding line, then, is as follows: the composition of this imaginative and sublime ode will not raise its poet to the status of the morally good
person; only honest living (one infers) can accomplish that aim. But the
writing of an ode such as this somehow raises him above political or merely
social distinction. Precisely how the writing of the poem achieves this last
aim remains obscure; Gray seems to be suggesting—in anticipation of aestheticist elitism—that the writing of a highly fanciful kind of poetry distinguishes the poet from the vulgar crowd. One recalls here the epigraph from
Pindar that Gray appended to this ode, and which, in his disdain for the
vulgar crowd, he significantly left untranslated: φωνᾶντα συνετοῖσιν. ἐς / δὲ
τὸ πᾶν ἑρμηνέων χατίζει [conventionally rendered, "vocal to the intelligent
alone; as for the crowd, they need interpreters"] (Olympian 2.86–87).[48]

---

46. London, 1636. I owe this observation to James Engell.

47. Cited by Lonsdale, ed., Poems of Gray, Collins, and Goldsmith, 177.

48. William H. Race disputes this traditional interpretation, which he believes is antithetical
to the open and profoundly public nature of Pindaric poetry, in "The End of Olympia 2: Pindar
and the Vulgus," California Studies in Classical Antiquity 12 (1980): 251–67. Race questions
the traditional understanding of ἐς δὲ τὸ πάν as "for the common herd" or in vulgus; "not one
parallel," he writes (252) "can be cited where τὸ πάν can possibly mean οἱ πολλοί." Glenn W.

While the writing of such verse may distinguish one from the crowd, the precise worth of such an activity remains unclear. The writing of such verse is not particularly conducive to the cultivation of moral virtue, Gray suggests, since it renders him "Beneath the Good how far." Yet somehow it also mysteriously leads him "far above the Great." However one interprets this line, what is clear is that Gray appears to share with Collins the vocational doubts spoken of by Fry. He does not make explicit what it is about the writing of modern poetry that makes it an activity worth pursuing, although the general ethical theme of the poem—a theme the logic of which was rightly challenged by Samuel Johnson[49]—is that the writing of great poetry tends to occur in an atmosphere of political liberty. Gray knows his Pindar

---

Most is in sympathy with Race's general point. Most remarks that "Pindar is discussed by many ancient poets, prose writers, and literary theorists—and not one provides even the slightest hint that Pindar's poetry might offer any obstacle whatsoever to the understanding. . . . As far as I know, only Fuhrmann . . . has apparently even recognized this fact" ("Pindar's Truth: Unity and Occasionality in the Epinician Ode" [Ph.D. diss., University of Tübingen, 1980], 3; revised as *The Measure of Praise* [Vandenhoeck and Ruprect: Göttingen, 1985]). Most refers to the essay by Manfred Fuhrmann, "*Obscuritas:* Das Problem der Dunkelheit in der Rhetorischen und Literarästhetischen Theorie der Antike," in *Immanente Ästhetik,* 46–72. In Most's opinion even Fuhrmann does not go far enough in absolving Pindar of the charge of obscurity. "Seit hellenistischer Zeit, als der größte Lyriker bewundert," Fuhrmann writes (71–72), "hat er in der Antike offenbar nicht durchaus als dunkler Dichter gegolten." Most believes that the phrase "nicht durchaus" is "misleading: 'durchaus nicht' would have been more accurate" ("Pindar's Truth," 3 n. 1). This charge of obscurity Thomas Gray, however, appears very much to have invited, as his inclusion of the untranslated Pindaric epigraph (as traditionally understood) makes abundantly clear. In some detailed and scholarly notes he wrote on Pindar's odes (preserved in the British Museum and dated March 20, 1747), Gray transcribed the Pindaric passage that eventually became the epigraph to "The Progress of Poesy." There he learnedly records the scholiast's opinion that Pindar is contrasting his own genius to the carping of Simonides. We can find many instances of Gray's courting of the obscure Muse in his letters. "The *still small voice* of Poetry was not made to be heard in a crowd," he writes to Walpole in January or February of 1748. "Suffer me then to tell you," he remarks to Warton on August 17, 1757, "that I hear, we are not at all popular. The great objection is obscurity, no body knows what we would be at . . . in short the Συνετοί appear to be still fewer, than even I expected." "I would not have put another note to save the souls of all the *Owls* of London," Gray writes to Mason on September 7, 1757, in reference to the notes that he was urged by his publisher (as T. S. Eliot was analogously urged to do and with analogous reluctance agreed to provide for that most famous of modern obscurantist poems, *The Waste Land*) to append to his two Pindaric odes, "The Progress of Poesy" and "The Bard"; "it is extremely well," Gray continues, "as it is. nobody understands me, & I am perfectly satisfied" (*Correspondence,* 1:296; 2:518, 522).

49. In the *Life of Gray* Johnson remarks: "His position is at last false: in the time of Dante and Petrarch, from whom he derives our first school of poetry, Italy was overrun by 'tyrant power' and 'coward vice'; nor was our state much better when we first borrowed the Italian arts" (*Lives of the English Poets,* ed. G. B. Hill, 3 vols. [Oxford: Clarendon Press, 1905], 3:437).

and he knows his Horace; and his confession of vocational doubt is not, as it is to a considerable degree in Horace, a sly means of commenting favorably on the virtues of his own modern poetic efforts.

Pindar's frequent remarks about his own poetic endeavors—such as the phrases from *Olympians* 9 and 2 that Collins and Gray use as the epigraphs for their own odes—were always designed specifically to enhance the glory of the victor. Such remarks, taken out of their original rhetorical context, became the very subject of these two important and influential eighteenth-century odes. The odes of Pindar were originally designed to perform the encomiastic function of praising athletes who had been successful in the games. These Pindarics of Collins and Gray now praise the poetic imagination itself, which these failed modern poets attempt, courageously, but in vain, to embody in their poems, poems that are—to adapt Wallace Stevens's representatively contemporary remark—purely the cry of their own failed occasions.[50]

50. John Sitter, *Literary Loneliness in Mid-Eighteenth-Century England* (Ithaca, N.Y.: Cornell University Press, 1982), 140–41, summarizes Harold Bloom's readings of Collins's poem in *The Visionary Company* (Ithaca, N.Y.: Cornell University Press, 1971) and Earl Wasserman's in "Collins' 'Ode on the Poetical Character,'" *English Literary History* 34 (1968): 92–115. According to Sitter, Bloom sees Collins as "one of the doomed poets in an Age of Sensibility" and Wasserman "sees the ending of the ode as a doubt-ridden retreat." The self-referential quality of many of Collins's odes was pointed out some years ago by S. Musgrove in "The Theme of Collins's *Odes,*" *Notes and Queries* 185 (1943): 214–17; 253–55. The self-referential nature of a number of odes by both Collins and Gray is extended into a thesis about the development of eighteenth-century poetry in general by Sitter in the book mentioned above and of the whole of the literature of the later eighteenth century by Frederic V. Bogel in *Literature and Insubstantiality in Later Eighteenth-Century England* (Princeton: Princeton University Press, 1984). Howard D. Weinbrot, in his review of Sitter's book, in *Journal of English and Germanic Philology* 83 (July 1984): 443–47, rejects Sitter's thesis that the poetry of the period as a rule cuts itself off from politics and history, from—in other words—its circumstantial context. Although Weinbrot gives convincing evidence for his claim, it cannot be denied that it was precisely the quest for the autonomy of poetry and of the poetic imagination that appealed to many in later generations. The young Coleridge, for example, was greatly stirred by Collins's "Ode on the Poetical Character": Coleridge wrote to Thelwall on December 17, 1796, that "Collins' Ode on the poetical character—that part of it, I should say, beginning with 'The Band (as faery Legends say) Was wove on that creating Day,' has inspired & whirled *me* alone with greater agitations of enthusiasm than any the most *impassioned* scene in Schiller or Shakespeare (*Collected Letters of Samuel Taylor Coleridge,* ed. E. L. Griggs, 6 vols. [Oxford: Clarendon Press, 1956], 1:164). And as Bogel comments, "Coleridge's conception of the poem as an organic unity, as a verbal structure obeying its own laws or as a created space analogous to the space of Creation itself, has obvious and well-documented links with the idealist cast of his metaphysical studies. But the literature of sensibility strengthened those links by providing concrete and literary examples of the way in which a work could begin to liberate itself from the exigencies of the historical or mimetic or referential" (*Literature and Insubstantiality,* 133).

Barbauld, Collins, Coleridge, and the Quest
for Pure Poetry

The term "pure poetry" first appears, in English, in Joseph Warton's well-known *Essay on the Genius and Writings of Pope,* the first volume of which was published in 1756. The term occurs again in Anna Barbauld's preface to an edition of Collins's poems, in which she distinguishes "pure Poetry, or Poetry in the abstract," from "didactic and dramatic compositions" (iii–iv). Barbauld's own amusing poem "Washing-Day" can be read as a spoof of the quest for the purity of the sublime. Her poem "To Mr. S. T. Coleridge" warns the young poet, in language reminiscent of Collins's ode, against the perils involved in the quest for evanescent metaphysical purity. Both of these poems by Barbauld were written in 1797, the year in which her edition of Collins's poems appeared. She was clearly living with Collins's poems, meditating on them, and it is thus possible to read her poems "Washing-Day" and "To Mr. S. T. Coleridge" as cautionary responses to that dangerously purified Pindaric, the "Ode on the Poetical Character."

In her description of "pure poetry" in the preface to her edition of Collins's poems, Barbauld describes rather than criticizes the evanescent nature of Collins's lyrics. The tone of controlled critical neutrality characteristic of the preface perhaps yields to a veiled critique through the imaginative abandon of "Washing-Day." The poem begins as a parody of the Miltonic high style so vainly pursued by Collins in the "Ode on the Poetical Character":

> The Muses are turned gossips; they have lost
> The buskined step, and clear high-sounding phrase,
> Language of gods. Come then, domestic Muse,
> In slipshod measure loosely pratting on
> Of farm or orchard, pleasant curds and cream,
> Of drowning flies, or shoe lost in the mire
> By little whimpering boy, with rueful face;
> Come, Muse, and sing the dreaded Washing-Day.
>
> $(1–8)^{51}$

Unlike Collins's odes, the subject matter of this poem is firmly rooted in the actual world. Collins longed, in vain, to write like Milton; Barbauld here

---

51. *Eighteenth-Century Women Poets,* ed. Roger Lonsdale (New York: Oxford University Press, 1990), 308. All quotations from Barbauld's poetry will be from this edition.

does just this, although in a mock-heroic context (note particularly 46–47, in which a "wet cold sheet" of laundry "Flaps in thy face abrupt"; cf. *Paradise Lost* 2.409, in which Satan is described as traveling "over the vast abrupt," the vast gap between hell and heaven). Collins longed to be original, to be relieved of the burden of the past; Barbauld has in fact written an original poem—at least I know of no previous poem in English that is exclusively devoted to doing laundry.

In addition, we must ask whether, for a woman writing poetry in the eighteenth century, the literary past is necessarily experienced as a burden. Whereas the tradition of poetry written by men was venerable and of long standing, the same was not the case for women. Even so relatively conservative a figure as Hannah More, as Anne Finch before her, attempted in her poetry to establish a literary genealogy for women poets in order to create a living tradition. Anna Barbauld, admittedly, was dismissive of the idea of a specifically women's poetry. It is possible, however, to see the ending of the poem as a response to the conclusion of Collins's "Ode on the Poetical Character," an ending which Barbauld might have considered as unduly maudlin about the burden of the past. Like Collins, Barbauld concludes with a reflection on the worth of her own poem. While "briskly the work" of washing-day went on, and "All hands" were "employed to wash, to rinse, to wring, / To fold, and starch, and clap, and iron, and plait," the poet muses:

> Then would I sit me down, and ponder much
> Why washings were. Sometimes through hollow bowl
> Of pipe amused we blew, and sent aloft
> The floating bubbles; little dreaming then
> To see, Montgolfier, thy silken ball
> Ride buoyant through the clouds—so near approach
> The sports of children and the toils of men.
> Earth, air, and sky, and ocean, hath its bubbles,
> And verse is one of them—this most of all.
>
> (75–86)

Barbauld likens the bubbles she would blow as a child on washing-day to the Montgolfier brothers' recent invention (1783) of the hot-air balloon. While, as Ann Messenger observes,[52] Barbauld was not hostile to the efforts

---

52. The style of Barbauld's Miltonic blank verse was no doubt influenced, as well, by Akenside; her edition of Akenside appeared in 1794. In *His and Hers: Essays in Restoration*

of balloonists, we can still perhaps detect a critique of male pride in her comparing such exploits to the blowing of bubbles on washing-day—a day lacking glamour but nevertheless of genuine importance to the life of eighteenth-century households and which was organized and carried out by women. Barbauld may well have considered Collins's grandiose and ultimately crippling conception of himself as doing battle with his literary forebears, such as John Milton, as another instance of male pride.[53]

Collins is overwhelmed by the achievement of his predecessors: "With many a Vow from Hope's aspiring Tongue, / My trembling Feet his guiding Steps pursue / In vain" (70–72). Heaven and the Imagination have "curtain'd close such Scene from ev'ry future View" (76). Barbauld does not entertain such potentially crippling aspirations for her poem: "Earth, air, and sky, and ocean, hath its bubbles, / And verse is one of them—this most of all." Her poem, like the soap bubbles to which she likens it, here bursts and vanishes. But unlike Collins, she gracefully and without mournful obsessiveness accepts its evanescence and its distance from the Miltonic sublime.

In her poem "To Mr. S. T. Coleridge," Barbauld warns the young poet—she is fifty-four years old at the time and Coleridge twenty-five—against the pursuit of pure poetry that had so frustrated Collins in his "quest [in Samuel Johnson's phrase] of mistaken beauties." What is remarkable about the poem for my purposes is how the older poet's attempt to steer Coleridge away from the very kind of paralysis that had beset Collins so precisely recalls the language of the "Ode on the Poetical Character," a poem of which Coleridge, in just the previous year, had expressed an inordinate degree of fondness. I

---

and Eighteenth-Century Literature (Lexington: University Press of Kentucky, 1986), Ann Messenger has an illuminating discussion of "Washing-Day" as a Miltonic parody (186–93). She sees (189–90) Barbauld's "abrupt" as a Miltonism, as well as the apposition "grandmother, eldest of forms," echoing Milton's "Night, eldest of things" (*Paradise Lost* 2.692).

53. Messenger (*His and Hers,* 191–92) points to a critique of masculine pride in an earlier poem of Anna Barbauld's "Written on a Marble." The poem contains the following lines:

> The world's something bigger,
> But just of this figure
> And speckled with mountains and seas;
> Your heroes are overgrown schoolboys
> Who scuffle for empires and toys,
> And kick the poor ball as they please,
> Now Caesar, now Pompey, gives law;
> And Pharsalia's plain
> Though heaped with the slain,
> Was only a game at *taw.*

shall italicize the words in Barbauld's poem which appear to be direct echoes of words, which I shall also italicize, in Collins's ode. In his ode, Collins speaks of the lure of *"Fairy* Legends" (23) and "inspiring *Bowers"* (75); Barbauld of the dangers of being "in *fairy bowers* entranced" (28). Collins speaks of the *"Gloomes"* that "embrown" the bower that protects Milton in his sublime isolation; Barbauld of the "unearthly forms" that, half-way up the hill of science, "glide through the *gloom"* (8) and of the "tender *gloom"* (29) that is so dangerously entrancing. Collins writes of how *"Strange Shades"* (58) are *"tangled* round the jealous *Steep"* (57), thus preventing the aspiring poet—whose *"Feet"* are "trembling" (71) from fear of failing to achieve perfection—from succeeding; Barbauld speaks of the "soothing soft / . . . *shades"* (23–24) that beckon the speculative thinker, of *"strange* enchantment," and warns Coleridge that "Midway the hill of science after *steep* / And rugged paths that tire the unpracticed *feet,* / A grove extends; in *tangled* mazes wrought" (1–3) and that he must beware of "dubious shapes" (4) that "lure the eager *foot* / Of youthful ardour to eternal chase."[54]

Hegel's Neoplatonic Pindar

I mentioned that, in the light of what Anna Barbauld means by lyric poetry in the preface to her edition of Collins's poems, Pindar would not be considered a true lyric poet at all. Viewed through Hegel's eyes, however, he is the pure lyric poet par excellence. Pindar, Hegel says,

> was frequently asked to celebrate this or that victor in the Games and indeed he made his living by taking money for his compositions; and yet, as bard, he puts himself in his hero's place and independently combines with his own imagination the praise of the deeds of his hero's ancestors. . . . He recalls old myths, or he expresses his own profound view of life, wealth, dominion, whatever is great and honor-

54. Lest we conclude that Barbauld's poem seems perhaps directed more at criticizing Coleridge's bent for metaphysical abstraction in general rather than specifically at his poetic practice, we should recall that it was Anna Barbauld who told Coleridge that she found "The Rime of the Ancient Mariner" wanting because it was "improbable" (*Table Talk,* ed. Carl Woodring [Princeton: Princeton University Press, 1990], 1:272), that is, not sufficiently grounded in the actual world.

able, the sublimity and charm of the Muses, but above all the dignity
of the bard [*vor allem aber über die Würde des Sängers*]. Conse-
quently in his poems he is not so much concerned to honour the
hero whose fame he spread in this way as to make himself heard. He
himself has not the honor of having sung the praises of victors, for it
is they who have acquired honor by being made the subject of Pindar's verse. This preeminent greatness of soul is what constitutes the
nobility of the lyric poet.[55]

Now Hegel is articulating something that is truly there in Pindar's poetry:
the poet is aware of the immortalizing effect of song and he sometimes
draws analogies between the efforts of the athletes he praises and the efforts
of the poet who sings these praises. Cowley was not insensitive to this
dimension of the poems, as we can infer from two lines he composed in his
ode "The Praise of Pindar." Pindar immortalizes those he praises, Cowley
writes,

> Whether the *Swift,* the *Skilful,* or the *Strong,*
> Be crowned in his *Nimble, Artful, Vigorous* Song.
>   (26–27)

The qualities of swiftness, skill, and strength of the athletes are duly praised
in verse that is correspondingly nimble, artful, and vigorous. For Hegel,
however, these qualities are not so much praised as completely eclipsed and
ultimately transcended by the corresponding qualities of the poet.

The "mastery" of lyric poetry, for Hegel, is derived not so much from the
poet's given "topic" as from the poet's "subjective enthusiasm" as it is "en-
grossed by the topic." And this creates a dialectical opposition between, on
the one hand, the "captivating might of the topic" [die hinreissende Macht
des Inhalts] and, on the other, "the poet's subjective freedom which flashes
out in the struggle against the topic which is trying to master it" [die

---

55. *Aesthetics: Lectures on Fine Art,* trans. T. M. Knox, 2 vols. (Oxford: Clarendon Press,
1975), 2:1129–30. The German is cited from *Hegels Werke,* 19 vols. (Berlin: Duncker and
Humbolt, 1834–87), 10:443. Hegel's lectures on aesthetics were reconstructed, E. H. Gom-
brich reminds us, by Hegel's student Hotho, "who used Hegel's notes for his lectures as well as
the notes that his students took. For this reason perhaps one ought not to weigh each word too
carefully, but on the whole they bear the stamp of indisputable authority" (" 'The Father of Art
History': A Reading of the *Lectures on Aesthetics* by G. W. F. Hegel," in *Tributes: Interpreters of
our Cultural Tradition* [Oxford: Phaidon Press, 1984], 55).

subjective poetische Freiheit, welche im Kampf mit dem Gegenstande, der sie bewältigen will, hervorbricht]. Hegel continues:

> It is mainly the pressure of this opposition which necessitates the swing and boldness of language and images, the apparent absence of rule in the structure and course of the poem, the digressions, gaps, sudden transitions, etc.; and the loftiness of the poet's genius is preserved by the mastery displayed in his continual ability to resolve this discord by perfect art and to produce a whole completely united in itself, which, by being his work, raises him above the greatness of his subject matter [*als sein Werk, über die Größe seines Gegenstandes hinaushebt*]. This sort of lyric enthusiasm is the origin of many of Pindar's odes.[56]

Let us return to the critical remarks of Paul Fry. The ode from its first appearance, he stated, "is a vehicle of ontological and vocational doubt." I have tried to show that this is hardly the case with the odes of Pindar. If we insist on seeing Pindar, however, as above all attempting to resolve a conflict between the demands of his recalcitrant material, on the one hand, and his own pursuit of "pure poetry," on the other. And if we further insist on seeing this conflict—as Hegel does—as the very subject of the odes, then we can view our critic's remarks as a restatement of those of Hegel in a depressed mood. Our critic's hypothetical writer of odes has doubts about his ability to handle his subject, and this dilemma becomes itself the subject of his ode, but he is not feeling as optimistic as Hegel about the possibility of resolving this dilemma with the free expression of his subjectivity.

Pindar's poetry, for Hegel, is about itself; it is "self-referential." As this attitude toward literature is axiomatic in much of contemporary critical theory, which, I believe, is often indebted to Hegel, it may be illuminating to relate Hegel's attitudes toward Pindar to his general system of the arts and their historical evolution, and to his view of the function of fine art in general, which he discusses in the introduction to his lectures on aesthetics.

Hegel divides the history of art into three stages: the symbolic, the classical, and the romantic. He judges the respective merits of these types of art in relation to their ability "to represent the idea [*die Idee*] to immediate vision in sensuous shape and not in the form of thought and pure spirituality in the strict sense." It is far from clear exactly what Hegel means by "the idea," but

---

56. *Aesthetics*, trans. Knox, 2:1141–42; *Hegels Werke*, 10:459.

it *is* clear that Hegel considers a work of art to be valuable to the extent that it makes available this "idea" to consciousness.

Echoing Kant's distinction between "free" and "dependent" beauty, Hegel says that he will discuss not that kind of art which is "subservient to certain objects" but rather that which "is free in its aims and its means," for "fine art is not art in the true sense of the term until it is also thus free." Art, for Hegel, has a content, and that content "is the idea." The "level and excellence . . . will depend upon the degree of intimacy and union with which idea and configuration appear together in elaborated fusion." In symbolic art there exists a related but not deeply intimate relation between what we might call form and content. When, in symbolic art, the idea is to be expressed in the form of a natural object, the idea is "imposed upon" such an object. A completely "adequate coalescence between the idea and its sensuous expression is not yet possible" in symbolic art, and "all that can be the outcome of such a relation is an abstract attribute, as when a lion is said to symbolize strength." The idea at this stage remains "more or less indeterminate . . . while the objects of nature are wholly definite in their shape."

In the second type of art, the classical, we are presented with "the free and adequate embodiment of the idea in the shape which . . . is uniquely appropriate to the idea itself." Classical art is itself a "concrete idea," an example of "the concrete spiritual" [*die concrete Geistigkeit*]. Classical art is, in other words—to paraphrase Hegel in terms familiar from our discussion of Aristotelian critical theory—a perfect coalescence of the particular and the universal.

The great virtue of symbolic art, for Hegel, is that it makes explicitly clear to the consciousness that "the idea stands relatively to natural phenomena as an alien." This very lack of intimate coalescence between the idea and its sensuous representation in symbolic art, that is, bespeaks the profound inadequacy of matter to express the idea. Classical art "no doubt attained the highest excellence of which the sensuous embodiment of art is capable"; but so perfect is the balance reached between form and idea, so perfect, that is, is the achievement of decorum, that the audience may temporarily forget— Hegel implies—that the idea has an abstract existence independent of the form that is for the moment allowing the idea its temporarily appropriate, but finally woefully inadequate, expression.

The following remarks by Hegel are very difficult, but their general significance is, I think, clear enough for our purposes. Whereas in the classical type of art we are presented with a perfect "coalescence of spiritual and sensuous existence as adequate conformation of both," Hegel writes, "as a matter of fact, however, in this fusion mind [*Geist*] is not represented agreeably to its true notional concept. Mind is the infinite subjectivity of the idea which, as absolute inwardness [*Innerlichkeit*], is not capable of freely expanding in its entire independence, so long as it remains within the mold of bodily shape, fused therein as in the existence wholly congenial to it." Romantic art, in brief, depicts the attempt of the spirit to free itself of its finally inadequate embodiment in works of art.[57]

Given these presuppositions, we may return to Hegel's discussion of Pindar with greater understanding. The Pindaric ode, as originally intended, is in reality an excellent example of what Hegel means by classical art, insofar that the ode is itself the perfect mediation between the particular occasion and the universal principles that may be found to be implicit in that occasion. But when Hegel actually comes to discuss Pindar's odes themselves they become, instead, brilliant examples of what Hegel means by romantic art. For what the odes record, for Hegel, is "the captivating might of the subject matter," on the one hand, and, on the other, "the poet's own subjective freedom which flashes out in the struggle against the subject matter which is trying to master it." The subject of Pindar's odes, for Hegel, is the attempt of the spirit to free itself of its inadequate material embodiment.[58]

---

57. These passages from Hegel's introduction to his lectures on aesthetics are translated by F. P. B. Osmaston, in Adams, ed., *Critical Theory Since Plato*, 534–45. The German is quoted from *Hegels Werke*, 10:99–100.

58. These Hegelian reflections are important for understanding those "deconstructive" literary attitudes—such as the ones expressed by Paul Fry in his book *The Poet's Calling in the English Ode*—that appear to have descended, at least in part, from Hegel. Much of the deconstructive enterprise can be seen as a reaction against the Hegelian quest for pure presence. The premises of deconstruction, as Grosvenor Powell writes, "have only been seriously entertained since the mid-eighteenth century. The possibility of direct experience (presence) could only be denied after it had been affirmed. Until recently, consciousness had always been regarded as contingent; final knowledge was never human knowledge ("Yvor Winters: A Poet Against Grammatology," *The Southern Review* 17 [October 1981]: 831–32). In a more recent article Casey Finch argues that Collins's *Odes* are obsessed with "the dream of full presence" and cites, as a response to such an alleged obsession, Paul de Man's reasonable statement that "unmediated expression is a philosophical impossibility" ("Immediacy in the *Odes* of William Collins," *Eighteenth-Century Studies* 20 [Spring 1987]: 291). For Martin Heidegger it was Hölderlin—the profound student and translator of Pindar—who records in his poetry the absolute presence of being and who, according to de Man, "finds himself in a position akin to that of the 'philosopher' who already possesses the Absolute Spirit in Hegel's *Phenomenology of Mind*" ("Heidegger's Exegesis of Hölderlin," in *Blindness and Insight: Essays in the Rhetoric of Contemporary Criticism* [Minneapolis: University of Minnesota Press, 1983], 251). "The problem of the relation between Hegel and Hölderlin"—who were friends and fellow students at Tübingen—"is," de Man writes, "inexhaustible" (263). Much of Hölderlin's poetry is concerned with the problem of the interpenetration of the human and the divine, of what Pindar speaks of as that privileged moment when the "Godsent brightness" shines briefly on mortals.

This is an ultimately Neoplatonic view of poetry, one that would reach its fulfillment in the "poésie pure" of Mallarmé. The poem—the material embodiment of the Idea—is at best a compromise. It offers a veiled glimpse of a spark from the emanations of the One, as the Idea has temporarily—in the words of Plotinus himself—"subdued the resistance of the material."[59] We find intimations of such a view in some nineteenth-century English odes, such as Keats's "Ode on a Grecian Urn" (cf. the famous lines "Heard melodies are sweet, but those unheard / Are sweeter"). But it was Mallarmé who, perhaps under the intoxicating influence of Hegel, was most notably entranced by the possibility of composing the absolutely pure poem, the poem of pure connotation and little or no denotative reference, "le poème tu, aux blancs."[60]

Paul Valéry and the Retreat from Purity

Paul Valéry, although a devout admirer of Mallarmé, came to believe that the attempt to compose the absolutely pure poem was bound to be frustrated—was, in fact, if pursued too rigorously, both a perilous and a prideful act: "A l'horizon, toujours, la poésie pure.... Là le péril; là, précisément, notre perte; et là même, le but.... Rien de si pur ne peut coexister avec les conditions de la vie.... La poésie absolue ... comme le vice parfait ... ne se [laisse] même approcher qu'au prix d'une progression épuisante d'efforts ... [et ne laisse] enfin que l'orgueil de n'être jamais satisfait.[61]

59. *Enneads* 5.8, trans. Stephen MacKenna, in Adams, ed., *Critical Theory Since Plato,* 106. True beauty, Plotinus says, is realized in a work of art—in this case a statue—"only to the extent that the stone has yielded to the art" [ὅσον εἶξεν ὁ λίθος τῇ τέχνῃ]. The Greek, which I have just rendered more literally than does MacKenna, is from *Plotini Opera,* ed. Paul Henry and Hans-Rudolf Schwyzer, 2 vols. (Oxford: Clarendon Press, 1977), 2:269. Very relevant to our discussion are the following remarks by M. H. Abrams: "Although Mallarmé's talk of the Absolute," Abrams writes, "was probably derived by hearsay from Hegel, he means by it very much what Plotinus had meant: the One 'is perfect because it seeks for nothing, and possesses nothing, and has need of nothing.' Mallarmé's aim was to achieve the sufficient poem, absolute in its purity in the sense that it is totally inhuman and unworldly, because independent not only of poet and audience, but even of reference to anyone or anything outside itself" ("Coleridge, Baudelaire, and Modernist Poetics," in *Immanente Ästhetik—Ästhetische Reflexion: Lyrik als Paradigma der Moderne* [Munich: Wilhelm Fink Verlag, 1966], 133).

60. "Crise de vers," in *Oeuvres complètes* (Gallimard: Paris, 1945), 136.

61. Quoted in Abrams, "Coleridge, Baudelaire, and Modernist Poetics," 136. Cf. Middleton Murry's statement that Collins's poetic principles "came near preventing him from having

His own great poem *Le Cimetière marin,* which I discuss at greater length in the next chapter, begins with an epigraph composed of some lines from Pindar's third Pythian ode that make this very point: "Do not, dear heart, yearn for immortal life, but use to the full the resources that are within your reach" [μή, φίλα ψύχα, βίον ἀθάνατον / σπεῦδε, τὰν δ' ἔμπρακτον ἄντλει μαχανάν] (61–62). Valéry is truly Pindaric in trying to articulate this piece of ancient wisdom in a modern context. Be very wary, Valéry suggests, about the delusive perils involved in attempting to achieve a state of pure and unmediated consciousness; and do not, dear heart, Valéry's poem further implies, try to write the perfect, absolutely pure poem. The pursuit of poetic purity is self-defeating. Such a relentless quest can end only in frustration, disillusionment, and an unhealthy detachment from life. "Il faut tenter de vivre"; one must try to live within mortal bounds, in the tangible, physical world, as Valéry states in the final stanza of the poem:

> Le vent se lève! . . . il faut tenter de vivre!
> L'air immense ouvre et referme mon livre,
> La vague en poudre ose jaillir des rocs!
> Envolez-vous, pages tout éblouies!
> Rompez, vagues! Rompez d'eaux réjouies
> Ce toit tranquille où picoraient des focs!

> [The wind is rising! . . . We must try to live!
> The huge air opens and shuts my book: the wave
> Dares to explode out of the rocks in reeking
> Spray. Fly away, my sun-bewildered pages!
> Break, waves! Break up with your rejoicing surges
> This quiet roof where sails like doves were pecking.][62]

The inevitable result of the relentless quest for unattainable poetic purity, we might in conclusion relevantly infer from Valéry's poem, would be none other than a severe case of vocational and even of ontological doubt.

---

anything to express at all" and that he tried to achieve "a perilous kind of purity that . . . hovers on the verge of emptiness" (*Countries of the Mind* [New York: E. P. Dutton, 1922], 86 and 94). This is, in essence, what Samuel Johnson means when he says in the *Life of Collins* that in his poems Collins was "in quest of mistaken beauties" (*Lives of the English Poets,* 3:338).

62. *Oeuvres de Paul Valéry,* 2 vols. (Paris: Librairie Gallimard, 1957), 1:151; trans. C. Day Lewis, in *Paul Valéry: Selected Writings* (New York: New Directions, 1950), 47.

6

POETRY AND THE IN-BETWEEN

Valéry's *Le Cimetière marin* and Pindar's Third Pythian Ode

> *The poet himself stands between the former—the gods, and the latter—the people. He is one who has been cast out—out into that* Between, *but only and for the first time in this Between is it decided, who man is and where he is settling his existence. "Poetically, dwells man on this earth."*
> —Heidegger, "Hölderlin and the Essence of Poetry"

> *Auprès d'un coeur, aux sources du poème,*
> *Entre le vide et l'événement pur*
> —Valéry, Le Cimetière marin

Pure Poetry and the Recovery of It-Reality

The doctrine of pure poetry has two consequences in terms of the history of the Pindaric tradition, one more salutary than the other. On the negative side, this notion of pure poetry has resulted in a loss of subject matter, in a formalism in which the poem tends to be about itself. I have devoted much of the previous chapter to tracing this historical development. Thus Collins and Gray write Pindaric odes on poetry—more specifically on the failure of contemporary poets to write sublime poetry. Thus Kant contrasts "the pure disinterested satisfaction in judgments of taste" with teleological judgments and argues that the aesthetic judgment can be satisfied by purely formal patterns that "have no meaning" and "depend on no definite concept."[1] And Schiller, in discussing the "ideal of aesthetic purity," can say that "subject matter,... however sublime and all-embracing it may be, always has a limiting effect upon the spirit."[2]

On the positive side, however, the concept of pure poetry has encouraged a notion of language that takes seriously into account what Voegelin calls It-reality, as I described Voegelin's articulation of the paradox of consciousness in the first chapter. In the pure poem, language is not restricted merely to denoting thing-reality. Although many of their poems are often not completely successful, both Collins and Gray, by moving away from the poetry of direct statement that characterizes much of Augustan verse, deserve credit for trying to link their efforts with the work of poets for whom language has the kind of richness and necessary ambiguity that Eric Voegelin describes in his analysis of the paradox of language. And in order to establish this link and achieve this end, Collins and Gray in their Pindarics both return, as does Voegelin, to Greece.

Devoted as he was to exploring the connotative powers of language, Collins never completely abandoned denotative reference. Even his almost purely suggestive poem, the "Ode to Evening," ends with an attempt to be explicit about the social importance of the mood evoked by twilight. But the French symbolists had no such qualms. As Valéry himself says in his essay "Mallarmé," poetry, for Mallarmé,

> ne s'agissait plus d'un divertissement, même sublime. Mais, au-dessus de ce que l'on nomme Littérature, Métaphysique, Religion, le nouveau devoir lui était apparu d'exercer et d'exalter la plus spirituelle de toutes les fonctions de la Parole, celle qui ne démontre, ni ne décrit, ni ne représente quoi que ce soit: qui donc n'exige, ni même ne supporte, aucune confusion entre le pouvoir verbal de combiner, pour quelque fin suprême, *les ideés qui naissent des mots.*

> [(was) no longer a question of amusement, however sublime. Over and above what is Literature, Metaphysics, Religion, he had perceived the new duty that consisted in exercising and exalting the most spiritual functions of all the functions of the Word, which neither demonstrates, nor describes, nor represents anything at all;

---

1. *Critique of Judgment,* trans. J. H. Bernard, *Critical Theory Since Plato,* ed. Hazard Adams, rev. ed. (New York: Harcourt Brace Jovanovich, 1992), 377.

2. *Critical Theory Since Plato,* 424–25.

which therefore does not require, nor even allow, any confusion between reality and the verbal power of combining for some supreme end *the ideas that are born of words.*][3]

Heidegger, in a similar attempt to get beyond a strictly referential and utilitarian view of language, remarks: "If we must, therefore, seek the speaking of language in what is spoken, we shall do well to find something that is spoken purely rather than to pick just any spoken material at random. What is spoken purely is that in which the completion of the speaking that is proper to what is spoken is, in its turn, an original. What is spoken purely is the poem."[4] Elsewhere Heidegger comments: "The more poetic a poet is— the freer (that is, the more open and ready for the unforeseen) his saying— the greater is the purity with which he submits what he says to an ever more painstaking listening, and the further what he says is from the mere propositional statement that is dealt with solely in regard to its correctness or incorrectness."[5] So far I have stressed the less positive aspects of the doctrine of pure poetry. It is time to consider its more positive dimensions.

We must say something, first of all, about the relation between symbolist poetics and the representation of "It-reality." Valéry was an advocate of "pure poetry," by which he meant a poetry that put a premium on the suggestive and connotative powers of language rather than on denotation and unambiguous referentiality. Another way to put this is to say that Valéry, following his master Mallarmé, sought a language for poetry that would be an index of participation in It-reality rather than reducing language to the intentionalist function of representing only thing-reality. Mallarmé's mistake, in my judgment, is that by attempting to focus at times almost exclusively on "It-reality"—and, like Hegel, by attempting to gain speculative control over It—he slighted "thing-reality" and hence became obsessed with the possibility of writing the silent poem, the poem that is sapped of all denotation, of all "thing-reality." Although Valéry subscribed to this spiritualist view of language,[6] one that has its roots in neoplatonic and Thomistic analogical think-

---

3. The French is cited from *Oeuvres de Paul Valéry,* 2 vols. (Paris: Bibliothèque de la Pléiade, 1957), 1:707; the English from *Paul Valéry: An Anthology,* edited and with an introduction by James R. Lawler (London: Routledge & Kegan Paul, 1977), 167.
4. "Language," in *Poetry, Language, Thought,* trans. Albert Hofstadter (New York: Harper & Row, 1971), 194.
5. " '. . . Poetically Man Dwells . . . ,' " in ibid., 216.
6. Valéry's spiritualism is implied in his remark to Gide of March 27, 1891: "All those who study 'man' in himself, make me sick. Only the church has an art. It alone gives a little comfort

ing about language rather than in Enlightenment/positivist nominalism, he apparently never abandoned the philosophical skepticism and atheism that might be seen as the ultimate result of the nominalist view of language. We might say: symbolist poetics is a poetics of faith, a poetics that implies that reality is ultimately mysterious, and that the most a poet can do is lovingly use a language that participates in and is an index of this mystery; Enlightenment and post-Enlightenment thought, cresting in Hegel, posits reality as thing to be known and mastered. It is the struggle between these two contradictory elements that is enacted in *Le Cimetière marin.*

From Plato, Voegelin borrows the term *metaxy* in order to articulate a reality that resists being reduced to either pure intentionalism ("thing-reality") or pure mystery ("It-reality"). Voegelin argues that Hegel's consciousness was deformed by making precisely the mistake of trying to bring the It under speculative control and thus to turn It into a thing. Voegelin points us to several passages in Hegel that describe this process. Hegel writes: "That truth is real only as a System, or that the substance is essentially subject, is expressed in the perception which pronounces the Absolute as *Geist*—this sublimest concept which belongs to the modern age and its religion."[7] And what is the *Geist?* It is "the Protestant principle to place the world of the Intellect into one's own mind, and to see, know, and feel in one's own self-consciousness all that was previously Beyond."[8] I would suggest that Paul Valéry's great poem *Le Cimetière marin* is a meditation—via Pindar's third Pythian ode—on the limitations of this Hegelian effort. And I would suggest further that Valéry associated this Hegelian effort with Mallarmé, of whose Hegelian idealism Valéry appears to have been critical, judging from some remarks he made in his *Cahiers.* There Valéry says of Mallarmé: "Il s'est malheureusement embarrassé d'ideés verbales venues des philosophes" (He is unfortunately encumbered by verbose ideas drawn from the philosophers [Hegel]).[9]

---

and detaches us from the world. I would say and shout: we are all children beside the liturgists and the theologians—since the greatest of us—Wagner and Mallarmé—bow before them and imitate them" (Agnes E. Mackay, *The Universal Self: A Study of Paul Valéry* [Toronto: University of Toronto Press, 1961], 29). Valéry was a religious skeptic, but as Mackay remarks, he took great "delight in the High Mass, and he often returned to his idea that it was the purest form of drama" (26–27).

7. From the preface to *The Phenomenology of Mind,* cited from Eric Voegelin, *In Search of Order,* vol. 5 of *Order and History,* 5 vols. (Baton Rouge: Louisiana State University Press, 1956–87), 5:62.

8. G. W. F. Hegel, *Geschichte der Philosophie,* 2:300; quoted in Voegelin, *In Search of Order,* 62.

9. *Cahiers, Édition Établie, Présentée et Annotée par Judith Robinson,* 2 vols. (Paris: Gallimard, 1973–74), 2:1115.

Le Cimetière marin is anti-Hegelian very much in the spirit of Paul Ricoeur's "Renoncer à Hegel" in *Temps et récit,* in which, as Eugene Webb has written, Ricoeur "speaks of Hegel's hope for total objectification of Spirit as a temptation to be renounced, but he also indicates that it is a temptation he has himself keenly felt. Explaining how 'we no longer think according to [*selon*] Hegel, but after [*après*] Hegel,' he says, 'what reader, once he has been seduced like us by his power of thought, would not feel the abandon-ment of Hegel as a wound, and one which, precisely in contrast to the wounds of the absolute Spirit, does not heal? To such a reader, if he is not to yield to the weaknesses of nostalgia, one must wish the courage for a labor of grief.' "[10] For Hegel's goal, as set out in the preface to *The Phenomenology of Mind,* was "the systematical development of truth in scientific form [which] can alone be the true shape in which truth exists." Hegel wished "to help bring philosophy nearer to the form of science—that goal where it can lay aside the name of *love* of knowledge and be actual *knowledge.*"[11]

Valéry appears to have felt the grief referred to above by Ricoeur, for in his essay "Au Sujet du *Cimetière marin*" he writes that he considers the poem "une méditation qui fait sentir trop cruellement l'écart entre l'*être* et le *connaître* que développe la conscience de la conscience" [a meditation that makes too cruelly felt the gap between *being* and *knowing* that is developed by the consciousness of consciousness].[12] The phrase "consciousness of con-sciousness" has a Hegelian ring, for "experience" [*Erfahrung*], according to Hegel in *The Phenomenology of Mind,* is the "dialectical process [*dia-lektische Bewegung*] that consciousness [*Bewußtseyn*] executes on itself."[13] As Voegelin comments, Hegel conceives of consciousness not in the Platonic, participatory sense, but "in the subject-object mode":[14] consciousness is the experience of the consciousness contemplating itself contemplating. Valéry's

10. Paul Ricoeur quoted in Eugene Webb, *Philosophers of Consciousness: Polanyi, Lonergan, Voegelin, Ricoeur, Girard, Kierkegaard* (Seattle: University of Washington Press, 1988), 154.

11. *The Phenomenology of Mind,* trans. J. B. Baillie (New York: Harper Torchbooks, 1967), 70.

12. *Oeuvres de Paul Valéry,* 1:1506; *The Collected Works of Paul Valéry,* trans. Denise Folliot, Bollingen Series 45 (New York: Pantheon Books), 7:151.

13. *The Phenomenology of Mind,* trans. Baillie, 142; the German from *Phänomenologie des Geistes,* ed. Wolfgang Bonsiepen and Reinhard Heede, in *Hegel: Gesammelte Werke* (Hamburg: Felix Meiner), 9:60.

14. *In Search of Order,* 55. Although Voegelin offers a critical analysis of Hegelian thought, he nevertheless has high praise for Hegel's "irreversible achievement" in resisting the deforma-tion of "Hellenic and Judaeo-Christian symbols . . . into intentionalist concepts to be manipu-lated by propositional thinkers" (64).

poem might be viewed as an expression of the grief experienced by the "subject" when the "object" of cognition is the Absolute. The poem is thus, by implication, a critique of the subject-object mode of cognition. Indeed, the entire aesthetic tradition—of which Valéry's poem and the doctrine of "la poésie pure" are the culmination—may be seen as a means of overcoming the subject-object problem and of returning to the classical experience of reason, which I discussed in Chapters 2 and 3.

Because of Valéry's commitment to symbolist poetics, in interpreting this particular poem one must—in the spirit of such a poetics—allow the language to resonate in suggestive ways. I hope, however, to avoid the extremes of interpretive anarchy suggested in Valéry's own remark that he made in response to questions about the meaning of his famous poem: "My verses have the meanings that my readers find in them."[15] Although I consider Valéry's remark as itself extreme in the interpretive freedom it grants to his readers, it may at least excuse what some might find rather speculative in the interpretation that follows.

Le Cimetière Marin: *A Response to Hegelian/Mallarmean Purism*

Mallarmé had suggested that poems should not have titles, for titles are too resounding. We may translate this as meaning: titles are too denotative, they reek too much of "thing-reality." Yet Valéry's poem has a title that situates the poem in the real world: a graveyard by the sea, which happens to be (although as readers we do not need to know this) in Valéry's own birthplace of Sète. The poem is not itself an ode, but it shares a good deal with the meditative ode tradition of the nineteenth century. We have the poet painting a scene from the natural world and reflecting on it. The poem can be divided into three sections. It begins with a meditation on the Absolute, symbolized by the roof of the temple the poet envisions glistening in the sea. The poet meditates on the graveyard and the dead buried there, and he then returns to his vision of the Absolute, from which he withdraws as the poem comes to a close. The poem is composed in twenty-four stanzas. I shall discuss the first three stanzas and the last six. My analysis of the first three stanzas focuses on the subtle ways

15. "Mes vers ont le sens qu'on leur prête"; quoted in Hans-Georg Gadamer, *Truth and Method* (New York: Crossroad, 1986), 509.

in which the poet anguishes about the gap he perceives between being in the world, on the one hand, and knowing in an absolute sense, on the other.[16] My analysis of the last six stanzas focuses on the poet's resolution of this conflict and how poetry can mediate it.

The poem begins as the poet describes the scene and introduces some of the poem's governing symbols:

> Ce toit tranquille, où marchent des colombes,
> Entre les pins palpite, entre les tombes;
> Midi le juste y compose de feux
> La mer, la mer, toujours recommencée!
> O récompense après une pensée
> Qu'un long regard sur le calme des dieux!
>
> [This quiet roof, where dove-sails saunter by,
> Between the pines, the tombs, throbs visibly.
> Impartial noon patterns the sea in flame—
> That sea forever starting and restarting.
> When thought has had its hour, oh how rewarding
> Are the long vistas of celestial calm.]

$$(1-6)^{17}$$

The poet is situated in the graveyard and is looking out at the sparkling Mediterranean at midday. The sea more than sparkles; it appears even to be on fire. Before we learn this, however, we are told at the very beginning of the poem of "Ce toit tranquille." The first question that a reader will have on

16. In her brilliant essay "Contexts for 'Being,' 'Divinity,' and 'Self' in Valéry and Edgar Bowers" (*The Southern Review* 13 [January 1977]: 48–82), Helen P. Trimpi sees Valéry struggling against his philosophical inheritance of neoplatonic essentialism. She speculates that in Valéry's often neoplatonic universe only pure intelligence has being and presence, and that Valéry therefore experiences the limitations of worldly existence as absence of being, for in his either/or dilemma there is no room for existence (as opposed to essence) in the Thomistic sense.

17. The English translation is from *Paul Valéry: Selected Writings* (New York: New Directions, 1950) and is by C. Day Lewis. I chose Lewis's blank verse translation because of its attempt to bring across Valéry's formal precision. The reader should be aware that this is not a literal translation. The French original was first published in *La Nouvelle Revue Française* in June 1920. It was published again later that year (August 31) with some of the stanzas reordered in their final arrangement and with the insertion of the Greek epigraph. In the December 1926 publication of *Charmes*, Valéry appended to the epigraph the name of the Greek poet and the particular poem from which the epigraph was drawn.

taking up this poem is: what is this "toit"? Is there an actual roof? We must wait before this question is answered. But what we are presented with is a "toit tranquille" on which doves—doves are often symbols of peace, and this is a peaceful scene—are walking. All we know about this "toit" so far is that it appears to throb ("palpite") "entre les pins" and "les tombes." But what sort of living thing is this "toit"?

In the second stanza the poet meditates on the source of the intense light that illuminates the scene:

> Quel pur travail de fins éclairs consume
> Maint diamant d'imperceptible écume,
> Et quelle paix semble se concevoir!
> Quand sur l'abîme un soleil se repose,
> Ouvrages purs d'une éternelle cause,
> Le temps scintille et le songe est savoir.

> [What grace of light, what pure toil goes to form
> The manifold diamond of the elusive foam!
> What peace I feel begotten at the source!
> When sunlight rests upon a profound sea,
> Time's air is sparkling, dream is certainty—
> Pure artifice both of an eternal Cause.]

> (7–12)

The poet acknowledges that this scene of "calme" alluded to in the concluding line of the first stanza is rather the *semblance* of calm: "Et quelle paix *semble* se concevoir!" The sun, as the source of all light, appears to represent the Absolute. But the Absolute, because we can only intuit it through perception, appears to the poet to be very possibly illusory. The ocean is referred to here ominously and ambiguously as "l'abîme"—ocean depths but also an abyss, complete emptiness, "le néant." And the sun is not "*le* soleil" but "*un* soleil"—the physical manifestation of *the* Absolute is thus diminished to the status of *an* Absolute, and the poet thus questions the ontological status of Absoluteness, or at least of our ability to perceive the Absolute. Both the sea and the sun are perceived to be "ouvrages purs d'une eternelle cause": but they are only so in perception, for, as the poet says in concluding this stanza, in his contemplation of the scene, the distinction between knowledge and dreaming has apparently been dissolved. Human beings, however, can never ultimately dissolve this distinction, for that would be to reduce It-reality to thing-reality in the Hegelian style. Language can hint at ultimate reality, but it cannot unambiguously depict It because It is not a thing. The most we can do is to articulate the paradox, which is what Valéry is doing, although he appears to want to do more than this.

In the third stanza the poet now explicitly questions the reality of his vision:

> Stable trésor, temple simple à Minerve,
> Masse de calme, et visible réserve,
> Eau sourcilleuse, Œil qui gardes en toi
> Tant de sommeil sous une voile de flamme,
> O mon silence! . . . Édifice dans l'âme,
> Mais comble d'or aux mille tuiles, Toit!

> [Sure treasure, simple shrine to the intelligence,
> Palpable calm, visible reticence,
> Proud-lidded water, Eye wherein there wells
> Under a film of fire such depth of sleep—
> O silence! . . . Mansion in my soul, you slope
> Of gold, roof of a myriad golden tiles.]

(13–18)

But before he questions the reality status of the vision, the poet describes the temple, which appears to be a shrine to perfect intelligence. Like the neoplatonic One, the roof is unchanging ("Stable trésor," "Masse de calme, et visible reserve") and is equivalent to pure intelligence ("temple simple à Minerve"; Minerva is of course the goddess of wisdom). So far all is relatively clear. But then in the third line of the stanza the sea is "eau sourcilleuse." What, exactly, is "haughty water"? Because this is a symbolist poem, in which a premium is put on suggestiveness, it is hard to pin down the meaning precisely, but several possibilities present themselves. "Sourcilleuse" here can mean "haughty," but the word can also mean "frowning" or "worried" and it can as well have the poetic meaning of "tall" or "lofty." All are possible; let us consider the possibilities in reverse order.

Since the poet envisions the shining water as the roof of a temple, then in fact, if that roof is imagined to be slanting upward, the water (roof) could be seen as "tall." But because the word that follows "sourceilleuse" is "Œil," the meaning of "worried" suggests itself, since the mention of physiognomy suggests the possible appropriateness of understanding the word as "worried" as in "worried brow" (*sourcil* is the word for "eyebrow"). But why would the water be worried? The poet, I suggest, in contemplating the Absolute, at first (as it later appears) deludes himself into believing in its *objective* presence, and then begins to worry—and projects this worry onto the object perceived—that his vision is in fact a *subjective* illusion. The water is at first perceived to be "tall" or "lofty," since at this moment the poet is entertaining a belief in the reality of the vision of the roof of a temple consecrated to the divine intelligence. As the faith in the reality of the vision recedes, the intermediate meaning of "worried" fleetingly but ominously suggests itself. The water then becomes "haughty" because the poet now concludes that he has projected his own narcissistic need for believing that he can envision the Absolute. Hence, it is the poet rather than the water— by virtue of a kind of transferred epithet—who is in fact "haughty" (*sourcilleux*), who is narcissistically entranced by the beauty of his own prideful projections.

And there is yet another possible meaning for "sourcilleuse": the word may be functioning as a pun ("sourcy water"), for the water is a "source" both literally and metaphorically in the sense that it is the source of the poet's own vision. That most stable structure of the temple, it now appears, is a projection of the poet's state of contemplation: "O mon silence!" The temple is indeed a structure, but it is a structure built by the poet's mind: "Édifice dans l'âme." The poet will not, however, relinquish the vision simply because it may be an illusion. Yes, the temple lives in the consciousness of the poet, *but*—"Mais" is the word that emphatically begins the last line of the stanza—he still envisions it as a "golden summit of a thousand tiles."

The stanza ends emphatically with "Toit," which appears after a comma that marks the most definite caesura in the line (the pause after "d'or" is very faint in comparison). "Toit" of course means "roof," but it sounds precisely like "toi"; moreover, because the poet rhymes "Toit" with "toi," he further suggests the possibility of a play on words. The subtle irony present here, I believe, is that the poet refers to the roof as "you" immediately after he has suggested that this very "Toit" is in fact a mere projection of "Moi"—of the poet's own mind, his subjective vision.

I have been discussing this poem in the kind of detail that is necessary to register the nuances of the symbolist style at its most delicately suggestive. To do this for the entire poem would swell this chapter out of all proportion—and no doubt tire the reader's patience. To adapt a line of Valéry's from the poem—a line that recalls the epigraph from Pindar's third Pythian—"La sainte patience meurt aussi!" Let me then proceed to the poem's conclusion, highlighting those parts which deal with what I take to be Valéry's anti-Hegelianism. The poem began with a meditation on the Absolute, symbolized by the roof of the temple, which the poet envisions glistening in the sea. The poet then meditates on the graveyard and the dead buried there, before returning to his vision of the Absolute, from which he withdraws as the poem comes to a close.

Let us reenter the poem at stanza 19, just before leaving the graveyard:

> Pères profonds, têtes inhabitées,
> Qui sous le poids de tant de pelletées
> Êtes la terre et confondez nos pas,
> Le vrai rongeur, le ver irréfutable
> N'est point pour vous qui dormez sous la table,
> Il vit de vie, il ne me quitte pas!

> [Ancestors deep down there, O derelict heads
> Whom such a weight of spaded earth o'erspreads,
> Who *are* the earth, in whom our steps are lost,
> The real flesh-eater, worm unanswerable
> Is not for you that sleep under the table:
> Life is his meat, and I am still his host.]
>
> (109–14)

The poet here declares that it is his obsession with the Absolute that destroys the reality of life in the In-Between. The dead are dead, they have become one with the earth. Although one may have visions of the horror of rats or worms feeding on the dead, the dead are in fact impervious to this process. It is the present living poet's obsession with the Absolute, his tendency to turn "It" into a "thing" that can be possessed, that—metaphorically, but with far more devastating results to the spirit—is "Le vrai rongeur, le ver irréfutable. . . . Il vit de vie, il ne me quitte pas!" The following stanza embroiders these ideas:

> Amour, peut-être, ou do moi-même haine?
> Sa dent secrète est de moi si prochaine
> Que tous les noms lui peuvent convenir!
> Qu'importe! Il voit, il veut, il songe, il touche!
> Ma chair lui plaît, et jusque sur ma couche,
> A ce vivant je vis d'appartenir!

['Love,' shall we call him? 'Hatred of self,' maybe?
His secret tooth is so intimate with me
That any name would suit him well enough,
Enough that he can see, will, daydream, touch—
My flesh delights him, even upon my couch
I live but as a morsel of his life.]

(115–20)

As one commentator suggests, "the 'worm' is Valéry's 'cogito ergo sum': the fact that the consciousness can regard itself is the only proof of life to oneself."[18] But the worm is, more specifically, associated with the serpent who in Genesis promises eternal knowledge to Eve, the "serpent" of Valéry's other great poem on the theme of the desire for absolute knowledge, "Ébauche d'un serpent." The pathological desire described by the poet is analogous to the Hegelian effort to become absolute spirit. But Valéry realizes that devotion to the absolute means relinquishing one's existence in time—which is the only existence one has.

The stanza that follows clarifies some of the important philosophical implications of the poem:

Zénon, Cruel Zénon, Zénon d'Élée!
M'as-tu percé de cette flèche ailée
Qui vibre, vole, et qui ne vole pas!
Le son m'enfante et la flèche me tue!
Ah! le soleil . . . Quelle ombre de tortue
Pour l'âme, Achille immobile à grands pas!

[Zeno, Zeno, cruel philosopher Zeno,
Have you then pierced me with your feathered arrow
That hums and flies, yet does not fly! The sounding
Shaft gives me life, the arrow kills. Oh, sun!—
Oh, what a tortoise-shadow to outrun
My soul, Achilles' giant stride left standing!]

(121–26)

18. G. D. Martin, *Paul Valéry, Le Cimetière Marin,* Edinburgh Bilingual Library (Edinburgh: Edinburgh University Press, 1971), 57.

Zeno is important here because he is associated with his teacher, Parmenides. Parmenides, we recall, championed the immobility of the One against those who would assign reality status to motion and the many.[19] Why is Zeno cruel? Perhaps because he answered the critics of Parmenides with the same kind of sarcasm with which these critics treated Parmenides' belief in the One. But in terms of our poem, Zeno is cruel because his proof that only the One exists causes our poet the same kind of pain he experiences in being gnawed by his Hegelian desire to turn the Absolute into a thing to be possessed. It is instructive to recall that Hegel, in the preface to the *Phenomenology,* referred to the *Parmenides* of Plato as "the greatest work of ancient dialectics" and "the true revelation and expression of the divine life."[20] One wonders if Hegel did not miss how Plato *satirized* the Parmenidean position, that only the One is real.[21]

Zeno criticized those who would prove the primacy of motion over the immobility associated with the One. Let us look at the two examples of Zeno's paradoxes referred to here. First, the flying arrow: G. S. Kirk and J. E. Raven reconstruct this paradox as follows: "An object is at rest when it occupies a space equal to its own dimensions. An arrow in flight occupies, at any given moment, a space equal to its own dimensions. Therefore an arrow in flight is at rest." At any given moment, the flying arrow is at rest, even though it appears to be moving: this is the paradox. Motion is therefore an illusion. Motion, however, is what makes the poet live, as both poet and human being; he appears to take great pleasure, for example, in writing the description of the arrow "qui vibre, vole" and to despair at having then to write "et qui ne vole pas." The sensually perceptible sound of the arrow is what gives him life ("Le son m'enfante") but the "point" (pun intended) of

19. On Zeno, see *The Presocratic Philosophers: A Critical History with a Selection of Texts* ed. and trans. G. S. Kirk and J. E. Raven (Cambridge: Cambridge University Press, 1971), 286–97. See also the revised edition, edited by Kirk, Raven, and Malcolm Schofield (Cambridge: Cambridge University Press, 1983), 263–79.

20. Trans. Voegelin, *In Search of Order,* 63.

21. One must take with a grain of salt Valéry's statement that he mentioned Zeno only to give his poem a little philosophical coloring—"Mais je n'ai entendu prendre à la philosophie qu'un peu de sa couleur" ("Au sujet du *Cimetière marin,*" in *Oeuvres de Paul Valéry,* 1:1506). This antiphilosophical doctrine of Valéry proceeds directly from the aestheticist stance of the pure poet for whom, as in the Kantian formulation (and restated by Poe), cognition must officially be separated off from pure aesthetic pleasure. Despite Valéry's disclaimers, *Le Cimetière marin* is one of the most philosophical poems ever written. As Pierre-Olivier Waltzer has written, "*Le Cimetière marin* est en outre un admirable poème philosophique, peut-être le plus pur de notre langue" (*La Poésie de Valéry* [Genève: Pierre Cailler, 1953], 348).

the paradox is what—like the "ver irréfutable"—kills him spiritually ("et la flèche me tue!"). He concludes these perceptions with the exclamation, "Ah, le soleil," evoking, once again, the symbol of the Absolute, the craving for which so consumes him.

The second paradox is paraphrased as follows by Kirk and Raven: "Achilles can never overtake a tortoise; because by the time he reaches the point from which the tortoise started, it will have moved on to another point; by the time he reaches that second point it will have moved on again; and so *ad infinitum.*"[22] The image of the swift-footed Achilles hopelessly "immobile à grands pas!" and defeated in a foot race by a tortoise might be acceptable as a purely intellectual construct, but the poet cannot accept it on an experiential level. And so the poem moves on to its concluding three stanzas.

> Non, non! . . . Debout! Dans l'ère successive!
> Brisez, mon corps, cette forme pensive!
> Buvez, mon sein, la naissance du vent!
> Une fraîcheur, de la mer exhalée,
> Me rend mon âme . . . O puissance salée!
> Courons à l'onde en rejaillir vivant.
>
> [No, no! Arise! The future years unfold.
> Shatter, O body, meditation's mould!
> And, O my breast, drink in the wind's reviving!
> A freshness, exhalation of the sea,
> Restores my soul . . . Salt-breathing potency!
> Let's run at the waves and be hurled back to living!
>   (127–32)

Motion may not be real "intellectually," but the poet encourages himself nonetheless to live in time ("dans l'ère successive"), even if temporal existence may pale before the brilliance of the Absolute.

Here then we have the theme of the limitations of human knowledge explicitly stated. The poet portrays his longing for complete knowledge, but draws back from this desire. He wishes now to experience reality in its sensuousness, even if he cannot comprehend it—in fact, it is precisely because he cannot comprehend it intellectually that he wishes now to experience it concretely and asks that the wave shatter "cette forme pen-

22. *The Presocratic Philosophers* (1971), 294–95.

sive." To live (exist)—note the word "vivant" which concludes this stanza—appears to mean, for Valéry at this point in the poem, to live in the In-Between and not to be derailed into equating living with absolute knowledge or absolute Being: "Courons à l'onde en rejaillir vivant" [Let's run at the waves and be hurled back to living].

In the next stanza the poet returns to his trance, but he imagines the sea now much more ominously than he had at the beginning of the poem:

> Oui! Grande mer de délires douée,
> Peau de panthère et chlamyde trouée
> De mille et mille idoles du soleil,
> Hydre absolue, ivre de ta chair bleue,
> Qui te remords l'étincelante queue
> Dans un tumulte au silence pareil,

> [Yes, mighty sea with such wild frenzies gifted
> (The panther skin and the rent chlamys), sifted
> All over with sun-images that glisten,
> Creature supreme, drunk on your own blue flesh,
> Who in a tumult like the deepest hush
> Bite at your sequin-glittering tail—yes, listen!]
>
> (133–38)

The poem ends with the following stanza:

> Le vent se lève! . . . Il faut tenter de vivre!
> L'air immense ouvre et referme mon livre,
> La vague en poudre ose jaillir des rocs!
> Envolez-vous, pages tout éblouies!
> Rompez, vagues! Rompez d'eaux réjouies
> Ce toit tranquille où picoraient des focs!

> [The wind is rising! . . . We must try to live!
> The huge air opens and shuts my book: the wave
> Dares to explode out of the rocks in reeking
> Spray. Fly away, my sun-bewildered pages!
> Break, waves! Break up with your rejoicing surges
> This quiet roof where sails like doves were pecking.]
>
> (139–44)

In the penultimate stanza of the poem, the vision of the sun-bedazzled sea as an image of Absolute being with which the poem began has given way to the ominous vision of that same sea as the skin of a panther, as a "chlamys" (a short cloak worn by men in ancient Greece) perforated by thousands and thousands of delusive images ("idoles") spawned by the sun, and finally as a serpent ("Hydre absolue") biting its own tail.[23] Valéry is here suggesting more explicitly than he has anywhere in the poem that the result of obsessively trying—as Hegel did—to gain speculative control of the It thereby turns It into a thing and thus demonically deforms reality. As difficult as the alternative remains, there remains only the alternative: consciousness exists in the In-Between. The sea had earlier in the poem been the symbol of the regal calm of eternity, a calm the poet strove to know and to share. Now, on closer inspection, the waves have a more turbulently physical presence, and the poet rejoices in how one of these waves "Dares to explode out of the rocks in . . . spray." It is the wave's daring, rather than the all-knowing and magisterial calm of the first vision of the sea ("Masse de calme et visible reserve"), that the poet now wishes to emulate.

It is the previous line, however, that most clearly makes an anti-Hegelian and, more specifically, an anti-Mallarmean point: "L'air immense ouvre et referme mon livre." Mallarmé wrote, "Le monde est fait pour aboutir à un beau livre" [All earthy existence must ultimately be contained in a book].[24] The "livre" of line 140 of *Le Cimetière marin* may be construed as an allusion to Mallarmé's Hegelian doctrine,[25] which Valéry here wishes to

23. The serpent, as I mentioned earlier, becomes the protagonist in Valéry's poem, "Ébauche d'un serpent," of the year following the publication of *Le Cimetière marin*.

24. "Sur L'Évolution Littéraire," in *Oeuvres Complètes* (Gallimard: Paris, 1945), 872; trans. Bradford Cook, in Adams, ed., *Critical Theory Since Plato*, 674.

25. For Mallarmé as successor to Hegel, see Barry Cooper, *The End of History: An Essay on Modern Hegelianism* (Toronto: University of Toronto Press, 1984), 283. On Hegel's notion of the Sage as articulated in the *Phenomenology*, Cooper writes: "The actual activity of the Sage was expressed in a dictum of one of Hegel's spiritual successors, Mallarmé: 'all earthly existence exists in order to end up in a book.' And, indeed, the Sage wrote a Book. It was not just any old book, however, but one that recapitulated conceptually the *Bewegung* [dialectical movement or process] of History. Henceforth, all dialectical movement existed within the Book and not within the World." Yvor Winters, in his poems that question the wisdom of the idealist tradition, makes much the same point. The price one must pay for such a relentless pursuit of purity is spiritual death; that is the only way out of the In-Between. See particularly the last line ("The mind's immortal, but the man is dead") of "Time and the Garden." Winters treats similar themes in "An Elegy (for the U.S.N. Macon)" and "An October Nocturne," two poems I discuss in Chapter 2. Janine D. Langan, in *Hegel and Mallarmé* (Lanham, Md.: University Press of America, 1986), argues, as does Cooper, for a direct and strong influence of the idealist philosopher on the symbolist poet. As I have mentioned, in a passage from his *Cahiers*, Valéry appears to

question. In his essay "Le Livre, Instrument Spirituel" (1896), Mallarmé writes:

> L'homme chargé de voir divinement, en raison que le lien, à volonté, limpide, n'a d'expression qu'au parallélisme, devant son regard, de feuillets.
>
> Sur un banc de jardin, où telle publication neuve, je me réjois si l'air, en passant, entr'ouvre et, au hasard, anime, d'aspects, l'extérieur du livre.

> [Man's duty is to observe with the eyes of the divinity; for if his connection with that divinity is to be made clear, it can be expressed only by the pages of the open book in front of him.
>
> Seated on a garden bench where a recent book is lying, I like to watch a passing gust half open it and breathe life into many of its outer aspects.][26]

In *Le Cimetière marin,* Valéry is associating the book with the solipsistic trance—rather than viewing the book, as did Mallarmé, as a complete embodiment of divine presence—that he is here asking the wave to shatter. The poet wishes that the "dazzled pages" ("pages tout éblouies") of this book fly away, that he reenter the tangible, physical world. And it is for this reason that the poem ends as it does with that strange and inelegant technical word "focs." The last line of the poem is a good example of what in archaic poetry is called ring composition: the last line echoes the first line, yet with a crucial difference. "Ce toit tranquille où marchent des colombes," the poet writes in the first line; "Ce toi tranquille où picoraient des focs!" he now writes in the last. "Où picoraient des focs" has replaced "où marchent des colombes." A "foc" is a technical nautical term for a kind of sail. The poet had begun the poem by imagining that the boats at sea were pigeons or doves sauntering along the roof of a temple. The poem ends with a demystifying admission that what appear to be pecking on this roof are not birds at all, but sailboats—and that therefore these "sailboats" are not in fact pecking at all. The last word is not very elegant and does not inspire a typically

---

criticize Mallarmé for his Hegelian idealism; there Valéry remarks of Mallarmé: "Il s'est malheureusement embarrassé d'ideés verbales venues des philosophes [Hegel]" (2:114–15). See also L. Austin, "Mallarmé et le rêve du livre," *Mercure de France* 1(1953): 81–108.

26. In *Oeuvres Complètes,* 378; trans. B. Cook, in Adams, ed., *Critical Theory Since Plato,* 674.

symbolist resonance. But the bald and rather awkward technical allusion serves to bring the poet back from dream to reality.

This reality, it is true, is not quite the "In-Between" (*metaxy*) of Plato. In fact, there is a disquieting anti-intellectualism in Valéry's all-or-nothing attitude toward the intellect. Since the poet has abandoned the Hegelian quest to perceive or to become pure spirit, he appears to want to become pure flesh. And yet, the poem itself exists as a means of mediating between pure presence and complete absence. Here, once again, we have a distinction between Valéry's poetics and Mallarmé's. It was Mallarmé's desire to write the absolutely pure poem, the ultimately invisible and silent poem. The perfect poem is the poem in which "it is clear that nothing lies beyond," where "silence is genuine and just." The space articulated by the poem "is a virgin space, face to face with the lucidity of our matching vision, divided of itself, in solitude, into halves of whiteness; and each of these is lawful bride at the wedding of the idea."[27] Pure spiritual presence can only be symbolized through pure absence of materiality. We have seen this paradox articulated by Hegel in his discussion of the history of art in the previous chapter. Valéry, however, appears to have accepted the In-Between nature of the poetic endeavor: "Entre la Présence et l'Absence," he writes in "Poésie et Pensée Abstraite," "oscille la pendule poétique" [The poetic pendulum oscillates *between* Presence and Absence].[28] The writing of poetry is, by implication, itself a means of living in the In-Between. As Gustave Cohen has argued, the conclusion of *Le Cimetière marin* can be read as an allusion to Valéry's opting to leave behind purity, silence, and nonbeing in favor of active living, which for Valéry at this time meant affirming the creative impulse to begin writing poetry again.[29]

And here, I think, we have established a link—one of many links— between *Le Cimetière marin* and the Pindaric ode from which Valéry draws the epigraph for his poem. I suggested that Valéry's poem is a meditation, via Pindar's third Pythian ode, on the Hegelian attempt to gain speculative control over It-Reality and thus to turn It into a thing. I have so far been

27. "Mystery in Literature," trans. B. Cook, in Adams, ed., *Critical Theory Since Plato,* 678.

28. *Oeuvres de Paul Valéry,* 1:1333. Cf. the remarks of Norman Suckling: "To Valéry the poem was not the *chose divinisée* that it appeared to Mallarmé, but the temporary depository of our intimations of divinity; set up for that purpose at the disposal of a reader, because no action of mind on mind is possible except through the medium of matter, and no progress towards the realization of divinity possible except by way of those incarnations of *le verbe,* those reciprocities of mind and matter, which we call forms" (*Paul Valéry and the Civilized Mind* [London: Oxford University Press, 1954], 46).

29. *Essai d'Explication du Cimetière marin* (Paris: Gallimard, 1958), 83–84. See also Martin, *Paul Valéry, Le Cimetière marin,* 67–68.

discussing Valéry's connections with Hegel and Mallarmé. It is time to consider the Pindaric connection.

Poetry and the In-Between: Pindar's Third Pythian Ode

It is remarkable that no one has scrutinized Pindar's third Pythian for its affiliations with Valéry's meditation. Scholars have noted the Lucretian feeling[30] of the poem and the other allusions to classical philosophy have been discussed,[31] but the relation of the poem to the Pindaric ode whose lines introduce *Le Cimetière marin* has been passed over in relative silence.[32] Valéry's Greek, it is true, was not as polished as a classical scholar's. The French poet himself remarks with characteristic modesty that "quant au grec, je suis malheureusement un écolier des plus médiocres" (with respect to Greek, I was never more than a most mediocre student),[33] but he knew the language and his poetic talent and intuitions no doubt helped to give him deeper insights into the meaning of Pindar's poem than, say, a dogged but uninspired scholarly interpreter of the poet.[34]

30. Of the phrase "le calme des dieux," which concludes the first stanza, Gustave Cohen observes that these are the "dieux d'Épicure, indifférents en leur *ataraxie* aux affaires humaines" (*Essai d'Explication du Cimetière marin,* 52). He also believes the eleventh stanza (beginning "Chienne splendide") marked by an "inspiration lucrétienne" (66).

31. Cohen remarks, for example, that the adjective "juste" in the phrase "Midi le juste" of line 3 is indebted to "la Δίκη, la justice, gardienne de l'Éternité dans la philosophie éléate" (ibid., 52). Valéry himself refers specifically to the presocratic philosopher Zeno in stanza 21.

32. Cohen does not mention it at all. Neither does D. J. Mossop in his commentary on the poem in *Pure Poetry: Studies in French Poetic Theory and Practice, 1746–1945* (Oxford: Clarendon Press, 1971), 230–48. G. D. Martin, in *Paul Valéry, Le Cimetière Marin,* is the exception; he realizes that, since Valéry introduces the poem with the lines from Pindar's third Pythian, they are part of the poem and deserve attention. His remarks, however, are brief. Martin writes: "We are at the start given two points of reference by Valéry himself, in the epigraph from Pindar: μή, φίλα ψυχά, βίον ἀθάνατον σπεῦδε, τὰν δ᾽ ἔμπρακτον ἄντλει μαχανάν. That is, 'Do not, my soul, seek immortal life, but exhaust the field of the possible.' The opposition between the absolute and the mobile present has been stated" (25). Suzanne Larnaudie makes some useful observations on Valéry and Pindar in *Paul Valéry et la grèce* (Geneva: Librairie Droz, 1992). See also Daniel Moutote, "La poésie grecque dans l'oeuvre de Paul Valéry," *Bulletin des Études Valéryennes* 35 (1984): 25–42, esp. 28–29.

33. Letter to Dontenville (January 20, 1934), *Lettres à quelques-uns* (Paris: Gallimard, 1952), 215.

34. The poem has its share of Grecisms. It begins, of course, with some lines, in Greek, from Pindar. Among the Greek-inspired archaisms in the language of the poem, Gustave Cohen

Pindar's poem and Valéry's have clear and obvious differences. Pindar's is a characteristically public performance; Valéry's, a private meditation. Pindar's shuns unnecessary ambiguity; Valéry's courts this ambiguity up to a point. But there are many similarities. Both poems are meditations on death, occasioned in Pindar's case probably by the failing health of his patron, Hieron; one of the motives for Valéry's poem may have been the declining health of his mother, who lived in Sète and raised the poet there.[35] Both poems articulate the same theme of the limitations of human striving; both poems relate this theme to the function and nature of poetry itself. Both Pindar and Valéry articulate with extraordinary sympathy the theme of the human quest for the absolute; both conclude that man must live in what Plato refers to as the *metaxy*. Both fully acknowledge and express the desire to transcend limitation, but both believe that such a desire must be held in check. We of course do not find the Pindaric triadic form in Valéry's poem, but it possesses a formal grandeur that recalls Pindar's restraint and precision rather than the impulsive exuberance that is often associated with Pindar's name. Like the third Pythian from which Valéry drew his epigraph and with which the poem now under discussion has so much in common, *Le Cimetière marin* is a meditation on death and the limits of the quest for pure and unmediated presence. One should not be surprised to discover a Pindaric feel to Valéry's poem, since Valéry was, according to Gustave Cohen, "si pétri de civilisation méditerranéenne et de culture classique, qu'on a quelquefois l'impression, comme chez Ronsard, qu'il pense en latin et en grec"[36] [so molded by Mediterranean civilization and by classical culture, that one sometimes has the impression, as with Ronsard, that he thinks in Latin and in Greek].

I shall stress those aspects of the third Pythian which might have struck a sympathetic chord in the poet of *Le Cimetière marin,* but I wish to do so within the context of a reading of the Pindaric poem as a whole. Since poetic unity has of late come under suspicion in discussions of literature, and since the problem of poetic unity has been an especially controversial topic with regard to the allegedly impetuous and fitful nature of Pindar's poetry, it is important to stress precisely how this ode is very carefully organized. Not a brief poem, it is brief enough (115 lines) to treat in its entirety.

---

mentions the words "idoles" (there meaning εἴδωλα, "images"), "chlamyde" (a cloak worn by men in ancient Greece), and "hydre" of stanza 23. See his *Essai d'Explication du Cimetière marin,* 95.

35. As Cohen surmises; see ibid., 58.

36. Ibid., 94.

The occasion for Pindar's poem is not entirely clear. No recent athletic victory is alluded to explicitly. The poem is a consolation for the ruler of Syracuse, Hieron, who appears to be in ill health. The ode consists of five triads, each consisting of a strophe, antistrophe, and epode. In order to express how he is himself implicated in the human desire to transcend limitation, Pindar begins the ode with a contrary-to-fact condition:[37]

> I would wish that Chiron, the son of Philyra—
> if it were permitted to utter a prayer
>   that is on everyone's tongue—
> I would wish—I say—that Chiron, who is now dead
>   and departed, were alive,
> Chiron, the once-widely ruling offspring of Uranian
>   Kronos. I would wish as well that this wild beast
>   who was kindly to men were still reigning in the
>   glens of Pelion,
> just as he was when he reared Asclepius,
> that gentle craftsman of remedies that strengthen the
>   limbs and give relief to pain,
> that hero who can protect men from all kinds of
>   diseases.
>
>   (1–7)[38]

Pindar opens the poem by making the very kind of impossible wish that the poem warns against: the first word of the poem is Ἤθελον, "I would wish." If it were permissible (εἰ χρεών, 2) to utter this prayer, he would utter it. It is not permissible, but he does so anyway, if only to acknowledge that such a desire is to be curbed.[39] Chiron, the poet says, reared Asklepios, who was a

---

37. Hayden Pelliccia, "Pindaricus Homericus: *Pythian* 3.1–80," *Harvard Studies in Classical Philology* 91 (1987): 39–63, argues against the view that Pindar's opening contains what might strictly be called a contrary-to-fact condition. David Young (*Three Odes of Pindar: A Literary Study of Pythian 11, Pythian 3, and Olympian 7,* Mnemosyne Supplement 9 [Leiden: E. J. Brill, 1968]) thinks otherwise.

38. The Greek is cited from the *Pindari Carmina,* ed. C. M. Bowra (Oxford: Clarendon Press, 1968); the English translation is my own. The Greek text of the complete poem can be found in the Appendix.

39. One of Pindar's best commentators, Basil L. Gildersleeve, remarks, "Hieron is victorious, but suffering, and he must learn that the gods give two pains for one pleasure, and be content to have only one against one. To expect more is to reach out to what is not and cannot be. To this lesson the poet leads up step by step. So in the very beginning of this ode he himself sets an

physician. As this ode will be a poem of consolation for the ailing Hieron, it is understandable why Pindar would mention Asklepios, but the reason for presenting him as an exemplum is not yet developed. Pindar concerns himself first with the mother of Asklepios, Koronis, the daughter of Phlegyas.

> Before the daughter of Phlegyas of the splendid horses
> bore him with the help of Eleithuia who attends to
>   mothers, she
> stricken in her chamber by the golden arrows of Artemis,
> went down into the house of Hades, through the workings
>   of Apollo.
> Not without purpose is the wrath of the children of Zeus.
> She, paying him slight regard, in the errors of her heart
> agreed to marry another without the consent of her
>   father—
> she who had before lain with Apollo of the unshorn hair
>
> and who was carrying the pure seed of the god.
> She did not wait for the arrival of the marriage feast,
> nor for the sound of full-voiced bridal songs,
> the sorts of things which innocent girls of her age
> like playfully to murmur on wedding nights. No,
> she longed for things that are remote, the sorts of things
> that many people long for. There is a most foolish type of
>   person who,
> scorning that which is familiar, gazes at what is far off,
> hunting down vain things with hopes that are not to be
>   fulfilled.
>   (8–24)

Koronis becomes the type of person who cannot live within human limitations, who is fatally impatient. She had, indeed, mingled with the divine and had the pure (καθαρόν, 15) seed of the god within her. But mediated purity is not enough for Koronis. She still kept longing for those things that are remote or absent (ἤρατο τῶν ἀπεόντων, 20). This longing for things that are remote is, Pindar goes on to suggest, typical of human nature. Koronis in her extremism is a representative figure. For many people have been infatuated (πάθον,

---

example of the impatient yearning he condemns" (*Pindar: The Olympian and Pythian Odes* [New York: Harper & Brothers, 1899], 268).

20) with the absent, including, one should add, the poet himself, who began this poem wishing fervently for that which was not. Indeed, there is the kind of person who habitually scorns that which is at his feet and, in a futile manner, hunts down the insubstantial. As David C. Young has noted,[40] this ode continually contrasts the near and the far, and in this epode the near is represented by the good-natured bantering of Koronis's friends. Koronis had, in fact, reached the pinnacle of human fortune by bearing the pure seed of the god, thus embodying the tension between the human and the divine, the near and the far. But she cannot live in the In-Between.

I am speaking as if Koronis had already been identified by the poet, but in fact she has not. She has been identified thus far only as "the daughter of Phlegyas of the splendid horses" (εὐίππου Φλεγύα θυγάτηρ, 8). Why does Pindar wait to identify her? Could it be that he wishes his audience to experience that same impatience that characterizes the yet unnamed Koronis? Must the audience, that is, wait until the beginning of the following strophe before the daughter of Phlegyas is named explicitly? Pindar constantly uses the technique of indirect naming to increase suspense before finally identifying the subjects of his praise. In the previous chapter we mentioned how Pindar, in the eleventh Olympian, first refers to the victor as Ὀλυμπιονίκης and then as "Son of Archéstratos" and finally, as we reach the climax of the praise, as "Hagesidámos." Pindar uses the same technique in this ode, but he appears to be using it in a particularly artful manner.

The second strophe begins as follows:

> This great infatuation
> The willfulness of fair-robed Koronis caught. She slept
> On the couch of a stranger from Arkadia.
>
> (24–26)

---

40. *Three Odes of Pindar,* especially appendix 1. For my understanding of *Pythian* 3, I have also found helpful William H. Race, *Pindar* (Boston: Twayne, 1986), 50–64, as well as Slater, "Pindar's *Pythian* 3: Structure and Purpose"; Pelliccia, "Pindaricus Homericus: *Pythian* 3.1–80"; Enrico Medda, "Ἤρατο τῶν ἀπεόντων, Prosperità e limitezza umana in una gnome pindarica (*Pyth. III 19 sqq.*)," in *Scritti in ricordo di Giorgio Buratti* (Pisa: Pacini, 1981), 295–309; and Thomas K. Hubbard, *The Pindaric Mind: A Study of Logical Structure in Early Greek Poetry* (Leiden: E. J. Brill, 1985), 23–26. Hubbard stresses, as do I, the mediating function of the poet, and qualifies what he takes to be Young's thesis that Pindar continually opts for the "near" as opposed to the "far." Rather than choosing the near over the far, Hubbard sees Pindar as mediating between these extremes. See particularly his analysis of the final epode of the poem, 25–26. Hubbard may be mistaking Young's intentions, for Young clearly suggests (62) that this poetic immortality offered by Pindar's poem combines qualities of the near (it is practically achievable; indeed it is being achieved in the present poem) and the far (it will last forever).

My translation does not do justice to the subtlety of Pindar's analysis of erotic passion here. Willfullness, Pindar appears to be saying, is not exactly free choice. In fact, it appears to be the opposite. The unwillingness to accept limitation, paradoxically, results in the submission to fate. It is not so much the person Koronis herself who is infected with this infatuation as it is her will or desire (λῆμα, 25), a personified force against which she herself seems helpless.

The triad continues:

> She did not escape the notice of the watcher. Loxias, the
>   king of the temple—
> Although he happened to be at the sheep-receiving shrine
>   of Pytho—
> perceived it in his all-knowing mind, and he was
>   convinced by this, his surest confidant. He does not
>   embrace falsehood,
> nor does god or mortal deceive him with either words or
>   deeds.
>
> He knew about her consorting with the stranger, Isychus,
>   son of Elatus, and her impious treachery,
> and he sent his sister [Artemis], raging with resistless
>   might,
> into Lakeria, for the maiden was living by the banks of the
>   Boebian lake.
> An evil *daimōn,* turning her towards disaster, subdued
>   her,
> and many of her neighbors shared the same fate, and
>   together they perished.
> Just so has a fire from a single spark ravaged a whole forest.
>
> But when her kinsmen had placed the girl within the
>   wooden wall of the pyre,
> and the fierce flame of Hephaistos encompassed it and
>   her,
> then Apollo said, "No longer shall I endure it my heart
> to allow my own child to die a most pitiable death along
>   with the grievous suffering of its mother."
> Thus he spoke, and with one step coming upon the child
>   he seized it from the corpse.

The kindling pyre opened up a path of light for him.
And bearing him [the child] away, he gave him to the
    Magnesian Centaur to teach him
how to heal those suffering from painful sicknesses.

                             (24–46)

The dominant image here is that of fire. It was not enough for Koronis to bear within her the pure seed (σπέρμα καθαρόν, 15) of the god. Her passion for the absolute, for the distant, compels her to consort with a foreigner from a distant land, Arkadia. This mad passion results in her destruction by fire. The fire is at first a mere metaphor: Koronis's destruction results in the destruction of others around her, just as a raging forest fire will begin from a single spark (Pindar actually says from a single seed, σπέρματος, 37). But the metaphor then, as so often in Pindar, becomes reality as we see the fire raging around the funeral pyre of Koronis. With this overwhelming brightness only a god can contend, and Apollo magisterially enters and saves the child—the child who will grow up to be a healer who will save so many others.

In the following strophe Pindar recounts in detail those whom Asklepios will heal:

Those who came to him with sores that arose from
    disease,
or with their limbs wounded either by hoary bronze or a
    boulder thrown from afar,
their bodies ravaged either by summer's heat or winter's
    cold—
these he delivered from diverse kinds of suffering,
attending to some with incantations, giving to others
soothing drugs to drink or swathing their limbs with
    healing ointments;
he restored others to health with surgery.

                             (47–53)

We have moved rapidly from disaster (for Koronis) and near disaster (for Asklepios) to salvation (for Asklepios and his patients). Disaster and triumph are inextricably intertwined in Pindar's poetry, and we should not be too surprised to learn that disaster may soon once again follow on the heels of this moment of calm as this triad concludes:

> But even skill lets itself be enthralled by profit.
> Gold—an alluring reward—appearing in his hand led
>   even Asklepios to bring back from death a man
>   already death's captive.
> Thus the son of Kronos, with his own hands hurling [his
>   shafts],
> quickly seized the breath of life from both their hearts
> and his gleaming thunderbolt hurled fate upon them.
>   (54–58)

Conceits are thought to be out of place in sublime poetry, at least according to neoclassical theory. But Pindar here shows how in his odes he is able to maintain sublimity at the same time that he makes use of balance and antithesis. We are here presented with two contrasting pictures: gold appearing in a patron's hand, a flaming thunderbolt in Zeus's. Asklepios is no sooner seduced by the first than he is punished by the second. The world of eternal brightness, of divine purity, can only be approached fitfully by humans. The attempt to possess it fully will result in disaster. Yet Pindar, as will Valéry, presents the quest sympathetically; he, too, as poet is implicated in the longing, as the word μισθῷ (reward, fee, 55) suggests: for Pindar elsewhere refers to the reward for his song as a μισθός,[41] just as he refers to his own craft—as he does Asklepios's craft—as σοφία (54). Pindar, like Asklepios, may be tempted to receive a reward that is excessive in return for the service of his art. Here Pindar begins to introduce the theme of the close relations between poetry and medicine; poetry, like medicine, is a powerful art, and both arts—it is implied—may be misused.

This third antistrophe ends with a gnomic reflection on the meaning of Asklepios's swift demise:

> We must seek from the gods those things that are suitable
>   to mortal thoughts,
> acknowledging that which is at our feet, what lot is ours.
>   (59–60)

With the word εἰμέν in line 60 (we are [of such an estate]), Pindar includes himself among those mortals who must curb the desire to possess the

---

41. *Pythian* 1.77 and 11.41.

absolute. The first person then modulates into the famous imperative to himself that will become the epigraph to *Le Cimetière marin*:

> μή, φίλα ψυχά, βίον ἀθάνατον
> σπεῦδε. τὰν δ ' ἔμπρακτον ἄντλει μαχανάν.

> [Do not, dear soul, seek eagerly for immortal life
> But use to the full the resources that are within your
>   reach.]

(61–62)

No sooner does Pindar issue this warning to himself than he flaunts it. The poem began with a contrary-to-fact condition ("if it were possible to utter the wish that is on the tip of everyone's tongue, I would wish that Chiron were still alive") that exemplified the poet's participation in the kind of longing for the impossible that characterizes the tragic Koronis and her son Asklepios. The poet now returns, even after explicating with gnomic certitude the moral lesson to be learned from heeding the very examples he has just narrated, to precisely this impossible wish:

> If only wise Chiron were still living in his cave,
> and if my honey-tongued songs had charmed his soul,
> I would have persuaded him to grant to good men, even
>   now, someone to heal them of their feverish
>   sicknesses—
> someone called Asklepios or even Apollo.
> And I would have come, cleaving the Ionian sea in my
>   ship,
> to the fountain of Arethusa and my Aetnean host.

(63–69)

The impossible wish is tactfully appropriate in this context, however. Hieron is ill, and what Pindar is saying is that he wishes that it were in his power to heal his patron. Poetry apparently is itself something of a healing agent, however, as the poem later emphasizes. We have already seen that one of the ways in which Chiron healed his patients was through "soft incantations" (μαλακαῖς ἐπαοιδαῖς, 51). Pindar's poem is itself an incantation[42] that, through its consolatory message, will at least help to heal Hieron's soul if not his physical health. Although Pindar is not able to bring Chiron back to life—such a desire to bring the dead back to life resulted, after all, in the doom of Asklepios himself—he does in a sense bring him back to life in a manner that is permissible and even beneficial to mortals; he brings him back to life *in the medium of poetry.* Poetry is Pindar's craft, as healing was Asklepios's. The purpose of healing is to restore balance to physical health, and we might say that it is one important purpose of poetry[43] to restore, through its powerfully soothing measures, a sense of balance to the moral and spiritual life and to warn against the kinds of extremes indulged in by Koronis and Asklepios as related in this poem.

Much of the remainder of the poem in fact praises Hieron for his sense of balance and tact, which—it is implied—will be further fostered by this balanced and tactful poem. As Pindar says in the first strophe of the fourth triad, as the syntax spills over from the preceding strophe, Hieron is a man

> Who as king watches over the Syracusans,
>   gentle to his citizens, not grudging to the nobility,
>   a man marveled at, like a father, by strangers.
>   (70–71)

One such "stranger" (ξεῖνος, 71)—that is, non-Aetnean—is of course Pindar himself. Hieron has been generous to both his own people and to those who are visitors to Syracuse, such as Pindar. That friendship Pindar wishes to reciprocate:

42. Valéry was himself in sympathy with Pindar's view of poetry as akin to incantation. In his essay on Mallarmé, he refers to the master's "conception of the Word" ("Verbe"), which would have "no meaning except in relation to a wholly spiritual universe, deeply similar to the universe of poetry: prayer, invocation, incantation create the beings to whom they speak. Language thus becomes an instrument of 'spirituality,' that is to say of the direct transmutation of desires and emotions into presences and powers that becomes 'realities' in themselves" [Du reste, se peuvent invoquer tous les usages de la parole qui ne satisfont point à des besoins de l'ordre pratique et qui n'ont de sens que par référence à un univers tout spirituel, de même nature profonde que l'Univers poétique: la prière, l'invocation, l'incantation, sont créatices des êtres auxquels elles s'adressent. Le Langage devient ainsi un agent de "spiritualité," c'est à dire de transmutations directes de désirs et d'émotions en présences et puissances comme "réelles"] (Lawler, ed., *Paul Valéry: An Anthology,* 168–69; *Oeuvres de Paul Valéry,* 1:708).

43. Especially a Pythian ode, since the patron of the Pythian shrine was Apollo, the patron of the arts, who was himself a healer.

> If I had come bearing the double blessings of both golden
>   health and a victory song—a brilliant adornment to the
>   victory wreaths from the Pythian contests
> which, in his excellence, Pherenikos [Hieron's horse] had
>   won at Kirrha once—
> I claim that, upon crossing the deep sea,
> I would have arrived as a light of deliverance more
>   brilliant than the sun.
>
>   (72–76)

The poet, like the patron, must accept limitation. The poet wishes that he could offer the twin blessings of medical aid for his patron and a victory song, but at this time he can offer neither, although he can express an intense desire to improve his patron's health and he can allude to Hieron's victories in the Pythian games.

What he *can* offer, however (apart, of course, from the present poem), is a prayer:

> But I wish to offer a prayer to the Mother Goddess,
> whose divine solemnity the maidens often celebrate—
>   along with Pan's—with song at night, at my front door.
> And since, Hieron, you know how to understand the gist
>   of sayings,
> Having learned this from the older poets, you know:
> For every blessing, the immortals mete out two griefs to
>   men.
> Fools are not able to bear these troubles gracefully,
> But noble men can, turning the fair part outward.
> The lot of good luck follows you.
> For if fortune looks with favor upon any man, it is upon
>   the leader of a people.
>
>   (77–86)

I mentioned how David C. Young has pointed to the importance of the theme of the near and the far in this poem, and Pindar is here associating himself with the near. He may not be able to sing a full-fledged victory song for Hieron at this moment, nor is he able to bring Hieron back to health. But he is able to offer a prayer to Magna Mater, or Rhea, who was apparently worshiped locally at Syracuse, the site of the present ode.[44] We are told that Koronis at the beginning of the poem had rejected the friendly and intimate marriage songs of her maiden friends and instead longed for the impossible. Here Pindar associates himself with the qualities of the "near" rejected by Koronis, for he as poet refuses to opt for the impossible and instead offers a humble prayer to a goddess—a goddess, however, from a distant land, Phrygia in Asia Minor—with whom he feels an intimate and a familiar relation. And the prayer is an apt one for the occasion of Hieron's ill health for, as Gildersleeve informs us, the scholiasts remark that Magna Mater was "the augmenter and reliever of sicknesses."[45]

Pindar suggests that he must work within the limitations of his own poetic possibilities. So, too, must Hieron learn to accept what the gods have meted out to him. And this has, Pindar suggests, been a generous allotment. Hieron enjoys the highest honor that can be bestowed upon a man: he is the leader of his people. Therefore he must accept misfortune when it comes, since all suffer, even those who are most blessed. Everyone who knows Homer realizes this. The fourth triad concludes:

> A secure life
> was allotted neither to Peleus son of Aiakos
> nor to godlike Kadmos. Yet they say
> that these reached the height of happiness permitted to
>   mortals,
> since they heard the Muses-with-golden-headbands
>   celebrating with song on the mountain
> and in seven-gated Thebes
> when Kadmos married ox-eyed Harmonia
> and Peleus married Thetis, the famed daughter of wise
>   Nereus.
>
>   (86–92)

---

44. A traditional interpretation of ἐμὸν πρόθυρον (78) is that "my portal" refers to Pindar's own house in Thebes. Cf. Gildersleeve, who tells us that Pindar worshiped "in front of his house [in Thebes] dedicated to the joint service of Rhea and Pan" (*Pindar,* 275). But cf. W. J. Slater, "Pindar's House," *Greek, Roman, and Byzantine Studies* 12 (1971): 141–52, who argues that the words more plausibly refer to Hieron's or to the chorus's own forecourt in Syracuse (145).

45. Gildersleeve remarks that "the Scholiasts tells us that Magna Mater was τῶν νόσων αὐξητικὴ καὶ μειωτική" (*Pindar,* 275).

We return in this fourth epode—in the ring composition that is so typical of Pindar—to the motif of marriage that we remember from the first epode. Koronis, in her longing for the distant, slept with the Arkadian stranger while she was still pregnant with Apollo's child, and she thus became the object of that god's wrath. Pindar here reminds Hieron that such unions between mortals and gods are the height of blessedness. These are those moments when, as Pindar unforgettably states it in the eighth Pythian ode, the αἴγλα διόσδοτος ("the Godsent brightness") shines on mortals. These moments—which Pindar's victory odes celebrate and thus perpetuate—are, however, fleeting and must be accepted as such. Men are not gods, and they must accept their in-between status. Those who reach such heights must be especially thankful and must accept with equanimity the misfortunes that will inevitably befall them.

We come now to the final triad of the poem in which the poet reminds Hieron graphically of the vicissitudes of human existence, and Pindar then concludes with a self-referential comment that expresses his understanding that he, too, is subject to the limitations of human existence. As the final strophe begins, we are attending the wedding of Peleus and Kadmos and listening in imagination to the Muses singing.

> And the gods banqueted with them
> and they saw the lordly children of Kronos on their
>   golden thrones
> and they received marriage gifts from them.
> And, through the favor of Zeus,
> they raised their hearts—crushed by former troubles—
>   again.
> But soon, because of their bitter sufferings, the three
>   daughters
> of Kadmos deprived him of his share of joy,
> although father Zeus entered the longed-for bed of white-
>   armed Semele.
>
> And the son of Peleus—the only son
> whom immortal Thetis bore in Phthia,
> an arrow having taken his life in battle—
> brought lamentation to the Greeks as his body burned in
>   his funeral pyre.
>
>   (93–103)

One of Pindar's great themes—a simple one but true enough and common in archaic Greek poetry—is the vicissitude of fortune: that victory
often contains the seeds of defeat, defeat of victory. A moment of joy is set
off in stark relief against past and future suffering. In a matter of moments
Pindar here interrupts the famous scene of the joyful wedding of Peleus
and Kadmos to place it within its more sober and universal context. Kadmos is now basking in his share of joy (εὐφροσύνας, 98), but three of his
daughters (Ino, Agaue, and Autonoë)—the fruits of the marriage with
Harmonia now being celebrated—we are told will meet tragic ends. And
in the same breath we are told that another of the daughters, Semele, will
become the privileged lover of Zeus. In the figure of Semele is concentrated precisely this motif of the rapid vicissitudes of fortune of which I
have been speaking, for Semele was indeed the lover of Zeus, but the
immediate result of this liaison was her death as a victim of Hera's jealousy.
Semele was, however, later restored to life—as Asklepios, we recall from
the third antistrophe of this poem, attempted tragically to restore a dead
man to life—and now lives (as Pindar portrays her in the second Olympian) on Olympus. Pindar now turns his attention in closing to the offspring of Peleus and Thetis, and once again—this time in the figure of the
famed Achilles—the poet emphasizes the profoundly mixed nature of what
the gods dispose to mortals. For the image of Achilles that Pindar leaves us
with in that last antistrophe is of the great warrior's body burning in his
funeral pyre as the joy of the wedding hymn is transposed into the grief
expressed in the wailing (γόον, 103) of the Greeks. Earlier in the poem
Pindar, in a brilliantly vivid description, tells his audience about how
Apollo with a single stride entered the funeral pyre of Koronis and
snatched his still living child Asklepios from the womb of the corpse of the
child's mother Koronis. Here there is no miraculous rescue. Pindar then
makes explicit the moral implications of the powerful *exempla* he has
depicted to his audience, and his patron:

> If any mortal knows the way of truth,
>   he knows that he should enjoy the good fortune that
>   comes from the gods.
>   Now this way and now that blow the gusts of the high-
>   flying winds.
>   Great prosperity—when it falls with its full weight from
>   above—does not come securely for very long.
>   (103–6)

In the final epode Pindar, as he typically does, expresses his own involve-ment in the ethical *topoi*[46] of his own poem:

> I shall be small when my fortunes are small, great when
>   they are great.
> Whatever divinity that is ministering to me I shall lovingly
>   honor,
> fostering it according to whatever means are at my
>   disposal.
> If God might once offer me splendid wealth,
> I would hope in future days to gain lofty fame.
> We know Nestor and Lykian Sarpedon, whose names are
>   household words,
> because of the resounding poems which skillful craftsmen
>   have shaped.
> Achievement endures through renowned song,
> but for few is the achievement easy.
>
> (107–15)

Pindar will accept whatever the gods dispose and adapt himself to the occa-sion. The medical motif recurs in this closing epode. Pindar, we recall, began this poem with a contrary-to-fact wish (that is on everyone's tongue) that Chiron were alive so that he could cure Hieron of his illness, and the poet reiterates this wish later in the poem. Pindar, like Hieron, must accept limita-tion. Hieron has had his rich share of good fortune. Pindar must also live within the realm of the possible. He repeats this truth here, but in a rhetori-cally complicated way that suggests that this consolatory poem is itself a kind of healing agent. Note, for example, the medical terminology Pindar uses: "Whatever divinity that is ministering [ἀμφέποντ', 108] to me," Pindar says, "I shall lovingly honor, fostering [θεραπεύων, 109] it according to whatever means are at my disposal [κατ' ἐμὰν . . . μαχανάν, 109]." The word ἀμφέποντ' recalls the manner in which Asklepios would minister (ἀμφέπων, 51) to his

---

46. The degree of the poet's involvement is somewhat qualified, as Andrew Miller has suggested to me, by David Young's observations on what he calls the "first-person indefinite" (*Three Odes of Pindar*, 58): "With the 'first-person indefinite,' the poet, by stating what he will do or hopes to do, suggests what intelligent people in general, often the laudandus in particular, do or ought to do. The statements made in the first person, therefore, may be applied to both the poet and the laudandus, and any differences in the degree of applicability to either or to men in general are determined by the immediate context" (58–59).

patients earlier in the poem. And how will Pindar in turn minister to—the word is θεραπεύειν (which can mean "treat medically")—this divinity? He will minister to it through whatever means are at his disposal, that is, through his poetic craft. The ending here recalls specifically the lines earlier in the poem that Valéry will choose for his epigraph: "Do not, dear heart, long eagerly for immortal life, but use to the full the resources that are within your reach" [τὰν δ' ἔμπρακτον . . . μαχανάν] (62). The resources that are within Pindar's reach are the resources of poetry. So they were for Valéry, who broke the purity of his poetic silence of twenty years with the publication of *La Jeune parque* in 1917 and who then published *Le Cimetière marin*—the conclusion of which poem may be viewed as affirming the life-giving quality of the writing of poetry—three years later.[47] To return to Pindar: human beings do not live forever, even with the best of medical attention, but the poetry—and poets, like physicians, are skilled craftsmen—that accepts this fact and celebrates achievement enables that achievement to live forever in men's memories. The poet can, through imagination, envision purity and perfection, and insofar as he does so he participates—and permits his audience to participate—in that divine realm. But the basis of poetry's power is its acceptance of human limitations and, specifically, of death.

Pindar's third Pythian is richly imaginative, but its imaginative reach is enlisted in the service of reminding men that they are not gods. The composition of the poem is Pindar's way of living within the means allotted to him. The poet imagines the beyond but the imaginer's feet are planted firmly on the ground. I have tried to suggest in this chapter and in the previous one how, in the neoplatonic/idealist tradition via Hegel and culminating in Mallarmé, this acceptance of the mediating role of language and of poetry yields to an impatience—one is reminded of Koronis's impulsiveness as depicted by Pindar in the third Pythian—with this mediating role and seeks to represent purity itself. The ideal poem, for Mallarmé, is the silent poem, the blank page; all else is a kind of compromise. One can—impatiently—attempt to escape from the In-Between nature of both reality and language, but as Paul Valéry reminds us in *Le Cimetière marin*, "la sainte impatience meurt aussi."

I do not wish to minimize the aestheticist leanings of Valéry and thereby draw too sharp a distinction between his own poetics and the poetics of his master, Mallarmé. Valéry never abandoned the symbolist emphasis on suggestion rather than denotation. He resisted to the end what Poe referred to as the didactic heresy. Poetry—in the famous Kantian formulation—was for

---

47. See Gustave Cohen, *Essai d'Explication du Cimetière marin*, 83–84.

Valéry like dancing as opposed to walking because, whereas walking has a definite end, dance "goes nowhere."[48] Valéry, like Mallarmé, wished to explore the capacity of language to evoke ultimate reality, but in *Le Cimetière marin* he deliberately stepped back from the extremes of the symbolist tradition.

There is a sense in which Mallarmé's poetics resemble Hegel's, as exemplified in Hegel's understanding of what he considered the essence of the Pindaric ode. We recall from our previous chapter that for Hegel the subject of Pindar's odes is the attempt of the spirit to free itself of its inadequate material embodiment. I contrasted this neoplatonic conception of the relation of subject to form with the more "Aristotelian" principles of literary theory implicit in Pindar's odes. For Pindar's odes may be viewed as exemplary mediations between particular, historical occasions and the universal principles that may be found implicit in those occasions. The "meaning" of Pindar's odes can be reduced neither to their moorings in particular historical occasions, nor to the general "philosophical" principles that emerge from the poet's reflections on the meaning of those occasions. A similar claim can be made for Valéry's poem, especially if we consider equating the "historical" (for the poet's perceiving psyche) facts of perception and sensation with the historical givens of Pindar's occasions. As Yvor Winters has observed of both *Le Cimetière marin* and *Ébauche d'un serpent*, there is in these poems "a good deal of abstract statement, so that there can be no real doubt as to their themes. The sensory details are a part of this statement—they are not ornament or background. The language is both sensory and conceptual at the same time. . . . The visual and intellectual are simultaneous—they cannot be separated in fact."[49] The meanings of Valéry's "symbols"—the sea, the sun, the temple, the graveyard—are reducible neither to their historically verifiable or merely perceptual truth, on the one hand, nor to some abstract philosophical scheme, on the other; and the poem attempts to maintain this tension between perception and intellection without yielding to one or the other pole. Unlike Mallarmé in his more extreme moments, Valéry appears to have accepted the In-Between nature of the poetic endeavor. And this acceptance—as we have seen from our close inspection of Pindar's third Pythian ode—is truly Pindaric and profoundly classical.

---

48. "Poetry and Abstract Thought," in Adams, ed., *Critical Theory Since Plato,* 922.
49. *Forms of Discovery: Critical and Historical Essays on the Short Poem in English* (Chicago: Alan Swallow, 1967), 252.

7

"ART WITH TRUTH ALLY'D"
Pope's *Epistle to a Lady* as Pindaric Encomium

Elroy Bundy's decisive work on Pindar teaches us to read the victory odes as encomia. Pindar's poems, Bundy argues, have a rhetorical structure; they are not to be understood as "aesthetic" objects in the Kantian/New Critical sense. What Bundy says about Pindar could just as easily be said about many other preromantic poems. I would like, in this chapter, to sketch out a Bundyan reading of Pope's *Epistle to a Lady,* which, like the typical victory ode of Pindar, is an encomium, in this case addressed not to a victorious athlete, but to an exemplary woman.

The poem's principle of order is not "aesthetic"—by which I mean purely formal and autonomous in a Kantian sense—but encomiastic and rhetorical, in the manner not only of Pindar[1] (whose odes Pope had once intended to translate) but of Dryden's great odes, particularly the "Song for St. Cecilia's Day, 1687" and "Alexander's Feast." Pope's genius was not particularly suited to the writing of sublime odes. Here Dryden is superior; like Pindar, Dryden is a great public poet. Pope's serious sublime mode often shades into bombast. Nor was Pope's genius suited to the encomiastic mode in general. Pope was more comfortable *refusing* to write encomia, as he does in his imitation of Horace's *recusatio* in *Satires* 2.1. There Pope's interlocutor, William Fortescue, has warned the poet to stay clear of potentially libelous satire. If "you needs must write," Fortescue warns Pope, "write CAESAR'S Praise" (21). Pope could not bring himself to be so mindlessly agreeable to authority, for he believed that "A vile Encomium doubly ridicules, / There's nothing blackens like the ink of fools" (*Epistles* 2:1, 410–11). We remember *Windsor Forest,* for example, not so much for its patriotic fervor as for the sympathy Pope shows for the victims of the hunt (the lapwings that "fall, and leave their little Lives in air," 134). In the Horatian mode, however, Pope is Dryden's superior; indeed, Dryden did not particularly care for Horace's plain style, which he perceived to be "groveling."[2] In the *Epistle to a Lady* Pope is able to combine Horatian ease and perceptual precision with the encomiastic intention that we can associate with the more elevated genre of the ode. The result is a stylistic masterpiece,[3] even if some of the sentiments about the characters of women will no doubt strike a modern reader, especially at first glance, as sexual stereotyping.

The poem is addressed to Martha (or "Patty") Blount, whom Pope praises explicitly beginning at line 249 ("Ah Friend! to dazzle let the Vain design"). The portraits of the unstable and contradictory women painted by Pope are interesting in themselves, but they are important, in terms of the poem's structure, chiefly insofar as they contrast with—in Bundy's terms, are "foil" for—the poet's depiction of the temperate Martha Blount. As Edward Young remarks to the dedicatee of his fifth *Satire* ("On Women"), apropos of the subject of much of that poem (which Pope knew), "satirizing those is prais-

---

1. For an enlightening discussion of the similarities between the encomiastic mode of the Pindaric ode and the rhetorical intentions of *Windsor Forest,* see Ruben Quintero, "Design in *Windsor Forest,*" in *Literate Culture: Pope's Rhetorical Art* (Newark: University of Delaware Press, 1992), 40–64.

2. *Essay on the Origin and Progress in Satire,* in *Of Dramatic Poesy and Other Critical Essays,* ed. George Watson, 2 vols. (London: Everyman's Library, 1962), 2:130.

3. Bolingbroke, according to a letter from Pope to Swift on February 16, 1732/3, considered the poem Pope's "*chef d'oeuvre.*"

ing thee" (12).⁴ I would like also to suggest how an encomiastic reading of the poem goes at least some distance toward qualifying what on the surface appears to be Pope's misogyny.

The poem begins with a statement that is surely, especially from today's point of view, not flattering to women:

> Nothing so true as what you once let fall,
> "Most Women have no Characters at all."
> (1–2)⁵

Although many late twentieth-century readers will be offended by this statement, we may assume that Martha Blount, to whom the poem is addressed, was not. After all, that second line is a direct quotation, casually dropped though it may have been, from her own lips.

What follows is a series of examples of the contradictory qualities of women:

> How many pictures of one Nymph we view,
> All how unlike each other, all how true!
> (5–6)

Line 6 contains, in miniature, the very contrariety that is the essence of the female character as Pope depicts it in this poem. The paradoxical truth about women is that they are untrue in the sense that they are not constant, and this quality of contrariety is enforced by Pope the poet through the metrical brilliance that has characterized his poetry from the beginning of his career. "How many pictures of one Nymph we view" hardly has a pause; "All how unlike each other, all how true!" is broken by an emphatic caesura that stresses the very contrariety that is the line's, and poem's, theme.

Here Pope is more than simply demonstrating his verbal and metrical brilliance. He is performing what could be called a Pindaric gesture. In his odes, Pindar at times sets up a comparison between the poet and the athlete praised by the poet. In order to establish a sense of reciprocity between *laudator* and *laudandus*, the encomiastic poet will sometimes, for example,

---

4. *The Complete Works, Poetry and Prose, of the Rev. Edward Young, LL.D.,* 2 vols. (London: William Tegg, 1864), 1:376.

5. *Epistle to a Lady* is cited throughout from *The Twickenham Edition of the Poems of Alexander Pope,* ed. John Butt et al., 11 vols. (New Haven: Yale University Press, 1938–68), vol. 3: *Epistles to Several Persons,* ed. F. W. Bateson (1951).

use metaphoric language drawn from the domain of the athlete whose accomplishments are being praised. Hence in the eighth Pythian, Pindar, in his role of encomiastic poet, uses a wrestling metaphor (in the fourth epode) in order to praise the athlete who had won the contest in wrestling. In *Nemean* 7, an ode for an athlete who had been victorious in the pentathlon, "Pindar's integrity and accuracy as a poet," as Gordon Kirkwood puts it, "are expressed in a metaphor of a javelin throw, which formed part of the pentathlon."[6] Cowley, a poet Pope admired,[7] in one of his Pindaric poems explicitly recognizes this as a Pindaric trope, as we can infer from two lines in his ode "The Praise of Pindar." Pindar immortalizes those he praises, Cowley writes,

> Whether the *Swift,* the *Skilful,* or the *Strong,*
> Be crowned in his *Nimble, Artful, Vigorous* Song.
> (26–27)[8]

The swiftness, skill, and strength of the athletes are duly praised in verse that is correspondingly nimble, artful, and vigorous. For Cowley, whose mediation of Pindar was deeply influential in the late seventeenth and eighteenth centuries, this reciprocity established by the poet between himself and his subjects was quintessentially Pindaric. So Pope in this poem is being Pindaric, in a manner noted by the influential Cowley, in part by establishing a reciprocity between his role as encomiastic epistolary poet and his (female) subjects.[9] Indeed, as Penelope Wilson observes, "there is often a hint of the

6. *Selections from Pindar* (Chico, Calif.: Scholars Press, 1982), 8.

7. We should not necessarily infer Pope's view of Cowley from the famous phrase "Who now reads Cowley?" (*Imitations of Horace,* 2.1.75), for Pope was there speaking of how tastes change, not criticizing Cowley. Indeed, Pope told Spence that "Cowley is a fine poet, in spite of his faults" (*Anecdotes,* 1:189). Moreover, in portions of his unfinished youthful epic on Alcander, prince of Rhodes, Pope took pride and pleasure in consciously imitating Cowley's style (*Anecdotes,* 1:18). It appears, from *Imitations of Horace,* 2.1.77–78 ("Forgot his Epic, nay Pindaric Art / But still I love the language of his Heart"), that Pope particularly admired the plain-style, Horatian side of Cowley. In the *Epistle to a Lady* Pope achieves the encomiastic intention of Cowley's Pindarics via Cowley's Horatian "language of the Heart."

8. *Pindarique Odes, Written in Imitation of the Stile and Manner of Pindar* (London, 1668), 18.

9. See Felicity Rosslyn, " 'Dipt in the rainbow': Pope on Women," in *The Enduring Legacy: Alexander Pope Tercentenary Essays,* ed. G. S. Rousseau and Pat Rogers (Cambridge: Cambridge University Press, 1989), 51–62. Indeed, Pope's ethical poem embodies the combination of precisely those contradictory qualities that he lauds (279) in Martha Blount: "Fix't Principles, with Fancy ever new." Gregory Nagy discusses the reciprocity Pindar establishes between the poet and his subject in *The Cambridge History of Literary Criticism,* vol. 1, *Classical*

androgynous in Pope's sense of his own creativity, reminding us of his characterization of himself to the Earl of Peterborough as 'abhominably Epicoene.'"[10]

The poem continues by presenting four brief portraits of two women whose characters are remarkable for their changeableness:

> Arcadia's Countess, here, in ermin'd pride,
> Is there, Pastora by a fountain side:
> Here Fannia, leering on her own good man,
> And there, a naked Leda with a Swan.
>
> (7–10)

Once again, the couplets perfectly embody the very contrariety they articulate: the ostentatious Countess of Arcadia in line 7 becomes Pastora—simplicity herself—in line 8; Fannia (the name of both a respectable Roman matron and a famous adulteress) at first directs her attention monogamously toward her husband and then, in the following line, metamorphoses into one of the many lovers of the adulterous Jove.

The following passage describes, at slightly greater length, the unfortunately stereotypical feminine extremes of sinner (Mary Magdalene) and saint (Cecilia):

> Let then the Fair one beautifully cry,
> In Magdalene's loose hair and lifted eye,
> Or drest in smiles of sweet Cecilia shine,
> With simp'ring Angels, Palms, and Harps divine;
> Whether the Charmer sinner it, or saint it,
> If Folly grows romantic, I must paint it.
>
> (11–16)

The reciprocity between the poet and his subject is stressed in the extraordinary lines that introduce the portrait gallery of women who make up the body of the poem:

Criticism (Cambridge: Cambridge University Press, 1989), 20–21. See also Leslie Kurke, *The Traffic in Praise* (Ithaca, N.Y.: Cornell University Press, 1991), esp. Nagy's foreword, viii.

10. "Engendering the Reader: 'Wit and Poetry and Pope' Once More," in *The Enduring Legacy*, 63–76. Cf. George S. Fraser, *Alexander Pope* (London: Routledge, 1978), 82: "There was something womanish in Pope himself."

> Come then, the colours and the ground prepare!
> Dip in the Rainbow, trick her off in Air,
> Chuse a firm Cloud, before it fall, and in it
> Catch, ere she change, the Cynthia of this minute.
>
> (17–20)

The poem is addressed to Martha Blount, but here Pope is addressing himself as poet in a manner reminiscent of how Pindar often addresses himself as poet in his odes. The point here is that the poet's verse must match in evanescent subtlety the subjects he paints. Indeed, Pope's success, like Pindar's, depends on the quality of his subjects. And Pope demonstrates that he is very much up to the task. He sums up the contradictory quality of the feminine character in the oxymoronic phrase "firm Cloud." To depict the elusiveness of his subject, he writes the most subtle verse.

> Chúse a firm Cloúd, befóre it fáll, and ín it
> Cátch, ere she chánge, the Cýnthia óf this mínute.

The feminine endings here are absolutely appropriate. The word "catch" spills over from the first line of the couplet until it is caught as the first word and syllable of the next line, a syllable after which there occurs a firm caesura, the first of two in this line, as there were two in the previous line. In Pope's verse the caesura or pause often occurs somewhere near the middle of the line, and there is usually only one clear pause per line. In the first line of this couplet caesuras appear after the fourth and eighth syllables; in the second, after the first and fourth. And the feminine endings—"female rhymes," as they were called in the eighteenth century—also serve to differentiate these lines from the firmly established norm of Pope's couplet verse and of eighteenth-century couplet verse in general. And it is Pope's subjects, "the Cynthia[s] of this minute," that elicit the supple verse.

Cynthia is shorthand for the Cynthian goddess, or Diana, the goddess of the moon, and the moon is a symbol of changeableness. The phrase "the Cynthia of this minute" is itself hard to pin down metrically. The second foot can be read three ways. "Cynthia" can be read as two syllables, and the second foot of the phrase would then be scanned and heard as "thyă óf." Or it can be read as three syllables, which is possible, although far from common in Pope: "thĭă óf." Both readings, however, stipulate that one vowel open onto another ("Cynthia" ends with a vowel and "of" begins with another), and Pope disparages exactly this practice in the *Essay on Criti-*

cism in the line "Tho' oft the Ear the *open Vowels* tire" (345). It is therefore possible that Pope intended that these vowels elide, as in classical Latin verse, and that the phrase should be heard as "the Cynthi' of this minute." This metrical "undecidability," to use a familiar contemporary critical term, just may be the point here. And the feminine ending gives an elusive quality to the line that also evades definiteness.

These contradictory subjects are portrayed in more lengthy detail in the following verses, lines 21–150. First Rufa (21–23) is described, then Sappho (24–28), then Silia (29–37), then Papillia (37–40). All of these portraits of inconsistent women are, in Bundy's terms, "foils" for Martha Blount's constancy of character.[11] Some of the details of these descriptions are, indeed, meant to be read as quite specific contrasts with Patty Blount. Sappho is Lady Mary Wortley Montagu, whose aggressively sarcastic nature, so different from Martha Blount's, Pope had come to dislike. The soft nature of Silia bears some resemblance to the character of Martha Blount, but unlike Martha, Silia is unpredictable. Her soft nature may turn violent. And what causes the sudden change?

> All eyes may see from what the change arose,
> All eyes may see—a Pimple on her nose.
>
> (35–36)

As Valerie Rumbold has observed, the implied contrast here is between Silia's vanity and Martha's resignation "to the effects of her smallpox and to the constant rashes with which her extremely fair skin responded to sun or stresses: as she tells Swift, the charms of the spirit are what matter."[12] Papillia, too, is drawn in contrast to Martha. For, as Rumbold also observes, whereas Martha was known for her love of trees and landscapes, Papillia is less constant in this regard:

> Papillia, wedded to her doating spark,
> Sighs for the shades—"How charming is a Park!"

11. Pope in 1733 wrote to Swift of Martha Blount's character: "Your lady friend is *semper eadem,* and I have written an epistle to her on that qualification in the female character" (*Correspondence,* 3:349); And to Caryll he wrote in 1732: "I see your god-daughter as constantly as I go to London, and I think nobody should be changed towards her, as she is always the same" (*Correspondence,* 3:274).

12. *Women's Place in Pope's World* (Cambridge: Cambridge University Press, 1989), 276.

> A Park is purchas'd, but the Fair he sees
> All bath'd in tears—"Oh odious, odious Trees!"
>
> (37–40)

The poem is in danger of becoming a mere list, and so the poet must remind Martha Blount of his reasons for discriminating the feminine character in the way he has:

> Ladies, like variegated Tulips, show
> 'Tis to their Changes that their charms they owe;
> Their happy Spots the nice admirer take,
> Fine by defect, and delicately weak.
>
> (41–44)

Women are charming, Pope rather patronizingly tells Martha Blount,[13] precisely because of their changeability. This defect of character captivates ("take[s]," 43) whoever observes these women, and the observer—in this case, the poet—must be subtly discriminating ("nice") in order to register the subtleties in character to be observed. It is significant that in her reading of the poem Mary Wollstonecraft misquotes line 44: for "delicately weak" she reads "amiably weak," thus failing to register the reciprocity established by Pope between the poet and his subjects. The delicacy of his female subjects, in the *Epistle to a Lady,* is reciprocated by the delicacy of the male poet. Delicacy was a positive critical term for Pope. "I scarce meet with anybody that understands delicacy," he remarked to Spence. And as James M. Osborn informs us, "Pope considered 'delicacy' a prime characteristic of Horatian satire: 'But *Horace,* Sir, was delicate, was nice.' "[14] The style of the *Epistle to a Lady* is the "delicate" style of Horatian satire.

As patronizing as these lines (41–48) appear to be, however, we should not take them at face value; rather we must attend to their rhetorical intention. Pope is here, to a great extent, setting up a foil—in Pindaric fashion—for the passage toward which the entire poem has been building, the direct compliment to Martha Blount. But before we reach that direct and heartfelt compliment, Pope paints some briefer portraits of women who are foils for

---

13. Mary Wollstonecraft, *A Vindication of the Rights of Women,* ed. Carol H. Poston, Norton Critical Editions (London, 1975), 106, found these lines particularly objectionable.

14. Joseph Spence, *Observations, Anecdotes, and Characters of Books and Men,* ed. James M. Osborn, 2 vols. (Oxford: Clarendon Press, 1966), 1:150; the phrase "But *Horace,* Sir, was delicate, was nice" is line 11 of *Dialogue* 1 of *Epilogue to the Satires.*

Patty's constancy: the cunning and artful Calypso, the whimsical Narcissa (in whom, as opposed to the consistently pious Martha, "Atheism and Religion take their turns," 66), the lewd and vicious Philomedé, the witty and refined Flavia, the stupid and silly Simo's Mate, and then the lengthiest and sharpest contrast to Patty's good temper, the powerfully unstable Atossa (115–50).

Martha emerges from her silence here to mention the exception of Cloe, rejected by Pope on the grounds that Cloe is *too* reasonable: "So very reasonable, so unmov'd, / As never yet to love, or to be lov'd" (165–66). And what of Queen Caroline, whose character may indeed be praised, as Edward Young rather fulsomely does at the conclusion of his sixth satire, for its "excess of goodness" ("Satire VI, On Women," 576)?[15] For she indeed, Pope says, may be described as "The same for ever!" (183). Pope continues:

> and describ'd by all
> With Truth and Goodness, as with Crown and Ball:
> Poets heap Virtues, Painters Gems at will,
> And show their zeal, and hide their want of skill.
> 'Tis well—but Artists! who can paint or write,
> To draw the Naked is your true delight:
> That Robe of Quality so struts and swells,
> None see what Parts of Nature it conceals.
> Th' exactest traits of Body or of Mind,
> We owe to models of an humble kind.
> If QUEENSBERRY to strip there's no compelling,
> 'Tis from a Handmaid we must take a Helen.
> From Peer or Bishop 'tis no easy thing
> To draw the man who loves his God, or King:
> Alas! I copy (or my draught would fail)
> From honest Mah'met or plain Parson Hale.
>   (183–98)

The true artist is not the person who portrays public figures with the requisite regal pomp. The real artist is rather the one who can depict human nature in its naked state: in an intimate epistle, for instance, written in the plain and honest style of Horace, such as this to Martha Blount.

In the final version of the poem, very possibly the result of William

15. *The Complete Works*, 1:403.

Warburton's editing rather than Pope's intentions,[16] follow two passages of general observations unrelieved by particularized portraits. The first contrasts the nature of men and women: men's "bolder Talents" are "in full light display'd"; women's "Virtues open fairest in the shade" (201–2). The second passage treats the "Ruling Passions" of women, which Pope states are "The Love of Pleasure, and the Love of Sway" (210). As Samuel Johnson has observed, Pope's theory of the ruling passion is a dangerously deterministic doctrine. And it is no more palatable here than in the *Essay on Man.* As to the poet's claim that women particularly love pleasure, Pope in a note somewhat qualifies the rigidity of his pronouncement by stating that "this is occasioned partly by their *Nature,* partly by their *Education,* and in some degree by *Necessity.*"[17] Whereas Nature, in the main, encourages women to seek pleasure, it is experience that has taught them to seek dominion. Once again, now, Pope qualifies his dogmatism, this time by the statement that women seek dominion because they are "by Man's oppression curst" (213). Pope continues with his encomium:

> Men, some to Bus'ness, some to Pleasure take;
> But ev'ry Woman is at heart a Rake.
> Men, some to Quiet, some to public Strife;
> But ev'ry Lady would be Queen for life.
>   (215–18)[18]

Next follow the sections that illustrate the effects of women's seeking power (220–30) and pleasure (231–42). What comes through in these lines is not condemnation but sympathy for the women who have been victims of their own society's narrowness: "Still round and round the Ghosts of Beauty glide, / And haunt the places where their Honour dy'd" (241–42). It is now, when the note of sympathy has been struck, that Pope finally addresses directly the poem's thus far only implicit subject:

---

16. As Frank Brady argues in "The History and Structure of Pope's *To a Lady,*" *Studies in English Literature* 9 (1969): 439–62.

17. *TE* 3:2, 65.

18. Warburton's gloss of the phrase "ev'ry Woman is at heart a Rake" is worth considering: "Some men (says the Poet) take to business, some to pleasure, but every woman would willingly make *pleasure her business:* which being the peculiar characteristic of the *Rake,* we must needs think that he includes (in his use of the word here) no more of the Rake's ill qualities than are implied in this definition, *of one who makes pleasure his business*" (*Works of Pope* [London, 1776], 2:135).

Ah Friend! to dazzle let the Vain design,
To raise the Thought and touch the Heart, be thine!
That Charm shall grow, while what fatigues the Ring
Flaunts and goes down, an unregarded thing.
So when the Sun's broad beam has tir'd the sight,
All mild ascends the Moon's more sober light,
Serene in Virgin Modesty she shines,
And unobserv'd the glaring Orb declines.

(249–56)

The flighty and contradictory "Cynthia[s] of this minute" of line 20, it now appears, were foil for "the Moon's more sober light" that the poet claims is emblematic of Martha Blount.

Oh! blest with Temper, whose unclouded ray
Can make to morrow chearful as to day;
She, who can love a Sister's charms, or hear
Sighs for a Daughter with unwounded ear;
She, who ne'er answers till a Husband cools,
Or, if she rules him, never shows she rules;
Charms by accepting, by submitting sways,
Yet has her humour most, when she obeys;
Lets Fops or Fortune fly which way they will;
Disdains all loss of Tickets, or Codille;
Spleen, Vapours, or Small-pox, above them all,
And Mistress of herself, tho' China fall.

(257–68)

Most women may, by Martha Blount's own admission, have no characters at all, but Martha, so the poet argues, clearly has character: "Oh, blest with Temper." "Temper" means "temperance," ethical balance, the cultivation of the mean, character in the old, Aristotelian sense. Indeed, Johnson in his *Dictionary* (1755) gives the following as his second definition of "temper": "middle course; mean or medium."[19] What character or moral virtue is, for Aristotle in the *Nicomachean Ethics* (2.5–7), is the habitual ability to choose a mean between extremes: courage is midway between cowardice and impulsiveness, and that mean is not merely arithmetic, but relative to

---

19. Johnson's first definition, "due mixture of contrary qualities," is equally relevant.

the individual having to make the choice. If by inclination you tend to be timid, Aristotle suggests, then you will have to accustom yourself to choosing a mean that is closer to impulsiveness than cowardice. Most women, according to Martha Blount, have no characters at all; they have not, for whatever reasons, accustomed themselves to choosing the mean between contrary extremes. Hence every portrait in the poem depicts women as wildly fluctuating between extremes. These women are not "blest with Temper"; they do not have character, *ēthos,* in the Aristotelian sense.

Martha Blount does possess character in the Aristotelian sense. Even Martha Blount, however, is a "Contradiction" (270). And here we come to the rhetorical center of the poem, the specific praise of Martha as a "contradiction" to be set within the context of the contradictoriness of her sex, as depicted by Pope, in general:

> And yet, believe me, good as well as ill,
> Woman's at best a Contradiction still.
> Heav'n, when it strives to polish all it can
> Its last best work, but forms a softer Man;
> Picks from each sex, to make its Fav'rite blest,
> Your love of Pleasure, our desire of Rest.
> Blends, in exception to all gen'ral rules,
> Your Taste of Follies, with our Scorn of Fools,
> Reserve with Frankness, Art with Truth ally'd,
> Courage with Softness, Modesty with Pride,
> Fix'd Principles, with Fancy ever new;
> Shakes all together, and produces—You.
>   (269–80)

Reading the poem as an encomium in the Pindaric manner as elucidated by Bundy, we would naturally see the contradictoriness of the previous portraits to be foil for this one, and Pope in a note makes this explicit: "The Picture" of Martha "is of an estimable Woman, with the best kinds of contrarieties." Martha is a "contradiction," but the word has lost its pejorative associations. Martha's contradictoriness means, in this context, that she combines the best qualities of both men and women and avoids the unfortunate extremes of both. She is no less than heaven's "last, best work." Two of the qualities she combines in her own character are "Fix'd Principles, with Fancy ever new." We recall here the Pindaric motif, as recognized by the influential Cowley, of articulating a reciprocity between *laudator* and *laudandus.* Is this line not a description as well of Pope as poet of this ethical epistle, a poem which combines the search for fixed principles of moral conduct with charming descriptions of his fanciful subjects? Earlier Pope mentioned how accurate depictions of his mercurial subjects demanded a subtly mercurial treatment:

> Pictures like these, dear Madam, to design,
> Ask no firm hand, and no unerring line;
> Some wand'ring touch, or some reflected light,
> Some flying stroke alone can hit 'em right:
> For how should equal [flat or uniform] Colours do the
>   knack?
> Chameleons who can paint in white and black?
>   (151–56)

The "reflected light" of this passage will later be seen to be foil for the moon, to whose "Modesty" Pope at the end of the poem compares Martha Blount. But here the poet's "reflected light" is that which must be a match for the Cynthia-like changeability of the female character, for the Cynthias of this minute; Cynthia, we recall, is the goddess of the moon, the very symbol of reflected rather than direct light.[20] And the poet whose fancy must be tested in order to paint successfully the mercurial portraits of women must now combine both "Fix'd Principles" and "Fancy ever new" in order faithfully to paint a portrait of Martha Blount.

There is no doubt that Pope draws on sexual stereotypes in this poem, and that the fame and reputation of the poet would thus work to enforce these stereotypes: woman is changeable and man more rational. And yet there is a sense in which Pope is not happy with the consequences of either of these stereotypical depictions. Women—with the exceptions of Cloe (who is cold and emotionless), perhaps Queen Caroline (although, as Pope suggests, who could ever tell the truth about so conspicuously public a figure?), and Martha Blount—may be changeable,[21] but men are tyrants

20. As Dryden states—although using the adjective "borrow'd" rather than "reflected"—in the great opening lines from *Religio Laici,* lines that Pope no doubt knew well: "Dim, as the borrow'd beams of Moon and Stars / To *lonely, weary, wandring* Travellers, / Is *Reason* to the *Soul.*"

21. The character traits of women, Pope believed (see his note to line 211 of *To a Lady*), were "occasioned partly by their *Nature,* partly by their *Education,* and in some degree by *Necessity.*"

(288) and women thus suffer "by Man's oppression curst" (213). The
encomiastic epistle that is a critique of women's character ends with a
criticism of the character of men.

> Be this a Woman's Fame: with this unblest,
> Toasts live a scorn, and Queens may die a jest.
> This Phoebus promis'd (I forget the year)
> When those blue eyes first open'd on the sphere;
> Ascendant Phoebus watch'd that hour with care,
> Averted half your Parents simple Pray'r,
> And gave you Beauty, but deny'd the Pelf
> Which buys your sex a Tyrant o'er itself.
> The gen'rous God, who Wit and Gold refines,
> And ripens Spirits as he ripens Mines,
> Kept Dross for Duchesses, the world shall know it,
> To you gave Sense, Good-Humour, and a Poet.
>
> (281–92)

Martha Blount is fortunate, the poet states, not to have married, for this
would have robbed her of her freedom; for marriage, he tells Martha, "buys
your sex a Tyrant o'er itself" (288). And despite Pope's traditional stance on
the wisdom of maintaining the appearance of women's subordination to
men as illustrated by lines 264–65 (where he praises the woman who
"Charms by accepting, by submitting sways, / Yet has her humour most,
when she obeys") of our poem, Pope recommended a different model to
Patty in a letter of 1714, in which he praised Lady Sandwich as an "easie,
lively, and independent Creature that a sensible woman always will be."[22]
Pope had earlier associated women with the moon (the typical woman is
"the Cynthia of this minute"; Martha is associated with "the Moon's more
sober light"), men with the more glaring light of the sun. An earlier passage
articulates this distinction:

> But grant, in Public Men sometimes are shown,
> A Woman's seen in Private life alone:
> Our bolder Talents in full light display'd,
> Your Virtues open fairest in the shade.
> Bred to disguise, in Public 'tis you hide;

---

22. From *Correspondence,* 1:261; quoted in Rumbold, *Women's Place in Pope's World,* 262.

There, none distinguish 'twixt your Shame or Pride,
Weakness or Delicacy; all so nice,
That each may seem a Virtue or a Vice.

(199–206)

Pope associates himself as poet at the poem's conclusion with Phoebus (Apollo), the god of the sun and of poetry—Apollo, whose sign was ascendant when Martha Blount was born. Martha thus partakes of both sun and moon. Ascendant Phoebus may have denied Martha a husband, but he has given her "Sense, Good-humour, and a Poet." Since husbands, Pope writes, are generally no more than tyrants, Phoebus Apollo's dispensation was no doubt a wise one. How much better to have given Martha a "Poet," who will compose the loving encomium that would become the second epistle of what would be called Pope's *Moral Essays,* than a tyrannical husband.[23]

I do not wish to create the impression that this poem is unproblematic, to glide over the kinds of difficulties that make it a touchy one for many modern readers—as it was for some although by no means the majority of Pope's contemporary readers—to respond to. The feeling of the poem, however, despite its traditional attitudes toward gender, is delicate rather than crude.[24] And if we attend, as I have tried to show, to the poem's encomiastic intention, its sexual stereotyping is to some degree qualified.[25]

---

23. My reading of "Tyrant" (288) as referring to the husband Martha Blount never had follows the suggestion of Aubrey Williams in a note in *Poetry and Prose of Alexander Pope* (Boston: Houghton Mifflin, 1969), 175. This reading would take "the Pelf / Which buys your sex a Tyrant o'er itself" (287–88) as referring to the riches ("Pelf") that would attract, for the wrong reason, a potential husband. For a similar use of the word tyrant, cf. *Epistle I: To Cobham,* 202.

24. As Maynard Mack has observed in remarking that "the tradition ultimately behind" the poem "is the genre of the satire against women, reaching back from some minor Restoration figures through Chaucer's Prologue to the Wife of Bath's Tale and certain excoriating Church Fathers to Juvenal's famous sixth satire—or diatribe, as it might more accurately be called. Pope alters the tradition almost past recognition, replacing its characteristic hostility with an attitude that moves from detached amusement (the stereotypical male response) to awe, wonder, and commiseration, accompanied by a sense of deepening personal understanding and involvement" (*Alexander Pope: A Life* [New York: W. W. Norton, 1985], 627).

25. For a vigorous reading of the poem that stresses how deeply Pope's poem participates in a consistent gender "ideology" that denies woman a being truly independent of man, see Ellen Pollak, *The Poetics of Sexual Myth: Gender and Ideology in the Verse of Swift and Pope* (Chicago: University of Chicago Press, 1985), chap. 4. There is no question that Pope's view of the nature of women is conventional. His conventional attitudes are to some degree qualified in the poem under discussion, however, not only by the kinds of reciprocity between male poet and female subject that I have been describing; but they are qualified as well by the moral point

We must, in reading the poem, try to imagine how Pope hoped Martha Blount would receive it. It is this illusion of heartfelt intimacy that the crafty (one is tempted to say Calypso-like) artist Pope wished to convey, as he nevertheless—in the masculine arena of the performing poet—made this poem available to the public. The man and artist, Alexander Pope, in combining in this poem the feminine quality of "Art" with the masculine quality of "Truth" (277)[26] is, as Pope says of Martha Blount, a contradiction still. This is the final Pindaric/encomiastic trope, as noted by the famous baroque Pindarist Abraham Cowley, of establishing a reciprocity between the (in this case, androgynous and thus contradictory) poet and the (in this case, similarly androgynous and contradictory) subject of his loving praise.

---

of *To Cobham,* a poem which appeared just before *To A Lady* as the first of the four *Epistles to Several Persons* in the 1735 edition of Pope's *Works.* And that moral point is explicitly antidogmatic: *men* are infinitely changeable and fickle; if we are looking for constancy, we must find it elsewhere: "God and Nature only are the same" (154). Although Pope certainly cannot be singled out in his time for his "essentialist" view of the differences between men and women, it is nonetheless true that, as Brean S. Hammond has remarked, "From the point of view of [today's] gender politics," the *Epistle to a Lady* "is in the end a disappointing poem" (*Alexander Pope* [Brighton, Sussex: Harvester, 1986], 193–94).

26. That Pope, in this passage, wishes to associate "Art" with women and "Truth" with men is clearly conveyed by strict verbal parallelism. Martha Blount, heaven's "last best work," is a combination of what Pope considered to be feminine and masculine qualities. In line 274, the poet tells Martha Blount that, in creating her, Heaven has combined "Your [sex's] love of Pleasure, our [sex's] desire of Rest." The order of naming first feminine and then masculine qualities is continued in both halves of lines 276 and 277, where Pope says that in Martha Blount, Heaven has blended "Your Taste of Follies, with our Scorn of Fools,/ Reserve with Frankness, Art with Truth ally'd." Hence, for Pope in this passage, "Art" is associated with women, "Truth" with men. Pope appears to be using the word "Art" in this passage chiefly in the following senses defined by Johnson in the *Dictionary:* "Artfulness; skill; dexterity"; "Cunning."

8

BONNE MUSIQUE OU BONNES MOEURS

Le Neveu de Rameau, the Good, and the Beautiful

After *Lui* in Diderot's *Le Neveu de Rameau* describes with enthusiastic approval a particularly vile act of opportunistic betrayal performed by a renegade from Avignon, he immediately goes on to sing an elaborate fugue, impersonating first one voice, then another. *Moi,* the *philosophe* of the dialogue, is shocked and amazed at what he perceives to be the unlikely combination of extraordinary aesthetic sensitivity and equally extraordinary moral turpitude and declares that it is clear that Rameau's nephew understands good music better than good morals. This realization, *Moi* goes on to say, filled his soul with horror:

> Je commençois à supporter avec peine la presence d'un homme qui
> discutoit une action horrible, un exécrable forfait, comme un con-
> noisseur en peinture ou en poésie, examine les beautés d'un ouvrage
> du goût. . . . Je devins sombre, malgré moi.

> [I was beginning to find almost unbearable the presence of a man
> who could discuss a dreadful deed, an abominable crime, in the way
> a connoisseur in poetry or painting discusses the fine points of a
> work of art. . . . I felt gloom overwhelming me.]

The *philosophe* articulates his perplexity with greater precision a few moments later. "Comment se fait-il qu'avec un tact aussi fin, une si grande
sensibilité pour les beautés de l'art musical, vous soiez aussi aveugle sur les
belles choses en morale, aussi insensible aux charmes de la vertu?" [How is it
that with such fineness of feeling, so much sensibility where musical beauty
is concerned, you are so blind to the beauties of morality, so insensible to
the charm of virtue?].[1]

What are the sources of this paradox posed by *Moi?* And how seriously
was Diderot himself concerned with it? In order to answer the second of
these questions, we should first of all look at these remarks in the context of
the dialogue itself. Diderot titled the work not *Le Neveu de Rameau,* but
Satire seconde, and it is a satire in both the ancient and modern senses of the
word. It is a satire, that is, in the sense that it is written in the tradition of
Horace's witty and conversational *sermones.*[2] And, like modern satire, it
looks with ironic and comical detachment at the subjects it surveys, including both central characters. It may well be the case that Diderot is poking
fun at *Moi* for even asking the question, for the very words with which it is
posed may themselves ironically imply Diderot's explanation of why *Moi*
would pose such a question in the first place. Let us look again at the text.
Here, at greater length, is the second passage from the dialogue cited above:

> MOI: Comment se fait-il qu'avec un tact aussi fin, une si grande
> *sensibilité* pour les beautés de l'art musical, vous soiez aussi aveugle

---

1. *Le Neveu de Rameau,* ed. Jean Fabre (Geneva: Librairie Droz, 1977), 76, 89; trans.
Jacques Barzun, in *Rameau's Nephew and Other Works* (Indianapolis: Bobbs-Merrill, 1975),
61–62, 71. All citations will be to these texts.

2. On the affinities of Diderot's prose satire with Horace's *sermones,* see E. R. Curtius,
"Excursus XXV: Diderot and Horace," in *European Literature and the Latin Middle Ages,* trans.
Willard Trask (New York: Harper & Row, 1963), 573–83.

sur les belles choses en morale, aussi *insensible* aux charmes de la vertu?

LUI: C'est apparement qu'il y a pour les unes uns *sens* que je n'ai pas.

MYSELF: How is it that with such fineness of feeling, so much *sensibility* where musical beauty is concerned, you are so blind to the beauties of morality, so *insensible* to the charm of virtue?

HE: It must be that virtue requires a special *sense* that I lack.[3]

As the words I have italicized—*sensibilité, insensible, sens*—suggest, we might see in this passage a critique of the notion of *sensibilité*, a critique that Diderot would bring to its fulfillment in *Le Paradoxe sur le comédien* (1773). A person who assumes that matters both ethical and aesthetic may equally be decided by so whimsical a faculty as "sensibilité," Diderot seems to be saying, will indeed be perplexed by what he perceives to be the moral turpitude of the aesthetically gifted nephew.

But the paradox is not so easily resolved, for throughout his life Diderot was himself deeply concerned—virtually obsessed, in fact—with the relation between the arts and morality. Diderot must himself, to some degree, have shared *Moi*'s perplexed sadness at the paradox embodied in Rameau's aesthetically gifted but deeply amoral nephew. One of the reasons that *Moi* is so distressed in general at what he sees in *Lui* is that *Lui* acts out, and thus makes perfectly clear, the practical consequences of many of the abstract, theoretical beliefs held by *Moi*, insofar as *Moi* is a representative *philosophe*. Diderot himself had come to agree with Boulanger's critique of the *philosophe*'s tendency to have begun "par où il aurait fallu finir" [where he ought to have finished], that is, "par des maximes abstraites, des raisonnements généraux" [with abstract maxims, with general arguments].[4] As it has long ago been suggested, for example, the nephew demonstrates the consequences of Diderot's own materialistic philosophy.[5] It is one thing to maintain formally a position of materialistic determinism and thus to proclaim that "plaisir et douleur sont et seront toujours les seuls principes des actions des hommes" [pleasure and pain are and will always be the sole principles of

3. *Le Neveu de Rameau*, 89; trans. Barzun, *Rameau's Nephew and Other Works*, 71.

4. Denis Diderot, *Oeuvres complètes*, ed. Jules Assézat and Maurice Tourneux, 20 vols. (Paris, 1875–77), 6:344.

5. Daniel Mornet, "La véritable signification du *Neveu de Rameau*," *Revue des deux mondes* 40 (1927): 889.

human behavior].[6] It is quite another to observe the concrete realization of this idea.

Just as the nephew's actions make clear the consequences of Diderot's own materialism and, by implication, the materialistic attitudes shared by many of Diderot's contemporaries—by Claude-Adrien Helvétius, for example—so does the nephew make clear the consequences of certain of the *Encyclopédie*'s implicit views on the relation of art to ethics. It is *Moi*'s awareness of these consequences which, I would suggest, causes the *philosophe* to feel such gloom at the spectacle of a man who, he believes, understands "bonne musique" better than "bonnes moeurs." What *Moi* is disturbed by is the phenomenon that Leo Spitzer has called "the moral paradox involved in all artistry, the amorality which stems from the artistic impulse itself."[7] The belief that the artistic or imitative faculty is inherently amoral and that the arts appeal chiefly to the senses rather than to the reason led Plato to threaten to banish the poets from his ideal republic. Many subsequent defenses of literature address themselves specifically to refuting Plato's objections, but the "paradox" of "the amorality which stems from the artistic impulse itself" was only reinforced by the place Diderot and d'Alembert found for the imitative arts among the categories of learning presented in the *Discours préliminaire* (1751) of the *Encyclopédie*. Throughout this chapter I assume, with Arthur M. Wilson,[8] that Diderot was in fundamental agreement with the principles expounded in d'Alembert's preface.

All human knowledge, d'Alembert writes, may be broken down into the categories of History, Philosophy, and the *Beaux-Arts,* areas of learning that correspond to the division of the world of letters into scholars (who attempt to establish facts), philosophers (who attempt to enlighten humankind), and *beaux esprits* (to whom society owes its principal enjoyments and who concern themselves with the arts of the imagination).[9] These divisions, in turn, correspond roughly to the True, the Good, and the Beautiful, that famous triad which has its distant origins in Plato (*Phaedrus* 246d–e). D'Alembert had earlier in the *Discours préliminaire* distinguished, among the liberal arts, the useful from the *beaux-arts,* whose principal object is to confer pleasure.[10] It is chiefly pleasure, then, that is the desired response

6. Diderot, *Oeuvres complètes,* 2:310.
7. "The Style of Diderot," in *Linguistics and Literary History* (Princeton: Princeton University Press, 1948), 157
8. *Diderot* (New York: Oxford University Press, 1972), 134.
9. *Encyclopédie* (Paris and Neuchâtel, 1751–65), 17 vols., 1:xviii.
10. Ibid., 1:xiii.

which, according to the program put forth by d'Alembert and endorsed by Diderot, should be evoked by the *beaux-arts*. Diderot frequently stressed the close relationship that he believed should exist between the true, the good, and the beautiful,[11] but the threefold division that the *Discours préliminaire* imposed on learning encouraged the eventual association of the arts exclusively with the realm of the beautiful (and their dissociation from the true and the good).

By asssuming that aesthetic pleasure distinguishes the fine arts from the mechanical, Diderot and d'Alembert were following the Abbé Batteux in his famous and influential treatise, *Les beaux arts réduits à un même principe* (1746). There Batteux, for the first time, established the modern system of the fine arts. As the Encyclopedists would after him, Batteux distinguishes between the fine arts and the mechanical arts, and the basis of this distinction is that the fine arts have pleasure rather than usefulness as their aim. He acknowledges a third group of arts, which includes rhetoric and architecture, the aim of which is to combine both usefulness and pleasure [*l'utilité et l'agrément*].[12] Although Diderot, in his *Lettre sur les sourds et muets* (1751), criticized Batteux for not distinguishing sharply enough between the respective methods by which poetry and painting imitated nature, he and the other Encyclopedists, substituting architecture for dance, accepted Batteux's system of the fine arts and with that the implication that the *beaux-arts* were not necessarily concerned with moral issues. This was an inheritance that posed great problems for Diderot, who wanted the *beaux-arts* to be not only *beaux* but *moraux* and *utiles* as well.

As P. O. Kristeller has shown[13]—in an essay that should be much better known than it is, especially given the contemporary interest in the rise of the so-called aesthetic "ideology"—the specialization of beauty as a purely aesthetic concept was not established until the eighteenth century. In Plato, for example, the word *kalon* was never distinguished from moral goodness, and the same may be said of the use of the term *beauty* in Proclus, Paenetius, Plotinus, and Augustine. Similarly, in the *Philebus,* Socrates argues that there is no such thing as pure pleasure—as pleasure purified of the ethical or cognitive activities of the soul, that very chimera of pure aesthetic pleasure that Kant chased and tried to pin down in *The Critique of Pure Judgment.* But

11. *Oeuvres complètes,* 1:32–36, 8:393, and 10:519.
12. *Les beaux arts réduits à un même principe,* 2d ed. (Paris, 1747), 6, 7.
13. "The Modern System of the Arts," in *Renaissance Thought,* 2 vols. (New York: Harper, 1965), 2:166–68.

Diderot, in his article "Beau" in the *Encyclopédie,* is concerned chiefly with the formal or aesthetic qualities of the concept of the beautiful: "J'appelle donc *beau,*" Diderot writes, "tout ce qui contient en soi de quoi réveiller dans mon entendement l'idée des rapports" [I call beautiful all that contains within itself anything that arouses in my understanding the idea of relations].[14] When Diderot goes on to discuss what he calls "le Beau morale," he imposes this purely aesthetic conception of beauty on the realm of ethics. It is grandeur ("la force"), Diderot writes, which makes goodness ("la bonté") beautiful. Hence, even a crime, he says, may be beautiful, since this presupposes in its perpetrator a sense of vigor, courage, audacity, constancy, profundity, and elevation. Here we have an explanation, from the pen of Diderot himself, of the source of the nephew's admiration for the criminal action of the renegade from Avignon. The very aesthetic sensitivity that enables him to appreciate great music also allows him to appreciate a great crime.

Diderot inherited, then, the notion of the *beaux-arts* from Batteux; and this definition implied a notion of the paradox of the inherent amorality of art. It is helpful to distinguish, however briefly, the pleasure a work of art was meant to evoke for an eighteenth-century connoisseur of poetry from the pleasure a work of art was meant to evoke according to the classical position presented by Aristotle in the *Poetics.* By viewing an imitation of a specific but hypothetical set of probable events, Aristotle says, we learn something in general about human experience. Since learning is pleasurable—it is, Aristotle says, the liveliest of pleasures (1448b17)—learning and pleasure are mutual parts of a single process. Pleasure is not sought, as is implied in the notion of the *beaux-arts,* as an end in itself. And here Aristotle shows himself to be in agreement with Plato, who, as I have mentioned, in the *Philebus* casts doubt on the ability to isolate a pleasure that is purified of ethical and cognitive concerns. As Bernard Weinberg observes, "[I]n such theories as those of Batteux . . . the poet has recourse only to his own taste for the discovery of means to please his singular audience. All utilitarian aims . . . disappear, and the only remaining end is that of a highly sophisticated pleasure on the part of a highly cultivated individual." What we have in effect reached in Batteux, Weinberg suggests, is "the end of the Aristotelian tradition."[15]

Now Diderot is not commonly known as an aesthetically oriented critic, for in his writings on the arts he insisted again and again that art had to be

14. *Encyclopédie,* 1st ed., 2:176.
15. "From Aristotle to Pseudo-Ariostotle," in *Aristotle's Poetics and English Literature: A Collection of Critical Essays,* ed. Elder Olson (Chicago: University of Chicago Press, 1965), 199.

moral. He championed Greuze, for example, over Boucher, not because he thought the former necessarily the superior painter, but on moral grounds. In his *Essai sur la peinture* (1766) he argued that it should be the chief objective of all writers, painters, and sculptors to render virtue desirable and vice odious.[16] The *philosophe* in *Le Neveu de Rameau* repeats this *desideratum:* the reading of literature, he says, should inspire "l'amour de la vertue; la haine du vice" [the love of virtue and the hatred of vice].[17] It is because he hoped the arts could achieve these ends that *Moi* is dismayed when he learns that the nephew's reading of La Bruyère and Molière has had precisely the opposite effect. What Tartuffe has taught him, the nephew says, is how to be as hypocritical as Molière's characters but still manage, unlike Tartuffe, to succeed. Diderot's own plays were extraordinarily moralistic. After *Le Père de famille* was performed at the Comédie-Française in 1761, Fréron characterized its author as assuming "l'air et le ton d'un législateur qui vient discipliner des sauvages" [the air and tone of a lawgiver who is about to discipline some savages],[18] and Laurence Sterne found Diderot's earlier play, *Le Fils naturel,* too didactic.[19] How are we to reconcile Diderot's didacticism with the aestheticism implied by the notion of the *beaux-arts* he inherited from Batteux?

The answer lies, I think, in observing that didacticism and aestheticism may, paradoxically, be viewed as symbiotic critical positions: a writer or artist may feel obliged to tack a moral onto a work, the appeal of which is mainly aesthetic, in order to lend to the work an air of moral respectability. This combination of the didactic and the purely aesthetic or hedonistic—articulated in antiquity in the famous Horatian recommendation that the poet mix the pleasurable with the useful—is found, for example, in one of Diderot's favorite authors, Samuel Richardson. Richardson claimed that his novel *Pamela* served the didactic purpose of teaching young women the virtues of preserving their chastity. But the great popularity of the book is due, at least in part, rather to Richardson's skill at turning his readers into voyeurs by titillating their sensibilities with extremely vivid scenes depicting nearly successful attempts at the seduction of Pamela by the son of her late mistress.[20] Diderot's moral didacticism, similarly, may be seen as an

16. *Oeuvres complètes,* 10:502.
17. *Le Neveu de Rameau,* 60; trans. Barzun, *Rameau's Nephew and Other Works,* 49.
18. *Année Littéraire* 5 (1761): 23–24.
19. Laurence Sterne, *Letters,* ed. Lewis Perry Curtis (Oxford: Clarendon Press, 1935), 162.
20. Cf. the remarks made by Richard Hurd to Cox Macro in a letter dated November 7, 1742. "As a draught of Nature," Hurd writes of *Pamela,* "I must read, love, & admire it, & stand

attempt to compensate for the aestheticism implicit in the very conception of the *beaux-arts.*

That the fine arts, unless made to serve some clearly defined useful purpose, would offer purely aesthetic pleasure is suggested again and again in many of the articles in the *Encyclopédie.* In the unsigned article "Art," first printed in the second edition of the *Encyclopédie,* for example, the author praises the talent required of practitioners of the fine arts, but concludes that they, as opposed to craftsmen whose work is useful, practice "des *arts* sans lesquels la société pourroit être heureuse, et qui ne lui ont apporté que des plaisirs de fantaisie, d'habitude et d'opinion" [those arts without which society could be happy enough, and which has resulted only in the pleasures of fantasy, custom, and opinion].[21] When d'Alembert, in his article on schools of painting ("École"), discusses the decline of painting in Italy in the eighteenth century, not a word is mentioned, as Franz Boas observes, about the comparative lack of explicit moral seriousness in artists such as Tiepolo, Canaletto, and Guardi.[22] And Louis, le chevalier de Jaucourt, in his article on modern painting, writes: "Le grand peintre pour nous, est celui dont les ouvrages nous font le plus de plaisir, comme le dit fort bien l'abbé du Bos" [The great painter, for us, is the painter whose works give us the most pleasure, as the Abbé du Bos has well said].[23]

Diderot's last important piece of art criticism, his *Pensées détachées sur la peinture, la sculpture, l'architecture, et la poésie* (1775–76), has a distinctly moralistic tone. There are "deux qualités essentielles à l'artiste" [two essential qualities for the artist] he says, and these are "la morale et la perspective" [morality and perspective]. "Je ne suis pas un capucin," he says elsewhere in the same work, but

---

amaz'd that any Reader of Taste should hazard his reputation so much as to own a dislike of it. But in it's moral capacity I am not so positive. On the other hand I incline to suspect more danger from it to the generality of young readers, than advantage. . . . The too lively representation warms & inflames—the passions kindle at the view, & want more than the fair complainants ejaculations, & reflections to cool them again. This, Sir, I cannot but fear will be the probable consequence of some part of Pamela's charming Journal to the unconfirm'd virtuous of both Sexes. I mention it not as an Objection to the work, (for I am satisfy'd 'tis the very perfection of it) but as a hindrance to it's moral Design" (BL, Addit. MS 32557, f.47).

21. *Encyclopédie,* 2d ed. (Geneva, 1777), 42 vols., 3: 482.

22. *Encyclopédie,* 1st ed., 5:314–35. The examples in this paragraph are cited by Boas in his article "The Arts in the *Encyclopédie,*" *The Journal of Aesthetics and Art Criticism* 23 (1964): 97–107.

23. *Encyclopédie,* 1st ed., 5:331.

j'avoue cependant que je sacrifierais volontiers le plaisir de voir de belles nudités, si je pouvais hâter le moment où la peinture et la sculpture, plus décentes et plus morales, songeront à concourir, avec les autres beaux-arts, à inspirer la vertu et à épurer les moeurs. Il me semble que j'ai assez vu de tétons et de fesses.[24]

[I am not a monk, but I avow nonetheless that I would gladly sacrifice the pleasure of seeing beautiful nudity, so long as I would thereby be able to hasten the moment when painting and sculpture, more seemly and moral, will dream of combining, with the other fine arts, to inspire virtue and to refine morals. It seems to me that I have seen enough breasts and behinds.]

It is significant that the title of this critical work includes, along with painting, three of the remaining four *beaux-arts,* as if Diderot were almost unconsciously implying that it is their very designation as *beaux-arts* that has led the arts to provide aesthetic pleasure alone and hence to their subsequent moral impoverishment. In the person of *Moi* the *philosophe* in *Le Neveu de Rameu,* Diderot had already experienced the paradox, as embodied in Rameau's nephew, of the person who is supremely sensitive to the beauties of art but who is at the same time a scoundrel. By harping so insistently on the moral component of art in this late critical work, Diderot appears to be making an ardent attempt to avert the separation of the good from the beautiful. But despite Diderot's constant efforts to relate morality to art, his acceptance—and the *Encyclopédie*'s promulgation—of Batteux's conception of the fine arts led to the gradual separation of the good from the beautiful, a separation that would be brought to its fulfillment before the end of the century through Kant's formulation, in his *Critique of Judgment* (1790), of the complete autonomy of aesthetic appreciation. It was Kant, who knew Batteux's work[25] and accepted the notion of the fine arts, who maintained that the purest kind of beauty must be devoid of ethical significance if it is to possess that "purposiveness without purpose"[26] of true art. What appeared to *Moi* in *Le Neveu de Rameau* as a paradox was to become, after Kant, a critical commonplace.

24. Denis Diderot, *Oeuvres esthéthiques,* ed. Paul Vernière (Paris: Garnier Frères, 1959), 765, 767.
25. Kant mentions him by name in section 33 of the *Critique of Judgment.*
26. *Critique of Judgment,* section 15.

9

THE PASTORAL TRADITION AND THE INHERITANCE OF ALEXANDRIAN PRECIOSITY

I have been speaking of literary formalism as if it had been invented in the eighteenth century—hinted at by Collins in his quest of mistaken beauties, nervously anticipated by Diderot in *Le Neveu de Rameau,* and finally given its paradigmatic articulation in the famous Kantian formulations in the *Critique of Judgment.* But literary formalism is a much older phenomenon. In this chapter I wish to discuss how the pastoral tradition, from its inception, encouraged the isolation of the quality of formal beauty from ethical and cognitive concerns. It is perhaps not a coincidence, therefore, that Paul Valéry found such a kindred spirit in the Virgil of the *Eclogues,* those early examples of pure poetry that Valéry brushed up his schoolboy Latin in order to translate.

The eighteenth century was crucial in the history of the pastoral. It is in the eighteenth century that the genre achieved an exquisite polish at the expense of a thinning out of a substance that was already fairly thin. The eighteenth century witnessed the flourishing of pastoral, but also its coup de grâce in the form of Samuel Johnson's critique of *Lycidas,* a critique that is anticipated in Gay's and Swift's pastorals and embodied in a moving modern pastoral poem, "Montana Pastoral" by J. V. Cunningham, which I discuss at the conclusion of this chapter. In order for us to understand Cunningham's poem as well as the reasons behind the debunking of pastoral in the eighteenth century in poets such as Swift and Gay and in the criticism of Samuel Johnson, it will be necessary to review the history of the pastoral genre, paying special attention to the genre's emphasis on poetic craft virtually for its own sake.

Pastoral as Motif and Genre

The first "official" pastorals are the *Idylls* of Theocritus, which would date the genre as emerging in the Hellenistic period, the first truly "literary" period in Western culture. But although the genre emerged rather late, there are clearly pastoral elements present in earlier literature, particularly if we define pastoral, as Samuel Johnson did when he spoke of Virgil, as "a poem in which any action or passion is represented by its effects upon a country life."[1] Whatever happens in the country, Johnson says, may afford a subject for a pastoral poet. And the country is associated with leisure and ease (*otium*), with what has become known as the "idyllic," a word derived from the name of Theocritus's pastoral poems or "idylls": an idyll, or *eidyllion,* a short descriptive poem.

One of the earliest appearances of pastoral poetry in the West occurs in the eighteenth book of the *Iliad:* on the shield of Achilles are represented "two herdsmen . . . taking pleasure in playing on their pipes" [δύω . . . νομῆες / τερπόμενοι σύριγξι,] (18.525–26). This idyllic moment does not last very long, however, for the two herdsmen are soon ambushed and killed by an enemy. And this awareness of the fleetingness of the pastoral moment is present throughout the Homeric poems, where such moments are set in the context of the active life. The gardens of Alcinoös in the seventh book of the

1. *Rambler* 37, in the *Yale Edition of the Works of Samuel Johnson,* 16 vols. (New Haven: Yale University Press, 1958–), 3:204.

Odyssey (112ff.) are magnificent, so magnificent that John Milton felt he needed to tell the readers of *Paradise Lost* that the Garden of Eden was a "Spot more delicious then those Gardens feign'd / Or of reviv'd *Adonis,* or renown'd / *Alcinous,* host of old *Laertes* Son."[2] Odysseus admires the gardens greatly, but he knows he cannot linger. He had been a captive of Calypso, whose grotto was so astoundingly beautiful that it evoked admiration even in a god; when Hermes came to persuade Calypso to release Odysseus, the god was astounded by the great beauty of the grotto and the surrounding grove. And the grotto and everything it suggests must have been very seductive to Odysseus, for he remained with Calypso for seven years until he finally felt ready to reenter the realm of experience, to endure whatever the gods would inflict on him on his way back home. The pastoral moment, in the *Odyssey,* as in the *Iliad,* is set in the context of trial and of the active life.

There are pastoral moments in the *Aeneid* also. One of the poignant themes in the final books is pastoral Italy's loss of innocence as it is forced to mobilize for war. In Plato, philosophy itself is often associated with the pastoral. In the *Phaedrus,* for instance, Socrates and Phaedrus begin their discourse on love while sitting under the shade of the plane tree by a lovely stream, with cicadas singing around them. But the idyllic setting is, once again, placed by the author within the context of the active life. "I am a lover of learning," Socrates tells Phaedrus, "and trees and open country won't teach me anything, whereas men in the town do" (230d).[3] Samuel Johnson will repeat this Socratic sentiment in the eighteenth century, perhaps most memorably in *Ramblers* 6 and 135.

The Idylls *of Theocritus: Primitivism and Decadence, Art for Art's Sake, Pastoral Elegy*

There are pastoral motifs present in much later literature, so many, in fact, that E. R. Curtius is justified in saying that of all the antique poetical genres,

---

2. *Paradise Lost,* 9.439–441, in *John Milton: Complete Poems and Major Prose,* ed. H. C. Beeching (New York: Oxford University Press, 1938). All quotations from Milton's poetry are from this edition.

3. *Phaedrus,* trans. R. Reginald Hackforth, in *The Collected Dialogues of Plato,* ed. Edith Hamilton and Huntington Cairns (Princeton: Princeton University Press, 1961), 479.

pastoral "has had, after the epic, the greatest influence."[4] Stesichorus sang of the Sicilian shepherd Daphnis, who scorned the love of a goddess for the sake of a mortal woman, in the seventh century B.C., but it was Theocritus in the first half of the third century B.C. who originated pastoral poetry as a genre. Theocritus's pastorals are set in Sicily, and Virgil, in his *Eclogues,* transports the genre to Arcadia, where it continues to reside through the Renaissance (Sidney's pastoral romance is titled the *Arcadia*). After Virgil, although pastorals in the Theocritean and Virgilian mode were still being written, the stock of pastoral motifs can be found as well in many different genres.

The pastoral was slow to become considered as a distinct literary genre. Aristotle said nothing about it. Even after Theocritus wrote, Hellenistic and Roman literary critics did not have a category for the pastoral. Longinus mentions Theocritus as a writer of "bucolics" (*On the Sublime* 33.4), but says nothing about the genre. Horace in the *Ars Poetica* is also silent on the topic. Quintilian (first century A.D.) in the *Institutes* (10.1.55) considers Theocritus in his discussion of the writers of epic. The pastoral *motif,* then, is perhaps more easily detected than the pastoral *as a literary genre.* Even in Theocritus there are many idylls that are not strictly bucolic. In fact, only about ten of the *Idylls* are strictly pastoral. *Idyll* 15, for example, is set in cosmopolitan Alexandria.

To someone unacquainted with the history of Greek literature, it might well appear that Theocritus's bucolic pastorals are very primitive in feeling: a representation, perhaps, of a golden age, of a rustic world before the complications of modernity have taken hold. And Theocritus, when read in the original, largely because of the Doric dialect of his poetry, may sound more archaic than Homer himself. But are these primitive poems? It is well to remember that Theocritus was a contemporary of Callimachus and that he was associated with the sophisticated *littérateurs* of the Alexandrian school. It must be remembered, too, that the *other* literary genre that emerged in Alexandria was the most self-conscious of them all, literary criticism itself. This suggests that Theocritus's idylls are not so much primitive as they are self-consciously primitive. It is hard to imagine Theocritus, in his contemporary Alexandria, speaking like one of the shepherds of his pastorals. One might question, then, Pope's belief that "as the keeping of flocks seems to have been the first employment of mankind, the most an-

4. *European Literature and the Latin Middle Ages,* trans. Willard Trask (New York: Harper & Row, 1963), 187.

cient sort of poetry was probably pastoral" and that all such poems "are full of the greatest simplicity in nature."[5]

What is the subject of pastoral? The answer to this question also suggests a relation between pastoral and that other late-to-emerge and—at times in our history—equally decadent genre, literary criticism. For the subject of the pastoral is often poetry itself. The characters in Theocritus's idylls are shepherds, cowherds, and shepherdesses. The shepherd writes poetry under trees, on the grass, by a brook. Why a shepherd as the type of a poet? Because, in this idyllic setting, it is the shepherd who has the time and leisure to write verse. Far from the concerns of the town, the shepherd alone has the σχολῆ or *otium* (leisure) to devote to song. If there is any one theme central to the bucolic idylls of Theocritus, it is the theme of the power of poetry, and the power of poetry to overcome the most sorrowful of experiences: the loss of a loved one. This theme in fact seems more pervasive in pastoral than the rustic motif itself, for Theocritus's second *Idyll,* for example, does not have a particularly rustic setting. Here a girl has been deserted by her lover; she tries to recall him with an elaborate charm and, when that does not bring him back, sends her maid to try one more spell and then confesses her unhappy story to the moon.

Poetry about poetry, then, and about love. This is the subject of virtually all of Theocritus's *Idylls.* In the first Thyrsis the goatherd sings his songs about Daphnis, who is dying of unrequited love. What does this have to do with poetry? According to one tradition, Daphnis was a Sicilian and the inventor of bucolic poetry. He was a herdsman and was loved by a nymph; a princess got him drunk, seduced him, and the nymph, because of his infidelity—an indiscretion committed not as the consequence of a conscious choice—blinded him, and he spent the rest of his life composing mournful songs on his sad fate, songs that some believe to be the origin of pastoral poetry.

In the first poem of Theocritus's *Idylls,* then, Thyrsis gives us a poem about a poet: we have a poem within the poem about a poet—the alleged founder of pastoral poetry. The eleventh *Idyll,* sung by the Cyclops, is addressed to Galatea, and the song itself, the Cyclops hopes, will alleviate the pain of unrequited love. The seventh *Idyll* is just as self-consciously poetic: here we have a singing contest between two shepherds, a device

---

5. *Pastoral Poetry and an Essay on Criticism,* vol. 1 of *The Twickenham Edition of the Poems of Alexander Pope,* ed. E. Audra and A. Williams (New Haven: Yale University Press, 1961), 23, 25. All citations from Pope's *Pastorals* will be from this edition.

(technically called the *carmen amoebaeum*), taken up by Virgil in his eighth *Eclogue;* by Pope in his third pastoral, *Autumn;* and spoofed by Gay in "Monday; or the Squabble" from *The Shepherd's Week.* Within the poem Lycidas sings a poem about the cowherd and poet Daphnis, and then Lycidas sings to us the song of how a wicked king had entrapped the goatherd Komatas:

> ἀσεῖ δ᾽ ὥς ποκ᾽ ἔδεκτο τὸν αἰπόλον εὐρέα λάρναξ
> ζωὸν ἐόντα κακαῖσιν ἀτασθαλίαισιν ἄνακτος,
> ὥς τέ νιν αἱ σιμαὶ λειμωνόθε φέρβον ἰοῖσαι
> κέρδον ἐς ἀδεῖαν μαλακοῖς ἄνθεσσι μέλισσαι,
> οὕνεκά οἱ γλυκὺ Μοῖσα κατὰ στόματος χέε νέκταρ.
> ὦ μακαριστὲ Κομᾶτα, τύ θην τάδε τερπνὰ πεπόνθεις.
> (78–83)[6]

[He will sing about how a wide coffer held a goatherd
still alive—this was a nasty trick of the king;
and he will sing of how the snub-nosed bees,
coming from the meadow
to the fragrant cedar box, fed him with soft flowers.
O most blessed Komatas, you have indeed suffered
    pleasantries.]

Here we have the familiar topos of the poet whose gift for song is said to be the result of the muses' filling his mouth with nectar. Komatas is, like Daphnis, a poet, and so, once again, we have a poem within a poem about a poet.

Poets had written before about the nature of poetry, but not with such self-consciousness. Odysseus narrates to the audience—is in fact the poet of—several books of the *Odyssey,* and we are meant to admire his gifts as a speaker of words; but his poetic skill is a crucial component of his status as a hero, one who is not only a doer of deeds but who is a speaker of words as well. Nor can we say—as we can of much of Theocritus's *Idylls*—that the subject of the *Odyssey* is poetry itself. Pindar often speaks of himself as poet and comments on his poetry, but each time he does this we can be fairly certain that his ultimate intention—however indirect this may appear at

---

6. *Theocritus,* ed. with translation and commentary by A.S.F. Gow, 2 vols. (Cambridge: Cambridge University Press, 1950), 1:60. Unless otherwise indicated, Theocritus will be cited from this edition. The translation is my own.

first sight—is to praise the athletic victor. But now, in the Hellenistic period, we get for the first time the appearance of a kind of art for art's sake. It was this preciosity that Longinus lamented: Hellenistic poetry, Longinus felt, succeeded more through its artfulness than its grandeur; it was, in fact, largely its very artfulness, its concern with literary formalism, with art for its own sake that, for Longinus, prevented it from achieving greatness. Robert Wells, a gifted translator of Theocritus, has recently made some extremely pertinent remarks about the Alexandrians and their affinities with the modern poetic formalism associated with Mallarmé:

> In the absence of other fixed points, their poetry is intent on making an absolute value of the words themselves. It aims at literary certainty—as if such a quality were capable of being isolated—and prides itself on a subtly heightened vocabulary and refined exactness of verse technique. In tone, on the other hand, it is habitually elusive and ambiguous; it refuses to allow itself to be judged just as it refuses to pass judgment. Mallarmé's remark that a poem is made with words, not ideas, and his insistence—playful but grounded in despair—that the world exists to be put in a book might have struck a chord with Theocritus and his contemporaries. They too were engaged in an attempt to "donner un sens plus pur aux mots de la tribu."[7]

The symbol of artfulness in Theocritus's first *Idyll* is the bowl that Thyrsis wins for his song about Daphnis. The bowl is itself an intricate work of art; if you sing of Daphnis's troubles, the goatherd tells Thyrsis, I will give you

> ... βαθὺ κισσύβιον κεκλυσμένον ἁδέι κηρῷ,
> ἀμφῶες, νεοτευχές, ἔτι γλαφάνοιο ποτόσδον.
> τῷ ποτὶ μὲν χείλη μαρύεται ὑψόθι κισσός,
> κισσὸς ἑλιχρύσῳ κεκονιμένος· ἁ δὲ κατ’ αὐτόν
> καρπῷ ἕλιξ εἰλεῖται ἀγαλλομένα κροκόεντι.
> ἔντοσθεν δὲ γυνά, τι θεῶν δαίδαλμα, τέτυκται,
> ἀσκητὰ πέπλῳ τε καὶ ἄμπυκι· πὰρ δέ οἱ ἄνδρες
> καλὸν ἐθειράζοντες ἀμοιβαδὶς ἄλλοθεν ἄλλος
> νεικείουσ’ ἐπέεσι · τὰ δ’ οὐ φρενὸς ἅπτεται αὐτᾶς·
> ἀλλ’ ὅκα μὲν τῆνον ποτιδέρκεται ἄνδρα γέλαισα,

7. *The Idylls of Theocritus* (Manchester: Carcanet, 1988), 22.

ἄλλοκα δ᾽ αὖ ποτὶ τὸν ῥιπτεῖ νόον· οἳ δ᾽ ὑπ᾽ ἔρωτος
δηθὰ κυλοιδιόωντες ἐτώσια μοχθίζοντι.
τοῖς δὲ μέτα γριπεύς τε γέρων πέτρα τε τέτυκται
λεπράς, ἐφ᾽ ᾇ σπεύδων μέγα δίκτυον ἐς βόλον ἕλκει
ὁ πρέσβυς, κάμνοντι τὸ καρτερὸν ἀνδρὶ ἐοικώς.
φαίης κεν γυίων νιν ὅσον σθένος ἐλλοπιεύειν,
ᾧδέ οἱ ᾠδήκοντι κατ᾽ αὐχένα πάντοθεν ἶνες
καὶ πολιῷ περ ἐόντι· τὸ δὲ σθένος ἄξιον ἄβας.
τυτθὸν δ᾽ ὅσον ἄπωθεν ἁλιτρύτοιο γέροντος
περκναῖσι σταφυλαῖσι καλὸν βέβριθεν ἀλωά,
τὰν δ᾽ ὀλίγος τις κῶρος ἐφ᾽ αἱμασιαῖσι φυλάσσει
ἥμενος· ἀμφὶ δέ νιν δύ᾽ ἀλώπεκες, ἃ μὲν ἀν᾽ ὄρχως
φοιτῇ σινομένα τὰν τρώξιμον, ἃ δ᾽ ἐπὶ πήρᾳ
πάντα δόλον τεύχοισα τὸ παιδίον οὐ πρὶν ἀνησεῖν
φατὶ πρὶν ἢ ἀκράτιστον ἐπὶ ξηροῖσι καθίξῃ.
αὐτὰρ ὅγ᾽ ἀνθερίκοισι καλὰν πλέκει ἀκριδοθήραν
σχοίνῳ ἐφαρμόσδων· μέλεται δέ οἱ οὔτε τι πήρας
οὔτε φυτῶν τοσσῆνον ὅσον περὶ πλέγματι γαθεῖ.
παντᾷ δ᾽ ἀμφὶ δέπας περιπέπταται ὑγρὸς ἄκανθος,
αἰπολικὸν θάημα· τέρας κέ τυ θυμὸν ἀτύξαι.

(27–56)

[. . . a deep, two-handed cup, new-made,
Washed in fresh wax, still fragrant from the knife.
About the lip of the cup an ivy pattern
Is carved, with golden points among the leaves:
A fluent tendril flaunting its yellow bloom.
Beneath is a woman's figure, delicately worked:
She is robed and wears a circlet to keep her hair.
On either side of her stand two bearded suitors
Arguing their claim. But she takes no notice,
Looks smilingly at one man, or so it appears,
Then at the other; while, hollow-eyed with love,
They struggle against her kindly indifference
On a jutting rock. He strains at the very edge
Of his strength to draw in a net with its heavy catch.
You can see the effort bunching in each tense limb
And in his neck as he gives himself to the task.
He has white hair, but his strength is supple and fresh.

A little distance from the old man's sea-labour
There is a vineyard hung with darkening clusters.
A small boy perches on a dry stone wall to guard them.
Two foxes shadow him. One sneaks along the rows
For plunder; another has fixed her tricky eye
On the quarter-loaf the boy keeps for his breakfast
And will not let him alone till she has snatched it.
Blithely intent, he shapes a cage for a cricket
From asphodel stalks and rushes. The bag with his food
Is forgotten; so are the vines. The toy absorbs him.
The base of the cup is overspread with acanthus.
A goatherd's treasure! It is too fine a thing.][8]

Here we have an excellent example of *ekphrastic* poetry, the emergence of which as a separate genre says much about the narrowing of poetic subjects in the Alexandrian period. Ekphrasis is, technically, the delineation of people, places, and, especially, of works of art, and is a species of epideictic oratory. The two other branches of oratory were the deliberative and the judicial or forensic. With the extinction of the *polis* and more democratic forms of government, there was really no occasion for the use of deliberative oratory, which concerned matters of state and was designed for large public gatherings. When rhetoric was taught, it was epideictic rhetoric, the oratory of display, a species of which is *ekphrasis,* elaborate description for its own sake.

Let us now turn to what Theocritus portrays on the cup in this excellent example of ekphrastic poetry. The two men contending for the woman (ἀμοιβαδὶς ἄλλοθεν ἄλλος, "alternately—now one, now the other," 34) are, in effect, pastoral poets singing the *carmen amoebaeum*—a song in which one shepherd/poet will sing a number of lines and the other will then answer with a corresponding number of lines. The woman is herself a work of art (δαίδαλμα, 32). And the boy sitting between the two foxes could well be a type of the poet, the practitioner of Hellenistic art for art's sake. His attention to his craft is so strong that he is unaware of what is going on around him. He is weaving a cricket cage (ἀκριδοθήραν, 52), and crickets are associated with pastoral poetry. Theocritus calls the bowl a "marvel of craftsmanship" (αἰολύχον θάημα, 56). What we have in the first idyll, then, is the following situation: in the poem (the work of art), Thyrsis, a poet, sings of Daphnis, the mythical founder of the art of bucolic poetry and receives, as a prize for his art, an extraordinarily detailed work of art that itself depicts, besides two men who are contending with each other (by implication) in pastoral song, a boy who is himself an artisan, weaving a cricket-cage for his own pleasure. Such mirrors upon mirrors of artistic self-referentiality invite the subtle speculations of the most deft postmodernist critic. As we shall see, it is precisely this cultivation of literary preciosity that would pose problems for later poets choosing to write in the pastoral genre. How can a poet say something significant about the world in a genre that, from its origins, seems to be so precious and self-enclosed?[9]

Along with this paean to art, the first *Idyll* presents a clear example of the distinct literary form of the pastoral elegy, a form that survives intact from Theocritus to Virgil to Spenser's *Shepheardes Calender* to Milton's *Lycidas* to Shelley's *Adonais* to Matthew Arnold's *Thyrsis*. The tripartite pattern of the pastoral elegy is fairly simple: (1) a shepherd-poet has either died or is dying of unrequited love; (2) nature, both animate and inanimate, bewails his death (this is the device which Ruskin called the "pathetic fallacy"); and (3) various figures come onto the scene and express their grief (Hermes, Priapos, and Venus to Daphnis in Theocritus's first *Idyll;* Triton, Camus, and St. Peter in Milton's *Lycidas*).

There is a clear connection between the pastoral elegy and the Hellenistic concern with art. As Moschus says in his lament for the dead pastoral poet Bion (who himself wrote a lament for the death of the mythical Adonis), various kinds of vegetation die, but these are reborn in the following spring. Human beings, however, are not resurrected. They die once and for all. Pastoral elegy at times affirms that song has an immortalizing effect. The poet achieves a kind of immortality through his verse, which, as Horace has said in one of his odes (3.30), he believed would be a monument more lasting than bronze. And it is not so much what the poet has to say as it is the extraordinary and painstaking craft with which he says it that confers immortality.

A word may be in order here about the origins of pastoral elegy and the relevance of such origins to Theocritus's first *Idyll*. The Daphnis myth has been viewed as a late Greek development of a symbol under which people mourned the withering vegetation of summer. The death of Daphnis or

---

9. A relatively recent attempt to relate the pastoral genre to historical contingency is Annabel Patterson, *Pastoral and Ideology: Virgil to Valéry* (Berkeley and Los Angeles: University of California Press, 1988).

Adonis symbolized, that is, the decay of spring in the scorching midsummer heat. For Theocritus's Daphnis, for example, the human passion of love withers the life of the shepherd in the way the midsummer heat withers the blooming plants of spring. This analogy is made explicit in the final couplet of Pope's *Summer:* "On me Love's fiercer Flames forever prey, / By Night he scorches, as he burns by Day" (91–92). Daphnis, then, is a type of Adonis. The death and resurrection of Adonis in the ancient East symbolized the cycle of the seasons. Thus, when a poet dies, his resurrection may take the form of the immortality he gains through his verse, through art.

Virgil's Eclogues: *Pastoral, Allegory, History*

Virgil's place in the history of pastoral is crucial. The Roman poet replaced Sicily as its setting with the distant and rather nebulous Arcadia and introduced an element that was to loom large in later pastoral: reference to the contemporary world through allegory, specifically through political allegory. It was through this device, through Virgil's allusions to contemporary events, that he attempted to keep the pastoral from becoming an exercise in preciosity.

In *Eclogue* 5 two shepherds—Menalcas and Mopsus—sing the death and apotheosis of Daphnis. The part that Mopsus sings is clearly modeled upon the first *Idyll* of Theocritus. The Menalcas section is *not* based on Theocritus, and this has encouraged the identification of Daphnis with Julius Caesar, who had recently been assassinated and then deified; this was how Servius read the poem, and his interpretation was transmitted to the Middle Ages and the Renaissance. Similarly, *Eclogue* 1 has been read allegorically. A slave named Tityrus has managed after many years to earn his freedom and is assured by a benefactor of some kind that he possesses a plot of ground, ample for his needs, although others around him are being forced to move. Meliboeus must leave his lands, but Tityrus, through the good offices of his benefactor, is secure. "Ah Meliboeus," Tityrus says, "the man to whom I owe this happy leisure [this *otium*] is a god" (6). Who is this god? In a few lines we learn that it is a young man whom Tityrus met at Rome, the city that "stands above all other cities" (24). It is in Rome that Tityrus meets the *deus* who offers to protect him and tells him: "pascite, ut ante, boves, pueri; submittite tauros" [Let your cattle graze, as they have always done, and put your bulls to stud] (45).[10] The name Octavian or Caesar is not mentioned, but it is likely that Virgil is here referring to the young Octavian, the man who will become Augustus Caesar. Tityrus is a shepherd and a poet. And what the allegory suggests is that the art of poetry—symbolized by the pastoral leisure enjoyed by Tityrus—is made possible only by favorable political events. But Virgil is not particularly explicit about what makes poetry worth pursuing.

Renaissance Pastoral, the Johnsonian Critique of Lycidas, and John Gay

Allegory remained part of the pastoral tradition through the Renaissance. Virgil, in the fourth *Eclogue,* declared that a new age was at hand and predicted the birth of a child during whose lifetime the ages will run quickly back until we return once more to the Golden Age and are at peace. Exactly who this child was has been a subject of debate, but many Christians had no doubt that Virgil meant Christ himself. Virgil here paved the way for Christian readings, not only of the fourth *Eclogue,* but of the entire pastoral genre.

The pastoral motif was easily assimilated by the Christian tradition. In Middle English works such as *The Second Shepherd's Play* (ca. 1385), Christ is portrayed as a good shepherd who protects his flocks from the wolves of Satan. The language of the Bible—beginning with its presentation of Moses as a shepherd of his people—itself encouraged this adaptation. Hence, the shepherd of ancient pastoral could become a Christ figure, a religious leader, a pastor, such as Edward King, Milton's Lycidas.

And we are now, after our survey of the history of pastoral, in a good position to confront Milton's poem and to attempt to consider the question of the justness of Johnson's famous criticism of *Lycidas.* For in Johnson's critique we have a pivotal moment in the history of the genre. Artifice, we have seen, had characterized the pastoral genre from its Theocritean beginnings. Virgil had attempted to bring the genre out of the shaded academic garden and into the sunlight of the forum by alluding to a large public world outside the poetic landscape, a world which made the practice of poetry possible. His introduction of allegory suggested to later practitioners of the

10. The Latin, as will be all quotations from Virgil, is cited from *P. Vergili Maronis Opera,* ed. R.A.B. Mynors (Oxford: Clarendon Press, 1969).

genre a way to save it from being consumed by its own preciosity. Milton's poem is the culmination of the Western pastoral tradition; Johnson's critique is a symptom—and perhaps even a principal cause—of its undoing.

Was Johnson correct to say of *Lycidas* that "its form is that of a pastoral, easy, vulgar, and therefore disgusting"?[11] By "easy" Johnson, in this instance, probably intended what the word means to us today: that which does not require much labor. But "easy" poetry could, for Johnson, be an object of his approval, for in *Idler* 77 he praised "easy" poetry for its plain-style Horatian quality of conversational suppleness and criticized the contrasting quality of unnecessary epic inflation. By "vulgar" he meant "common" rather than crude, and by "disgusting" he meant "displeasing." Since, for Johnson, freshness and originality were essential qualities of good poetry, to write in the hackneyed pastoral genre was to guarantee that a poet would fail to evoke any feelings beyond the conventional; since art demands a degree of originality, an evocation of the unexpected (which, as Aristotle frequently remarked, is the cause of pleasure), the pastoral will fail to please: it will be, in other words, "disgusting." One important source of pleasure, for Johnson, was novelty or variety, and pastoral had by the eighteenth century become so conventional and predictable—so common or "vulgar"—that only very limited pleasure, from Johnson's point of view, could be gained through it. Pope's *Pastorals,* for instance, are exquisite but predictable; as Johnson in the *Life of Pope* remarked in their defense: "To charge these *Pastorals* with want of invention is to require what was never intended."[12]

We must now consider Johnson's claim that the poem lacks sincerity. Perhaps we should hear Johnson's words themselves, for certainly in them sincerity and conviction are not lacking. *Lycidas,* Johnson writes, "is not to be considered as the effusion of real passion; for passion runs not after remote allusions and obscure opinions. Passion plucks no berries from the myrtle and ivy, nor calls upon Arethuse and Mincius, nor tells of 'rough satyrs and fauns with cloven heel.' Where there is leisure for fiction there is little grief."[13] One way to answer Johnson's objection is to suggest that he is inappropriately applying the critical doctrine of "sincerity" to a kind of poem that achieves its intended effects via a thoroughgoing conventionality.[14] And certainly in contrast to Johnson's own moving and deeply felt

---

11. *Lives of the English Poets,* ed. G. B. Hill, 3 vols. (Oxford: Clarendon Press, 1905), 1:163.
12. Ibid., 3:224.
13. Ibid., 1:163.
14. John Crowe Ransom discusses the impersonality of *Lycidas* in "A Poem Nearly Anonymous," *American Review* 4 (1933), 179–203; reprinted in *Milton's Lycidas,* ed. C. A. Patrides

elegy for Dr. Robert Levett, Milton's poem seems impersonal and even ostentatious. Where Johnson gives his readers a clear sense of Levett's character and virtues, Edward King remains completely anonymous.

It is true that Milton may not have known King very well. The actual degree of this kind of personal sorrow—a critique of Johnson's critique might well argue—is perhaps not entirely relevant. The occasion of the poem is familiar: Edward King died in a shipwreck on the Irish Seas in 1637. He was a classmate of Milton's at Cambridge and was preparing to take holy orders. When he died, some of his friends solicited elegies from various people and collected them in a single volume; Milton's *Lycidas* is one of these.

The best way to read the poem is, as Douglas Bush has suggested,[15] as a kind of trial by fire of Milton's religious faith, of his belief in divine providence and in Christian revelation. King was in this sense a figure precisely analogous to Milton: he was a poet, a virtuous man, and was studying for the priesthood (an occupation that Milton, perhaps at this very time, was considering). Is so virtuous a life worth all the trouble, if God can snuff it out in a moment? One of the things which lends to *Lycidas* its great power is Milton's close personal identification, not so much with King himself as with what King represents. He is, in other words, what T. S. Eliot referred to as an "objective correlative," in this case an objective correlative of Milton's projection of himself as poet/pastor.

Milton begins the poem with a lament over Lycidas's early death, then makes his identification with King explicit. Just as he is lamenting the death of his friend, Milton says,

> So may som gentle Muse
> With lucky words favor my destin'd urn,
> And as he passes turn,
> And bid fair peace be to my sable shrowd.
>
> (19–22)

And the poem continues—in a passage that imitates sections of Theocritus's first *Idyll* and Virgil's tenth *Eclogue*—but in an angry vein:

(New York, 1961), 64–81. In *The Green Cabinet: Theocritus and the European Pastoral Lyric* (Berkeley and Los Angeles: University of California Press, 1969), Thomas G. Rosenmeyer suggests that this quality of anonymity is typical of the pastoral tradition from Theocritus onward.

15. *John Milton: A Sketch of His Life and Writings* (New York: Collier Books, 1967), 58–66.

Where were ye Nymphs when the remorseless deep
Clos'd o're the head of your lov'd *Lycidas?*
For neither were ye playing on the steep,
Where your old *Bards,* the famous *Druids,* ly,
Nor on the shaggy top of *Mona* high,
Nor yet where *Deva* spreads her wizard stream:
Ay me, I fondly dream!
Had ye bin there—for what could that have don?
What could the Muse herself that *Orpheus* bore,
The Muse herself, for her enchanting son
Whom Universal nature did lament,
When by the rout that made the hideous roar,
His goary visage down the stream was sent,
Down the swift *Hebrus* to the *Lesbian* shore.
    Alas! What boots it with uncessant care
To tend the homely slighted Shepherds trade,
And strictly meditate the thankless Muse.
Were it not better don as others use,
To sport with *Amaryllis* in the shade,
Or with the tangles of *Neaera's* hair?
Fame is the spur that the clear spirit doth raise
(That last infirmity of Noble mind)
To scorn delights, and live laborious dayes;
But the fair Guerdon when we hope to find,
And think to burst out into sudden blaze,
Comes the blind *Fury* with th'abhorred shears,
And slits the thin spun life.

(50–76)

King is here identified not only with Daphnis of ancient pastoral, but with Orpheus as well, the poet and singer par excellence. Should the poet then seek fame, Milton asks? But, he immediately answers, death may end life before fame is won. True fame is not earthly glory, but true and lasting fame in heaven.

Further testing of providence occurs in the poem. The poet then tries to find some natural cause for the death, but fails. Both water and air were calm on the day of the wreck. And then, when St. Peter remarks on how much more worthy was King was than so many of the clerics that at present infest his church, Milton is once again questioning the workings of God's providence. Even if Johnson had read the poem in this way—as an occasion of the testing of Milton's faith in God's divine providence via the death of King as an "objective correlative" for Milton's own career objectives and religious aspirations—it is likely that he would not have been persuaded of the poem's alleged greatness for at least two reasons.

First, such an argument would not have lessened the impression he received from the poem that the unfortunate King was not so much, for Milton, an actual human being who tragically suffered an untimely death by drowning as he was an opportunity for the young poet to exercise his eloquence. And there is much to be said for this claim. Milton's style, as Johnson remarks elsewhere, "was not modified by its subject."[16] Or, as Coleridge said of Milton—although with no adverse criticism intended—in his comparison of Shakespeare and Milton in the *Biographia Literaria:* whereas Shakespeare "darts himself forth, and passes into all the forms of human character and passion, the one Proteus of the fire and the flood," Milton "attracts all forms and things to himself, into the unity of his own IDEAL. All things and modes of action shape themselves anew in the being of MILTON; while SHAKESPEARE becomes all things, yet for ever remaining himself."[17] We have in Milton, in other words, the first example of what has been called the egotistical sublime. Milton's is indeed a strangely personal impersonal poetry, where the borderline between the poet and his subject matter is often blurred to the point of identity.

And, second, Johnson would have objected to the presumption of any poet who questioned the wisdom of divine providence, even if that poet concluded with an affirmation of faith.

The poem does indeed end with a final affirmation of belief in the triumph of immortality in the Christian sense. The list of flowers (132–53) that strew the hearse of Lycidas, Milton ironically remarks, is a mere fiction, for there was no hearse: the body was never found. Yet the mortal body is seen, in Christian terms, as unimportant. As Daphnis in Virgil's fifth *Eclogue* is transported to heaven and becomes divine, so Lycidas is apotheosized as "the Genius of the shore" (183), a symbol of the Christian notion of death as rebirth.

Does the ending work? It certainly did not for Johnson. Not only did Milton's poem, for Johnson, lack novelty and sincerity, as we have seen, but

16. *Lives of the English Poets,* 1:190.
17. *Biographia Literaria,* ed. James Engell and W. Jackson Bate, 2 vols. (Princeton: Princeton University Press, 1983), 2:27–28.

it had "yet a grosser fault"—the mingling of "trifling fictions" with "the most awful and sacred truths, such as ought never to be polluted with such irreverent combinations." Johnson continues: "The shepherd likewise is now a feeder of sheep, and afterwards an ecclesiastical pastor, a superintendent of a Christian flock. Such equivocations are always unskillful; but here they are indecent, and at last approach to impiety, of which, however, I believe the writer not to have been conscious."[18] What Johnson is objecting to in general is true of this passage. Milton has mingled a trifling fiction—in this case the hackneyed pastoral convention of the resurrection of the drowned Lycidas as the "Genius of the shore" who will somehow watch over and protect all those "that wander in that perilous flood"—with the most awful and sacred truth of the resurrection of Christ.

It is the mingling of Christianity and paganism that Johnson objects to here. Shelley in his *Adonais* is in this sense more consistent, for in his elegy for Keats his contention that the dead poet receives a kind of immortality by becoming one with the universe is truer to the pantheistic vision of ancient pastoral elegy than is the Christian vision of Milton. But even if Milton had composed a more consistently coherent allegory, such religious allegory would not necessarily have pleased Johnson, who believed that religious truths were too lofty for poetic ornamentation. The pastoral genre, however, if it is denied an allegorical dimension, may well revert to the kind of preciosity we discussed earlier and that Longinus criticized in his treatise on poetic elevation. Once Christian belief begins to wane, or once it is considered irreverent or superfluous for poets to allude to Christian beliefs in the predominantly secular mode of poetry, then the allegorical or religious significance of pastoral begins to disappear. By the early eighteenth century, pastorals had become completely secularized; they were once again pure art, and they could be found "disgusting" (or displeasing) to great critics because they had nothing new in them. Nor were pastorals such as Pope's— exquisitely crafted though they might be—redeemed by allusions to history or to political realities, such as we find in Virgil's *Eclogues*.

Pastoral, then, did become "easy, vulgar, and therefore disgusting" by Johnson's time. Probably the most successful of pastorals from the early eighteenth century are antipastoral pastorals, poems which spoof the pastoral genre as being mere escapism and contrast pastoral fantasies with the harsh realities such fantasies attempt to evade. One of the most brilliant of these antipastorals is John Gay's *Shepherd's Week* (first published in 1714).

18. *Lives of the English Poets,* 1:165.

The shepherds of Pope's *Pastorals* (1709) spoke in elegant, polished Augustan English. But did they sound rustic? Did they evoke the "primitive" feeling of Theocritus's own pastorals? Gay's poems present examples of English poetry that delicately violate Augustan decorum, using the kind of "low" words that Pope had shunned. What Gay gives his reader is a delicately indelicate rendition of the crude realities of country life, not an idealized world. Gay in fact reminds one of Robert Wells's observation, made in the introduction to his translation of Theocritus, that "inherent in bucolic poetry is the paradox of a graceful clumsiness,"[19] although Gay's intentions are more directly and consistently humorous than those of Theocritus. And although Gay invites allegorical interpretation by depicting the days of the shepherds' week—thus recalling Spenser's allegorical *Shepheardes Calender*—his poems defy such interpretation. Consider, for example, the introductory lines of "Monday; or, the Squabble," the "squabble" being Gay's satiric equivalent of the *carmen amoebaeum*; the characters are Lobbin Clout, Cuddy, and Cloddipole:

> *LOBBIN CLOUT.*
> Thy Younglings, *Cuddy,* are but just awake,
> No Thrustles shrill the Bramble-Bush forsake,
> No chirping Lark the Welkin sheen invokes,
> No Damsel yet the swelling Udder strokes;
> O'er yonder Hill does scant the Dawn appear,
> Then why does *Cuddy* leave his Cott, so rear?

> *CUDDY.*
> Ah *Lobbin Clout!* I ween, my Plight is guest,
> For *he that loves, a Stranger is to Rest;*
> *If Swains belye not, thou has prov'd the Smart,*
> And *Blouzelinda's* Mistress of thy Heart.
> This rising rear betokeneth well thy Mind.
> Those Arms are folded for thy *Blouzelind.*
> And well, I trow, our piteous Plights agree,
> Thee *Blouzelinda* smites, *Buxoma* me.

19. *The Idylls of Theocritus,* 29. As Margaret Doody reminds us, "Gay's affection for Theocritus, who is quoted in the 'Proeme' [to *The Shepherd's Week*], seems genuine" (*The Daring Muse: Augustan Poetry Reconsidered* [Cambridge: Cambridge University Press, 1984], 107).

LOBBIN CLOUT.

Ah *Blouzelind!* I love thee more by half,
Than Does their Fawns, or Cows the new-fall'n Calf:
Woe worth the Tongue! may Blisters sore it gall,
That names *Buxoma, Blouzelind* withal.[20]

The contrast Gay achieves in these poems between delicacy of form and
crudeness (though a sensual crudeness, utterly unlike Swift's, or even that of
the more delicate Pope in his bitter satirical poems) of content is masterful:
"No chirping Lark the Welkin sheen invokes, / No Damsel yet the swelling
Udder strokes." Here we have juxtaposed the delicate and the gross: "chirping Lark" juxtaposed with the lumbering because antiquated phrase "Welkin
sheen" ("shining sky"); the delicate "Damsel" whom Gay depicts stroking
the "swelling Udder" of a cow. Only in an age when the rules governing
stylistic decorum were so clearly defined—"swelling Udders" will not appear in lofty heroic verse of the English Augustan period—could such have
been wrought. But the brilliance of the parody suggests that the form paro-
died is dead.

J. V. Cunningham's "Montana Pastoral" *and the Pastoral Tradition*

The form comes alive again in "Montana Pastoral" by J. V. Cunningham, but
in a way that once again suggests that—paradoxically—it is lifeless. Cunningham himself states the principles by which his poem may be perhaps
best apprehended. In a brief and typically incisive statement of his views
on what constitutes graduate training in English, Cunningham explained
what he took to be the proper way to pursue literary scholarship. "If what I
read has any real reference," Cunningham writes, "I should know something of the referent. We call this history. If the referent is, in part, as it is in
Lycidas, prior literature, I should know that. We call this literary history."[21]
Cunningham, who was a professional scholar of the Renaissance, seems to
have known *Lycidas* well. And he also knew the prior literature to which

---

20. John Gay, *The Shepherd's Week* (London, 1714).
21. "Graduate Training in English," in *The Collected Essays of J. V. Cunningham* (Chicago:
Swallow, 1976), 272–73.

Lycidas refers. He was, in other words, familiar with the literary history that makes up the pastoral tradition. "Montana Pastoral" is written, in its own unique way, in the pastoral tradition of *Lycidas* and its antecedents. The poem is, moreover, an antipastoral in the general spirit of Samuel Johnson's critique of *Lycidas.* Since the poem is an implicit rejection of the often effete formalism characteristic of the genre since its inception in Alexandrian Greece, a discussion of "Montana Pastoral" presents itself as a fitting conclusion to this chapter.

Here is the poem:

> I am no shepherd of a child's surmises.
> I have seen fear where the coiled serpent rises,
>
> Thirst where the grasses burn in early May
> And thistle, mustard, and the wild oat stay.
>
> There is dust in this air. I saw in the heat
> Grasshoppers busy in the threshing wheat.
>
> So to this hour. Through the warm dusk I drove
> To blizzards sifting on the hissing stove,
>
> And found no images of pastoral will,
> But fear, thirst, hunger, and this huddled chill.[22]

The poem's organization is tight and very clear: it consists of five stanzas, each comprised of a single couplet. The final couplet recapitulates the poem's principle of organization when the poet states that in his recollection of the Montana landscape he has "found no images of pastoral will, / But fear, thirst, hunger, and this huddled chill." The subject of the first stanza is "fear," evoked by the "coiled serpent." The subject of the second stanza is "thirst," evoked by "the grasses" that "burn in early May." "Hunger" is the subject of the more difficult third stanza, where the poet sees "in the heat / Grasshoppers busy in the threshing wheat." To "thresh" is to separate the grains of a cereal from the husk, and "threshing wheat" is wheat that is in the process of being threshed. But it is being threshed not by farmers but by "grasshoppers" and the presence of these devastating locusts means the destruction of the crop; hence, the subject of this stanza is the "hunger" that will result from this destruction. The subject of the fourth stanza is the

---

22. *The Exclusions of a Rhyme: Poems and Epigrams* (Denver: Swallow Press, 1960), 37.

"chill" of the Montana landscape during a snowstorm, a landscape that is no mere pastoral symbol of the icy indifference of a reluctant lover; it is a landscape that is actually inhabited by those who find themselves "huddled" around a stove for meager protection against savage blizzards.

By trying to place Cunningham's poem within the context of the pastoral tradition, I do not wish to create the impression that the poem is pedantically allusive in the tradition of Eliot's *Waste Land* or Pound's *Cantos.* Cunningham is not, in the manner of Eliot, pointing us to particular passages from previous poetry and then perhaps implicitly castigating us for our ignorance when the sources of these allusions are not immediately ringing in our ears. Cunningham is not that kind of poet. But Cunningham's poem does allude to the pastoral tradition through both specific details and in its general conception, and it behooves us to try to re-create a probable context for understanding the poem by reconstructing that context. Let us first attend to the details.

In Virgil's second *Eclogue,* the shepherd Corydon is pining away for love of Alexis and complains:

> O crudelis Alexi, nihil mea carmina curas?
> nil nostri miserere? mori me denique coges?
> nunc etiam pecudes umbras et frigora captant,
> nunc viridis etiam occultant spineta lacertos,
> Thestylis et rapido fessis messoribus aestu
> alia serpylumque herbas contundit olentis.
> at mecum raucis, tua dum vestigia lustro,
> sole sub ardenti resonant arbusta cicadis.
>
> (6–13)

[O cruel Alexis, don't you care for my songs?
Do you have no pity for me? Will you thus drive me to my
    death?
Now even the cows court the shade and cool places,
now the thorn-hedges conceal the green lizards,
and Thestylis, for those reapers wearied by the violent
    heat,
is crushing herbs redolent of garlic and thyme.
But as I pore over your footprints, along with my voice
the vineyards resound with the cicadas under the blazing
    sun.]

Cunningham, who was a fine Latinist, appears to have drawn on several of these conventional details of the pastoral tradition.

Now is the time to indulge in the amorous dalliances offered by the *otium* of bucolic peace, Corydon pleads to the reluctant Alexis, since "nunc viridis etiam occultant spineta lacertos" [now the thorn-hedges conceal the green lizards]. The feared "coiled serpent" of line 2 of *Montana Pastoral* is perhaps an ironic allusion to these harmless green lizards, who appear in other contexts of cool pastoral and amorous repose, as in Horace, *Carmina* 1.23.6–7. The more likely literary source of Cunningham's "coiled serpent" is, however, Virgil's *Eclogue* 3.93, where the shepherd Damoetas issues his warning, "frigidus, o pueri (fugite hinc!), latet anguis in herba" [Flee from here, boys; a chilly snake is hiding in the grass!] The third *Eclogue* is a typical pastoral singing match and here two rival shepherds, Damoetas and Menalcas, meet and challenge each other. Each shepherd speaks a set of two verses that is answered by the other in a corresponding set of two verses, in what is technically called, as I have mentioned, a *carmen amoebaeum.* It is in this context that Damoetas speaks his lines:

> Qui legitis flores et humi nascentia fraga,
> frigidus, o pueri (fugite hinc!), latet anguis in herba.
>
> (92–93)
>
> [You who pick flowers and strawberries that grow close
>   to the ground,
> Flee from here, boys; a chilly snake is hiding in the grass!]

The snake (*anguis*) mentioned by Damoetus is less important for the actual danger it poses than it is for the bravura of its artistic effect in the singing match, an effect that Menalcas attempts to counter in his reply. Damoetus urges the boys to *flee* because a snake lurks in the grass; Menalcas responds by urging the sheep to *stay* lest they wander too close to the river bank and fall over the edge into the water, as the ram himself has done. Cunningham's serpent, unlike Virgil's, is dangerously real. As the adjective "coiled" suggests, the "serpent" is not an artistic ploy but an imminent threat. Nor is Cunningham's "coiled serpent" the "snake" that the shepherd Thomalin fearfully—and mistakenly, as it turns out—

surmises to be "peeping close into the thicke" and "mouing of some quicke"[23] in Spenser's *March Aeglogue* from *The Shepheardes Calender* (73–74). The snake makes a late appearance in the pastoral tradition in Alexander Pope's *Summer: The Second Pastoral,* in which Alexis, pining away for love of Rosalinda, says, in an adaptation of *Eclogue* 3.93, "This harmless Grove no lurking Viper hides, / But in my Breast the Serpent Love abides" (67–68).

Later in our passage from *Eclogue* 2, Virgil goes on to say, "Thestylis et rapido fessis messoribus aestu / alia serpyllumque herbas contundit olentis" [and Thestylis, for those reapers wearied by the violent heat, is crushing herbs redolent of garlic and thyme] (10–11). In the second stanza of Cunningham's poem, the scorching heat (Virgil's "rapidus aestus") is no mere metaphor—as it chiefly is in Virgil—for the unrequited love of a surmised shepherd; the "grasses" that "burn in early May" are rather a literal fact that evokes for the poet the reality that drinking water is now a rare and precious commodity. And in Montana, as opposed to Virgil's Arcady, in place of the fragrant herbs and thyme ("serpyllumque herbas olentis"), one is presented with the less appetizing but persistent "thistle, mustard, and the wild oat." Such vegetation is also, of course, a stark contrast to the catalog of luscious flowers to be found in Milton's *Lycidas* (132–51) and to the vegetation of the Sicily of Theocritus's *Idylls,* for this Sicily was, as Erwin Panofsky in a well-known essay on the pastoral has remarked, "richly endowed with . . . flowery meadows, shadowy groves and mild breezes."[24]

The cicada is the insect long associated with pastoral leisure. It appears, for example, in Plato's *Phaedrus* (230c), when Socrates invites Phaedrus to join him for a philosophical discussion in the shade of a plane tree by a stream: "τὸ εὔπνουν τοῦ τόπου ὡς ἀγαπητόν καὶ σφόδρα ἡδύ· θερινόν τε καὶ λιγυρὸν ὑπηχεῖ τῷ τῶν τεττίγων χορῷ" [How satisfying and exceedingly sweet is the fragrance of the place; summer-like and shrilly it echoes with the cicada-choir]. The cicada (ὁ τέττιξ) can be heard later in Plato's dialogue (258e) and in Theocritus's *Idylls* (e.g., 5.29, 110), and it reappears at the conclusion of our passage from the *Eclogues* (2.12–13): "raucis . . .

23. *The Works of Edmund Spenser: The Minor Poems,* ed. C. G. Osgood and H. G. Lotspeich, 2 vols. (Baltimore: Johns Hopkins University Press, 1943), 1:32. All quotations from Spenser will be taken from this edition.

24. "*Et in Arcadia Ego:* Poussin and the Elegiac Tradition," in *Meaning in the Visual Arts: Papers in and on Art History* (New York: Anchor Press, 1955), 298.

sole sub ardenti resonant arbusta cicadis" [the vineyards resound with the cicadas under the blazing sun]. In Theocritus's *Idyll* 4.16, the cicada, as was proverbially held, feeds on dewdrops. These charming dew-eating cicadas of the pastoral tradition have become, in Cunningham's poem, those devouring locusts, the "Grasshoppers busy in the threshing wheat." And it is these that have taken the place of the human reapers (*messores*) of Virgil's *Eclogue* 2.10.

Cunningham's "grasshoppers" are, then, ominous descendents of the sweet-sounding cicadas of the pastoral tradition. But they are descendents, as well, of the ἄκρις or "locust," which, although often mentioned as similarly sweet-sounding and harmless (*Idylls* 5.32, 7.41), is occasionally depicted in Theocritean pastoral as dangerous to crops (*Idyll* 5.108), as they certainly are so depicted in Exodus 10.4, where Moses warns the Pharaoh that, if he refuses to let God's people go, the Lord will inflict a plague of locusts upon Egypt. In the Septuagint the Greek translation of the Hebrew word for locust is the same word (ἡ ἄκρις) that appears in *Idyll* 5.108.

The "blizzards" of the fourth stanza are not a metaphor for the hardened heart of the loved one who coolly rejects the lover's advances as in, for example, Gallus's lament for Lycoris in Virgil's tenth *Eclogue,* or of Alexis's for Rosalinda in Pope's *Summer,* in which Alexis complains, "The sultry *Sirius* burns the thirsty Plains, / While in thy Heart Eternal Winter reigns" (21–22). Nor are these "blizzards" strictly a symbol of a state of spiritual despair, as in the winter experienced by Colin Cloute in Spenser's *January Aeglogue.* There Colin laments:

> Thou barrein ground, whom winters wrath hath wasted,
> Art made a myrrhour, to behold my plight:
> Whilome thy fresh spring flowrd, and after hasted
> Thy sommer prowde with Daffadillies dight.
> And now is come thy wynters stormy state,
> Thy mantle mard, wherein thou maskedst late.
>
> Such rage as winters, reigneth in my heart,
> My life bloud friesing with vnkindly cold:
> Such stormy stoures do breede my baleful smart,
> As if my yeare were waste, and woxen old.
> And yet alas, but now my spring begonne,
> And yet alas, yt is already donne.
>
> (19–30)

The "blizzards" of "Montana Pastoral" are, rather, a terrible physical reality—with profound emotional consequences—for those who are forced to endure them.

In my analysis of Cunningham's poem I have so far discussed the details of the pastoral tradition. Informing this tradition in a more general sense was the myth of the death of Adonis, a myth which symbolized the decay of spring in the scorching midsummer heat. In Theocritus's first *Idyll*, for example, the passion of unrequited love withers the life of the shepherd Daphnis in the way the midsummer heat withers the blooming plants of spring. This analogy is made explicit in the final couplet—which I cited earlier—spoken by the rejected lover Alexis in Pope's *Summer:*

> On me Love's fiercer Flames for ever prey,
> By Night he scorches, as he burns by Day.
> (91–92)

Daphnis and Alexis are types of Adonis, and the death and resurrection of Adonis in the ancient East symbolized the cycle of the seasons, a cycle that Pope can still allude to in his four pastorals, "Spring," "Summer," "Autumn," and "Winter."

"Montana Pastoral" also alludes to this cycle of the seasons, each of which is suggested in the compass of this one brief poem. Yet these seasons do not divide the year with the clarity we are accustomed to find in the idealized pastoral tradition, for "There is dust in this air." The springtime alluded to in the "early May" of the second stanza—a springtime in which "the grasses burn"—more closely resembles the blistering heat of summer. The wheat that is usually harvested in autumn is, in the third stanza of the poem, being threshed—by locusts—"in the heat" one normally associates with summer. And shortly after the onset of "the warm dusk" in the fourth stanza, the "blizzards" usually inflicted by winter suddenly appear "sifting on the hissing stove," a reference, it would seem, to the dramatic and terrifying changes in weather one can experience in Montana. Here is a brutal climate that, in the concluding words of Cunningham's poem "August Hail," "Denies the season":

> In late summer the wild geese
> In the white draws are flying.
> The grain beards in the blue peace.
> The weeds are drying.

> The hushed sky breeds hail.
> Who shall revenge unreason?
> Wheat headless in the white flail
> Denies the season.

The cycle of the seasons, in traditional pastoral, symbolizes not only death but, more important, rebirth. The cycle of the seasons alluded to in "Montana Pastoral" is no romanticized image of "pastoral will"; it is, rather, a grim reminder of a different kind of eternity, one more akin to the "infinite regress" Cunningham speaks of in "The Phoenix":

> More than the ash stays you from nothingness!
> Nor here nor there is a consuming pyre!
> Your essence is in infinite regress
> That burns with varying consistent fire,
> Mythical bird that bears in burying!
>
> I have not found you in exhausted breath
> That carves its image on the Northern air,
> I have not found you on the glass of death
> Though I am told that I shall find you there,
> Imperturbable in the final cold,
>
> There where the North wind shapes white cenotaphs,
> There where snowdrifts cover the fathers' mound,
> Unmarked but for these wintry epitaphs,
> Still are you singing there without sound,
> Your mute voice on the crystal embers flinging.

The perverse and jumbled cycle of the seasons has, in "Montana Pastoral," always run its harsh and ineluctable course and continues—even now—to run its course: "So to this hour."

"Montana Pastoral," like other poems in the pastoral tradition, does not describe nature for its own sake. The details of the Montana landscape of the poet's youth are significant not for their merely descriptive value, but for their emotional resonance. "Montana Pastoral," Cunningham has written in *The Quest of the Opal,* is "a curt autobiography, . . . in which the details of fear, thirst, hunger, and the desperation of this huddled chill were hardly a just summary of [the poet's] first twenty years but rather an epigrammatic presentation of the salient motives those years communicated to his later life."[25] I have suggested that "the details of fear, thirst, hunger, and the desperation of this huddled chill" were mediated by the details of the pastoral tradition, and that a full reading of the poem asks that we apprehend it—as Cunningham has said in praise of a poem by Wallace Stevens—as "both modern and traditional."[26] "Montana Pastoral" has the elegiac tone of much of the pastoral tradition, and it is as carefully crafted as any Alexandrian poem. Its modernity consists, in large part, in its rejection of the idealization that often accompanied the pastoral genre from its Theocritean beginnings. By rejecting formalism for its own sake, Cunningham's poem is more of a classic—in my definition of that term—than many of the allegedly "classical" pastoral poems of Greece and Rome and the poems that less than critically follow this tradition.

25. *Collected Essays,* 418.
26. "Tradition and Modernity," in ibid., 242.

PART III

RESISTING THE DIDACTIC HERESY

10

THE AMBIVALENCE OF THE *AENEID* AND THE ECUMENIC AGE

Part 1 of this study was devoted to elucidating fundamental assumptions of classical *noēsis;* Part 2, to considering how formal beauty, while always a requirement of a classic work, is never the whole story. I discussed how literature in the classic sense has traditionally resisted reduction to the principle of formal beauty and coherence. In Part 3 I consider how literary works resist what Poe called "the heresy of 'the didactic' "[1]—the reduction

1. "The Poetic Principle" [delivered as a lecture in 1848 and 1849; published posthumously in 1850], in *Critical Theory Since Plato,* ed. Hazard Adams, rev. ed. (New York: Harcourt Brace Jovanovich, 1992), 577. Poe continues: "It has been assumed, tacitly and avowedly, directly and indirectly, that the ultimate object of all poetry is truth. Every poem, it is said, should inculcate a moral; and by this moral is the poetical merit of the work to be adjudged. . . . We have taken it

of literature, that is, to ideology, propaganda, or to some previously conceived abstract moral truth. The *Aeneid* was composed in order to glorify
the Rome of Augustus. Apuleius's *Metamorphoses* (or *The Golden Ass*) has
the avowed intention of persuading its audience to accept the "truth" of the
religion of Isis. Defoe in the preface to *Moll Flanders* insists that he has
written the book with the explicit intention of presenting a negative example to his readers so that they might live more pious lives. I shall argue that
each of these three authors subverts his explicitly avowed didactic aims.

I begin with Virgil's *Aeneid.* No work on the meaning of the classic can
overlook Virgil; for, as Eliot believed, if there ever were a classic author, then
that author must be Virgil. What made Virgil a classic for Eliot was, first,
Virgil's "maturity." In "What Is a Classic?" Eliot writes: "I shall distinguish
between the universal classic, like Virgil, and the classic which is only such
in relation to the other literature in its own language, or according to the
view of life of a particular period. A classic can only occur when a civilization is mature; when a language and a literature are mature; and it must be
the work of a mature mind."[2] What most of all made Virgil a classic for Eliot
was a quality that is related to this criterion of maturity: the Roman poet's
intuited sense of where he fit in the history of what was to become Western
European literature and Christendom. For Eliot, Virgil in effect made that
literature possible because he made the idea of Europe possible. This self-
sacrificing quality of Virgil as an author is, for Eliot, the culmination of Latin
literature itself, "a literature unconsciously sacrificing, in compliance to its
destiny in Europe, the opulence and variety of later tongues to produce, for
us, the classic."[3]

My own approach is less ambitious than Eliot's, and in some ways it is
antithetical to Eliot's view of what makes the *Aeneid* a classic. Much of the
nobility of the *Aeneid* results from our privileged position of knowing how
the Middle Ages, and Dante in particular, viewed Virgil. If we are chauvinis-
tic Westerners, then this is the poem that foretells our destiny as leaders of
the civilized world. If we are Christians, then this is a poem that foreshadows
the Christian empire. From the vantage point of post-Hegelian (including
postmodern) thought, however, what makes the work so appealing a classic

---

into our heads that to write a poem simply for the poem's sake, and to acknowledge such to
have been our design, would be to confess ourselves radically wanting in the true poetic
dignity and force" (ibid.).

2. *On Poetry and Poets* (London: Faber & Faber, 1957), 55.

3. Ibid., 70.

is how the grandiose historical claims in it are themselves so frequently undercut by the famous Virgilian pathos. I realize in saying this that I am speaking of what, in my personal judgment, makes the poem a classic in our time. And yet I would want to generalize from my own personal observations and state that it is not the obligation of literature in the classic sense to teach a specific moral lesson. As Yvor Winters observes in the forward to *In Defense of Reason,*[4] if we are to reduce literature to its moral content, then the question must be raised as to whether or not it would be more efficient to bypass literature altogether and go directly to ethical tracts for our moral edification. Moreover, Virgil himself knew nothing of Christianity, nor could he have predicted the birth of Europe from the idea of Rome. In this chapter I shall emphasize how much of what makes Virgil's poem so great—in fact, a classic—is the extreme qualification of its own ideological message, an ideological message that, until fairly recently, many readers took at face value. The great English neoclassical poets Dryden and Pope, for example, saw the *Aeneid* as essentially didactic in intention. For Dryden this was a positive quality. Pope was less charitable: "The *Aeneid* was evidently a party piece, as much as [Dryden's] *Absalom and Achitophel.* Virgil [was] as slavish a writer as any of the gazetteers. I have formerly said that Virgil wrote one honest line."[5] One of my purposes here is to point to those qualifications contained within the *Aeneid* that make the poem less of a party piece than Pope had believed.

Far more than by the Homeric poems, the Western epic tradition was influenced by, shaped by, the *Aeneid* of Virgil. The word "epic" and the name "Virgil" were, for the medieval, Renaissance, and Augustan periods, virtually synonymous—for several reasons. First, not many people—not even many educated people—could read Greek very well, and sometimes, as was the case with Dante, they could not read it at all. Second, many people who could read Greek, such as the famous Renaissance critic Julius Caesar Scaliger, felt that the Homeric poems, when compared with Virgil's, were barbaric in both style and content. The style, they felt, was crude and unrefined—ignorant as they were of the modern theories of oral composition and presumably unaware of Aristotle's distinction (*Rhetoric* 3.12) between the oral style (which is meant to be perceived at a distance, in which all refinements and niceties are lost) and the written style (which the eye may scrutinize at its leisure).

---

4. *In Defense of Reason* (New York: Swallow Press and William Morrow, 1947), 3–4.
5. Joseph Spence, *Observations, Anecdotes, and Characters of Books and Men,* ed. James M. Osborn, 2 vols. (Oxford: Clarendon Press, 1966), 1:229–30.

And such critics felt as well that Homer's heroes were crude and unrefined; Odysseus, they often remarked, was a wily opportunist and Achilles no more than a brutish killer. If asked about the twenty-fourth book of the *Iliad* and Homer's depiction of Achilles as a civilized man, even a philosopher, they would respond by saying that Achilles, by accepting Priam's many and luxurious gifts of ransom, was showing himself to be thoroughly mercenary. Aeneas, they would respond, would never comport himself in this manner. For them the real epic hero was not Achilles, not Odysseus, but Aeneas, the wanderer with a definite goal, who could not be accused, as could Odysseus, of loving wandering merely for wandering's sake; Aeneas was the warrior with a clearly defined social purpose.

Perhaps no one would have been more surprised at having become the inspiration and model of the Western epic tradition than the young Virgil himself. Publius Virgilius Maro was a man who by nature appears to have preferred the shaded repose of the academic garden to life in the glaring sunlight of the public forum. An ancient biographer, Donatus, tells us that Virgil was a student of the law. But to be an effective and successful pleader one would have to have been born more in the Ciceronian mold: robust, forthright, aggressive, worldly. A Cicero Virgil was not; his career as a pleader, according to Donatus,[6] was rather short-lived. He appeared before a jury exactly once, and then abandoned the public life for the academic garden: he turned his attention to philosophy and to poetry.

The poetry he wrote was not the poetry of the forum. Virgil began his poetic career as a follower in the Alexandrian tradition of Callimachus, a tradition whose slogan was μέγα βίβλιον μέγα κακόν [big book, big pain]. Callimachus, who lived about two hundred years before Virgil, rejected epic poetry and the themes associated with it in favor of the short, subtle, and original poem that deals with slighter and less pretentious subject matter. The best description of the kind of poem advocated by Callimachus is contained in the prologue to his *Aetia.* "I know that the Telchines, who are ignorant of the Muse and hardly her friends, grumble about my poetry because I did not accomplish the task of composing a single continuous song in thousands of lines on kings and heroes, but like a child I spin out a little story—although the decades of my life are not few. To these Telchines," Callimachus continues, "I say this":

---

6. See *Vita Donati* (50–51) in *Vitae Vergilianae Antiquae,* ed. Colin Hardie (Oxford: Clarendon Press, 1966), 9.

Away, Jealousy's destructive brood. Henceforth
judge poetry by its craft and not the Persian league;
don't seek from me the thumping song:
thunder is not my part, that is for Zeus.
The very first time I put the tablet on my knee
Apollo said to me, the Lupine god,
"Poet, let your sacrifice be as fat as you can,
but your muse, my friend, keep her slim.
This too I say: where the waggon does not trample
there you should tread, not by others' common tracks
nor the broad highway, but on unworn paths—
no matter that you take a narrower course."
Amongst those we sing who love the clear note
the cicada makes, not the uproar of the ass;
like the long-eared beast others may bray,
I would be slight, the winged one.[7]

Or as Ezra Pound, impersonating the Callimachean Propertius, says in the
first poem of the *Homage to Sextus Propertius:*

> Out-weariers of Apollo will, as we know, continue their
> > Martian generalities,
> > > We have kept our erasers in order. . . .
>
> Annalists will continue to record Roman reputations,
> Celebrities from the Trans-Caucasus will belaud Roman
> > celebrities
> And expound the distentions of Empire,
> But for something to read in normal circumstances?
> For a few pages brought down from the forked hill
> > unsullied?
> > I ask a wreath which will not crush my head.[8]

7. The section in verse is translated by Anthony Bulloch, "Hellenistic Poetry," in *The Cambridge History of Classical Literature,* vol. 1, *Greek Literature,* ed. P. E. Easterling and B.M.W. Knox (Cambridge: Cambridge University Press, 1985), 559. The prose translation of the Greek, as contained in *Callimachus: Aetia, Iambi, Hecale, and other Fragments,* ed. C. A. Trypanis (Cambridge: Harvard University Press, 1958), is my own. The prose section translates lines 1–7; Bulloch's translates lines 17–32. The Greek text is fragmentary.

8. *Collected Shorter Poems* (London: Faber & Faber, 1968), 225.

A true believer in the Callimachean manifesto, then, would not write an *Aeneid,* for that would be a continuous poem of many thousands of lines on kings and heroes. And there was no path wider or more heavily traveled than the path beaten by Homeric epic. The Callimachean poet writing Latin verse in Virgil's time would avoid, at all costs, braying like an ass. The last thing he would try to write would be a patriotic epic with a heavy didactic message, a Roman stars and stripes.

He might rather retreat to the academic garden and begin his serious poetic career by writing a group of short pastoral poems modeled on the *Idylls* of Theocritus. He might, in other words, write the *Eclogues* or *Bucolics.* In the seventh of his *Idylls* Theocritus had declared his allegiance to the Callimachean creed. And Virgil, in the opening lines of his sixth *Eclogue,* declares, in the person of Tityrus, his own allegiance to this creed. The lines are in fact virtually a translation of Callimachus's *Aetia:*

> Prima Syracosio dignata est ludere versu
> nostra neque erubuit silvas habitare Thalea.
> cum canerem reges et proelia, Cynthius aurem
> velit et admonuit: 'pastorem, Tityre, pinguis
> pascere oportet ovis, deductum dicere carmen.'
> nunc ego (namque super tibi erunt qui dicere laudes,
> Vare, tuas cupiant et tristia condere bella)
> agrestem tenui meditabor harundine Musam.

[My earliest muse saw fit to play with light Sicilian verse. She dwelt among the woods, and did not blush for that. Later, when kings and battles filled my thoughts (i.e. when I began to think about writing an epic), Apollo plucked my ear and gave me his advice. "Tityrus," he said, "a shepherd ought to let his sheep grow fat, but court a slender Muse." Now, Varius, since plenty of poets will volunteer to sing your praises and to compose sad and serious chronicles of war, I will take up my slender (*tenuis*), rustic reed.][9]

No kings or battles for Virgil; his was the slender, Callimachean muse. And in his next major poem, the *Georgics,* he remains true to his Callimachean principles. The *Georgics* is a longer work, a didactic poem on farming in four

---

9. Translation adapted from that of E. V. Rieu, *Virgil: The Pastoral Poems* (Harmondsworth, Middlesex: Penguin, 1949), 53.

books, but is the kind of longer poem of which Callimachus would have approved. It was, in the manner of the collective poem of Hesiod admired by Callimachus, avowedly not "a single, continuous poem" or narrative. And its subject was not war, rulers, or kings.

The *Eclogues* were published in 37 B.C., the *Georgics* some eight years later (around 29 B.C.). Then Virgil began to write, probably at Augustus's behest, an epic poem in praise of the Roman Empire. Callimachus would not have been pleased. Virgil had, it is true, praised Rome in his poems before. The *Georgics* virtually begins with a panegyric to Augustus, a panegyric that is expanded at the beginning of book 3; and there is some political allegory even in Virgil's earlier *Eclogues*. But now Virgil was to devote an entire poem to this end of praising Rome. The poet who had sung the praises of the rustic life was now about to enter the forum once again.

From the Middle Ages through the nineteenth century, the *Aeneid* was read as the perfect epic poem; Aeneas was seen as the perfect hero; Virgil was viewed as one who deeply and without reservations believed in the Roman Empire, in its goals and aspirations. And there is much in the poem to support this view. But it is also, in some ways, a prejudiced view, for such readers tended to interpret the poem in ways that confirmed their own beliefs and aspirations. The Middle Ages, for example, saw in Aeneas the prototype of Christ, a man who sacrificed himself for the good of his nation; and the center of this nation happened to be Rome, which would become the seat of the papacy and hence the center of the Christian world.

It is largely for this reason that Dante chose Virgil as his guide in *The Divine Comedy*. And in the Renaissance poets wanted to write poems that would, above all, inspire men to perform noble actions. To model yourself on the behavior of Achilles or even Odysseus was a dangerous thing to do. When young people read or listen to literature read aloud, Plato argued in the third book of the *Republic*, they would, he felt, be encouraged to imitate the heroes whose actions were represented in the work. If impressionable minds were to read the *Iliad*, for example, they might be encouraged to imitate the often disreputable behavior of Achilles. Literature, therefore, Plato suggests, should either be censored or removed from the curriculum entirely.

And many of the writers of Renaissance epic tacitly agreed with Plato's objections. Homer's Achilles could not be appropriated for this purpose; Odysseus was a more promising candidate, but he was still a questionable model for an earnest Christian, unless the poem were read allegorically. But

Aeneas was a man remarkable for his *pietas,* for his deep sense of moral responsibility both to his fellow men and to the gods; and Aeneas was thus eminently adaptable to the aims of the writers and critics of Renaissance epic. The view of Sir Philip Sidney in the sixteenth century is typical. Heroic or epic poetry, Sidney writes in his *Apology for Poetry,* is the noblest kind of poetry because "the lofty image" of the epic hero "inflameth the kind with desire to be worthy." Sidney continues:

> Only let *Aeneas* be worn in the tablet of your memory; how he gouerneth himselfe in the ruine of his Country; in the preseruing his old Father, and carrying away his religious ceremonies; in obeying the Gods commandement to leaue *Dido,* though not onely all passionate kindnes, but euen the humane consideration of vertuous gratefulnes, would haue craued other of him; how in storms, howe in sports, howe in warre, howe in peace, howe a fugitiue, how victorious, how besiedged, how besiedging, howe to strangers, howe to allyes, how to enemies, howe to his owne; lastly, how in his inward selfe, and how in his outward gouernment; and I thinke, in a minde not preiudiced with a preiudicating humour, hee will be found in excellencie fruitefull, yea, euen as *Horace* sayth,
>> *Melius Chrisippo et Crantore.*[10]

So Spenser in *The Faerie Queene* models Sir Guyon of book 2 in part upon Virgil's Aeneas. Spenser's poem, as a Renaissance courtesy book, is meant to inculcate into its readers the twelve moral virtues, which medieval commentaries on the *Nicomachean Ethics* had attributed to Aristotle. Each of the projected twelve books (of which six were actually completed) was meant to inculcate one of these virtues by representing, in each of these books, the actions of a hero who embodies it. The second book, for example, concerns the virtue of temperance and the hero who represents this trait is Sir Guyon, who is in many ways modeled on Virgil's Aeneas.

In the nineteenth and twentieth centuries Virgil's poem had among its defenders the descendents of the idealist/didactic Renaissance view: Aeneas, these readers believe, represents the civilized values of the Augustan age, *ratio, humanitas,* and *pietas,* and in this sense he indeed offers a model for all civilized people to imitate. "I have read," C. S. Lewis writes, that Virgil's Aeneas

---

10. *The Apology for Poetry,* in *Elizabethan Critical Essays,* ed. G. G. Smith, 2 vols. (1904; rpt., London: Oxford University Press, 1971), 1:179–80.

is hardly the shadow of a man beside Homer's Achilles. But a man is precisely what he is: Achilles had been little more than a passionate boy. You may, of course, prefer the poetry of spontaneous passion to the poetry of passion at war with vocation, and finally reconciled. Every man to his taste. But we must not blame the second for not being the first. With Virgil European poetry grows up. For there are certain moods in which all that had gone before seems, as it were, boys' poetry, depending both for its charm and for its limitations on a certain naivety.[11]

So much for the idealists, whose view of the poem was challenged by those who believed that Virgil, in his heart of hearts, simply could not wholeheartedly embrace the aims of the Roman Empire. The *Aeneid,* they claimed, is more than a profoundly ambiguous work; it consistently subverts its avowed intentions. If Virgil was so unqualifiedly pro-Augustan, readers in this tradition of interpretation have asked, why does Virgil present Aeneas as such a cad in his behavior toward Dido in book 4? Why also does Virgil not only end Aeneas's trip to the underworld in book 6 with the sad reference to the early death of Marcellus, but then have the supposedly rejuvenated hero leave the underworld not through the Gate of Horn, but rather through the Gate of Ivory—the Gate of False Dreams? And why, finally, does the poem end on so dissonant a chord? Aeneas wins the hand of Lavinia. The work does not, however, end with their marriage, but rather, with Aeneas poised over the body of his enemy Turnus who, having just begged for Aeneas's mercy, receives instead Aeneas's sword through his chest while *cum gemitu fugit indignata sub umbras* [with a groan his spirit, disdainful, fled to the shades below]. Which reading of the poem best represents Virgil's own intentions, the idealistic or the cynical? Was Virgil a propagandist or a subversive?[12] As Philip R. Hardie observes, "modern criticism of the *Aeneid* has

11. "Virgil and the Subject of Secondary Epic," in *A Preface to Paradise Lost* (Oxford: Oxford University Press, 1942), 37.
12. The ominous side of the *Aeneid* is well brought out in W. R. Johnson, *Darkness Visible* (Berkeley and Los Angeles: University of California Press, 1975), and A. J. Boyle, "The Meaning of the *Aeneid:* A Critical Inquiry," *Ramus* 1 (1972): 63–90. A recent attempt to make what I have called the "idealist" case is Phillip Hardie, *Virgil's Aeneid: Cosmos and Imperium* (London: Oxford University Press, 1986). In *Virgil* (London: Oxford University Press, 1986), Jasper Griffin offers a balanced view that draws attention to the ambiguity of the *Aeneid.* Also notable for its balanced view is G. B. Conte, *The Rhetoric of Imitation: Genre and Poetic Memory in Virgil and Other Latin Poets* (Ithaca: Cornell University Press, 1986), edited and with a foreword by Charles Segal; chapters 5 through 7 deal specifically with the *Aeneid.* Conte's work is

largely structured itself around two opposing assessments of the poem, which see it as either a panegyric of Rome and its hero, Augustus, or as a tragedy of the individual caught up in the remorseless processes of history; an epic of optimism or an epic of pessimism."[13]

I would like to look closely at the three scenes mentioned above— Aeneas's parting from Dido, the ending of Aeneas's trip to the underworld, and the death of Turnus—and to offer a reading that tries to mediate between the extremes I have described. In trying to understand Virgil I shall be seeking help from some of his translators and from political theory. I shall conclude the chapter by attempting to analyze some aspects of Virgil's political theory and to account for the poem's ambivalences—the poet's way of resisting the didactic heresy—as resulting, in part, from problems associated with this political theory.

First of all, Dido and Aeneas. The idealists, such as Sidney, see this episode as a clear example of Aeneas's piety, of his determination to follow the commands of the gods at the expense of his personal pleasure. Dido represents a conglomeration of all the female temptors of Odysseus. She threatens Aeneas not by offering him eternal life, as Calypso had offered Odysseus, but rather by nearly upsetting the plan to found the Roman Empire. And Dido has almost gotten her way when Mercury reminds Aeneas that Jupiter has other plans for him. Mercury finds the Trojan hero "founding towers and building houses anew" [Aenean fundantem arces ac tecta novantem / conspicit] (4.260–61).

Aeneas, of course, decides (if that is the right word) to leave Dido after the promptings of Mercury. A heroic victory over the forces of temptation, the idealists would say. Aeneas is here forgoing his personal pleasure in order to found the Roman Empire. Before Jupiter sends down the messenger of the gods in order to prod Aeneas into action, he asks Mercury

> si nulla accendit tantarum gloria rerum
> nec super ipse sua molitur laude laborem,
> Ascanione pater Romanas invidet arces?
>   (4.232–34)

---

extremely sensitive to how Virgil uses allusions (especially to Homer) to establish a tone that mediates between the extremes of political propaganda and subversiveness. A sensitivity to the formal complexities of the poem must, however, be supplemented by a discussion of political philosophy, since the poem explicitly addresses this subject.

13. *Virgil's Aeneid: Cosmos and Imperium,* 1.

[if the glory of such great achievements does not inspire him, if he is not moved to exert himself to preserve his own reputation, will he, as a father, deny his son what is to become the Roman city?]

If Jupiter gives such a command, the idealists say, it must be right and it must be obeyed. Certainly the words of Jupiter in John Dryden's version would tend to confirm this view:

> "Go, mount the Western Winds, and cleave the Skie;
> Then, with a swift descent, to *Carthage* fly:
> There find the *Trojan* Chief, who wastes his Days
> In sloathful Riot and inglorious Ease,
> Nor minds the future City, giv'n by Fate;
> To him this Message from my Mouth relate:
> 'Not so fair *Venus* hop'd, when twice she won
> Thy Life with Pray'rs, nor promis'd such a Son.
> Hers was a Heroe, destin'd to command
> A Martial Race, and rule the *Latian* Land;
> Who shou'd his ancient Line from *Teucer* draw;
> And, on the conquered World, impose the Law.'
> If Glory cannot move a Mind so mean,
> Nor future Praise from fading Pleasure wean,
> Yet why should he defraud his Son of Fame,
> And grudge the *Romans* their Immortal Name!
> What are his vain Designs? what hopes he more
> From his long ling'ring on a hostile Shore?
> Regardless to redeem his Honour lost,
> And for his Race to gain th' *Ausonian* Coast?
> Bid him with Speed the *Tyrian* Court forsake;
> With this Command the slumb'ring Warrior wake."[14]

Aeneas "remains waiting in Tyrian Carthage" [Tyria Karthagine . . . exspectat] (224–25), Virgil says. Dryden's moral judgment is more severe; Aeneas, for Dryden, "wastes his Days / In sloathful Riot and inglorious Ease."[15]

14. Dryden's translation of the *Aeneid* is cited from vols. 5 and 6 of *The Works of Virgil in English 1697,* ed. William Frost and Vinton A. Daring (Berkeley and Los Angeles: University of California Press, 1987). This passage (lines 328–49) is from 5:462–63.

15. Dryden, in his translation, is more didactic than Virgil. Cf. Dryden's translation of *Aeneid* 4:220–21. In the original, Virgil says that Jupiter, having been made aware of Aeneas's tarrying

But part of what complicates Virgil's moral judgment of the Dido and Aeneas affair is that Dido is Virgil's re-creation not only of the female temptresses of the *Odyssey*—of Calypso, of Circe, of the Sirens—but also of Nausikaa, for it is Dido who, like Nausikaa, first receives the hero after he has been battered by the sea in the aftermath of many adventures and just before he is about to sail home (Italy will be Aeneas's new home). Virgil stresses the similarities between the two heroines in the beautiful simile with which he introduces his readers to Dido. Aeneas, inside the walls of the temple, has been gazing at the murals depicting the mournful scenes of the Trojan War when Dido appears:

> regina ad templum, forma pulcherrima Dido,
> incessit magna iuvenum stipante caterva.
> qualis in Eurotae ripis aut per iuga Cynthi
> exercet Diana choros, quam mille secutae
> hinc atque hinc glomerantur Oreades; illa pharetram
> fert umero gradiensque deas supereminet omnis
> (Latonae tacitum pertemptant gaudia pectus:)
> talis erat Dido, talem se laeta ferebat
> per medios instans operi regnisque futuris.
>
> (1.496–504)

> [The queen paced toward the temple in her beauty.
> Dido, with a throng of men behind.
> As on Eurotas bank or Cynthus ridge
> Diana trains her dancers, and behind her

---

in Carthage, "oculosque ad moenia torsit / regia et oblitos melioris amantis" [turned his eyes toward the royal walls and the lovers who had become forgetful of their nobler fame]. The phrase "oblitos famae melioris amantis" Dryden judgmentally renders with the following: Jupiter, having "cast his Eyes on *Carthage,* found / The lustful Pair in lawless pleasure drown'd: / Lost in their Loves, insensible of Shame; / And both forgetful of their better Fame" (322–25). As Robin Sowerby has remarked in the introduction to his edition of Dryden's *Aeneid,* "It is a criticism of Dryden's translation that he has ironed out basic ambiguities that are present not merely as nuances in particular passages ... but in the larger meaning of the whole poem" (*Dryden's Aeneid: A Selection and Commentary* [Bristol: Bristol Classical Press, 1986], 19). Dryden sees the poem as essentially an encomium to Augustus, who he believed was represented by Aeneas. Steven Zwicker discusses how Dryden's politics find their way into the poet's translation of the *Aeneid* in *Politics and Language in Dryden's Poetry* (Princeton: Princeton University Press, 1984), esp. chap. 6. See also James A. Winn, *John Dryden and His World* (New Haven: Yale University Press, 1957), 486–92.

On every hand the mountain nymphs appear,
A myriad converging; with her quiver
Slung on her shoulders, in her stride she seems
The tallest, taller by a head than any,
And joy pervades Latona's quiet heart:
So Dido seemed, in such delight she moved
Amid her people, cheering on the toil
Of a kingdom in the making.][16]

Virgil's simile is drawn from *Odyssey* 6. Before she spots Odysseus, Nausikaa and her female attendants come down to shore to wash some clothes, picnic, and then play by the water:

αὐτὰρ ἐπεὶ σίτου τάρφθεν δμῳαί τε καὶ αὐτή
σφαίρῃ ταί γ᾽ ἄρα παῖζον, ἀπὸ κρήδεμνα βαλοῦσαι·
τῇσι δὲ Ναυσικάα λευκώλενος ἄρχετο μολπῆς.
οἵη δ᾽ Ἄρτεμις εἶσι κατ᾽ οὔρεα ἰοχέαιρα,
ἢ κατὰ Τηΰγετον περιμήκετον ἢ Ἐρύμανθον,
τερπομένη κάπροισι καὶ ὠκείῃς ἐλάφοισι.
τῇ δέ θ᾽ ἅμα νύμφαι, κοῦραι Διὸς αἰγιόχοιο,
ἀγρονόμοι παίζουσι—γέγηθε δέ τε φρένα Λητώ—
πασάων δ᾽ ὑπὲρ ἥ γε κάρη ἔχει ἠδὲ μέτωπα,
ῥεῖά τ᾽ ἀριγνώτη πέλεται, καλαὶ δέ τε πᾶσαι.
ὣς ἥ γ᾽ ἀμφιπόλοισι μετέπρεπε παρθένος ἀδμής.

[Princess and maids delighted in that feast;
then, putting off their veils,
they ran and passed a ball to a rhythmic beat,
Nausikaa flashing first with her white arms.
So Artemis goes flying after her arrows flown
down some tremendous valley-side—Taygetos,
    Erymanthos—
chasing the mountain goats or ghosting deer,
with nymphs of the wild places flanking her;
for, taller by a head than nymphs can be,

16. The translator here is Robert Fitzgerald (New York: Random House, 1984), who is sensitive to the Virgilian pathos and ambivalences. Unless otherwise stated, the English translation of the *Aeneid* cited in the remainder of this chapter will be his.

the goddess shows more stately, all being beautiful.
So one could tell the princess from the maids.]

$$(6.99-109)^{17}$$

The passage from Virgil, when viewed in the light of its Homeric model, is deeply portentous. Homer most innocently compares the beautiful unmarried Nausikaa to Diana, the chaste goddess. Dido, it is true, may also be compared to Diana in the sense that, since the death of her husband Sychaeus, she has perforce been chaste, but what establishes that typically Virgilian tone of tragic pathos is that *this* Diana is about to meet the lover who will cost her both her chastity and her life.

And how does Aeneas treat this Nausikaa? It is difficult to say just how Aeneas could have gracefully and tactfully broken the news to Dido that, as the future father of the Roman race, he must leave her, but Aeneas does not come off particularly well. As Dryden mentions in the introduction to his translation, even Segrais—Virgil's staunch defender and seventeenth-century French translator—confessed that "he might have shewn a little more sensibility when he left her; for that had been according to his Character."[18] In the difficult speech he must make to Dido he starts off well, sounding like a lover: "I never shall deny all you can say, / Your majesty," he tells her, "of what you meant to me. / Never will the memory of Elissa / Stale for me, while I can still remember / My own life, and the spirit rules my body" [negabo / promeritam, nec me meminisse pigebit Elissae / dum memor ipse mei, dum spiritus hos regit artus] (4.334–36). But Aeneas then begins speaking legalese: "pro re pauca loquor" (concerning this matter, this *res,* 337), I will say a few things. A *res* is, technically in this context, the subject matter of an accusation in court. This legalistic tone is caught by two of Virgil's modern translators. Rolfe Humphries has his Aeneas say, "I have a point or two to make."[19] And one of Virgil's more recent translators, Allen Mandelbaum, makes the legal connotations fully explicit: "I'll speak brief words that fit the case."[20]

Aeneas then goes on to defend himself against the accusation (Dryden's

17. The Greek is cited from the Oxford Classical Text. The translator, again, is Fitzgerald (New York: Doubleday, 1963). Unless otherwise stated, the English translations of the *Iliad* and the *Odyssey* will be those of Fitzgerald.

18. *Dedication of the Aeneis,* in *The Works of Dryden,* ed. Earl Miner (Berkeley and Los Angeles: University of California Press, 1969), 5:296.

19. *The Aeneid of Virgil,* trans. Rolfe Humphries (New York: Scribner's, 1951), 99.

20. *The Aeneid of Virgil,* trans. Allen Mandelbaum (New York: Bantam, 1972), 92.

Aeneas says, "This only let me speak in my defense") that he, Aeneas, had deceived Dido: "Do not think / I meant to be deceitful and slip away" [neque ego hanc abscondere furto / speravi (ne finge) fugam, 4.337–38], he declares to her, a few moments after he had told his men to make ready the ships but to conceal—the word in Latin is *dissimulent* (4.291)—the true reasons for their preparations. Do this, Aeneas told them, while I (in Mandelbaum's translation) "try out approaches, seek the most tactful time for speech, [quis rebus dexter modus] whatever dextrous way might suit my case" (4.294). In his translation Dryden has attempted to tone down what he might have felt was Aeneas's opportunism, and to stress that it is fate and not personal choice that has brought Aeneas to do what he must do. Dryden's Aeneas says that it is his intention "to move" Dido's "tender Mind, by slow degrees, / To suffer what the Sov'reign Pow'r decrees." There is no mention of the decree of the "Sov'reign Pow'r" in the original. But we were married, Dido pleads to Aeneas; no, Aeneas answers, "I never held the torches of a bridegroom, / Never entered upon the pact of marriage" [nec coniugis umquam / praetendi taedas aut haec in foedera veni] (338–39): I never entered into such an agreement or compact; I never (in effect) signed on the dotted line. Dido is not convinced. Having cursed Aeneas and his fated mission, she kills herself and is consumed by a funeral pyre, which Aeneas sees from the distance as his ship leaves the shores of Carthage. Dido dies, Virgil tells us, a death she did not deserve [merita nec morte peribat] (4.696).

And what of the trip to the underworld? Aeneas is supposed by many to have changed here, to have finally accepted and understood his divine mission. And he does learn of the future and history of Rome: he learns that, if other nations have been graced with more gifted sculptors or philosophers, the distinctively Roman art is to rule other nations, to extend the empire. He also encounters Dido again here, who—in one of the most poignant scenes in the poem—is impervious to his expressions of regret and, by her silence, graphically expresses the reality that even in death she has not forgiven him. And the long parade of Roman propaganda ends not on a positive note, but with the description of the sad death of the promising young Marcellus, Augustus's son-in-law and a prospective ruler of the Roman empire. "Oh, do not ask / About this huge grief of your people, son," Anchises, in tears, tells Aeneas; "Fate will give earth only a glimpse of him, / Not let the boy live on" (6.868–70). But Aeneas is not, it appears, daunted by this sad fact. Anchises tells him about the wars he must wage to win Italy and "fired his love / Of glory in the years to come" (6.889). As Wendell

Clausen has remarked, what Virgil presents us with at the conclusion of the sixth book is "a long Pyrrhic victory of the human spirit."[21]

But then comes the puzzling conclusion to book 6 and to this trip to the underworld. One can leave the underworld through one of two gates, the gate of horn or the gate of ivory. The gate of horn is an easy exit given to true shades, but through the gate of ivory "false dreams" are sent by the spirits to the world above. Why does Aeneas leave Hades through the gate of false dreams? Is Virgil calling into question the wisdom of Aeneas's prospective ventures? Various solutions have been offered to the problem. The gate of horn is closed to Aeneas, one critic has suggested, because he is not a true shade, that is, he is still alive. Another critic recalls the ancient belief that the gate of horn opened to send forth dreams only after midnight, and that Virgil is mentioning the gate of horn in order to tell us the time—that it is not yet midnight.[22] But it seems unlikely that Virgil would give his readers the time of day Aeneas returned to the upper world so precisely and neglect to tell them how to respond emotionally to this episode.[23]

And there is another difficulty in coming to a too innocent reading of this episode. Virgil evokes Homer throughout the *Aeneid,* and the Homeric allusion here only deepens our confusion. In book 19 of the *Odyssey* Penelope dreams of the twenty geese who are killed by an eagle, and Odysseus, still disguised as a beggar, interprets this as predicting the death of the suitors by Odysseus's hand. Penelope accepts his interpretation, but still ponders whether or not the dream will become a reality. "Friend," Penelope says to Odysseus, who at this point in the poem is still dressed as a beggar,

> many and many a dream is mere confusion,
> a cobweb of no consequence at all.
> Two gates for ghostly dreams there are: one gateway
> of honest horn, and one of ivory.
> Issuing by the ivory gate are dreams
> of glimmering illusion, fantasies,
> but those that come through solid polished horn
> may be borne out, if mortals only knew them.

---

21. "An Interpretation of the *Aeneid,*" *Harvard Studies in Classical Philology* 68 (1964): 164.

22. See ibid., 147.

23. Two fairly recent attempts to solve the problem are D. C. Feeney, "History and Revelation in Vergil's Underworld," *Proceedings of the Cambridge Philological Society,* n.s., 32 (1987): 1–24, and R. J. Tarrant, "Aeneas and the Gates of Sleep," *Classical Philology* 77 (1982): 51–55.

> I doubt it came by horn, my fearful dream—
> too good to be true, that, for my son and me.

Circumspect Penelope was, however, a little too circumspect in this case, for her pessimism was unfounded. The dream of the geese was, it turned out, a true dream; it had issued from the Gate of Horn. The Gate of Ivory, the Gate of False Dreams, is reserved for the exit of Aeneas. Odysseus would return, had in fact already returned, to save his homeland, and his return is associated in this simile with the Gate of Horn. Aeneas, before he is to found his own homeland, leaves the underworld through the Gate of False Dreams.

Does Virgil's attitude become any clearer in the final scene of the poem? In order to win the hand of Lavinia, Aeneas must defeat Turnus and his allies, for it was to Turnus that Lavinia's hand had been promised, and it is Turnus whom Lavinia's mother, Amata, still favors as her daughter's future husband, despite the protestations of Amata's husband, King Latinus. After much fighting on both sides, in book 12 the fierce Turnus meets Aeneas in man-to-man combat. Jupiter sends down from Olympus one of the Furies, who distracts Juturna, Turnus's sister and now his charioteer, and separates her from her brother. Turnus is helpless, and Aeneas now sees his chance: he wounds Turnus in the thigh; the Rutulians are stunned; but Turnus has not been mortally wounded, and now he begs Aeneas to feel mercy for him and to spare his life. The scene is meant to recall the death of Hector from the *Iliad*. But Turnus's touching words recall as well the great scene at the end of the *Iliad* when Priam comes to Achilles as a suppliant begging for the body of his son. "The man brought down, brought low" [ille humilis supplexque], Virgil says of Turnus, "lifted his eyes / And held his right hand out to make his plea" [oculos dextramque precantem / protendens]:

> "Clearly I earned this, and I ask no quarter.
> Make the most of your good fortune here.
> If you can feel a father's grief—and you, too,
> Had such a father in Anchises—then
> Let me bespeak your mercy for old age
> In Daunus, and return me, or my body,
> Stripped, if you will, of life, to my own kin.
> You have defeated me. The Ausonians
> Have seen me in defeat, spreading my hands.
> Lavinia is your bride. But go no further
> Out of hatred."

['equidem merui deprecor' inquit;
'utere sorte tua. miseri te si qua parentis
tangere cura potest, oro (fuit et tibi talis
Anchises genitor) Dauni miserere senectae
et me, seu corpus spoliatum lumine mavis,
redde, meis. vicisti et victum tendere palmas
Ausonii videre; tua est Lavinia coniunx,
ulterius ne tende odiis.']

(12.931–38)

At the conclusion of the *Iliad* Priam succeeds in melting Achilles' angry soul into compassion by asking Achilles to see, in Priam's sorrows, the sorrows of Achilles' own father:

μνῆσαι πατρὸς σοῖο, θεοῖς ἐπιείκελ' Ἀχιλλεῦ,
τηλίκου ὥς περ ἐγών, ὀλοῷ ἐπὶ γήραος οὐδῷ.
καὶ μέν που κεῖνον περιναιέται ἀμφὶς ἐόντες
τείρουσ', οὐδέ τίς ἐστιν ἀρὴν καὶ λοιγὸν ἀμῦναι. . . .
ἀλλ' αἰδεῖο θεούς, Ἀχιλεῦ, αὐτόν τ' ἐλέησον,
μνησαμάμενος σοῦ πατρός. ἐγὼ δ' ἐλεεινότερός περ,
ἔτλην δ' οἷ' οὔ πώ τις ἐπιχθόνιος βροτὸς ἄλλος,
ἀνδρὸς παιδοφόνοιο ποτὶ στόμα χεῖρ' ὀρέγεσθαι."
   Ὣς φάτο, τῷ δ' ἄρα πατρὸς ὑφ' ἵμερον ὦρσε γόοιο.
ἁψάμενος δ' ἄρα χειρὸς ἀπώσατο ἦκα γέροντα.
τὼ δὲ μνησαμένω, ὁ μὲν Ἕκτορος ἀνδροφόνοιο
κλαῖ' ἀδινὰ προπάροιθε ποδῶν Ἀχιλῆος ἐλυσθείς,
αὐτὰρ Ἀχιλλεὺς κλαῖεν ἑὸν πατέρ', ἄλλοτε δ' αὖτε
Πάτροκλον. τῶν δὲ στοναχὴ κατὰ δώματ' ὀρώρει.
   (24.486–89, 503–12)

["Remember your own father,
Akhilleus, in your godlike youth: his years
like mine are many, and he stands upon
the fearful doorstep of old age. He, too,
is hard pressed, it may be, by those around him,
there being no one able to defend him
from bane of war and ruin. . . .
                    Akhilleus,
be reverent toward the great gods! And take

pity on me, remembering your own father.
Think me more pitiful by far, since I
have brought myself to do what no man else
has done before—to lift to my lips the hand
of one who killed my son."

Now in Akhilleus
the evocation of his father stirred
new longing, and an ache of grief. He lifted
the old man's hands and gently put him by.
Then both were overborne as they remembered:
the old king huddled at Akhilleus' feet
wept, and wept for Hektor, killer of men,
while great Akhilleus wept for his own father
as for Patróklos once again; and sobbing
filled the room.]

In the Virgilian passage Turnus asks Aeneas to recall *his* father, Daunus, who will grieve terribly over the death of his son. Through many of the final books of the *Aeneid* the Homeric prototype for Turnus had been Achilles. The Sibyl, in fact, in book 6, when predicting for Aeneas the strife he would face in Italy, referred to Turnus as *alius Achilles*, "a new Achilles," and by this Virgil was implying that Turnus's single-minded dedication to glory and warfare could be compared only to that of Achilles himself. But now Turnus becomes, not a new Achilles, but a new supplicating Priam of the twenty-fourth book of the *Iliad.* In this scene it is Aeneas who becomes "a new Achilles."

The great victory of *Iliad* 24, of the whole of the *Iliad* itself, is the achievement of humanity and compassion displayed by the fierce Achilles to the father of the man who had killed his greatest friend. That astounding moment is being alluded to here, and it was a moment the significance of which did not go unappreciated by Virgil. We recall how, in book 2 of the *Aeneid,* Priam berates Achilles' son Pyrrhus—who has just murdered one of Priam's sons before the father's very eyes—for failing to live up to his father's example. For Achilles, Priam says,

iura fidemque
supplicis erubuit corpusque exsange sepulcro
reddidit Hectoreum meque in mea regna remisit.

(2.541–43)

> [Blushed for shame and respected that which was just, and he respected as well the protection due to the suppliant; and he gave back Hector's body, in its bloodless coffin, to me and he sent him back to my own kingdom.][24]

Virgil is here distinguishing Pyrrhus from his father. Pyrrhus becomes true to the color implied by his name through his bloody murder of Priam's family. Achilles, by contrast, would have blushed or "reddened with shame" (*erubuit*) had he not treated Priam with the respect due to him. Achilles was an angry and violent man throughout most of the poem, and his fury becomes embodied—in the *Aeneid*—in the character of Turnus. But, Virgil implies here, we have a different Achilles at the end of the poem. The redness of Achilles' furor has modulated into a blush for shame lest he fail to treat Priam with the proper degree of humanity.[25]

How does Aeneas, this scene's "new Achilles," respond to the plea for mercy of Turnus, this scene's "new Priam"? How, that is, does Virgil, the new Homer, rewrite perhaps the greatest scene in Greek literature? Here is how Aeneas responds to Turnus's supplications:

> stetit acer in armis
> Aeneas volvens oculos dextramque repressit;
> et iam iamque magis cunctantem flectere sermo
> coeperat, infelix umero cum apparuit alto
> balteus et notis fulserunt cingula bullis
> Pallantis pueri, victum quem vulnere Turnus
> straverat atque umeris inimicum insigne gerebat.
> ille, oculis postquam saevi monimenta doloris
> exuviasque hausit, furiis accensus et ira
> terribilis: 'tune hinc spoliis indute meorum
> eripiare mihi? Pallas te hoc vulnere, Pallas

---

24. My own translation.

25. Virgil alludes to the famous scene of supplication as early as book 1 (484–87), when Aeneas, on the walls of the temple in Carthage, is deeply moved by a depiction of the startling meeting between Achilles and Priam in *Iliad* 24. What Virgil emphasizes in this particular passage, however, is the mercenary rather than merciful quality of Achilles' yielding, for Virgil says that Achilles "was selling his [Hector's] lifeless body in exchange for gold" [exanimumque auro corpus vendebat Achilles] (1.486). It was at this point in the narrative necessary for Virgil to establish a contrast between Greek callousness and incipiently Roman mercy and piety. A different counterpoint between Greek and Roman character will be created in the closing scene from the *Aeneid*.

immolat et poenam scelerato ex sanguine sumit.'
hoc dicens ferrum adverso sub pectore condit
fervidus; ast illi solvuntur frigore membra
vitaque cum gemitu fugit indignata sub umbras.

                                    (12.938–52)

                    [Fierce under arms, Aeneas
Looked to and fro, and towered, and stayed his hand
Upon the sword-hilt. Moment by moment now
What Turnus said began to bring him round
From indecision. Then to his glance appeared
The accurst swordbelt surmounting Turnus' shoulder,
Shining with its familiar studs—the strap
Young Pallas wore when Turnus wounded him
And left him dead upon the field; now Turnus
Bore that enemy token on his shoulder—
Enemy still. For when the sight came home to him,
Aeneas raged at the relic of his anguish
Worn by this man as trophy. Blazing up
And terrible in his anger, he called out:
"You in your plunder, torn from one of mine,
Shall I be robbed of you? This wound will come
From Pallas: Pallas makes this offering
And from your criminal blood exacts his due."
He sunk his blade in fury in Turnus' chest.
Then all the body slackened in death's chill,
And with a groan for that indignity
His spirit fled into the gloom below.]

End of *Aeneid.* The poem does not conclude with an act of mercy, as did the *Iliad.* The Homeric model for Pallas was Patroclus. Just as Achilles sought to avenge Patroclus's death by killing Patroclus's vanquisher, so Aeneas avenges Pallas's death by killing Pallas's vanquisher. In the opening six books of the poem, Virgil consistently compares Aeneas's wanderings and trials to the wanderings and trials of Odysseus; in the final books Virgil compares Aeneas's military prowess to that of Achilles. And in this passage the allusions to Achilles are extraordinarily clear: Aeneas is described as ferocious (*acer,* 12.938)—one of the words which Horace uses to describe Achilles in the *Ars Poetica* (121)—and as "blazing up / And terrible in his anger" [furiis accensus et ira / terribilis] (12.946–47). But whereas the *Iliad* ends with an Achilles whose anger has been assuaged, the *Aeneid* ends with a "new Achilles" whose anger is at the boiling point.[26]

Hero myths often involve two elements: a contest for civilization and the final marriage of the hero to the king's daughter to create a civilized order. After Odysseus wins the contest involving the bow and the axes and defeats the suitors, a marriage hymn is sung in Odysseus's house and civilization is restored. But the *Aeneid* ends not with a marriage but with a violent death. So disturbed by the ending of the poem was one of Virgil's early fifteenth-century readers, the Italian humanist Maffeo Vegio, that he himself wrote a book 13 in Latin in which the marriage of Aeneas does indeed take place and in which the poem ends on an unequivocally positive note.

Virgil's *Aeneid* does not. Does this then leave us with a subversive *Aeneid*? If so, the obvious question is: how could such a poem have gotten past Augustus? Perhaps a subtler reading of the poem is possible, a reading that is neither wholly propagandistic nor subversive. At the end of this chapter I shall turn to the puzzle of why Virgil has Aeneas leave the underworld through the gate of false dreams. At this time I would like to try to steer a middle course between the idealist and cynical readings of the Dido and Aeneas episode and the final scene in the poem.

When Aeneas tells Dido that the gods have ordered him to leave her, she sarcastically replies, "What fit employment / For heaven's high powers! What anxieties / To plague serene immortals!" [scilicet is superis labor est, ea cura quietos / sollicitat] (4:379–80). This sentiment is explicitly Epicurean. When Aeneas, although moved by the love he feels for Dido, obeys the gods' commands, even though he cannot concretely envision what his future will be, he is being explicitly Stoic in his actions. The Epicureans believed that the gods existed, but that they existed in a realm of calm far beyond the human and would never deign to become involved in earthly affairs; the ultimate aim of life for the Epicureans was to seek pleasure and to avoid pain. Good and evil, truth and nontruth were reduced to the principle of seeking pleasure or avoiding pain. The Stoic believed that everything happens in conformity with universal fate; the word *fatum* appears again and again in the *Aeneid*. In order to avoid a rigid determinism, the Stoics distinguished between the principal cause and the initiating cause. Any event

---

26. On this passage, see the last chapter ("The Death of Turnus") in Wendell Clausen, *Virgil's Aeneid and the Tradition of Hellenistic Poetry* (Berkeley and Los Angeles: University of California Press, 1987), 83–100.

requires both sorts of causes. Thus, Oedipus's murder of his father, the Stoic might explain, was caused not only by the chain of events that brought the two men together (the initiating cause), but also by Oedipus's decision to strike (the principal cause). Fate sets up networks of initiating causes, but the need for principal causes leaves some room for the operation of free will. The cosmos, the universe, is good, but the good of the whole may sometimes involve the suffering or the destruction of the individual; he or she may struggle against Fate, but that struggle will not alter the outcome. Or as Chrysippus explains Stoic philosophy: man is like a dog tied behind a moving cart, which he may choose to follow or be dragged by.[27] Aeneas's leaving Dido represents, perhaps, the victory of Stoicism over Epicureanism. Aeneas chooses, reluctantly, to leave Dido; he is not quite dragged by the cart, but he follows it less than enthusiastically. And that choice involves the individual suffering of both Aeneas and Dido in the interest of the greater good of founding the Roman Empire. Dido not only suffers but is destroyed, and it is the destruction of Dido for which Virgil, in his attempt to mythologize history, appears to find Aeneas in some sense morally responsible; for Virgil depicts Aeneas's deserting Dido as the origin of the Punic Wars, which Dido predicts (6.621–29).

If Aeneas is more or less dragged by the cart of *fatum* in the first six books, in the final six books, after the future is revealed to him in the underworld, he chooses willingly to follow it, even if this involves his own suffering or the destruction of engaging individuals, such as Camilla or Turnus. Turnus represents an older kind of heroism, a more self-seeking heroism that Virgil associates with Achilles; it is a heroism that seeks glory but is blind to *fatum*. Aeneas must defeat this kind of heroism and embody in himself a heroism that works in harmony with *fatum*. Virgil is constantly reminding his readers of the suffering and destruction that is the necessary price to be paid. Thus he ends the parade of lofty Roman figures in the underworld with the touching portrait of the young Marcellus. And thus he ends the *Aeneid* not with a marriage, but a murder. Aeneas killed Turnus,

---

27. Hippolytus, *Refutation of All Heresies* 1.21, in *The Hellenistic Philosophers*, ed. A. A. Long and D. N. Sedley, 2 vols. (Cambridge: Cambridge University Press, 1987), 1:386: "They too [Zeno and Chrysippus] affirmed that everything is fated, with the following model. When a dog is tied to a cart, if it wants to follow it is pulled and follows, making its spontaneous act coincide with necessity, but if it does not want to follow it will be compelled in any case. So it is with men too: even if they do not want to, they will be compelled in any case to follow what is destined." This is a translation of the relevant section of *Stoicorum Veterum Fragmenta*, ed. Hans Friedrich August von Arnim, 4 vols. (Leipzig: Teubner, 1903), 2:284.

yes, but he also was killing, he felt, the forces of chaos, of misguided *furor.* It is his seeing the picture of the brutal slaughter of the fifteen sons of Aegyptus by the Danaids—a clear symbol of chaos, of blind fury (*furor*) unleashed—that checks Aeneas's sympathy for Turnus in that final scene.

And perhaps it is that same nagging reluctance but ultimately Stoic acceptance so characteristic of Aeneas that may be seen as characterizing the author of the *Aeneid.* Aeneas, by nature a retiring and peace-loving man, is appointed by fate to lead the future Roman race in war. Virgil, by nature a pastoral poet, a man who lost the only law case he ever pleaded, is asked by Augustus to dismiss his Alexandrian principles and write a national epic. Virgil had grown up in a world beset by civil wars, and Augustus held out the promise of a Pax Romana. And Virgil, like his hero Aeneas, ultimately chose to follow the cart rather than to be dragged by it. But when we read the *Aeneid* it is hard not to miss the tone of nagging reluctance. Reading the poem is like driving a car with one foot on the accelerator and the other on the brake. Virgil, to be sure, formally affirmed the Rome of Augustus; but was his writing the *Aeneid* more an act of Stoic will rather than the fruit of a profound and unqualified commitment of his soul?[28]

To answer this question we must turn to philosophy and political theory. One of the fundamental tenets of Platonic philosophy is that history cannot be known as a whole, but that the philosopher's soul is open to the mystery of existence. This insight is memorably stated by Plato at the conclusion of the *Apology.* The court has sentenced Socrates to death, an end considered by many to be the worst possible fate. But even this may be a good, Socrates states: "So I go to die, and you to live; and which of us is going to the more fortunate end is unclear to everyone, except to the god" (42). Plato is here playing with the meaning of "life" and "death," but he is also making the case for rational mysticism: we cannot know with certainty what the future will bring; history cannot be known as a whole; the philosopher's existence is one of participation in the mystery, a participation that requires a faith that precedes understanding. The conception of mankind that the *Aeneid* officially supports is what Dante Germino, following Eric Voegelin, has called the ecumenic rather than the universal (or spiritual) conception of mankind. For it is in the tension between these two conceptions that Virgil's

---

28. For a view of Virgil similar to the one articulated here, see Adam Parry, "The Two Voices of the *Aeneid,*" *Arion* 1 (1963): 66–80, who, as G. B. Conte remarks, "reads the *Aeneid* as an Augustan national poem within which a private voice (the poet's) insinuates itself sorrowfully and without assimilation" (*The Rhetoric of Imitation,* 156).

poem uneasily lives. This important distinction, and its relevance to an understanding of the *Aeneid,* requires some explanation.

Ecumenic humankind, as it received its formulation by Polybius, who recorded the years of Roman expansion from 220 to 144 B.C., is—in the words of H. C. Baldry—"an aggregate, the sum-total of individual human beings spread over all the various countries of the inhabited world [Polybius's *oikoumenē*]—mankind, in fact, viewed *geographically,* as we find it easy to see today."[29] Germino describes how this Polybian view of humankind, which was inherited by the political thinkers influential in the Roman Republic, "as the aggregate of human beings presently living in the inhabited world, or *ecumene,* prevails over the insight—gained in classical Greece and in Israel—of man's humanity as derivative from his capacity for experiencing the divine presence in his soul."[30] Germino is here paraphrasing the insights articulated by Eric Voegelin in *The Ecumenic Age:*

> This term *ecumene,* which originally means no more than the inhabited world in the sense of cultural geography, has received through Polybius the technical meaning of the peoples who are drawn into the process of imperial expansion.... This ecumene, as Polybius understands it, is an object of organization rather than a subject; it does not organize itself for action like Egypt, or the Chosen People, or an Hellenic polis. Moreover, it does not develop a symbolism by which its thinkers articulate their experience of the new order.... [A]bove the ecumene there rises no cosmological symbolism as from the Near Eastern Empires, no symbolism of world history as from Israel's present under God, no philosopher's theory of the polis as from the Athens of Plato and Aristotle.[31]

29. H. C. Baldry, *The Unity of Mankind in Greek Thought* (Cambridge: Cambridge University Press, 1965), 167; quoted in Dante Germino, *Political Philosophy and the Open Society* (Baton Rouge: Louisiana State University Press, 1982), 96.

30. *Political Philosophy and the Open Society,* 97.

31. *The Ecumenic Age,* vol. 4 of *Order and History* (Baton Rouge: Louisiana State University Press, 1974), 124–25. In *Virgil's Aeneid: Cosmos and Imperium,* Philip Hardie, in a work of remarkably thorough research, elucidates how Virgil in the *Aeneid* attempts to draw analogies between Augustan imperial order and cosmic order. What Hardie does not discuss, however, are the origins of political cosmological symbolism in Egypt. As Germino remarks, "In the cosmological style of thought, society was a *microcosmos,* a little *cosmos,* a copy of the order of the visible heavens.... [T]he pharaonic conception of society as a microcosm did not imply a program for world conquest and could tolerate the existence of rival cosmological empires. Egyptian society was conceived as an order analogous to that of the order of the visible world, or *cosmos,* itself experienced as divine. The divine order was mediated by the Pharaoh to the

To use the terminology that Voegelin will later develop in the final volume of *Order and History,* ecumenism reduces the human soul—with its capacity for experiencing itself as participating in the mysterious unfolding of the It—to one more of the "things" among the other "things" of the infinitely expanding political world of the ecumenic empires. As Germino adds, citing Baldry's *Unity of Mankind,* "It is the Romans who made history 'an organic whole' moving towards a *telos* (end) rather than a series of disparate events. Fortune is said to have 'guided nearly all of the world's affairs in one direction and made all incline toward one and the same end' [Polybius, *Universal History,* I, 4]—i.e., the Roman conquest of virtually the entire *ecumene.* Thus, Polybius anticipates Virgil's celebration of Rome as an *imperium sine fine.*"[32]

One of the purposes of Virgil's *Aeneid* is to provide for the citizens of the empire a "symbolism of world history" such as "Israel's present under God" that Voegelin feels is lacking in the Polybian account. But in the Virgilian conception what replaces the sense of the eternal as symbolized in the world-transcendent God of Israel is the pragmatic and earthly realization of the Roman "empire without end." And it is precisely this transcendental status which Virgil confers on the founding and expansion of the Roman Empire that gives—at least to many of today's readers—such a presumptuous and, ultimately, even hollow ring to the proclamations uttered throughout the poem about Rome's manifest destiny. Virgil had lived through a period of continual civil war, and he had high hopes that the establishment of the empire would bring with it the assurance of political stability. And this is sound political thinking as far as it goes, for, as Eugene Webb has written, "imperialism recognizes . . . that, however spiritual mankind may be, it always retains its physical dimension and its situation in the cosmos made up

---

peoples in his realm. The cosmological symbolism of the Pharaoh lacked any sense of an activist, imperialist mission to conquer the entire known world" (*Political Philosophy and the Open Society,* 95).

32. *Political Philosophy and the Open Society,* 98. In *Epic and Empire: Politics and Generic Form from Virgil to Milton* (Princeton: Princeton University Press, 1993), David Quint notes the Polybian roots of Virgil's political theory. "Epic takes particularly literally," Quint writes, "that history belongs to the winners. Imperial conquest of geopolitical space—the imposition of a single, identical order upon different regions and peoples—becomes a process of history making. The *Aeneid* appears to identify history itself with a new idea of universal history. Polybius, the Greek historian of the second century B.C., argued that Rome's emerging empire had for the first time made such a history possible, a history in which 'the affairs of Italy and Africa have been interlinked with those of Greece and Asia, all leading up to one end' [Polybius 1:7–9]" (30).

of world and society as well as of man and the gods, and it requires ordering on its lower as well as its higher levels."[33] Virgil is far more spiritually sensitive than Polybius, who records the brute fact of Rome's imperial expansion with a detached sense of its inevitability in the world of power politics. But in the *Aeneid* the great poet's understanding and exploration of universal humankind is continually burdened with the mortgage of ecumenic humankind.

In at least one episode, however, Virgil leaves ecumenism open to question in what appears to be an allusion to Plato. We recall that at the conclusion of *Aeneid* 6, Virgil writes:

> Sunt geminae Somni portae, quarum altera fertur
> cornea, qua veris facilis datur exitus umbris,
> altera candenti perfecta nitens elephanto,
> sed falsa ad caelum mittunt insomnia Manes.
> his ubi tum natum Anchises unaque Sibyllam
> prosequitur dictis portaque emittit eburna.
>
> (6.893–98)

> [Two Gates the silent House of Sleep adorn;
> Of polish'd Iv'ry this, that of transparent Horn:
> True Visions through transparent Horn arise,
> Through polish'd Iv'ry pass deluding Lyes.
> Of various things discoursing as he pass'd,
> *Anchises* hither bends his Steps at last.
> Then, through the Gate of Iv'ry, he dismiss'd
> His valiant Offspring and Divining Guest.[34]

What Virgil may have intended by having Aeneas leave the underworld through the gate of false dreams has been elucidated by R. J. Tarrant. Tarrant suggests that Virgil's underworld is marked by Platonic associations. Since, for Plato, physical reality, due to the soul's entrapment in the body, clouds our

---

33. *Eric Voegelin: Philosopher of History* (Seattle: University of Washington Press, 1981), 252.

34. Dryden's translation (*Works of Dryden,* 5:568), which I have used here because of its appropriate grandeur in rendering this haunting passage. The Latin may be translated, fairly literally, thus: "There are two gates of sleep. One, they say, is of horn, where true shades easily make their way out; the other polished and gleaming with white ivory, but false are the dreams that the spirits send to the world above [through this gate]. With these words Anchises sees off both his son and the Sibyl, and he dismisses them through the ivory gate."

vision of truth, a person who is physically alive is less real (and participates more in the realm of *falsa insomnia*) than are "true shades" (*verae umbrae*) who have been freed of the distortions forced on us by bodily existence. The Platonic symbolism here, which finds expression in Anchises' speech in *Aeneid* 6 (see esp. 733–34), places the worldly aspirations of Roman ecumenism within an appropriately mystical context. That which immediately follows on the heels of the proto-Hegelian predictions about the ultimate shape of history dominated by Rome is a Platonic allusion that hints at the mystery of history. As Tarrant says, "Virgil seems to have found Plato's view of the physical world as a mere shadow of a purer world a useful structure of thought by which to express his own sense of the evanescence of mortal aspirations."[35] This is the Virgil who would appeal to Bernardus Silvestris for whom, as Frank Kermode remarks, "the journey of Aeneas becomes an allegory for what the human soul undergoes in the body, while his descent to the underworld figures a liberation from sense and an education in philosophy."[36]

If Tarrant is correct in his reading, then Virgil at the end of book 6 is being openly mystical in his understanding of the destiny of humankind. But the explicitness even of this unusual passage is a topic of scholarly dispute. And for most of the poem, Virgil's explicit message is ecumenic and imperialist. As Robin Sowerby remarks, depicted on the shield that Aeneas carries with him into battle in book 8 are "the rape of the Sabines and the conquest of Gaul" concluding with "the victory of Augustus and the gods of Rome against Antony and the forces of Cleopatra backed by the strange deities of the East. The final image is of the parade of Eastern peoples through the streets of Rome in the official triumph of Augustus, who appears not as civiliser but as the conqueror who victoriously asserts Roman power. The images on the shield triumphantly represent the still pictures of the relentless Roman will to power."[37]

Donatus, Virgil's biographer, tells us that Virgil, just before he died, was planning to spend three years revising the *Aeneid.* One wonders what revisions he would have made. Would he perhaps have had Aeneas appear less wooden in his scene of farewell with Dido? Would he have cleared up the ambiguities surrounding the gate of false dreams through which Aeneas leaves the underworld in book 6? Would he have ended the poem on a more

---

35. "Aeneas and the Gates of Sleep," 54. Tarrant goes on to say: "This awareness, however, coexists with an equally strong feeling that the mission of Aeneas will have a permanent and beneficent influence on human history" (ibid.).

36. *The Classic* (London: Faber & Faber, 1975), 39.

37. *Dryden's Aeneid,* 30.

unequivocally positive note? Yet these ambiguities remain in the text as we have it. When Augustus asked to hear part of the poem in progress, Virgil responded that he had nothing to show that was worthy of Augustus's attention. And it was only after much prodding by the emperor that Virgil did finally read three books aloud to him. Why was Virgil so reluctant to read his work to Augustus? On his death bed, Virgil asked that the poem be burned. Again, one wants to know why. Was he simply a perfectionist, or did he feel that his own ambivalences had not yet been sufficiently resolved? Had Virgil's poem a clearer imperialist and ideological message, however, it would correspondingly have been more propagandistic and hence less of the sort of classic I have been trying to elucidate throughout this book.

11

PHILOSOPHY AS DOCTRINE, RHETORIC AS PANACHE?

The *Metamorphoses* of Apuleius

In the *Aeneid* Virgil has his Jupiter predict that the Roman Empire will be vast and powerful. "Imperium sine fine dedi" (I have granted [to the Romans] empire without end), Jupiter confidently proclaims to Venus (1.279). And there was much to Jupiter's prophecy. The empire encompassed virtually all of Europe, including Britain, Asia to the borders of Persia, and North Africa south to the Sahara. And it was in northern Africa, probably in the town of Madauros—which lay in what is now eastern Algeria, near Tunisia—that Apuleius was born. Madauros was a thriving center of education and culture in the time of Apuleius, but it was located far from Rome, and the empire itself, it appears, could not always provide its subjects with what they needed, especially on the spiritual plane. For the age of Apuleius—and particularly the period between the accession of Marcus Aurelius (A.D. 161) and the conversion of Constantine (A.D. 312)—saw the rise of many religious sects, which suggests that universal or spiritual humankind was resisting its diminution to ecumenic humankind.

We get a sense of the bunglings and ineffectiveness of the Roman bureaucracy in the scene—which Erich Auerbach discusses in *Mimesis*[1]—with the official in the market in the very first book of Apuleius's *Metamorphoses*. The official whom Lucius meets by chance in the market was a former fellow student who is happy to see his old friend and wishes to be of service to him. Lucius has just bought some fish in the market. The official takes a look at the fish, is convinced that Lucius has overpaid, and we are presented with the following scene:

> His actis et rebus meis in illo cubiculo *conditis,* pergens ipse ad balneas, ut prius aliquid nobis cibatui prospicerem, forum cuppedinis peto inque eo piscatum opiparem expositum *video,* et percontato pretio, quod centum nummis indicaret, aspernatus viginti denarios praestinavi. Inde me commodum egredientem continuatur Pythias condiscipulus apud Athenas Atticas meus, qui me post aliquantum multum temporis amanter agnitum invadit, amplexusque ac comiter deosculatus, "Mi Luci," ait, "sat pol diu est quod intervisimus te, at hercules exinde cum a Clytio magistro digressi sumus. Quae autem tibi causa peregrinationis huius?" "Crastino die scies" inquam. "Sed quid istud? Voti gaudeo. Nam et lixas et virgas et habitum prorsus magistratui congruentem in te video." "Annonam curamus" ait "et aedilem gerimus, et si quid obsonare cupis utique commodabimus." Adnuebam, quippe qui iam cenae affatim piscatum prospexeramus. Sed enim Pythias, visa sportula successisque in aspectum planiorem piscibus, "At has quisquilias quanti parasti?" "Vix," inquam "piscatori extorsimus accipere viginti denarium."
>
> Quo audito, statim arrepta dextera postliminio me in forum cuppedinis reducens, "Et a quo," inquit "istorum nugamenta haec comparasti?" Demonstro seniculum—in angulo sedebat quem confestim pro aedilitatis imperio voce asperrima increpans, "Iam iam" inquit "nec amicis quidem nostris vel omnino ullis hospitibus parcitis, quod tam magnis pretiis pisces frivolos indicatis et florem

1. *Mimesis: The Representation of Reality in Western Literature,* trans. Willard Trask (Garden City, N.Y.: Doubleday, 1957), 52–55.

Thessalicae regionis ad instar solitudinis et scopuli edulium caritate deducitis? Sed non impune. Iam enim faxo scias quem ad modum sub meo magisterio mali debeant coerceri." Et profusa in medium sportula iubet officialem suum insuper pisces inscendere ac pedibus suis totos obterere. Qua contentus morum severitudine meus Pythias ac mihi ut abirem suadens, "Sufficit mihi, o Luci," inquit "seniculi tanta haec contumelia."

His actis consternatus ac prorsus obstupidus, ad balneas me refero, prudentis condiscipuli valido consilio et nummis simul privatus et cena, lautusque ad hospitium Milonis ac dehinc cubiculum me reporto. (1.24–25)

[After this was arranged and my belongings put in my room, I set out by myself for the baths. But first, since I wanted to procure something for our supper, I headed for the provision-market. I saw some elegant fish on display there, and when I asked the price and was told they cost a hundred sesterces, I refused and bought them for twenty denarii. Just as I was leaving I came upon Pythias, who had been a fellow-student of mine at Athens in Attica. With a loving gleam of recognition after such a long time, he rushed up to me and kissed me affectionately. "My friend Lucius," he said, "by heaven, it has been a long time since I saw you. Yes, by Hercules, it was when we took leave of our teacher Clytius. What brings you here in your travels?" "You will find out tomorrow," I replied. "But what's this? Congratulations! I see you have attendants and the rods of office and the dress of a magistrate." "I am an administrator of food supplies," he said, "and market inspector, and if you wish to do any shopping I am at your service." "No thanks," I replied, since I had already provided quite enough fish for supper. But Pythias saw my basket and shook the fish up so that he could see them more clearly. "How much did you pay for this rubbish?" he asked. "I just managed to twist a fishmonger's arm to take twenty denarii for them," I answered.

When he heard this, he instantly grabbed my hand and led me back to the provision-market. "And from which of these merchants," he asked, "did you buy that junk?" I pointed to a little old man who was sitting in a corner, and Pythias immediately began to berate him in an extremely harsh tone befitting the authority of his office as inspector. "So now!" he shouted. "You do not even spare my friends, or indeed any visitors to this place. You mark up worthless fish at high prices,

and you are reducing this flower of Thessalian territory to the semblance of a deserted, barren cliff by the costliness of your wares. But
you will not get away with it, because now I am going to show you
how rogues are going to be checked while I am magistrate." Then he
emptied the basket out on the open pavement and ordered his assis-
tant to trample on the fish and crush them to a pulp with his feet.
Content with this display of stern morality, my friend Pythias advised
me to be off, saying, "I am satisfied, Lucius, just to have abused the
old fellow that way."

Speechless and utterly dumbfounded at these events, I went on to
the baths, having been robbed of both money and supper by the
authoritative counsel of my wise fellow-student. When I had bathed,
I returned to Milo's house and then went to my room.][2]

What is the function of this scene? It is clearly, on one level, a spoof of
bureaucracy. The official makes a show of his concern, but his concern gets
Lucius absolutely nowhere; in fact, it leaves him far worse off than he was
before. Perhaps he was overcharged, but now he has neither money nor fish.
The Roman Empire does not seem to be living up to Anchises' high expectations as declared to Aeneas in book 6 of the *Aeneid.*

Rome seems to have failed to live up to Anchises' expectations in more
ways than one. Let us look at this scene again. Could it have happened in, say,
Homer's *Odyssey?* The comparison is not inappropriate, for Lucius is a
latter-day Odysseus. In Homer people generally earn the ends that they
meet: we may feel that Poseidon is harsh toward Odysseus, that the vengeance he seeks for the blinding of Polyphemos is excessive, but Homer also
shows us how Odysseus, at least to some degree, has earned Poseidon's
wrath, just as the suitors have earned the brutal treatment they receive from
Odysseus and Telemachus at the conclusion of the poem.

What we see in Homer is a world ruled, to a large degree, by cause and
effect. Actions are not simply gratuitous; they are motivated, they are—to

2. The Latin text and English translation, is cited, as will be all quotations from *The Golden
Ass,* from *Apuleius: Metamorphoses,* 2 vols., edited and translated by J. Arthur Hanson, Loeb
Classical Library (1989). As Hanson mentions in his introduction, he has modernized and
regularized the Latin spelling. The standard text of the *Metamorphoses* has been the Teubner,
ed. R. Halm (Leipzig, 1931). I wish to dedicate the present chapter to the memory of J. Arthur
Hanson, whose friendship and humanity I remember with affection, and whose stimulating
lectures on Apuleius I had the privilege of hearing at Princeton University in the late 1970s and
early 1980s. My reading of Aristomenes' tale is indebted to Professor Hanson's lectures.

recall our paradigm of the classical understanding of literature—rationally comprehensible. This is part of what makes Homer a classic, especially in the proto-Aristotelian sense of the fictional plot as embodying a sequence of cause and effect.[3] Gratuitous sensationalism is a characteristic not only of the episodic and often violent plot of the *Metamorphoses,* but it is a characteristic of the style of Apuleius as well. The style is not the style of a classic; it is not the balanced, dignified, and restrained style of a Cicero or a Virgil. Eduard Norden found it truly abominable.[4] And it is not difficult to understand why. When, to take just one example out of too many to be cited, Charite discovered that her beloved husband Tlepolemus had been murdered, she was so grief-stricken, Apuleius says—in an inappropriate play on words given the tragic circumstances in which the words are uttered— "invita remansit in vita" [she unwillingly remained alive] (8.6). Apuleius himself—in the persona of Lucius—at the very beginning of the work apologizes for his stylistic indecencies: "En ecce praefamur veniam, siquid exotici ac forensis sermonis rudis locutor offendero" [I ask your pardon, if I—as a rude and uncultivated speaker of a foreign language—offend you] (1.4).[5] Latin, Lucius claims, is not his native tongue; he taught himself the language, with great difficulty, only after he arrived at Rome.

What sort of world are we presented with in Apuleius? Why did the official act as he did? If this were a scene in Homer we would ask what Lucius did to deserve such harsh treatment. But in the case of Lucius we simply do not know. We are presented with effects, but the causes are left unspoken. Erich Auerbach mentioned the Kafkaesque quality of Apuleius's *Metamorphoses.* We might now add: Monty Pythonesque, as well, especially in its sadism. One thinks of the scene from one of the Monty Python episodes in which a man goes to his insurance agent to file a claim after experiencing a particularly devastating loss. "I'm sorry," his agent tells the claimant, "but the reason your payments were so low was that you had a 'no-claim' policy." "A 'no-claim' policy?" laments the poor victim, reeling from yet another piece of sudden and unexpected adversity, "Oh, no!" As he

---

3. See *Poetics* 9.11–12, 10.4, 23.2, as cited by Kathy Eden in her entry "Fiction," in *The New Princeton Encyclopedia of Poetry and Poetics,* ed. Alex Preminger and T.V.F. Brogan (Princeton: Princeton University Press, 1993), 407.

4. *Die Antike Kunstprosa,* 2 vols. (Leipzig and Berlin: Teubner, 1923), 2:600–605.

5. In *Auctor and Actor: A Narratological Reading of Apuleius' The Golden Ass* (Berkeley and Los Angeles: University of California Press, 1985), John J. Winkler suggests that the speaker of the prologue, from which this sentence is drawn, is neither Lucius nor Apuleius but rather perhaps "some itinerant Greek now working as a storyteller in Rome" (203). Winkler, in his brilliant and supple study, at times attempts to imitate the playful aspect of Apuleius's own style.

begins sobbing uncontrollably, the agent looks him in the eyes, and with seeming compassion places his hand on the man's shoulder: "I can't stand to see a grown man cry. So, shove off!"

Or consider the story the curious Lucius is told by Aristomenes at the very beginning of the book. Here Aristomenes tells the tale of a friend named Socrates, who became romantically involved with an old woman named Meroe, a witch who used her magical powers to punish faithless, and not so willing, lovers. Socrates and Aristomenes decide to escape from Meroe's grasp, but before they do Meroe and her sister Panthia break into the lodgings of Socrates and Aristomenes. Aristomenes says,

> video mulieres duas altioris aetatis. Lucernam lucidam gerebat una, spongiam et nudum gladium altera. Hoc habitu Socratem bene quietum circumstetere. Infit illa cum gladio, 'Hic est, soror Panthia, carus Endymion, hic Catamitus meus, qui diebus ac noctibus illusit aetatulam meam, hic qui meis amoribus subterhabitis non solum me diffamat probris, verum etiam fugam instruit. At ego scilicet Ulixi astu deserta vice Calypsonis aeternam solitudinem flebo.' Et porrecta dextera meque Panthiae suae demonstrato, 'At hic bonus' inquit 'Consiliator Aristomenes, qui fugae huius auctor fuit et nunc morti proximus iam humi prostratus grabatulo succubans iacet et haec omnia conspicit, impune se relaturum meas contumelias putat. Faxo eum sero, immo statim, immo vero iam nunc, ut et praecedentis dicacitatis et instantis curiositatis paeniteat.'
>
> "Haec ego ut accepi, sudore frigido miser perfluo, tremore viscera quatior, ut grabatulus etiam successu meo inquietus super dorsum meum palpitando saltaret. At bona Panthia 'Quin igitur' inquit 'soror, hunc primum bacchatim discerpimus vel membris eius destinatis virilia desecamus?'
>
> "Ad haec Meroe—sic enim reapse nomen eius tunc fabulis Socratis convenire sentiebam—'Immo' ait 'supersit hic saltem, qui miselli huius corpus parvo contumulet humo.' Et capite Socratis in alterum dimoto latus, per iugulum sinistrum capulo tenus gladium totum ei demergit, et sanguinis eruptionem utriculo admoto excipit diligenter, ut nulla stilla compararet usquam. Haec ego meis occulis aspexi. Nam etiam, ne quid demutaret, credo, a victimae religione, immissa dextera per vulnus illud ad viscera penitus cor miseri contubernalis mei Meroe bona scrutata protulit, cum ille impetu teli praesecata gula vocem, immo stridorem incertum, per vulnus effun-

deret et spiritum rebulliret. Quod vulnus qua maxime patebat spongia offulciens, Panthia 'Heus tu,' inquit 'spongia, cave in mari nata per fluvium transeas.' His editis abeunt et una remoto grabatulo varicus super faciem meam residentes vesicam exonerant, quoad me urinae spurcissimae madore perluerent."

[I saw two women of rather advanced age, one carrying a lighted lamp and the other a sponge and a naked sword. Thus equipped they surrounded the soundly sleeping Socrates. The one with the sword began: 'This, sister Panthia, is my darling Endymion, my Ganymede. This is the one who made sport of my tender youth day and night, the one who disdained my love and not only slandered me with his insults but even plotted to escape. Shall I, forsooth, deserted like Calypso by the astuteness of a Ulysses, weep in ever-lasting loneliness?' Then she stretched out her hand and pointed me out to her friend Panthia. 'And this,' she said, 'is the good counsellor Aristomenes, who advised this escape and now lies near death, stretched out on the ground, sprawling under his little cot and watching all this. He thinks he is going to report these insults against me with impunity. Later—no, soon—no, right now—I will make him regret his past raillery and present inquisitiveness.'

"When I heard that, my poor body dissolved in cold sweat, and my insides quivered and trembled so that the cot, disturbed by my own shaking, swayed and danced on top of my back. 'Well then, sister,' replied the gentle Panthia, 'why not take him first and tear him limb from limb in a Bacchic frenzy, or at least tie him up and cut off his genitals?'

"Meroe—since I perceived her name in fact matched Socrates' stories—answered her. 'No,' she said, 'let him at least survive to bury this poor wretch's corpse with a little earth.' And with this she bent Socrates' head to one side and plunged her sword down through the left side of his neck all the way up to the hilt. Then she placed a leather bottle to the wound, carefully collecting the spout of blood so that not a single drop appeared anywhere. I saw all this with my very own eyes. Next, so as not to deviate, I suppose, from the ritual of sacrificing a victim, she inserted her right hand through that wound all the way down to his insides, felt around for my poor comrade's heart, and pulled it out; at this he emitted a sound from that throat slashed open by the weapon's stroke, or rather poured out an inarticulate squeal through the wound and gurgled forth his life's breath. Panthia staunched the wound at its widest opening with her sponge, saying, 'Listen, o sponge, born in the sea, take care to travel back through a river.' After these words they left him; and both of them removed my cot, spread their feet, and squatted over my face, discharging their bladders until they had drenched me in the liquid of their filthy urine.] (1.12–13)

What kind of world is this? It is a world in which a man named Socrates, who obviously possesses none of the august dignity of his famous namesake, seduces and is seduced by a witch, a world in which this Socrates has his heart literally cut out—and replaced by a sponge—by two supernatural female creatures, and the contents of his blood collected in a bottle. It is a world, in brief, in which—perhaps at best—a man can expect to be suddenly turned, in effect, into a tortoise and get himself urinated upon. At the worst (and this is perhaps not even the worst), it is a world in which a beautiful, innocent young woman is faced with the very real threat of being stuffed into the belly of a dead ass, stitched in with only her head protruding, and then exposed, on some cliff edge, to the full force of the sun. Nor are we finished with Socrates here. For apparently he has survived the heart transplant. Or *thinks* he has survived, at any rate, until the next day, when he leans over a stream to drink. The wound gapes open and he falls, lifeless, to the ground. Aristomenes' companion doesn't take the tale seriously, but our hero Lucius most certainly does, and it makes him all the more anxious to learn more about magic, to indulge his characteristic trait of curiosity.

Is all this violence simply gratuitous? Is Apuleius trying to revolt our sensibilities? Or does he have some higher objective in mind? We must recall that the entire last book of the *Metamorphoses* recounts the conversion of Lucius to the cult of Isis. Is our author's chief intention to persuade us, as readers, to adopt the same faith lest we suffer the same kind of degrading experiences suffered by Lucius before his conversion? Is Apuleius's chief intention, that is, to entertain (if that is the right word) or to instruct? For if we read the work as one that is pointing symbolically to the redemption from the evils of the world, then even the gruesome scene just quoted above contains motifs and symbols that loom large in the work.

To understand Apuleius's artistic intentions we should recall that he was born, as I have mentioned, probably in Madauros in northern Africa around A.D. 125 and traveled widely throughout the ancient Mediterranean world. He was apparently known to his native countrymen as a "philosopher," for during some excavations a commemorative statue of him was found with a dedication reading "to a Platonic philosopher."[6] Yet in what sense was Apuleius a "philosopher"? And if he was a philosopher, how is it possible that he was also a "sophist"? He was a sophist in the sense that he was an orator who delivered eloquent speeches for set fees, and who delighted in the spoken word for its own sake. We must of course recall here that, according to Plato, philosophy and the sophistic love of rhetorical display for its own sake could not mix.

Apuleius was in fact part of the movement that has come to be known as the Second Sophistic. Oratory or rhetoric had once been an elevated genre of literature. This was especially the case in the days of the Athenian democracy, as is clearly evident in so many of the rousing speeches in Thucydides, for example. But by the Hellenistic period and in Rome after the republic, oratory had lost most of its practical importance, since there were no longer any significant popular assemblies in which an orator could move an audience to important decisions with his eloquence. The usual form in which one displayed one's rhetorical skills was through the set speech or declamation, delivered often before great crowds, in theaters, or in public buildings. And what one delivered was the epideictic speech, the speech in which an orator displayed his rhetorical skills and his learning.

We have in the *Florida,* a selection from Apuleius's set speeches, an anthology left us from this aspect of our author's literary career. It contains speeches suggesting the wide range of topics taken up by the Second Sophistic, topics from the sublime to the ridiculous, from a discourse about Alexander the Great to one about a parrot.

It was also helpful for a sophist to be a polymath, to convince his audience that he was learned in many fields. Here is how, in his *Apology,* Apuleius describes his credentials—in effect, gives us a brief version of his curriculum vitae: I have drunk, Apuleius tells us, from many goblets of learning at Athens, from

> the inventive cup of poetry, the limpid one of geometry, the sweet one of music, the rather austere one of dialectic, and above all the cup of universal philosophy—inexhaustible and nectareous. For Empedocles composes poems; Plato, dialogues; Socrates, hymns; Epicharmus, mimes; Xenophon, histories; Crates, satires; your Apuleius embraces

---

6. See James Tatum, *Apuleius and the Golden Ass* (Ithaca, N.Y.: Cornell University Press, 1979), 106.

all these genres and cultivates the nine Muses with equal zeal. And if he does so with obviously greater goodwill than talent, for that very reason perhaps is he all the more to be praised.[7]

Apuleius was, then, an eloquent speaker and a polymath who had serious interests in Platonic thought. So eloquent a speaker was he that he may well have managed to get himself cleared, through his wit, of serious charges brought against him in a court of law. He was accused of dabbling in magic, of cajoling a wealthy widow into marrying him, and of depraved living in general.

That Apuleius was a neoplatonic "philosopher" has profound significance for our interpretation of the work as a whole. Consider the following interpretation of the Cupid and Psyche episode as a neoplatonic allegory. Venus is jealous of Psyche because of her great beauty. She condemns her to a rock and leaves her there to be approached by her husband, who will take the form of a serpent. Zephyrus wafts the beautiful young woman to the home of her new husband, who happens to be Cupid, and who tells her that she must never see his face. But she cannot restrain her curiosity: she views her husband by lamplight, but a drop of oil spills and burns his shoulder; he wakes and angrily flies away. Psyche is permitted to earn another chance. Of the tasks she has to perform, the last is to descend to Hades and to bring back from Proserpina a jar containing divine beauty. After despairing almost to the point of suicide about her ability to perform this task, she accomplishes it, but cannot resist peeking into the jar. As soon as she opens the jar she is about to be overcome by a deathlike stupor; but Cupid intervenes to save her and requests that Jove free Psyche from Venus's wrath. Jove agrees, and Psyche is made immortal. Cupid and Psyche are wed and have a child named Voluptas (pleasure).

Psyche clearly stands for the soul, Cupid for love (or *erōs*). Cupid's appearance at the end of the tale suggests that the soul cannot survive without love—and that, through love, the divine intervenes and saves the soul. However hard the unaided soul tries to work out its own salvation, it cannot do so without the intervention of some divine power. Like Lucius, the soul (Psyche) is naturally curious.[8] Love can serve as an intermediary, but only a

7. From ibid., 125.

8. The theme of curiosity has recently been well discussed by Joseph G. DeFilippo, "*Curiositas* and the Platonism of Apuleius' *Golden Ass*," *American Journal of Philology* 3, no. 4 (1990): 471–92.

divine decree can make the soul immortal. In the Cupid and Psyche story it is Jove who so decrees, and Jove—as the most powerful Olympian god—can be taken as pointing forward to Isis. True happiness is achieved only when the soul acquires knowledge of the divine. At the center of this work, then, is a tale that can be taken as an allegory explicable in neoplatonic terms. And the importance of the episode suggests that the work as a whole is susceptible to the same kind of allegorical, or at least symbolic, reading.

Yet there are crucial differences between the Platonism of Plato and the neoplatonism of a figure such as Apuleius. And one of the most fundamental differences has to do with the attitude toward knowledge itself. For Socrates, the experience of questioning and openness is the core of philosophy; philosophy is quite simply the love of wisdom. A philosopher is not so much one who knows but one who knows he does not know. What we meet in this later period is the philosopher who knows he knows and deigns to teach others. Apuleius in his speeches—he did not, so far as we know, write dialogues—presents himself as one who already knows the truth.

This attitude can be seen in the work of another writer associated with the Second Sophistic, Apollonius of Tyana. When a member of the audience to whom he had just given a speech asked Apollonius why he asked them no questions, Apollonius is reported to have replied, "Because when I was a boy I asked questions; there is no need for me to ask questions now, but rather to teach the things I have discovered." To which the other responded again, "How then, Apollonius, will a wise man discourse?" "Like a lawgiver," Apollonius answered, "for the lawgiver should deliver to the many those instructions about which he has persuaded himself."[9] Apuleius did not, of course, say this, but the attitude toward knowledge that this passage reveals is typical of the Second Sophistic. This is not the Platonic attitude, for it was Plato who held that it was the wrong kind of educator who believed he could "put into the soul the knowledge that was not there before, like sight into blind eyes" (*Republic* 518c). The dialogue—and not the set speech—is the medium in which the philosopher engages with truth. Apuleius, then, was an "orator" (a sophist), and he was a "philosopher" (of the neoplatonic rather than the Socratic type). He wrote a treatise *On the God of Socrates,* which is about the nature of Socrates' *daimōn.* He also wrote a philosophical work titled *On the Doctrine of Plato,* which was a survey of Plato's life and teachings. The philosophical doctrines discussed here are, moreover, important in under-

---

9. Quoted in Tatum, *Apuleius and the Golden Ass,* 127.

standing the probably neoplatonic allegory of Cupid and Psyche, which is the centerpiece of his *Metamorphoses.*

Now these two interests of Apuleius—oratory and "philosophy"—are central to the *Metamorphoses.* The work is, on the one hand, the brilliantly crafted product of a first-rate verbal talent; the style is engaging (though bizarre) and the stories are attention-getting, even if frequently repulsive or gratuitously violent. And there is a strong philosophical intention—it is better described as a *didactic* intention—that governs the work as a whole. It is, in other words, a combination of "oratory" and "philosophy," although we must be careful to define what these terms mean in the Apuleian context, for oratory here means, for the most part, verbal flourish and philosophy, a particular doctrine. We have moved very far from the Aristotelian understanding of rhetoric as a rational means of persuasion as well as from the Platonic (and Aristotelian) understanding of philosophy as a search for truth.

We can think of the work, then, as a kind of extended symbolic tale, a romance in the sense defined by Henry Knight Miller,[10] in which the narrative we are witnessing is meant to be seen from the perspective of the governing deity, Isis. All we see, until book 11, is the flux of the phenomenal world, which has meaning only insofar as it points toward salvation through Isis. The entire work, in other words, is virtually an allegory of the cupidinous soul that is doomed to suffering so long as it rivets its attention on, and indulges its insatiable curiosity in, the world of the flesh and the senses.[11] With this in mind, let us look at the symbolic significance of some of the details in the gruesome tale of Aristomenes.

First, the motif of metamorphosis. Aristomenes feels he has, in effect, been turned into a tortoise, which might be seen as a foreshadowing of Lucius's transformation into an ass and then back into a human being through the agency of Isis.

Second, the figure of Socrates. In the realm of mere becoming, on the surface level of the text, he appears to be the very opposite of Socrates as we

10. "Henry Fielding's *Tom Jones* and the Romance Tradition," *English Literary Studies,* no. 6 (Victoria, B.C.: University of Victoria, 1976).

11. The religious intentions of the work are stressed by Pietro Scazzoso, *Le Metamorfosi di Apuleio: studio critico sul significato del romanza* (Milan, 1951) and R. Merkelbach, *Roman und Mysterium in der Antike* (Munich, Berlin, 1962), both cited by John J. Winkler in *Auctor and Actor,* 5. Two critics who see specific adumbrations of the Isiac religion in episodes prior to book 10 are Merkelbach, 79–86, and G. C. Drake, "The Ghost Story in *The Golden Ass* by Apuleius," *Papers on Language and Literature* 13 (1977): 12–14, also cited in Winkler, *Auctor and Actor,* 58.

know this austerely self-controlled figure from the dialogues of Plato. But the very inclusion of a figure named Socrates may suggest a context of Platonic—or at least of neoplatonic—thought.

Third, the theme of curiosity. Lucius cannot keep himself from wanting to hear this tale. His curiosity results in his transformation into an ass. Extreme curiosity is itself a form of greed or gluttony and, as James Tatum informs us,[12] Plato specifically associates the ass with gluttony. In the *Phaedo* Socrates, in talking about metempsychosis, says that a soul may be imprisoned in a body that corresponds to its former life. As an example, Socrates says, "the kinds who have cultivated gluttony and violence and drunkenness and have not taken pains to avoid them are likely to assume the bodies of asses and other animals of that sort."[13] And, as Tatum also informs us, the figure of the ass itself has special significance to the religious theme, for Set, the rival deity of the goddess Isis, was often depicted as a man with the head of an ass. We ourselves, moreover, as readers are implicated in the truancy of vain curiosity by desiring to read the *Metamorphoses.* We are caught in the act of being "audeurs."

Fourth, there is the theme of magic. Meroe is a witch. Lucius wants to learn about magic. Magic will ultimately be seen, in the *Metamorphoses,* as a desire to control reality, rather than to submit to it under the aegis of Isis. Magic is the humanistic attempt to do without the divine help that can only come through submission to Isis.

Fifth, there is the power of the female. Meroe is powerful, but her power will pale in contrast to the ultimate power of Isis. Indeed, the book presents us with a sequence of female figures of increasing spiritual significance: we progress from the purely sensual Fotis to the admirable and noble Charite (whose presence evokes the tale of Cupid and Psyche) to Isis herself.

All this, then, leads us to the conclusion that Apuleius wrote *The Golden Ass* with the chief intention of converting followers to the faith of Isis. All the tales leading up to the conclusion, by this reading, would be taken not as pure entertainment but as symbolic foreshadowings of the final book. We have read the work correctly only if we ourselves become, as a result of reading it, disciples of the cult of Isis. In the first three books Lucius suffers many warnings not to indulge his propensities for sexual activity and magic; in books 4–10 he suffers the consequences of his actions; and in book 11 he is redeemed.

12. *Apuleius and the Golden Ass,* 43–47.
13. Ibid., 30.

The final book, even in its more transparent style, indeed appears to be different in feeling from the preceding books and this might well lead us to conclude that Apuleius intends that his readers take his didactic—indeed messianic—message with the utmost seriousness. But Apuleius cannot maintain the tone of pious seriousness, for the conclusion of the work, following a passage in which the author elaborates in great detail the process of initiation into the cult of Isis, may strike us as a little odd:

> Denique post dies admodum pauculos deus deum magnorum potior et maiorum summus et summorum maximus et maximorum regnator Osiris, non in alienam quampiam personam reformatus, sed coram suo illo venerando me dignatus affamine per quietem recipere visus est: quae nunc incunctanter gloriosa in foro redderem patrocinia, nec extimescerem malevolorum disseminationes, quas studiorum meorum laboriosa doctrina ibiden exciebat. Ac ne sacris suis gregi cetero permixtus deservirem, in collegium me pastophorum suorum, immo inter ipsos decurionum quinquennales allegit. Rursus denique quaequa raso capillo collegii vetustissimi et sub illis Sullae temporibus conditi munia, non obumbrato vel obtecto calvitio, sed quoquoversus obvio, gaudens obibam.

> [Finally, after just a few days, he that is mightiest of the great gods, the highest of the mightiest, the loftiest of the highest, and the sovereign of the loftiest, Osiris, appeared to me in a dream. He had not transformed himself into a semblance other than his own, but deigned to welcome me face to face with his own venerable utterance, bidding me unhesitatingly to continue as now to win fame in the courts as an advocate and not fear the slanders of detractors which my industrious pursuit of legal studies had aroused in Rome. Furthermore, to avoid my serving his mysteries as an undistinguished member of the faithful, he elected me to the college of his *pastiphori,* and even made me a member of the quinquennial board of directors. Then, once more shaving my head completely, neither covering up nor hiding my baldness, but displaying it wherever I went, I joyfully carried out the duties of that ancient priesthood, founded in the days of Sulla.] (11.30)[14]

14. "The days of Sulla," as Hanson notes, refers to "the early first century B.C."

There is something a little grotesque about our hero's so conspicuously "exposing" his bald head wherever he goes [calvitio... quoquoversus obvio]. Baldness should be a sign of humility, of the renunciation of sensuality associated with the flowing hair of a Fotis. Lucius has become a successful lawyer. We have here none of the feeling of the Platonic or Judeo-Christian renunciation of the world, no sense of an exodus from a false to a truer understanding of reality such as we find in the Platonic parable of the cave, or in the Exodus from Egypt. Lucius was transformed from an ass back into a man by eating rose petals. Does Apuleius want, as it were, to have his rose petals and eat them, too? Does Apuleius feel, in other words, that acceptance of the Isiac faith cannot only coexist with, but even enhance, one's attempts to make it in the world? And, if so, is he a serious philosopher in the Platonic sense and/or a convert to the Isiac faith?

Or is all of the *Metamorphoses,* including the final book, an elaborate joke that is based on—and intended to engender in the reader—a profound philosophical skepticism?[15] On this reading, the work is a critique of the desire for certainty, of the desire to control reality through such means as Lucius's interest in magic, or, later, his belief in the divinity of Isis. After all, it was Psyche's desire to see Cupid, to be certain about his identity rather than to accept his beneficence on trust, that resulted in near tragedy. One senses that Apuleius felt that even philosophical nihilism was preferable to absolutism, and that he believed literature was truest to itself when it resisted the didactic heresy even as it seemed to be claiming to uphold it; for the entire work is written from the perspective of a converted Lucius in the same manner that, centuries later, *Gulliver's Travels* will be written from the perspective of an obviously demented, because true-believing, Gulliver. Or did Apuleius himself perhaps possess so superficial a capacity for spiritual experience that he was unaware of just how unserious he was? Is Apuleius, in other words, so superficial a thinker that he is unaware of his own superficiality?

We have discussed, in the previous chapter, a work—Virgil's *Aeneid*—that many would consider a classic; we have now concluded a discussion of a work from one of the Western classical literatures that many would argue is

15. This is Winkler's argument: "The intertextual grid I use in screening the novel is constructed from the classics of Skepticism: Sextus Empericus, Cicero's *Academics,* and Timon's poetry on Pyrrho. I suspect that there are lines of research that would connect the novel of Apuleius *Platonicus philosophus* with the history of Skepticism, both Academic and popular, and above all with its elusive founding author, Plato/Socrates" (125). Winkler believes that *The Golden Ass* is "an open-ended problem text that the reader must supplement" (241).

not. It is not only that the style of Apuleius's *Metamorphoses* is gratuitously bizarre. Nor is it only that the plot is full of gratuitous violence. What mars the work from the perspective of the present study is how it implicitly claims to be offering up absolute philosophical and religious truth in the form of the doctrine of belief in Isis, on the one hand; and, on the other, its reduction of the rhetorical devices of fiction to a means—however indirect—of convey-ing such a truth. In such a reading, Apuleius would thereby have reduced philosophy to the adherence to a specific doctrine and rhetoric to the means of persuading one to accept such a doctrine. If the work is, rather, a spoof of Isiac (and, by implication, any other sort of) fundamentalism, this would render much of it—despite its extraordinary wit and inventiveness—gratuitously sensationalistic and hence hardly possessing the kind of balance we associate with the classic. It would then be a classic of indeterminacy, resisting at virtually every turn the reduction of literature (and philosophy) to ideology or propaganda, but it would leave the reader with nothing to hold onto apart from his or her profound skepticism, a skepticism bordering on nihilism.

12

GENRE, DIDACTICISM, AND THE ETHICS OF FICTION IN
MOLL FLANDERS

Part of the problem of *Moll Flanders* is the question of what it is. The notion of genre is essential to an appropriate apprehension of most of the works of the English Augustan period. And, despite the modernist dogma of the so-called intentional fallacy, Augustan writers generally meant what they said. To understand a given work is, for them, to understand the author's intention. So Alexander Pope believed, who articulated this conviction with characteristic precision and elegance in the *Essay on Criticism:* "A perfect Judge will *read* each work of wit / With the same Spirit that its author *writ*" (233–34). And he goes on to say:

> In ev'ry Work regard the *Writer's End,*
> Since none can compass more than they *Intend;*

> And if the *Means* be just, the *Conduct* true,
>
> Applause, in spite of trivial Faults, is due.
>
> (255–58)[1]

The great problem with reading the prose fiction of that un-Augustan writer Daniel Defoe, however, is to decide what he intended. What was this *Writer's End?*

There are those who doubted that Defoe himself knew what he was doing, or even that he cared very much about literary artistry. "Two-thirds of each of his 'novels' *Roxanna, Colonel Jack,* and *Moll Flanders,*" Leslie Stephen writes, "are deadly dull." "The remainder," Stephen continues, "though exhibiting specimens of genuine power, is not far enough above the commonplace to be specially attractive. In short, the merit of Defoe's narrative bears a direct proportion to the intrinsic merit of a plain statement of facts."[2] For William Minto *Moll Flanders* "is only a string of diverting incidents, the lowest type of book organism. . . . There is no unique creative purpose in it to bind the whole together."[3] For Mark Schorer, as well, it is not for artfulness that we go to Defoe, whose claim to literary fame consists in his being "our classic revelation of the mercantile mind."[4] What Schorer perceives to be the alleged "deficiencies" of the work lead him to conclude that "this is not, after all, the first English novel."[5] Ian Watt, in *The Rise of the Novel,* gives Defoe ample credit for his earthy realism and for being the master of the "brilliant episode." Watt leaves it open to question, however, whether or not this particular talent in the end outweighs Defoe's shortcomings as a novelist, such as his "weaknesses of construction" and his "lack of moral or formal pattern."[6] But perhaps we should ask: is it accurate to describe Defoe's *Fortunes and Misfortunes of the Famous Moll Flanders* as a "novel"?

One of the things we expect of a novel is verisimilitude. In some ways we get this in *Moll Flanders,* particularly through Defoe's inclusion of so much everyday detail. But in many ways we do not. She has an extraordinary number of husbands (five) and not a few lovers (at least twenty)—extraordinary,

---

1. *The Twickenham Edition of the Poems of Alexander Pope,* ed. John Butt et al., 11 vols. (New Haven: Yale University Press, 1938–68), 1:268–69.

2. *Hours in a Library,* 3 vols. (London: John Murray, 1917), 1:29.

3. *Daniel Defoe* (London: Macmillan, 1887), 141.

4. Introduction to the Modern Library edition of *Moll Flanders* (New York: Random House, 1950), xiii.

5. Ibid., xvi.

6. *The Rise of the Novel* (Chatto and Windus, London: 1957), 130.

that is, by eighteenth-century standards. She first marries the youngest son in the house of a family whose mother takes in the destitute Moll to be a companion to her two daughters. Before she marries that particular son (Robin), however, she has an affair with the older brother. After the death of Robin, Moll takes a new husband, a gentlemen-tradesman who turns out to be a big spender and an irresponsible rake and is declared bankrupt. All is well and happy with her third husband in Virginia until she realizes that *his* mother is *her* mother, that he is also her brother, and that with him she has been committing incest. We may easily accept such a coincidence in the romance tradition, but if we come to Defoe with our expectations formed by the "realistic" novel, then our sense of credulity is being stretched. Her fourth husband—between husbands three and four she had been the mistress of a married gentleman (a banker) with whom she lived in Bath—is Jemmy, who she thinks is rich, but who turns out to be penniless and is in fact a member of a gang. She returns to the banker, who has now divorced his wife, and lives with him for five years; he dies suddenly, and Moll's thieving begins. She then remarries Jemmy, and the couple then move to America and live happily and successfully on a plantation before ultimately returning to England.

The realistic novel, of course, is shot through with romance conventions; the emotional effect of wonder, which is the emotional effect most espe-cially evoked by the romance, is indeed often evoked by the novel, but certainly less often than in the romance.[7] Indeed, the numerous and often "unbelievable" relationships and coincidences of the plot of *Moll Flanders* evoke the wonder and surprise more often associated with the romance than with the novel. In terms of form and character as well *Moll Flanders* is closer to the romance than the novel. For in *Moll Flanders* there appear many incidents—the kind of digressions we often find in the romance—that

7. For a very helpful discussion—to which I am indebted—of the distinctions between the romance and the novel, see Henry Knight Miller, "Henry Fielding's *Tom Jones* and the Romance Tradition," *English Literary Studies*, no. 6 (University of Victoria, 1976). Miller explicitly discusses the relevance of the romance tradition to *Moll Flanders* in "Some Reflections on Defoe's *Moll Flanders* and the Romance Tradition," in *Greene Centennial Studies: Essays Presented to Donald Greene in the Centennial Year of the University of Southern California,* ed. Paul J. Korshin and Robert R. Allen (Charlottesville: University Press of Virginia, 1984), 72–92. For the standard description of the "realistic" novel, I continue to find Ian Watt's *Rise of the Novel* very useful. Even a revisionist essay such as J. Paul Hunter's "Novels and 'the Novel': The Poetics of Embarrassment," *Modern Philology* 85 (1988): 480–98, which acknowledges how the rediscovery of Mikhail Bakhtin's "Discourse in the Novel" forces us to rethink the centrality of Watt's paradigm, argues nevertheless that "both credibility and probability . . . are crucial to the novel. They represent a basic conceptual difference from romance: things that cannot happen or seem to happen in an ordinary world do not happen in novels" (483–84).

do not seem particularly relevant to the work's overall intention or effect. Moreover, the representation of the emotions in *Moll Flanders* is sometimes believable, but from a novelistic point of view—in which we expect a gradual psychological development of character—only sometimes.

It appears, then, that *Moll Flanders* may not be a novel at all, if we consider the elements of plot and character. And it looks even less like a novel if we consider the question of moral intention. A novel can be distinguished from the romance by how ethical significance is expressed in it. In the novel we expect the author's moral perspective to be conveyed implicitly, but the romance is often explicitly allegorical and didactic.[8]

Defoe was very clear about the didactic intentions of his own work; in the preface he writes:

> But as this Work is chiefly recommended to those who know how to read it, and how to make good Uses of it which the story all along recommends to them; so it is to be hop'd that such Readers will be more pleas'd with the Moral than the Fable, with the application than with the Relation, and with the end of the Writer than with the Life of the Person written of.[9]

The *"Writer's End"* (to recall Pope's phrase) stated explicitly here, is to instruct, to teach a lesson about the kind of fate that awaits those who transgress moral boundaries. Defoe clearly advises that the reader should not be distracted by the story itself or sympathize inordinately with Moll; what matters is the moral. He then goes on in the preface to ally his own intentions with "the Advocates of the Stage" who

> have, in all Ages, made this the great Argument to perswade People that their Plays are useful, and that they ought to be allow'd in the

---

8. See Miller, "Henry Fielding's *Tom Jones* and the Romance Tradition," chapter 5.

9. *The Fortunes and Misfortunes of the Famous Moll Flanders,* 2 vols. (Oxford: Basil Blackwell, 1927), 1:viii. I believe that Defoe means this passage seriously. I could accept an ironic reading of it were the author an Apuleius or a Jonathan Swift, but Defoe's literary moralism is explicitly and undeniably revealed as late as 1728 when, in the social tract *Augusta Triumphans,* he berates Gay's *Beggar's Opera* for its questionable morality (see William Schultz, *Gay's Beggar's Opera: Its Content, History, and Influence* [New Haven: Yale University Press, 1923], 237). A useful summary of the question of whether or not Defoe makes use of irony in *Moll Flanders* is Maximillian E. Novak, "Conscious Irony in *Moll Flanders:* Facts and Problems," in *Twentieth-Century Interpretations of Moll Flanders,* ed. Robert C. Elliot (Englewood Cliffs, N.J.: Prentice-Hall, 1970), 40–48.

most civiliz'd, and in the most religious Government; namely, that they are applyd to vertuous Purposes, and that by the most lively Representations, they fail not to recommend Virtue, and generous Principles, and to discourage and expose all sorts of Vice and Corruption of Manners; and were it true that they did so, and that they constantly adhered to that Rule, as the Test of their acting on the *Theatre,* much might be said in their Favour.

"Throughout the infinite variety of this Book," Defoe goes on to say, "this fundamental is most strictly adhered to" (*Moll Flanders,* 1:ix).

If the recommendation of virtue and the exposure of vice were the chief intentions of Defoe's fiction, then one must ask, Why does the author show so much sympathy for Moll? Why does he so continually soften the indictment against Moll the loose woman and accomplished thief by presenting her throughout as a victim of the most unfortunate circumstances? A possible answer might be: because the moralistic author wants to make the point that a transgressor will be punished regardless of how dire the circumstances might have been that originally drove the sinner into evil. A possible answer, but not a very satisfying one.

It is undeniable that despite Defoe's self-proclaimed adherence to a reductive didacticism, he had a great deal of sympathy for Moll and he presents her as very much the victim of circumstances beyond her control. Moll from the very start of the book is portrayed as a helpless victim of an uncaring social system. She was an orphan. Had she been born "in France or where else I know not," she tells us, where orphans "are immediately taken into the Care of the Government" and are looked after so that they are eventually "able to provide for themselves by an honest industrious Behaviour," she would not have been forced into thievery. "Had this been the Custom in our Country," she says,

> I had not been left a poor desolate Girl without Friends, without Cloaths, without Help or Helper, as was my Fate; and by which, I was not only expos'd to very great Distresses, even before I was capable, either of understanding my Case or how to amend it, but brought into a Course of Life which was not only scandalous in itself, but which in its ordinary Course tended to the swift Destruction both of Soul and Body. (1:2)

Such was Moll's unfortunate start in life. Nor did fortune continue to treat her any more kindly. The immediate incident that precipitated Moll's descent into crime was the death of her fifth husband, the sober banker, after which she claims she was left "Friendless and Helpless." She had money enough for a short while, but with no livelihood to support her, her prospects, she tells us, were bleak. "In this Distress," she says,

> I had no Assistant, no Friend to comfort or advise me, I sat and cried and tormented myself Night and Day, wringing my Hands, and sometimes raving like a distracted Woman; and indeed I have often wonder'd if it had not affected my Reason, for I had the Vapours to such a degree, that my Understanding was sometimes quite lost in Fancies and Imaginations.
>
> I liv'd two Years in this dismal Condition, wasting what little I had, weeping continually over my dismal Circumstances, and as it were only bleeding to Death, without the least hope or prospect of Help; and now I had cried so long, and so often, that Tears were exhausted, and I began to be Desperate, for I grew poor apace. (2:3)

What is Moll to do now? Where is she to turn? Thievery seems to be the only answer.

It is difficult not to be sympathetic to Moll's plight to the point of excusing her altogether. She is desperate and what she engages in is, after all, only petty crime. What the reader is presented with here is a virtually unresolvable antagonism between the author's avowed moral intention in the work—"to discourage and expose all sorts of vice and corruption of manners"—and the moral stance that is *implied* (in a way characteristic of the novel) by the work itself. And our suspicion of the deep sympathy that Defoe feels for his protagonist only increases if we realize how much of Defoe there is in Moll. Both are outsiders in their societies, and must make their ways by their wits; both aspire toward becoming "gentle persons"— Defoe, after all, added that classy (or so he thought) "De" to his surname "Foe."

Moll Flanders seems, then, to be a work that undermines its author's avowed intentions, a work whose ethical implications undercut rather than deepen his moral aim. George Starr has written well on Defoe's debt to "spiritual autobiography," and whether or not we accept his specific thesis, I think we can say that Moll's character is in many ways depicted in a manner that has much in common with the prenovelistic conventions of narrative fiction—is conceived, in other words, "ontologically" or "typologically" rather than "psychologically."[10] What we would look for in trying to apprehend the moral intention of a work written in this older tradition is the author's method of depicting the spiritual status of his characters, a method that might well jar with our modern sense of the lifelikeness of gradual psychological development.

A possible way to read the work, then—and it is a way that certainly allows us to apprehend the work's structure—is to see it in "spiritualist" terms: to see it as the process of the hardening of the soul to sin, followed by attempts at false repentance, and, finally, true repentance. Thus we see that Moll is at first morally sensitive to her crimes. "It is impossible to express the Horror of my Soul all the while I did it" (2:4), she comments just after her first transgression. But then her soul becomes gradually hardened until slowly, in Newgate Prison, the truth begins to dawn on her. Previously inured to her surroundings in Newgate, the experience that will change her is her recognizing the presence there of her Lancashire husband, who was driven to crime because Moll had deceived him into believing that her dowry would be considerable:

> I was overwhelm'd with Grief for him; my own Case gave me no Disturbance compar'd to this, and I loaded myself with reproaches on his Account; I bewail'd my misfortunes, and the Ruin he was now come to, at such a Rate, that I relish'd nothing now, as I did before, and the first Reflections I made upon the horrid Life I had liv'd began to return upon me, and as these Things return'd, my Abhorrence of the Place, and of the Way of living in it, return'd also; in a Word, I was perfectly chang'd, and became another Body.
>
> While I was under these Influences of Sorrow for him, came Notice to me that the next Sessions there would be a Bill preferr'd to the Grand Jury against me, and that I should be tried for my Life: My Temper was touch'd before, the wretched Boldness of Spirit which I had acquired, abated, and conscious Guilt began to flow in my Mind. In short, I began to think, and to think indeed is one real Advance from Hell to Heaven; all that hardened State and Temper of Soul, which I have said so much of before, is but a Deprivation of Thought; he that is restor'd to his Thinking, is restor'd to himself. (2:106–7)

10. See Miller, "Henry Fielding's *Tom Jones* and the Romance Tradition," chap. 5. Here Miller suggests that the idea of a "gradual 'evolution' or 'development' " of character, while appropriate to the psychologizing standards of the nineteenth-century novel, is not what one generally finds in the romance tradition, which often depicts the soul as undergoing "a series of crucial leaps into [ontological] states that were radically different from what had gone before" (57).

What we have here is the beginning of a conversion experience ("I was perfectly chang'd, and become another Body"). To "think" is to be conscious of one's moral being, of the presence of the divine in one's own soul; Moll recognizes that she has been suffering from "Deprivation of Thought," a virtual translation of the Augustinian notion of "privation of being."[11] She now realizes, in other words, that she had been attempting to eradicate the image of God in her soul. Quite rapidly from here to the end of the book she awakens from her "Lethargy of Soul" (2:104); she is reborn in Newgate (where she had been physically born). She leaves for America—literally but, more important, spiritually "a new World" (2:167)—with her Lancashire husband, where she becomes successful and happy.[12]

Such, in very broad outline, would be a reading of the work that accords with the intentions of the author as enunciated in the preface. George A. Starr has shown us, thoroughly and precisely, how convincingly such a reading can be supported by the religious writings of the time.[13] If Defoe were an allegorical writer—a Spenser or a Bunyan—such a reading would be completely convincing. But what seems to be of equal or even of greater interest to Defoe are those circumstantial factors that often mitigate against a strictly "spiritualist" reading of the book. Seen "allegorically," for instance, Newgate Prison is important as a symbol of hell, of what Defoe refers to as complete "Deprivation of Thought." And yet, as a reformer, Defoe was also interested in the physically horrific character of Newgate. These need not, of course, be mutually exclusive concerns, but in Defoe's fiction realistic detail often jostles uneasily against symbolic intention.[14] A "symbolic" and "spiritualist" reading of the book, then, confirms the author's avowed inten-

11. In which evil is defined, not as a substance, but as privation of complete being. For an expression of this doctrine, which became conventional in Christian thought, see the early chapters of Augustine's *Confessions*.

12. Moll's "transportation" to this new world is perhaps another instance of how Defoe's vocabulary has both a literal and a spiritual meaning. Moll is transported both literally to America and spiritually into a state of religious joy.

13. *Defoe and Spiritual Autobiography* (Princeton: Princeton University Press, 1965). Paula R. Backscheider, in *Daniel Defoe: Ambition and Innovation* (Lexington: University of Kentucky Press, 1986), appears to be in sympathy with Starr's spiritualist reading; see esp. 175–77.

14. Cf. Lee Edwards, "Between the Real and the Moral: Problems in the Structure of *Moll Flanders*," in *Twentieth-Century Interpretations of Moll Flanders*: "In his attempt to create a work which would be at once a moral fable and an accurate account of the realities of a particular life, Defoe created a double perspectival structure but failed to provide a sequence of narrative events which would either develop one point of view in terms of the other or generate a wider view which could contain the two. The real and the moral are not yoked to pull together, but are harnessed so that first the one pulls and now the other" (106).

tions as articulated in the preface: ". . . to recommend Virtue and generous Principles, and to discourage and expose all sorts of Vice and Corruption of Manners"; and we as readers should "be more pleas'd with the Moral than the Fable, with the Application than with the Relation, and with the end of the Writer than with the Life of the Person written of." And yet the "relation" of events often qualifies so extremely the "moral" intention of the author, that we are overcome with sympathy for Moll.

Perhaps we should resist the temptation, however, to reduce fiction to its "moral" or "religious" content. Kathy Eden, following the suggestive analysis of Wesley Trimpi, argues that Aristotle's conception of fiction "clearly emerges in the course of the *Poetics* as the literary counterpart to 'equity' in the disciplines of ethics and law." She continues: "As logical constructs, both fiction and equity are designed to qualify ethical action by negotiating between universal propositions—the general ethical presuppositions of the poet's audience or the advocate's legal code—and particular circumstances—the details of the plot or the events of the individual legal case."[15] Equity, as Aristotle makes clear in the *Nicomachean Ethics,* is the attempt to arrive at a balanced judgment of a particular legal case through a consideration of the qualifying circumstances.

Although there have been recent attempts to relate literature to law, the analogies that exist between literary and legal analysis continue to be obscured by our inheritance of eighteenth-century aestheticism (discussed in Part 2 of this book). And when such analogies are made in criticism that rejects such formalism, there is a tendency—particularly in New Historical criticism—to fail to discriminate between the distinctive methods of various forms of "discourse." The references to the law in literature, for example, may be viewed in some New Historical/Marxist accounts as highlighting the particular ideological affiliations implicitly or explicitly advocated by the text.[16] The current climate of opinion thus makes it necessary for me to be explicit about two points pertinent to the following analysis. First, fiction considered as fiction need not entail a formalism, as in the case of Kant, that excludes cognitive and ethical concerns. And second, the efficacy of fiction lies precisely in its ability to judge human action from a philosophically

15. "Poetry and Equity: Aristotle's Defense of Fiction," *Traditio* 38 (1982): 17. The same author develops her thesis on the connections between poetry and equity in *Poetic and Legal Fiction in the Aristotelian Tradition* (Princeton: Princeton University Press, 1986), particularly in chap. 2, 25–61.

16. For a criticism of New Historicism in this regard, see, e.g., Edward Pechter, "The New Historicism and Its Discontents: Politicizing Renaissance Drama," *PMLA* 102 (1987): 292–303.

flexible, nonideological point of view. The validity of these two assertions will, I hope, become apparent in the following discussion of the similarities that exist between fiction and equity.

To elucidate these similarities and to articulate their relevance to *Moll Flanders,* it will be necessary to discuss relevant passages from Aristotle's *Nicomachean Ethics* and Quintilian's *De institutione oratoria* in some detail and afterward to offer some suggestions about their relation to Defoe's intentions in *Moll Flanders.*

Aristotle's discussion of equity in the *Nicomachean Ethics* (5.10.3–7) reads as follows:

> Law is always a general statement, yet there are cases which it is not possible to cover in a general statement. In matters therefore where, while it is necessary to speak in general terms, it is not possible to do so correctly, the law takes into consideration the majority of cases, although it is not unaware of the error this involves. And this does not make it a wrong law; for the error lies not in the law nor in the lawgiver, but in the nature of the case: the material of conduct is essentially irregular. When therefore the law lays down a general rule, and thereafter a case arises which is an exception to the rule, it is then right, where the lawgiver's pronouncement because of its absoluteness is defective and erroneous [ἥμαρτεν ἁπλῶς εἰπών], to rectify the defect by deciding as the lawgiver would himself decide if he were present on the occasion, and would have enacted if he had been cognizant of the case in question. Hence, while the equitable is just, and is superior to one sort of justice, it is not superior to absolute justice, but only to the error due to its absolute statement. This is the essential nature of the equitable: it is a rectification of the law where law is defective because of its generality. In fact this is the reason why things are not all determined by law: it is because there are some cases for which it is impossible to lay down a law, so that a special ordinance becomes necessary. For what is itself indefinite [ἀόριστος] can only be measured by an indefinite standard, like the leaden rule used by Lesbian builders; just as that rule is not rigid but can be bent to the shape of the stone, so a special ordinance is made to fit the circumstances of the case.[17]

17. *Nicomachean Ethics,* trans. Harris Rackham, Loeb Classical Library (1968), 316–17.

Let us relate these comments to *Moll Flanders*. It is wrong to steal: this statement is correct, speaking absolutely. In the majority of cases, the rule can be enforced in an unproblematic way. But there are cases that are not covered in the general statement of the law. This does not mean that the law is a bad one or that the lawgiver erred when framing it. But when someone like Moll Flanders, who is clearly a victim of society, steals merely for survival, in judging her action we—the readers of the "novel"—would have to decide her guilt or innocence "as the lawgiver would himself decide if he were present on the occasion." Human behavior cannot always be judged by rigid categories of right and wrong. In some instances, if we judge by the flexible Lesbian rule, a special ordinance becomes necessary. As Trimpi observes, equity—and the arts in general—corresponds to qualitative measurement, which "is 'substantial,' particular, applicable, and casuistic," whereas "the quantitative measure is abstract, general, inflexible, and impersonal."[18]

Moreover, as Trimpi remarks, "it is precisely in its 'equitable' function that the fictional example [καθ᾽ ὑπόθεσιν] is useful for Aristotle and Quintilian when considerations of quality [i.e., the true ethical nature of an action that cannot be understood in purely quantifiable terms] enter a case."[19] It is precisely fiction that, in the classical articulation, mediates between universal principles and particular examples—as I elucidated in Chapter 5 in my discussion of the principles of literary theory implicit in the Pindaric ode.

In *De institutione oratoria* Quintilian suggests the importance of fictional examples in ascertaining the "quality" of an action. The example he gives is that of a person who violated the law by not supporting his parents. In order to persuade the jury that he should not go to prison for his actions, such a man, Quintilian says, "advances the hypothesis [*utitur fictione*] that he would be exempt from such a penalty if he were a soldier, an infant, or if he were absent from home on the service of the state." These hypotheses are fictions in the sense that they do not truly reflect the man's own situation, but if we entertain such fictions there may be others that do in fact apply to this particular case and would encourage the judge to look beyond the strict letter of the law. These fictional hypotheses are particularly useful, according to Quintilian, when "we argue against the letter of the law" [*contra scriptum*] or when "we

---

18. *Muses of One Mind: The Literary Analysis of Experience and Its Continuity* (Princeton: Princeton University Press, 1983), 268. As Trimpi points out, Aristotle's views on equity are an extension of Plato's views on the necessity of flexible measurement in legal and ethical matters as expressed in the *Statesman* (283d–85b, 294–97).

19. *Muses of One Mind,* 272.

are concerned with the quality of an act" (5.10.95–99).[20] So with Moll Flanders. It is clearly a violation of the law to steal. But what if one is an orphan and a woman—in a society in which women are not granted privileges of education and ownership—who has the misfortune of being left in poverty by her husband(s) with virtually no legitimate means of securing her survival? As we flesh out a fictional account of this kind of person, the rigidity of the law becomes qualified by our consideration of mitigating circumstances, and we have also managed to write an extended narrative called *The Fortunes and Misfortunes of the Famous Moll Flanders*.[21]

Defoe was greatly interested in the law. As Ian Watt observes in his *Rise of the Novel*, Defoe's characters often exhibit qualities of "forensic ratiocination"[22] as they weigh their actions, and Defoe also draws extensively on contemporary canon and common law.[23] Defoe was particularly interested in problems of casuistry or equity. As George Starr in his excellent book on the subject informs us, the works of the casuists William Perkins, William Ames, and Richard Baxter were part of the standard curriculum at the Newington Green Academy, which Defoe attended. In Perkins Defoe would have read that "the circumstances of time, place, person, and manner of doing, doe serue to enlarge or extenuate the sinne committed," a concept that, Starr comments, Defoe "frequently reiterates," such as in the following remark from *The Compleat English Tradesman*: "Circumstances, Time, and Place alter things very much." "At times, Moll's story tends to subvert 'classical moralism,'" Starr observes, "and casts doubt on the legitimacy of rigid distinctions between 'goodness and badness.' With this object, considerable emphasis is put on the principle that circumstances alter cases."[24] Starr's remarks are very much to the point, but I would take issue with what he

20. These passages from Quintilian are quoted in ibid., 255–56.

21. The relation of equity to the eighteenth-century novel is mentioned by John P. Zomchick, "'A Penetration Which Nothing Can Deceive': Gender and Juridical Discourse in Some Eighteenth-Century Narratives, *Studies in English Literature, 1500–1900* 29, no. 3 (1989): 535–61. In his discussion of *Tom Jones,* Zomchick cites Sir Robert Chambers's definition of equity as "that branch of English jurisprudence that supplies the deficiencies of law" by doing "what the law requires but cannot perform" (*A Course of Lectures on the English Law,* ed. Thomas M. Curley, 2 vols. [Madison: University of Wisconsin Press, 1986], 2:31, 551). Although he discusses *Moll Flanders* in his article, Zomchick does not explicitly treat the relations between Defoe's fiction and equity in law.

22. P. 80.

23. See Spiro Peterson, "The Matrimonial Theme of Defoe's *Roxana,*" *PMLA* 70 (1955): 166–91, and *Defoe and the Nature of Man* (Oxford: Clarendon Press, 1963).

24. *Defoe and Casuistry,* 112–13. The phrase "classical moralism" is taken from Carl Van Doren's introduction to *Moll Flanders* (New York: Alfred A. Knopf, 1923), xiii.

appears to mean by "classical moralism," since you cannot get any more classical than Aristotle, for whom it was precisely equity—a less objectionable name for casuistry—that attempted to arrive at a balanced judgment by negotiating between the strict letter of the law and particular cases.

Defoe is generally seen as an anti-Augustan, or at least as an un-Augustan—that is, as an "unclassical"—writer. And to a large extent this is true, especially if we think of the English Augustan achievement as the triumph of form and the English Augustan work of art as the perfectly realized formal embodiment of its author's intention. I am not arguing that Defoe went to Aristotle or to Quintilian in the way Pope or Johnson went to Horace or Juvenal. What I am suggesting is that Defoe was greatly interested in casuistry and that he read the texts of casuistical writers; that fiction and equity or casuistry perform analogous functions; and that, as in Aristotle and Quintilian, a fictional account—in Defoe's case, of Moll's plight—is a means of analyzing and qualifying the strict letter of the law that, if applied rigidly and without regard to circumstances, might very well judge a defendant far too harshly. Much of *Moll Flanders* is therefore a classic in the Aristotelian sense that I have been trying to define and exemplify throughout this book. Defoe has, in this regard, resisted the didactic heresy. Defoe was also, however, tied to the moralistic and overwhelmingly didactic nature of spiritual biography and of the romance tradition and was careful to portray the steps by which Moll hardened her soul to sin and then, through repentance, was spiritually reborn. The tension between these two principles of order—which we might call the classically ethical, on the one hand, and the allegorical/moralistic, on the other—is never fully resolved.

PART IV

RESISTING MIMETIC LITERALISM

13

DRYDEN'S *OF DRAMATIC POESY* AND THE ANCIENT ANTAGONISM BETWEEN ELEVATION AND VERISIMILITUDE

In Part 3 I dealt with how works of literature often resist being reduced to abstract philosophical precepts. In Part 4 I will now consider the issue of mimetic literalism. The first full-length discussion of the mimetic nature of literature occurs in Plato, and I shall reexamine Plato's argument—which I believe has often been misunderstood—in the final chapter of this book. One of the most significant treatments of the theme of the limitations of mimetic literalism is to be found in Cervantes's *Don Quixote,* which can be viewed as a reaction against the reduction of literature to the represen-tation of purely material reality, and specifically against the excesses of Renaissance (neo-Aristotelian) literary theory, which sought to reduce literature to history.[1] The pursuit of mimetic literalism would be continued in the seventeenth and eighteenth centuries through Corneille's addition of the unities of time and place to the original (and liberally expressed) Aristotelian unity of action. In defense of Shakespeare, Samuel Johnson would concede that "to the unities of time and place he has shewn no regard, and perhaps a nearer view of the principles on which they stand will diminish their value, and withdraw from them the veneration which, from the time of Corneille, they have very generally received by discovering that they have given more trouble to the poet, than pleasure to the auditor." Johnson then goes on to argue—against mimetic literalism—that "it is false, that any representation is mistaken for reality; that any dramatic fable in its materiality was ever credible, or, for a single moment, was ever credited."[2] Joshua Reynolds, in his *Discourses,* continues to make the case against mimetic literalism, in this instance with regard to the visual arts. "Even in portraits," Reynolds says in his *Discourse* 4, "the grace and ... the likeness consists more in taking the general air, than in observing the exact similitude of every feature."[3] In the present chapter I shall consider the issue of mimetic literalism in an earlier document of the neoclassical period, Dryden's *Essay of Dramatic Poesy* (1668). I shall place this issue within the context of the history of literary theory, and then, in the concluding chapter, I shall return to one of the earliest and most influential statements against mimetic literalism in Plato's *Republic.*

After Lisideius has pleaded the case for French drama in Dryden's famous dialogue, Neander comes to the defense of the drama of his native England. Lisideius has just praised French drama for, among other things, its superior elevation to English drama. Here is a crucial point in Neander's response:

> For the lively imitation of nature being in the definition of a play, those which best fulfill that law ought to be esteemed superior to the others. 'Tis true, those beauties of the French poesy are such as will raise perfection higher where it is, but are not sufficient to give it where it is not: they are indeed the beauties of a statue, but not of a

---

1. On this issue, see Alban K. Forcione's brilliant study, *Cervantes, Aristotle, and the Persiles* (Princeton: Princeton University Press, 1970).

2. *The Yale Edition of the Works of Samuel Johnson,* 16 vols., ed. Arthur Sherbo (New Haven: Yale University Press, 1958–57), 7:75–76.

3. *Discourses on Art,* edited and with an introduction by Robert W. Wark (London: Collier Books, 1969), 56–57.

man, because not animated with the soul of poesy, which is imitation of humour and passions.[4]

Neander is admitting here that French drama *is* more elevated than English drama. " 'Tis true," he says, that "those beauties of French poesy are such as will raise perfection higher where it is." But English drama, Neander suggests, is more "lively," which means, for Dryden, more lifelike, more realistic.[5] Thus, English drama gives you the image of a man, French the "beauties of a statue."

In the final section of Dryden's *Essay of Dramatic Poesy,* Crites and Neander debate the virtues and propriety of using rhyme in serious plays. Since a play, Crites says, "is an imitation of nature; and since no man without premeditation speaks in rhyme, neither ought he to do it on the stage" (1.78). "Verse, 'tis true," Neander admits in response, "is not the effect of sudden thought." But, Neander continues, "A play, as I have said, to be like nature, is to be set above it; as statues which are placed on high are made greater than the life, that they may descend to the sight in their just proportion" (1.88). Where Neander had previously made the case for realism in drama, he is here arguing for its very opposite. He had just condemned French drama for its failure to be sufficiently "lively," that is, realistic; the beauties it offers, he had remarked, were those "of a statue, but not of a man." Neander now reverses the evaluative connotations of the analogy of the drama to a statue. A play, he now says, must be set above nature as "statues . . . placed on high are made greater than the life."[6] Such an apparent reversal in the position of Neander—whose views many critics take to be those of Dryden himself—suggests that Dryden's claims of critical impartiality and even confusion might well be taken as more than a rhetorical or literary device.[7] "It will not be easy to find in all the

---

4. *Of Dramatic Poesy and Other Critical Essays,* ed. George Watson, 2 vols. (New York: Everyman's Library, 1962), 1:56. Further references to this edition will be made parenthetically in the text.

5. H. James Jensen, *A Glossary of Dryden's Critical Terms* (Minneapolis: University of Minnesota Press, 1969), 74.

6. By "nature" Neander is here referring to "common nature," and he is suggesting that a serious play should be elevated above this "common nature." For a discussion of the various meanings which Dryden attaches to the term "nature," see Mary Thale, "Dryden's Critical Vocabulary: The Imitation of Nature," *Publications in Language and Literature* 2 (1966): 315–26.

7. The epigraph to the *Essay of Dramatic Poesy,* from Horace's *Ars Poetica*—"fungar vice cotis, acutum / reddere quae ferrum valet, exsors ipsa secandi" [I shall play the whetstone's part, which sharpens steel, but is itself incapable of cutting] (304–5)—initiates the theme of critical impartiality. In "The Academic Nature of the *Essay of Dramatic Poesy,*" *Papers on Language and Literature* 8 (1972), Richard V. Leclerq argues that Dryden's

opulence of our language," Johnson shrewdly remarked in a very Johnsonian manner, "a treatise so artfully variegated with successive representations of opposite probabilities."[8]

Why does Neander argue first on naturalistic and then on anti-naturalistic grounds? Several answers suggest themselves. He may simply be defending Dryden's own efforts at writing the rhymed heroic play, which was more naturalistic than the French drama but more stylized than the blank-verse drama of his Elizabethan and Jacobean predecessors. Dryden had written *The Rival Ladies* (1664) partly in rhyme and *The Indian Emperor* (1665) entirely in rhyme. A second and related answer is that Neander feels himself and his contemporaries to be oppressed by what W. J. Bate has called "the burden of the past" and Harold Bloom "the anxiety of influence." The dramatic achievements in blank verse of Jonson, Fletcher, and Shakespeare are so decisive, Neander remarks, that "this therefore will be a good argument to us either not to write at all, or to attempt some other way." "This way of writing in verse," Neander continues, referring to the heroic couplet, "they have only left free to us" (1.85). By remaining true to the tradition of English "liveliness" and at the same time writing their plays in the as yet unperfected dramatic medium of the heroic couplet, the playwrights of Restoration England could thereby distinguish themselves from—and even surpass—their daunting Renaissance predecessors.

There is, however, a perhaps less obvious though more fundamental answer to the question. The whole of the *Essay of Dramatic Poesy* may be viewed, as Robert D. Hume has proposed, as "a struggle between literal and ideal representation"[9] and it is this struggle that Neander—by arguing first in favor of extreme naturalism and then against it—is trying to resolve. Dryden would go on attempting to resolve this problem throughout his career as a writer, often trying to strike a balance between a vigorous and

---

impartiality must be viewed as a philosophical pose characteristic of the method of the New Academy rather than his actual position. Even if we do equate Dryden's position with that of Neander, Dryden's adherence to Neander's principles would appear to be somewhat tentative, for when he came to write the dedicatory epistle Dryden was already questioning the correctness of the views he had only recently held: "I confess," he tells Lord Buckhurst, "I find many things in this discourse which I do not now approve; my judgment being a little altered since the writing of it, but whether for the better or the worse, I know not: neither indeed is it much material in an Essay where all I have said is problematical" (*Of Dramatic Poesy,* 1:13). Dryden concludes his dedicatory epistle by stating that it was not his intention "to reconcile, but to relate" (ibid., 16) the various views expressed in the *Essay.*

8. *Lives of the English Poets,* ed. G. B. Hill, 3 vols. (Oxford: Clarendon Press, 1905), 1:412.

9. *Dryden's Criticism* (Ithaca: Cornell University Press, 1970), 195.

earthy realism and a dignified sense of elevation. Before discussing how Dryden attempted to do this, it will be helpful to trace the problem back to its source, where the water is clearest, and to place this "struggle between literal and ideal representation" within the context of the history of literary theory. In order to understand why Dryden was so perplexed by this problem, I shall begin by looking at some passages that, at first glance, may appear to have little to do with the question of the decorum of literary representation.

It will be necessary, first of all, to recall some basic formulations made in antiquity about the objects of knowledge and their representation. In the Platonic dialogue that bears his name, Critias tells Timaeus, who has just given his account of the creation of the universe:

> The accounts given by us all must be, of course, of the nature of imitations and representations; and if we look at the portraiture of divine and of human bodies as executed by the painters, in respect of the ease or difficulty with which they succeed in imitating their subjects in the opinion of onlookers, we shall notice in the first place that as regards the earth and mountains and rivers and woods and the whole of heaven, with the things that exist and move therein, we are content if a man is able to represent them with even a small degree of likeness; and further, that, inasmuch as we have no exact [ἀκριβές] knowledge about such objects, we do not examine closely or criticize the paintings, but tolerate, in such cases, an inexact and deceptive sketch. On the other hand, whenever a painter tries to render a likeness of our own bodies, we quickly perceive what is defective because of our constant familiar acquaintance with them, and become severe critics of him who fails to bring out to the full all the points of similarity. And precisely the same thing happens, as we should notice, in the case of discourses: in respect of what is celestial and divine we are satisfied if the account possesses even a small degree of likelihood, but we examine with precision [ἀκριβῶς] what is mortal and human. (106e)[10]

The epistemological principle that Critias is implying here is the following: there is an inverse relation between the degree of verisimilar accuracy that should be expected in any representation, on the one hand, and the degree of elevation or the importance of the subject matter, on the other. In other

---

10. *Critias,* trans. R. G. Bury, Loeb Classical Library (1929), 260–63.

words, the more sublime the object of knowledge, the less accurately can it be rendered or known.

This formulation is stated again and again in antiquity. In his treatise *On the Parts of the Animals,* Aristotle says:

> Of things constituted by nature some are ungenerated, imperishable, and eternal, while others are subject to generation and decay. The former are excellent beyond compare and divine, but less accessible to knowledge. The evidence that might throw light on them is furnished scantily by sensation; whereas respecting perishable plants and animals we have abundant information, living as we do in their midst. . . . The scanty conceptions to which we can attain of celestial things give us, from their excellence, more pleasure than all our knowledge of the world in which we live. (1.5, 644b 23–645a)[11]

And in his treatise *On the Soul:* "We regard all knowledge as beautiful and valuable, but one kind more so than another, either in virtue of its accuracy [κατ' ἀκρίβειαν], or because it relates to higher and more wonderful things [θαυμασιωτέρων]."[12] There are two criteria for judging the value of knowledge: knowledge is valuable either by virtue of its exactitude or because its objects possess a "higher dignity and greater wonderfulness."[13] That which can be known or rendered with exactitude and experienced by the senses will, therefore, inspire less wonder than that which is more difficult to know or render with exactitude. This principle becomes the epistemological basis of the ancient characters or levels of style and their corresponding literary genres.

11. *On the Parts of Animals,* trans. W. Ogle, in *The Basic Works of Aristotle,* ed. R. McKeon (New York: Random House, 1941), 656.

12. *On the Soul,* trans. W. S. Hett, Loeb Classical Library (1936; rpt., 1964). For my awareness of the significance of the ancient epistemological principle that there is an inverse relation between, on the one hand, the degree of accuracy to be expected in any representation and, on the other, the degree of elevation or the importance of the subject matter, I am indebted to Wesley Trimpi, *Muses of One Mind: The Literary Analysis of Experience and Its Continuity* (Princeton: Princeton University Press, 1983), 97–102, where Trimpi cites the Platonic and Aristotelian passages quoted here.

13. J. A. Smith's translation, in McKeon, ed., *Works of Aristotle,* of the Greek phrase βελτιόνων τε καὶ θαυμασιωτέρων. Cf. the following reasons given by Samuel Johnson, in the famous comparison between Dryden and Pope in the *Life of Pope,* for his belief that Dryden's "acquired knowledge" was superior to that of Pope: "The notions of Dryden were formed by comprehensive speculation, and those of Pope by minute attention. There is more dignity in the knowledge of Dryden, and more certainty in that of Pope" (*Lives of the English Poets,* 3:222).

As in Plato's and Aristotle's formulations about the objects of knowledge and their representation, so with regard to the classical levels of style, there is an inverse relation between the degree of verisimilar accuracy that should be expected in any representation, on the one hand, and the degree of elevation, on the other. The high style is appropriate to the genres of tragedy and epic; it is elevated above the concerns of the everyday and it is meant to evoke—through the grandeur of its language and of its subject matter—the emotion of wonder. The low style—the style appropriate to comedy, the epigram, the epistle, and satire—depicts everyday, "realistic" details. And these styles should not, if at all possible, be mixed. Although levels of style may occasionally be combined, Horace says toward the beginning of the *Ars Poetica,* this should be the exception rather than the rule:

> versibus exponi tragicis res comica non volt;
> indignatur item privatis ac prope socco
> dignis carminibus narrari cena Thyestae.
> singula quaeque locum teneant sortita decentem.

> [A theme for comedy refuses to be set forth in verses of tragedy; likewise the feast of Thyestes scorns to be told in strains of daily life that are more fitting to the comic sock. Let each style keep the becoming place allotted to it.][14]

Lofty tragic verse is simply not compatible, Horace is suggesting, with the depiction of realistic detail.

There is, in fact, an antagonistic relation in ancient literature between elevation and realism, between πάθος (strong emotion suitable to tragedy) and ἦθος (realistic character description suitable to comedy), and this antagonism is discussed again and again by ancient critics such as Aristotle, Longinus, and Quintilian. In his famous comparison between the *Iliad* and *Odyssey* in the *Peri hypsous,* Longinus praises the consistent sublimity of the *Iliad* but says that "in the *Odyssey* one likens Homer to the setting sun; the grandeur remains without the intensity" (9.10).[15] Why is the *Odyssey* less grand than the *Iliad?* Because, in part, it depicts

---

14. Both the Latin and the translation, which I have slightly adapted, are from *Horace: Satires, Epistles, and Ars Poetica,* trans. H. Rushton Fairclough, Loeb Classical Library (1926; rpt., 1970), 458–59.

15. *"Longinus" on the Sublime,* trans. W. Hamilton Fyfe, Loeb Classical Library (1927; rpt., 1965), 153.

everyday detail, that is, it is more "realistic" and hence more like comedy. As Longinus concludes his comparison between the Greek epics, he says that great writers and poets, with the decline of their emotional power (πάθος), give way to realistic character-study (ἦθος). And he then says that "the realistic description of Odysseus' household forms a kind of comedy of manners" (9.15).[16] Aristotle anticipates these remarks when he says, in the *Poetics* (1459b14), that the *Iliad* may be characterized as "pathetic" (παθητικόν) and the *Odyssey* as "ethical" (ἠθική). Aristotle's and Longinus's association of the *Iliad* with πάθος and of the *Odyssey* with ἦθος is, then, as D. A. Russell has suggested, fundamentally a distinction between the intensely elevated and the "more realistic, nearer to everyday life" and "milder in emotional tone."[17]

The antagonism between the appropriateness of representing that which is elevated and that which is more particularized is present in all classicizing periods and becomes especially acute in the poetry of the English Augustan period. Every reader of *The Rape of the Lock*, for example, or of Pope's poems written in the conversational Horatian style, cannot help being struck by the poet's extraordinary gift for the depiction of minute, vivid, realistic detail. When Pope came to translate the *Iliad*, however, he felt that he had to purge the translation of those very kinds of details which enliven *The Rape of the Lock* and the Horatian poems. For Longinus, no poem was more elevated than the *Iliad*. Pope, however, believed that much of the poem's diction was not sufficiently elevated for his contemporary audience, as he explains in commenting on his translation of one of Homer's similes: "The Lowness of this Image . . . will naturally shock a modern Critick, and would scarce be forgiven in a Poet of these Times. The utmost a Translator

---

16. Ibid., 155.

17. For other discussions in antiquity of the contrast between πάθος and ἦθος, see Dionysius of Halicarnassus, *Demosthenes* 2, 8, 43, 53; Cicero, *Orator* 128; and Quintilian, *De institutione oratoria* 6.2.8–24. These passages are cited in D. A. Russell's commentary upon Longinus's comparison between the *Iliad* and *Odyssey* in *Peri hypsous* 9.11–15, *"Longinus" On the Sublime* (Oxford: Clarendon Press, 1964), 99. Dean T. Mace, in one of the finest pieces written on Dryden's *Essay*, argues that it is the conflict between his allegiance to representing external events (characteristic of native English drama) and his allegiance to representing the "passions" (characteristic of French seventeenth-century drama) that most perplexes Dryden; see "Dryden's Dialogue on Drama," *Journal of the Warburg and Courtauld Institutes* 25 (1962): 87–112. This chapter may be taken as supplementing Mace's article by suggesting that the seventeenth-century notion that the higher genres such as tragedy and epic should imitate not chiefly an action but rather the "passions" themselves is an extreme development of the ancient antagonism between ἦθος and πάθος.

can do is to heighten the Expression, so as to render the disparity less observable: which is endeavour'd here, and in other Places."[18] Hence, for example, Homer's "persistent horsefly" (*Iliad* 17.570) becomes, in Pope's translation, a "vengeful Hornet" (17.642).

The sublime and the everyday, then, are not very compatible in classicizing periods, and their incompatibility becomes a central theme in such important neoclassical treatises as the *Discourses* of Sir Joshua Reynolds. "Whatever is familiar, or in any way reminds us of what we see and hear every day," Reynolds characteristically observes in his *Discourse* 13, "perhaps does not belong to the higher provinces of art, either in poetry or in painting."[19] It is for their concentration on the depiction of common, everyday objects that Reynolds in *Discourse* 7 regards Rembrandt and the Dutch painters—"who introduced into their historical pictures exact representations of individual objects with all their imperfections"[20]—as incapable of achieving the grand style.

In the Middle Ages, however, when the ancient levels of style were not so rigorously separated, the sublime and the everyday could be found in the same literary work, as they are, for example, in the *Divine Comedy* and in the plays of Shakespeare, whose methods of literary representation owe much to the later Middle Ages. This is, of course, the profound insight of Erich Auberbach and is the central theme of *Mimesis.*[21] The tragedies of Racine and Shakespeare both inhabit what Reynolds refers to as "the higher provinces of art"; but Shakespeare, unlike the neoclassical Racine but like

18. *The Twickenham Edition of the Poems of Alexander Pope,* ed. John Butt et al., 11 vols. (New Haven: Yale University Press, 1938–68), 7:153. For a fuller discussion of the problems of stylistic decorum considered in relation to Pope's translation of Homer, see my *Pope's Iliad: Homer in the Age of Passion* (Princeton: Princeton University Press, 1983), 55–73. Homer's depictions of the familiar and the everyday were not always considered indecorous. Aristotle, for instance, in discussing how an argument may be rendered as clearly as possible, suggests in the *Topics* (157a14–16) that "examples and illustrations should be adduced, the examples being to the point and drawn from things which are familiar [οἰκεῖα] to us, of the kind which Homer uses and not of the kind that Choerilus employs" (trans. E. S. Forster, Loeb Classical Library [1960], 686–87).

19. *Discourses on Art,* 207.

20. Ibid., 111.

21. The ancient antagonism between realism and elevation is resolved in medieval literature, Auerbach suggests, because "the story of Christ, with its ruthless mixture of everyday reality and the highest and most sublime tragedy . . . had conquered the classical rule of styles" *Mimesis: The Representation of Reality in Western Literature,* trans. Willard Trask [Garden City, N.Y.: Doubleday, 1957], 409). See also *"Sermo Humilis,"* in *Literary Language and its Public in Late Latin Antiquity and the Middle Ages* (Princeton: Princeton University Press, 1965), 5–66.

the medieval Dante, can in his tragedies deal as well with "whatever is familiar, or in any way reminds us of what we see and hear every day." In the course of the Renaissance, when what Auerbach refers to as "the Christian-figural scheme" began to lose its hold, "antique models . . . and antique theory reappeared, unclouded."[22]

Viewed against this background, we can begin to understand Neander's criticism of French drama for resembling a statue in his first speech, and his seemingly contradictory recommendation, in his second and final speech, that plays must be set above ordinary nature "as statues . . . placed on high are made greater than the life." Neander is trying to resist the ancient and often mutually exclusive claims of elevation, in his first speech, and of everyday, earthy realism in his last. Lisideius, who argues the case for French drama before Neander comes to the defense of the native English tradition, may be viewed in broader terms as a neoclassicist, as one who believes that the depiction of realistic detail and elevation are mutually exclusive, and he is willing to eliminate any realistic details and particularities in order to achieve the highest elevation possible.

It might be thought that Lisideius's defense of the unities suggest that he believes the drama should, above all, imitate an action with as much verisimilar accuracy as possible. For, as Corneille writes in his *Discourse on the Three Unities:*

> A dramatic poem is an imitation, or, to put it better, a portrait of men's actions; and without doubt the portraits are more excellent to the degree that they resemble the original. The representation lasts two hours; and it would resemble the original perfectly if the action it represents did not demand any longer in the imitation itself. Thus let us not at all stop at twelve or at twenty-four hours. But let us confine the action of the poem in the least time that we can, so that the representation resembles it more closely and is more perfect.[23]

The more pressing reason that Lisideius defends the unities, however, is that he feels once the eye's exacting demands for verisimilitude are placated, the stage can be cleared for highly emotional speeches, which ap-

---

22. *Mimesis,* 279.
23. In W. J. Bate, *Criticism: The Major Texts* (1952; rpt., New York: Harcourt Brace Jovanovich, 1970), 119. The translation is by Bate.

peal to the ear, whose demands for verisimilitude are traditionally less exacting than those of the eye.[24] For apart from his advocacy of the unities, Lisideius wants as little realistic detail as possible depicted on the stage, although it may be considered decorous to have such details narrated. Hence Lisideius says:

> I have observed that, in all our tragedies, the audience cannot forbear laughing when the actors are to die; 'tis the most comic part of the whole play. All *passions* may be lively represented on the stage, . . . but there are many *actions* which can never be imitated to a just height; dying especially is a thing which none but a Roman gladiator could naturally perform on the stage, when he did not imitate or represent, but naturally do it; and therefore it is better to omit the representation of it.
>
> The words of a good writer, which describe it lively, will make a deeper impression of belief in us than all the actor can persuade us to when he seems to fall dead before us; as a poet in the description of a beautiful garden, or a meadow, will please our imagination more than the place itself can please our sight. When we see death represented, we are convinced it is but fiction; but when we hear it related, our eyes (the strongest witnesses) are wanting, which might have undeceived us, and we are willing to favour the sleight when the poet does not too grossly impose on us. (1.51)

The principle that the eye demands greater clarity and exactness than does the ear helps to explain, for example, the convention of the messenger speech in ancient and in neoclassical tragedy. Violence occurs offstage in Greek tragedy. We do not see Clytemnestra kill Agamemnon in his bath, we do not see Oedipus blind himself, for neither of these actions can ever, in the words of Lisideius, "be imitated to a just height." Thus Aristotle says in the twenty-fourth chapter of the *Poetics* that astonishing incidents can more easily be incorporated into epic than into tragedy, since in epic "we cannot

24. Dio Chrysostom, for example, in his *Twelfth, or Olympic Discourse,* has an imaginary Phidias compare his own art with that of Homer. Phidias argues that the literary artist is freer from the strictures of verisimilitude than is the visual artist, for the eyes "are harder to convince and demand greater clearness" than do the ears. Phidias goes on to say that although it was easy enough for Homer to describe Zeus as he performs miraculous acts, in "our art it is absolutely impossible, for it permits the observer to test it with his eyes from close at hand and in full view" (*Discourses,* trans. J. W. Cohoon, Loeb Classical Library [1939], 2.75, 83).

actually see the person performing the action. Because the incidents in the pursuit of Hector would show themselves to be absurd if they were put on the stage—the Achaeans standing there, not pursuing him, and (Achilles) signaling to them to stand back—whereas in epic we do not notice this" (1460a11).[25] Horace recalls this observation in the *Ars Poetica* when he says, in a passage that Lisideius himself cites, that astonishing events should be narrated rather than acted, since "less vividly is the mind stirred by what finds entrance through the ears than by what is brought before the trusty eyes" [segnius irritant animos demissa per aurem / quam quae sunt oculis subiecta fidelibus]. Horace goes on to say:

> Yet you will not bring upon the stage what should be performed behind the scenes, and you will keep much from our eyes, which an actor's ready tongue will soon narrate in our presence; so that Medea is not to butcher her boys before the people, nor impious Atreus cook human flesh upon the stage, nor Procne be turned into a bird, Cadmus into a snake. Whatever you show me, I discredit and abhor. (180–88)[26]

Lisideius's desire to exclude all verisimilar details that will strain the eye's exacting demands for credibility is, therefore, firmly within the neoclassical tradition of the decorum of representation.

Neander, like Lisideius, is aware that the depiction of realistic detail and elevation are traditionally held to be mutually exclusive within what I have described as the neoclassical tradition. But Neander, unlike Lisideius, is willing—at least in his first speech—to sacrifice elevation for the sake of depicting realistic detail. Hence, Neander opposes the long speeches in French drama because such speeches are not lifelike. "It is unnatural," Neander says, "for any one in a gust of passion to speak for so long a time, or for another in the same condition to suffer him without interruption" (1.60). English comedy is superior to the Old Comedy of Aristophanes because it is more lifelike than Aristophanic comedy. Aristophanes' portrayal of Socrates was more ridiculous than realistic, for "the τὸ γελοῖον of the Old

25. In Gerald F. Else, *Aristotle's Poetics: The Argument* (Cambridge: Harvard University Press, 1967), 622. The translation is Else's.
26. *Horace: Satires, Epistles, Ars Poetica,* trans. H. Rushton Fairclough, Loeb Classical Library (1926), 464–67. I have slightly modified the translation.

Comedy, of which Aristophanes was chief, was not so much to imitate a man as to make the people laugh at some odd conceit which had commonly somewhat of unnatural or obscene in it" (1.72). It is this gift for realistic description for which Neander praises Ben Jonson. The "peculiar genius and talent of Ben Jonson," Neander comments, is "the description of... humours, drawn from the knowledge and observation of particular persons" (1.73). And Neander praises Shakespeare, as I have mentioned, for his extraordinary capacities for lifelike description. "All of the images of nature were present to him," Neander says; "when he describes anything, you more than see it, you feel it, too" (1.67).

At the end of the *Essay,* Crites and Neander address themselves to the question of whether rhyme is allowable in serious plays. Crites opposes rhyme because it is unnatural. For, Crites says, a play being an imitation of nature, "since no man without premeditation speaks in rhyme, neither ought he to do so on the stage" (1.78). Such an argument in favor of naturalism—that is, for "liveliness"—could well have been made by Neander, but Neander in fact argues the opposite case. He believes that rhyme and not blank verse should be used, since a serious play is an imitation not of ordinary life, not of common nature, but of "nature wrought up to an higher pitch. The plot, the characters, the wit, the passions, the descriptions, are all exalted above the level of common converse, as high as the imagination of the poet can carry them" (1.87).

That it is Neander rather than Lisideius who argues in favor of rhyme; and that it is Neander as well who argues in favor of the lifelike drama of Shakespeare and Ben Jonson, suggests that Dryden—who had been raised with neoclassical critical principles but was deeply affected by his own native and largely unneoclassical dramatic tradition—wished above all to resist the potentially mutually exclusive claims of the sublime, on the one hand, and the realistic or the verisimilar, on the other. I would call Dryden's effort "classical" in the best sense, especially if we remember the qualities of the best kind of style as Aristotle describes it in chapter 22 of the *Poetics.* There Aristotle says that this is a style that will avoid the extremes of excessive meanness and undue elevation. The clearest style—the most lively and "realistic" style—will use current words, but the problem with such a style is that it will never rise above the mean or lowly. In order to elevate a style above the everyday, a writer must use unusual words, but if a style departs too sharply from common usage, it will become merely enigmatic. So Sainte-Beuve in "What Is a Classic?" suggests that "a true classic" will be written "in a style which is new without neologisms, new and ancient, easily contemporaneous with every age."[27]

As a dramatist, Dryden was perhaps never really able to steer successfully between these two extremes. In accordance with Neander's advice (see *Of Dramatic Poesy,* 1.82 and 84), Dryden attempted to negotiate this middle course by making rhyme as "natural" and "easy" as possible through avoiding unnatural word order, varying the position of the caesura, and frequently enjambing his lines. But apparently he found even this liberalized use of rhyme to be stilted and confining in his plays, for he abandoned the rhyming heroic play after writing *Aureng-Zebe,* which was performed in 1676, and turned to a more naturalistic Shakespearean model. *All for Love* is generally considered to be Dryden's best serious play, but it suffers, as do Dryden's heroic plays, from the inheritance of the ancient antagonism between verisimilitude and elevation, for it is an uneasy blend of the familiar and the sublime, of sentimentalized melodrama and the ideal. Dryden has removed from Cleopatra many of those moral blemishes which are so conspicuous in the Shakespearean play, and has thereby created a more idealized image of her. But he has in the process transformed the glorious Queen of Egypt into a frail hausfrau whose greatest regret is that her public role has frustrated her desire to be what she naturally is, "A wife, a silly, harmless household dove, / Fond without art, and kind without deceit."[28]

As Dryden himself admitted after his long career as a dramatist had ended, "my genius never much inclined me" to "the stage" (2.91). It is significant that Dryden makes this confession in his *Discourse Concerning the Original and Progress of Satire* (1693), for it is in his satires rather than in his plays that Dryden manages to write successfully in a manner that is both elevated and particularized. In the *Discourse Concerning Satire* Dryden, by contrasting the satirical style of Juvenal with that of Horace, is in effect defending his own satirical style. "The low style of Horace," Dryden says, "is according to his subject, that is, generally grovelling"; he follows the "humble way of satire" (2.130–31), the *sermo pedestris.* Juvenal, on the other hand, is "much more elevated. His expressions are sonorous and more noble; his verse more numerous, and his words are suitable to his thoughts, sublime and lofty. . . . Juvenal excels in the tragical satire, as does Horace in the comical" (2.140).

The phrase "tragical satire," considered from the point of view of the ancient levels of style, is virtually an oxymoron, for tragedy and satire

27. "What Is a Classic?" trans. A. J. Butler, in *Critical Theory Since Plato,* ed. Hazard Adams rev. ed. (New York: Harcourt Brace Jovanovich, 1992), 569.

28. *All for Love,* ed. David M. Vieth (Lincoln: University of Nebraska Press, 1972), 91.

inhabit—strictly speaking—opposite ends of the stylistic scale. The subject matter of tragedy consists of legendary figures from a distant past and the tragic style is correspondingly lofty, whereas the current affairs of everyday life provide the subject matter for satire and its style is correspondingly low and plain. Juvenalian satire, however, combines qualities of the *genus grande* and the *genus humile,* for Juvenal rails, in an impassioned and elevated style, at particular persons he observes in the Rome of his day. Juvenal's subject matter, in other words, is that of the *genus humile,* but his style is best described as a version of the *genus grande.* It is precisely for this Juvenalian ability to combine qualities of the high and the low styles that Dryden singles out for praise his own satire, *MacFlecknoe* (1682). "If anything of mine is good, 'tis *Mac-Fleckno,*" Dryden is reported to have said, "and I value myself the more upon it, because it is the first piece of ridicule written in heroics."[29] If the phrase "tragical satire," when judged by the strictest classical standards, implies an unconventional mixture of styles, it is equally unconventional to regard satire, as Dryden does, as "undoubtedly a species" of "heroic poetry" (2.149). In describing Boileau's manner of writing satire in *Le Lutrin,* Dryden is once again implicitly defending his own procedures in his great satires, *MacFlecknoe* and *Absalom and Achitophel.* "This," Dryden writes in the *Discourse Concerning Satire,* "I think . . . to be the most beautiful and most noble kind of satire. Here is the majesty of the heroic, finely mixed with the venom of the other; and raising the delight which otherwise would be flat and vulgar, by the sublimity of the expression" (2.149). Let us recall the opening lines of these poems by Dryden. First, *MacFlecknoe* (1682):

> All humane things are subject to decay,
> And, when Fate summons, Monarchs must obey:
> This *Fleckno* found, who, like *Augustus,* young
> Was call'd to Empire, and had govern'd long:
> In Prose and Verse, was own'd, without dispute
> Through all the Realms of *Non-sense,* absolute.[30]
>
> (1–6)

And then *Absalom and Achitophel* (1681):

29. Joseph Spence, *Observations, Anecdotes, and Characters of Books and Men,* ed. James M. Osborn, 2 vols. (Oxford: Clarendon Press, 1966), 1:274.

30. *The Works of John Dryden,* ed. Edward Niles Hooker, H. T. Swedenberg, Jr., et al. (Berkeley and Los Angeles: University of California Press, 1956–), 2:54.

> In pious times, e'r Priest-craft did begin,
> Before *Polygamy* was made a sin;
> When man, on many, multiply'd his kind,
> E'r one to one was, cursedly, confind:
> When Nature prompted, and no law deny'd
> Promiscuous use of Concubine and Bride;
> Then, *Israel*'s Monarch, after Heaven's own heart,
> His vigorous warmth did, variously, impart
> To Wives and Slaves: And, wide as his Command,
> Scatter'd his Maker's Image through the Land.[31]
>
> (1–10)

It is in verse satires such as *MacFlecknoe* and *Absalom and Achitophel* rather than in his plays that Dryden managed to find the via media between earthy realism and elevation sought by Neander in the *Essay of Dramatic Poesy.* And it is the poet's achievement of this delicate and difficult mean in stylistic decorum that in part renders these poems classics of English poetry.

---

31. Ibid., 2:5.

14

PLATO'S "ATTACK" ON POETRY RECONSIDERED

As I suggested in the first chapter, I believe Plato's attitude toward literature has been misunderstood. He has been presented, especially in histories of literary theory, as the enemy of poetry, and Aristotle has been put forth as poetry's champion. In their understanding of Plato's literary theory, the poets have been more consistently on the right track. So Sidney, who in his *Apology* says, "I have ever esteemed [Plato] most worthy of reverence, and with great reason, since of all Philosophers he is the most poeticall." Sidney says that what Plato was criticizing and indeed banishing was not poetry itself: he was rather "banishing the abuse, not the thing, not banishing it, but giving due honor unto it." He then goes on to declare, in a defense of poetry that is largely Aristotelian, that in his treatise he will consider Plato "our Patron and not our adversary."[1] So Shelley in his *Defense of Poetry* declared that "Plato was essentially a poet—the truth and splendor of his imagery, and the melody of his language, are the most intense that it is possible to conceive."[2]

Plato's dialogues, it is true, are not metrical compositions, but Aristotle in the first chapter of the *Poetics* (1447b) argues that it is a work's mimetic quality, and not the fact that it is composed in verse, that renders it poetry, and he includes Plato's dialogues among his examples of mimetic art. Plato himself suggests, however indirectly and implicitly, that his own dialogues are indeed philosophical poetry. At the beginning of the *Republic* (367), for example, Socrates laments that no poet or prose writer has ever treated the problem of whether justice is desirable in itself. Only in the prose poem that is the *Republic,* Plato replies, does this question finally receive its appropriate treatment. The Athenian stranger in the *Laws* (811d) is more explicit: he refers to this dialogue as "just like a kind of poem" [παντάπασι ποιήσει τινὶ προσομοίως].

In this final chapter, in the spirit of ancient ring composition, I wish to return to the subject of the first chapter, that is, to Plato, and to suggest that Plato was indeed a poet in the ways intuited by Sidney and Shelley, and that many of his reservations about poetry can be viewed as criticisms of how the poetry of his own time failed to embody key elements in the classical understanding of poetry, as I have tried to define the classic in this book. In other words, there is a real sense in which for Plato poetry was (or should be) "a formally coherent, compelling, and rationally defensible representation that resists being reduced to either the literal representation of material reality, on the one hand, or to the bare exemplification of an abstract philosophical precept, on the other." As Sidney argued, so will I, that Plato objected not so much to poetry itself, but to its abuse. Indeed, Plato, even in his critique of poetry, is deeply classical in precisely the manner in which I am defining the classic. In the first chapter I considered the importance, for a fresh assessment of Plato's literary theory and its relevance to contemporary critical concerns, of some of the dialogues—such as the *Cratylus, Symposium, Sophist,* and *Parmenides*—that are often not considered by students of literary criticism. I wish now to return to more familiar ground: the *Ion* and books 2, 3, and 10 of the *Republic.*

1. *Apology for Poetry,* in *Elizabethan Critical Essays,* ed. G. G. Smith, 2 vols. (1971; rpt., London: Oxford University Press, 1904), 1:190–91.
2. *Critical Theory Since Plato,* ed. Hazard Adams, rev. ed. (New York: Harcourt Brace Jovanovich, 1992), 518.

The Ion: *The Case for a Rationally Defensible Poetics*

In the *Ion,* Plato criticizes both literature and the sophistic misuses of it. Ion is a rhapsode, a traveling singer who specializes in the Homeric poems, but when pressed by Socrates about what exactly it is that defines his art, he is at a loss to respond. The occupation of the rhapsode, Socrates suggests, is questionable on at least two counts. First, the rhapsode is not in control of his rational faculties and his appeal is to the passions, not to the reason, of his audience. If his audience is moved to tears, he is successful; if it is not, he has failed. Of the moral implications of the actions narrated by Homer, Ion is completely ignorant and unconcerned. His shortcomings are similar to those of the sophist, from Plato's point of view. Like the sophists, he performs his duties for pay. And like the professional rhetorician Gorgias of Leontini, Ion is more concerned with the effects of his words on his audience than with their truth or falsehood. To recall our paradigm: the Homeric poems, according to Plato in the *Ion,* may well be representations that are *emotionally compelling,* but they are not *rationally defensible,* at least not by Ion, who depicts himself as an unconscious link in a chain of inspiration descending from the gods to the poet himself to the rhapsode and reaching outward, finally, to the audience.

This particular Platonic dialogue itself, however, *is* emotionally compelling; it is, at the very least, quite amusing to see how poorly Ion defends his métier. One of the things that is compelling about the dialogue is, in fact, something it has in common with Homer himself, Ion's specialty. Part of the pleasure we receive from reading the *Odyssey* is viewing the contest between the arrogant suitors and the recently returned and supremely intelligent Odysseus disguised as a beggar, a contest that is the origin of the antagonism between the *alazōn* (boaster) and the *eirōn* (dissembler). The Homeric example must have had a profound effect on Plato the artist, and specifically on that inveterate *eirōn,* Socrates, who is modeled, in some ways, after the Odysseus of the second half of the *Odyssey.* Plato alludes to Homer throughout his work, and in this dialogue presents Socrates as quoting from memory a passage from the *Odyssey* (*Ion* 539; *Odyssey* 20.351–57) in which the prophet Theoklymenos predicts the bloody, imminent demise of the suitors just before Odysseus and Telemachos are about to take their just revenge; the response of the suitors to the dire prophecy is ignorant and complacent laughter. Socrates doubtless understands that the arrogance of the suitors brought about their downfall, but the relevance of this passage to Ion's own present existential situation escapes the rhapsode. In this sense, the *Ion* is truer to the meaning of Homer than are the mindless rantings of the rhapsode. Indeed, the unspoken theme of the dialogue is, "Who is the true heir to Homer, the rhapsode or the philosopher?" "You are so much more experienced with Homer than I am," says the *eirōn* Socrates (539e) after he has just cited, from memory, two long passages from Homer, the first being the Theoklymenos prophecy about the death of the suitors. The dialogue itself, then, is emotionally compelling in a Homeric (specifically, in an *Odyssean*) way.

There is another passage in which Socrates suggests that his understanding of Homer is superior to Ion's. Toward the end of their encounter, Ion, by this time utterly overwhelmed by Socrates' superior powers of reasoning, makes the absurd and groundless assertion that the art of the rhapsode and the art of the general are one and the same. "You are just like Proteus," Socrates tells Ion; "you twist and turn, this way and that, assuming every shape, until finally you elude my grasp and reveal yourself a general. All in order to impress me [ἐπιδείξῃς] with how skilled you are concerning Homer" (542a).[3] It is Ion who can recite the Proteus passage (*Odyssey* 5.365–570) from memory to stir the desired emotions in his captive audience, but it is Socrates who understands Homer's thought and the significance of the Proteus episode and who, like Menelaus, strives to pin down an elusive antagonist.

The dialogue has been taken as both a serious defense of inspiration and as a spoof of this ancient claim for poetry. As we recall from our discussion of the classical experience of reason (νοῦς) in Chapters 2 and 3, to be reasonable—from a Platonic/Aristotelian perspective—is to participate in the divine. Aristotle, we recall, referred to the life of the questioning consciousness as one of immortalization (ἀθανατίζειν) of the psyche. Plato, in the *Symposium*, refers to the life of the philosopher as existing between the poles of mortality and immortality. The *Ion* is dated earlier than the *Symposium*, but in it we can see adumbrated the area of the In-Between articulated in the later dialogue. The rhapsode, like the philosopher, exists between the realm of the divine and the human, in fact mediates between them. But he does not do so consciously. The philosopher, on the other hand, is conscious of his existence in the In-Between. Plato was serious about Ion's theory of divine inspiration, but he attempted to replace the rhapsode/poet with the philosopher/poet. It is rationality—in the sense of classical *noēsis*—that serves as a mediator between the divine

---

3. *Ion*, trans. Paul Shorey, in *The Collected Dialogues of Plato*, ed. Edith Hamilton and Huntington Cairns (Princeton: Princeton University Press, 1961). Translation slightly modified.

and the human. The *Ion,* as a dramatic work, is both emotionally compelling and its philosophical stance is rationally defensible.

In the dialogue the *Ion,* then, Plato gives us a representation that is— unlike Ion's account of how Homeric poetry works—rationally defensible. Moreover, to recall the subject of the second part of this study on the limitations of formalism, Ion has reduced Homer, in Plato's view, to a formalist who offers his audience a poem of inexplicable and indeed mindless beauties.

The Ion: *The Limitations of Mimetic Literalism*

Socrates next argues against some of the sophistic uses of literature. The sophists often regarded the Homeric poems as an encyclopedia of arts and sciences, of the various *technai* that the sophists themselves taught, and this tradition of regarding Homer as a teacher of specialized skills continued long after Plato's time. In his poems, Socrates says, Homer speaks of many arts, such as medicine, divination, fishing, and horse racing. If a person wanted to learn any of these specialized skills, Socrates suggests, would he not be better off going to a specialist in the field rather than to the Homeric poems? Taken at face value, Plato's argument here is clear. If poetry is meant to teach (in this case, to teach specific skills), then it teaches them poorly in comparison with experts in any of the specialized fields. But poetry is, by its very nature, an unspecialized form of discourse. Plato knew this; being himself a great literary artist, Plato was well aware that one does not go to poetry for information about this or that particular *technē*. If this is what poetry was being reduced to in his time, then poetry should be replaced, Plato is suggesting, with philosophy as the form of discourse that treats unspecialized subject matter[4]—but with Plato's own kind of *poetic* philosophy.

A mimetically literalist reading of Plato's *Ion* yields predictable results. Plato here is opposed to poetry, particularly to Homeric poetry, because it appeals only to the emotions and because it has no particular subject matter to teach. A less literalist reading of the dialogue, however, suggests some-

---

4. Cf. David Roochnik, "Plato's Critique of Postmodernism," *Philosophy and Literature,* no. 2 (1987): esp. 283–84. There Roochnik argues that Socrates, "much like the poets and rhapsodes" (285), has devoted himself to understanding human nature in general rather than becoming a specialist in any particular *technē*.

thing rather different: Plato is in fact attempting to question the distinction between poetry and philosophy, and he is, thereby, implicitly defending his own form of philosophical *poiēsis*. What the dialogue explores is the question: who better understands Homer's intentions, the philosopher or the rhapsode? And who, therefore, is the true heir to Homer and the tragic tradition, the rhapsode or the philosopher? Ion has just returned from Epidaurus where he attended the festival of Asklepios, the god of healing, and where the rhapsodes have had a contest (ἀγῶνα) in honor of that god. "And were you competing for some prize, I wonder, and how did you fare in the competition?" [ἠγωνίζου τι ἡμῖν; καὶ πῶς ἠγωνίσω;] (530b). Within the first few lines of the dialogue Plato has mentioned the word ἀγών and its cognates three times. We recall that the tragic poets entered their plays into competitions. The effete Ion—Plato is no doubt associating the Ionic rhapsode from Ephesus with Asiatic luxury rather than Hellenic discipline and rationality—competed and won the first prize. But what kind of contest was this? Clearly, Plato implies, this contest was a mere shadow in comparison with the contest enacted in this dialogue between the rhapsode and the philosopher over the question of who is the true heir to Homer and the tragic tradition. This is an *agōn* far more worthy of comparison to the contests between playwrights in the tragic competition during tragedy's days of glory.

There exists an *agōn*, then, between the poet and rhapsode, on the one hand, and the philosopher (who, in this dramatic dialogue, shows himself to be a gifted poet) on the other. What they are competing for is the prize of who shall be considered the inheritor of the true poetic tradition. The festival of Asklepios is important in this respect, for poetry had been considered an art of healing, a therapeutic experience for the listener.[5] Plato is asking: is poetry, as interpreted by Ion, the art of healing, or is rather philosophy such an art? Moreover, Ion as a non-Athenian—as many of the sophists were—has taken over the mantle of tragedy, whereas the tragedies used to be a Athenian affair. The rhapsodes have usurped an art with profound implications for the public welfare and diminished it to an aesthetic diversion. This, I believe, is the point of Plato's having Ion claim, desperately and inexplicably, that the art of the rhapsode and the art of the general are the same (539d). Ion's logic is flawed, but Plato's irony is exquisite: the effete Ion can hardly be viewed as the kind of person who could protect a city from military attack.

---

5. Cf. Pindar, *Olympian* 2.14–15, *Pythian* 1.6–14, 3.63–67, and my discussion of this last poem in Chapter 6; see also *Nemean* 4.1–5 and Hesiod, *Theogony* 98–103.

In sum, then, what Plato is objecting to in the *Ion* is (1) the tendency of literature to appeal not to the rational faculty, but to the emotions; and (2) the sophistic notion that one can learn specialized skills from poetry. The implication of this second point is that the aim of philosophy—like poetry before it, as I have argued in Part 3 of this study—is not necessarily to inculcate specific informational or doctrinal points through a mimetically literalist representation.

The Republic: *Some of Plato's Objections to Poetry Reconsidered*

Plato's first discussion of mimetic representation in the *Republic* appears toward the end of book 2 and at the beginning of book 3. Here Socrates is discussing the guardians of his ideal republic and the place and function of literature in their education. Literature is a positive educational tool, Socrates suggests, so long as it provides exemplary models of behavior that the future guardians can imitate. Therefore we must expurgate all passages that depict supposedly heroic characters, such as Achilles, performing actions that are anything less than exemplary. And since we know divinity is good, we must censor as well all references, in Homer and elsewhere, that suggest that the gods are evil or in any way responsible for evil in the world.

Nor shall the gods be shown to be in any way fallible. They should not be depicted as weeping. Here Socrates criticizes Homer for portraying Zeus, in *Iliad* 16, as wailing helplessly over the imminent death of his son Sarpedon during one of the battles of the Trojan War. And the picture Homer paints is not, admittedly, a very dignified one. Would not a young person's confidence in the divine order be shaken if he or she heard the father of gods and men so audibly moaning, in a time of crisis, about his own personal bad luck?

> Oh no! How can it be that Sarpedon, dearest of men,
> Is now fated to be vanquished by Patroklos, son of
>   Menoitios.
>
>   (387b)

The full force of the wailing can, however, only be felt if one hears this passage in the original, with its onomatopoetic imitations of sounds of wailing:

ὤ μοι ἐγών, ὅτε τέ μοι Σαρπηδόνα, φίλτατον ἀνδρῶν,
μοῖρ' ὑπὸ Πατρόκλοιο Μενοιτιάδαο δαμῆναι.

(16.433–34)

Gods should not be seen wailing, nor should they be the objects of laughter. Hence it is an act of impiety for Homer to describe how the gods laugh at Hephaestus at the end of the first book of the *Iliad,* as—when he fills the cups of the gods with divine nectar—he comically limps around, huffing and puffing.

In the nineteenth century, in the literary theory of Poe and particularly of Keats, one of the chief criteria for determining the excellence of a literary work was its "intensity," its potential for sending a shiver down the spine. Poetry must, above all, be emotionally compelling—irresistibly so. It is this sheer poetic power whose influence Plato fears, and he therefore has Socrates decide that

> we must further taboo in these matters the entire vocabulary of terror and fear [τὰ δεινὰ τε καὶ φοβερά], Cocytus named of lamentation loud, abhorred Styx, the flood of deadly hate, the people of the infernal pit and of the charnel house, and all other terms of this type, whose very names send a shudder through all the hearers every year. And they may be excellent for other purposes, but we are in fear [φοβούμεθα] for our guardians lest the habit of such thrills make them more sensitive and soft than we would have them. (387c)[6]

And in book 10 he goes on to say that if impressionable minds develop the habit of pitying (ἐλεεῖν) the heroes of Homer and tragedy, they will not easily restrain their pity (ἐλεεινόν) when they themselves suffer hardships (606b).

Plato's desire to eliminate all unfavorable representations of the gods should not be taken as mere fourth-century puritanism or bowdlerization. What Plato objects to here is, largely, the tendency to view the gods in an anthropomorphic manner. The subject of the *Republic* is *dikē,* the due measure or right order of the soul. The human soul is well ordered (possesses *dikē*) if it is open to inquiry. This openness Plato symbolizes as receptivity to the divine, and hence, if divinity is thought to be evil or even

---

6. *The Republic,* trans. Shorey, in Hamilton and Cairns, eds., *The Collected Dialogues of Plato,* 632.

fallible, as Homer might seem to suggest, the souls of human beings—and particularly of the young, who are Plato's concern in this section of the *Republic*—will close themselves to the divine, that is, to the search for truth, and hence not possess *dikē*. As Heraclitus had remarked: "Through lack of faith the divine escapes being known."[7]

By rejecting Homer's indecorous representation of the gods, Plato placed himself in a tradition that begins with Xenophanes (born sometime in the middle of the sixth century B.C.). "Homer and Hesiod," Xenophanes writes, "have attributed to the gods everything that is a shame and reproach among men, stealing and committing adultery and deceiving each other." The reasons for such misrepresentation, Xenophanes says, was the naïveté of the early poets. "Mortals consider," he writes, "that the gods are born, and that they have clothes and speech and bodies like their own." Humans create gods in their own image, down to racial differences. "The Ethiopians say that their gods are snub-nosed and black, the Thracians that theirs have light blue eyes and red hair." And, he says, "if cattle and horses or lions had hands, or were able to draw with their hands and do the works that men can do, horses would draw the forms of the gods like horses, and cattle like cattle, and they would make their bodies such as they each had themselves." In contrast to these ways of symbolizing the divine, Xenophanes proposes his own, in anticipation of Plato: there is "one god, greatest among gods and men, in no way similar to mortals either in body or in thought." In contrast to what one might deduce from the manifestations of divinity in the Homeric poems, God "always . . . remains in the same place, moving not at all; nor is it fitting for him to go to different places at different times, but without toil he shakes all things by the thought of his mind."[8]

Xenophanes rejects the myths of Homer and Hesiod because he feels they are untrue to the nature of divinity as he experiences it, just as Plato will reject these same myths because he believes they are false representations of the nature of the divine. What both Xenophanes and Plato are rejecting here is, in part, the mythic tendency toward anthropomorphism, toward experiencing and symbolizing divinity as merely an extension of the human realm of being. The gods, Xenophanes suggests, are endowed with improper attributes because humans created gods in their own image. The intention

---

7. Diels-Kranz, B86; quoted in Eric Voegelin, *Order and History,* vol. 2, *The World of the Polis* (Baton Rouge: Louisiana State University Press, 1987), 228.

8. *The Presocratic Philosophers,* trans. G. S. Kirk, J. E. Raven, and Malcolm Schofield (Cambridge: Cambridge University Press, 1983), 168–70.

of Socratic dialectic is to leave anthropomorphizing behind, realizing, however, that since human beings are not God, "transcendent" truths can be approached only through human means, that is, by analogy and not as literalist signs of (in Derrida's terms) a "transcendental signified."

Another objection to poetry leveled by Plato in this early section of the *Republic* is the possibly deleterious effect on the young soul of sympathetic identification with ignoble characters. Such absorption in other personalities can be harmful. If the future guardians are to devote their energies to contemplating the forms of true being, then works of literature will—the suggestion is—impede their progress. For such works will encourage the listeners to imitate, to impersonate all things and types of people, good or bad, and such an activity will serve only to implicate the future guardians in the labyrinthian flux of the phenomenal world, in the world of becoming that, in the course of the *Republic,* Plato will distinguish from the world of true being.

Socrates' final objection to literature in this early section of the *Republic* revolves around a term—*mimēsis,* "imitation"—which, used in a different and broader sense, becomes central to his discussion in book 10. Here Socrates argues that there are certain forms or styles of poetry that are more harmful to moral health than are others. He divides all narrative poetry into three kinds: (1) the purely narrative kind, represented by dithyrambs, in which the poet simply tells a story; (2) the "imitative" kind, poetry in which the poet conducts his narrative solely by means of impersonation, of which tragedy and comedy are examples; and (3) the mixed kind, represented by the epic, in which the poet speaks partly in his own person, and partly through characters. Socrates here condemns the kinds into which *mimēsis* enters, whether wholly or partially (and this is a condemnation of nothing less than the great literary forms that had preceded Plato: epic, tragedy, and comedy). In all such compositions, the poet for a time identifies himself with other characters and compels the hearer or reader to share sympathetically in that identification. Such absorption in the personalities of others is seen by Plato as being harmful. As will Aristotle, so Plato here recognizes that the imitative faculty is instinctive; if that faculty is indulged, Socrates suggests, a person's character could completely dissolve. We have seen, in our chapter on Diderot's *Neveu de Rameau,* the dangers of such absorption, for in the character of Rameau's nephew Diderot presents us with a person of extraordinary mimetic gifts who—virtually as a consequence of these gifts—is morally confused and unstable.

Plato's most famous attack on literature occurs toward the end of the *Republic* (595a–608b). Socrates has by this time discussed the so-called theory of the forms and the tripartite division of the soul, and his criticism of poetry here gains additional force when it is viewed from the perspective of these important discussions. In order to suggest the illusory nature of poetic representation, Plato draws on an analogy from the visual arts. Only the forms or "ideas" of things have absolute being. A bed[9] made by a carpenter participates in the world of becoming rather than of being. It is a particular example of a bed, but it is not bedness itself. The artist who depicts a bed on a canvas is, therefore, a step further removed from bedness. His image exists at a third remove from true being. Not only does painting—and, by analogy, poetry—exist at a third remove from true being, but, because of its illusory nature, poetry attempts to fool the calculating or reasoning element of the soul. Poetry appeals, rather, to the passions.

Socrates and Plato were not dogmatists. True to their method of dialectic, they were open to further revelation. Toward the end of the discussion of the defects of mimetic representation, Socrates and Glaucon agree that poetry should be banished from the ideal republic. Socrates suggests that poetry has no cognitive value, but he is willing to be shown otherwise. And so he says that it is entirely fitting that if poetry should want to return from exile, she might plead her defense, either in lyric or some other measure. "And we would allow her advocates who are not poets but lovers of poetry," Socrates continues, "to plead her cause in prose without meter, and show that she is not only delightful but beneficial to orderly government and all the life of man. And we shall listen benevolently, for it will be a clear gain for us if it can be shown that she bestows not only pleasure but benefit" (607d).[10]

Plato's challenge was taken up by a long line of defenders of poetry. One of the earliest of these was Plato's protégé, Aristotle. In response to Plato's objection that literature does not provide exemplary types, Aristotle implies that it is not the function of poetry to provide ethical models. A tragedy is a generalized representation of an action. Plato, for example, might have criticized Sophocles' portrayal of Odysseus in *Philoctetes*. Is it proper, Plato might have asked, to paint such an unfavorable image of one of the founding fathers of Hellenic civilization? What if the future guardians of the Republic, having been exposed to such a model, were to imitate him? But, Aristotle might in turn respond, the play is an imitation of an action, not of character.

---

9. R. G. Steven, in "Plato and the Art of his Time," *Classical Quarterly* 27 (1933): 149–55, suggests that the κλίνη (couch or bed) of *Republic* 10 has a precise visual analogue in an actual vase fragment on which an illusionistic image of a κλίνη is painted.

10. *The Republic*, trans. Shorey, in Hamilton and Cairns, eds., *The Collected Dialogues of Plato*, 832.

And to any intelligent reader or listener it is clear, through the structure of events in the play, that Sophocles is implicitly criticizing the actions of Odysseus, as he is represented in this play.

For Plato's demand for poetic justice, Aristotle substitutes—as I discussed in Chapter 4—the doctrine of *katharsis*. For the emotions of pity and of fear, Aristotle says (*Poetics* 13), are not aroused best by a dramatization of straightforward retribution. The downfall of a villain would doubtless satisfy the moral sense, but it would inspire neither pity nor fear. For pity is aroused by unmerited misfortune, fear by the misfortune of a person like ourselves. To keep one's emotions of pity and fear in good working order, Aristotle might say, is one of the chief moral functions of tragedy. Unless we have the capacity to pity others and fear the gods, our own lives may end in a tragedy that could perhaps have been avoided. Hence, to Plato's objection that poetry does not engage the rational part of the soul but agitates the lower passions, Aristotle responds that there are some passions that should indeed be agitated, as I suggested in Chapter 4 in my analysis of the principles of literary theory implicit in the tale Odysseus tells to Antinoös in *Odyssey* 17.

There is yet another Platonic objection to poetry to which Aristotle responds. It is the aim of poets to please, Plato says, by addressing the passions rather than the intellect. An important pleasure derived from poetry, Aristotle answers, is an intellectual pleasure. By viewing a generalized imitation of a probable set of events, we can learn something about the particulars of our own experience. And learning, Aristotle says, is itself pleasurable; it is, in fact, the liveliest of pleasures. But this pleasure is not sought as an end in itself; it is the by-product of the experience of learning. Pleasure, as Aristotle says in the *Nicomachean Ethics,* "completes the activity . . . as an end which supervenes as the bloom of youth does on those in the flower of their age" (1174b33).[11] Pleasure is the natural by-product, for the doer, of any activity done well.

The Republic: *A Response to Mimetic Literalism*

The challenge laid down by Socrates for those who wish to defend poetry to come forward was, then, nobly accepted by Aristotle. And the history of literary theory—indeed, of the history of literature in the West—can be

---

11. *Nicomachean Ethics,* trans. W. D. Ross, in *The Basic Works of Aristotle,* ed. Richard McKeon (New York: Random House, 1941), 1099.

construed as a series of responses to Socrates' invitation in the *Republic.* But Aristotle was not really the first theorist to respond to Plato's criticisms, for all of Plato's dialogues are themselves mimetic, and thus contain implicit principles of literary theory that often answer Plato's own objections. It is therefore clearly questionable to say that Plato objected to mimetic representation per se given that his own dialogues are themselves so clearly mimetic representations[12] of hypothetical moments in the life of Socrates. In them we see Socrates taking a leisurely walk with Phaedrus, Socrates at a banquet discoursing on love, Socrates defending himself in an intensely dramatic trial, Socrates in prison refusing to make an ignominious escape and, on the threshold of death, explaining patiently to the disordered soul of Crito precisely why such an escape would be an unjust and foolish thing to undertake.

Plato had objected to Homer's presentation of those performing less than virtuous actions for fear that untutored minds might then imitate these actions in their own lives. But this did not prevent Plato from presenting a detailed portrait, in the *Symposium,* of the raucous Alcibiades, who enters the house of Agathon in a state of total inebriation, full of *hybris.* Surely Plato must have feared that impressionable minds might imitate the actions of Alcibiades, who, as we learn from Thucydides, was an extremely charismatic personality. There is, however, another character in the dialogues whom Plato puts forth as a model for imitation, and this, of course, is Socrates himself. Toward the end of the *Republic* it is agreed that no poetry will be admitted into the polis except for "hymns to the gods and encomia to noble souls" [ὕμνους θεοῖς καὶ ἐγκώμια τοῖς ἀγαθοῖς] (607a). As Eric Voegelin has suggested, surely all of the Platonic dialogues may be seen as encomia to Socrates and the words and speeches of Socrates as he searches for truth are themselves hymns to the gods.[13]

Not only are the dialogues examples of mimetic representation, but Plato often uses myth in the dialogues. Plato's second major attack on literature in the *Republic,* in which he brands the great mythmaker Homer as a mere imitator of imitations, precedes the concluding section of the work, which is

12. Cf. Allen H. Gilbert, "Did Plato Banish the Poets?" in *Medieval and Renaissance Studies* 2 (Durham: Duke University Press, 1968), 35–55. Plato's writings, Gilbert observes, "are all imitative, in the sense that Socrates and the others speak for themselves. Yet, though all expositors know they are dialogs, I know of none who fully treats them as such. Hence manifold error in dealing with Plato's writings" (37).

13. *Plato and Aristotle,* in *Order and History,* 5 vols. (Baton Rouge: Louisiana State University Press, 1956–87), 2:134.

itself a myth: the myth of Er. What distinguishes the kind of myth Plato implicitly recommends from the kind of myth he criticizes? With this question we come to the main point of this chapter: I would argue, following Paul Friedländer, that Plato is here rejecting myths that ask to be understood simply as "realistic"—that is, mimetically literalist—adventure stories, devoid of philosophical content.[14]

In the tenth book of the *Republic,* Socrates says that the painter is like a person carrying a mirror and turning it around in all directions, thus producing images of the sun, stars, and earth and oneself and all the other animals, plants, and lifeless objects (596e). As Friedländer suggests, Plato may be referring here not to an old master such as Polygnotos—the "good artist who paints a model of what might be the most beautiful human being" (472d). What Plato "had in mind," Friedländer continues,

> was the younger generation of painters, who in their manners as well as their products are rightly compared to the "Sophists": Apollodorus, for example, the inventor of the illusionistic paintings with shadows [σκιγραφία] rejected by Plato as deceitful; Zeuxis, who in Aristotle's judgment lacked the "ethos" of Polygnotos, and who took delight in the portrayal of the individual, concrete object, painting grapes with such an illusion that birds came to pick at them; or Parrhasios and Pauson.[15]

Nor was Plato referring to Egyptian statues, which he loved. As Friedländer suggests, Plato may well be alluding to the younger generations of painters,[16] those illusionists who, through their extremely realistic depic-

---

14. Ibid., 119–25. With Friedländer are Kurt Hildebrandt, *Platon* (Berlin, 1933), and Eric Voegelin, *Plato and Aristotle,* vol. 3 of *Order and History.* Hans-Georg Gadamer disagrees with Friedländer's position in his essay "Plato and the Poets," in *Dialogue and Dialectic: Eight Hermeneutical Studies on Plato,* trans. P. Christopher Smith (New Haven: Yale University Press, 1980): "Also mistaken is the defense of Plato which would argue that his critique is not of poetry as such but only of a degenerate contemporary form of it which contented itself with scenes from real life. For it is precisely Homer and the great tragedians who enthrall Socrates and his friends but who are criticized nonetheless" (47). T.B.L. Webster, in "Greek Theories of Art and Literature," *Classical Quarterly* 33 (1939): 166–79, suggests that Plato objected primarily to the extreme realism of contemporary art and drama. Webster's view is questioned by Eric A. Havelock, *Preface to Plato* (Cambridge: Harvard University Press, 1963), 8.

15. *Plato: An Introduction,* 119.

16. Cf. Hermann Wiegemann, "Plato's Critique of the Poets and the Misunderstanding of His Epistemological Argumentation," trans. Henry W. Johnstone Jr., *Philosophy and Rhetoric* 23, no. 2 (1990): 220: "When Plato, in the *Republic,* ranks art as at third remove from reality—still

tions, thereby implied—as sophists such as Protagoras said quite explicitly—that man was the measure of all things. Both the sophists and these painters of mundane and literal realism, whose attention was riveted wholly upon the world of appearances, would—from Plato's perspective—be closed to the investigation of more general truths. What Plato is objecting to are the mimetic literalists of fourth-century Greece, and to the kind of viewer who admires a particular painting only for its achievement of a remarkable degree of mimetic accuracy. Aristotle, in the *Poetics,* will say that poetry depicts the universal, history the particular; and that poetry is therefore more philosophical than history. *What Plato is suggesting here is that art has, in effect, become "history" in the sense of its being a mere recording of material reality.* It is not the generalizing or philosophical power of art that is appreciated by the populace: they enjoy only that which confirms the manner in which they see things.

Such mimetic literalism had also invaded the high art of tragedy. Much of the work of Euripides, when compared with the drama of Aeschylus or even with a Sophoclean tragedy, is approaching a kind of bourgeois realism, a tradition that was continued by the successors of Euripides. The Homeric poems are profoundly philosophical and are certainly not mere mirror images of mundane reality. But since the prevailing style of the arts during Plato's time was naturalism, there was a tendency to read the Homeric poems (and tragedy) as if they, too, were merely naturalistic. Their philosophical implications, their ability to point beyond themselves, had been lost. They were now often experienced as realistic adventure stories, or they were ransacked for extraliterary reasons. As mentioned above, it was said that the Homeric poems could teach various technical skills and that students could extract useful maxims from them. Those who were not philosophers would, like Ion, not be capable of understanding the meaning of Homer's poetry. What was necessary, now, was a historical understanding of Homer from the perspective of the philosopher, with his myth of the human soul. Plato must have believed that this truly historical understanding of Homer was, because of the pressures exerted by the contemporary climate of opinion, very difficult to achieve. Rather than run the risk of misunder-

---

presupposing the skill of a craftsman, because art means *mimēsis* of mere images—a determinate kind of *mimēsis* is intended, perhaps that of the portrait artist (*Cratylus* 432b–d; cf. *Sophist* 236b). But the superior and real *mimēsis* is that of Beauty (*Sophist* 236b, *Laws* 668b, *Timaeus* 80b, *Symposium* 205c), the representation designed with the help of the Muses."

standing,[17] he may have felt it was better to take the "official" position that poetry itself was—from a philosophical perspective—a suspect medium.

The prevailing trend in the arts of Plato's time, then, was toward naturalism. It might be helpful to return here to Eric Voegelin's analysis of consciousness. Consciousness must be aware of the two ways in which it interacts with reality. Consciousness intends objects, and in this capacity of intentionality, reality consists of the "things" intended by consciousness, of "thing-reality." But a thinker will be engaging in what Voegelin calls an act of "imaginative oblivion"[18] if she or he takes thing-reality for the whole picture. For consciousness has its participatory dimension as well; that is, it not only, as a subject, intends objects, but is also a participant in It-reality. A flattened naturalism, with its exclusive emphasis on reality in its thingness, may seduce the soul into performing an act of imaginative oblivion by suggesting that reality is equivalent only to thing-reality. Indeed, that which distinguishes the tales or stories narrated in Plato's dialogues from much of the literature written in his own time is that Plato does not indulge in such flattened naturalism. The stories and tales in his dialogues move beyond naturalism to describe (for example) the rewards and punishments for the good and bad souls in Hades, as well as the consequences which their previous development and nurturing of *aretē* has for the choice of a future life.

Socrates had earlier complained that poetry was to be condemned because it stirred up emotions such as fear and pity as well as inappropriate laughter (387c, 389a). But it is precisely these emotions that Plato stirs up in the myth of Er. Er reports how a soul, who had been insufficiently schooled by previous suffering, freely chooses to become a despot, but then—realizing that this choice will bring along with it other less dazzling accoutrements (such as the fate that he would devour his own children)— beats his breast and loudly laments his choice (κόπτεσθαί τε καὶ ὀδύρεσθαι τὴν αἵρεσιν, 619c), precisely the kind of unheroic behavior that Socrates had criticized in Homer's depiction of Achilles and Zeus (388b–d). The despot Ardiaeus and others, because of their heinous crimes, are not permitted to leave the underworld but are found and flayed, and every time they wish to ascend, a frightening voice blows them back down. Plato refers to

---

17. Given the latitude in interpretive practices in much current literary criticism, one sympathizes with Plato's point. "Once a thing gets put into writing," Socrates says in the *Phaedrus*, "the composition, whatever it may be, drifts all over the place, getting into the hands not only of those who understand it, but equally of those who have no business with it" (275e, trans. R. Reginald Hackforth, in Hamilton and Cairns, eds., *The Collected Dialogues of Plato*, 521).

18. *Order and History*, vol. 5, *In Search of Order*, 61.

these as events inspiring fear (φοβῶν, 616a). The sight of these souls choosing their next life, Er says (620a), was one that moved pity (ἐλεινήν), laughter (γελοίαν), and astonishment (θαυμασίαν). Plato approves of the eliciting of these emotions in the present context, however, because he feels they are not gratuitously evoked, that the fictions that evoke them are *rationally defensible.* As I suggested in Chapter 1, the attack on poetry in *Republic* 10 must be read in the context of the work as a whole, and this means reading the *Republic* itself as a formally coherent and symbolically evocative *poēsis* culminating in the myth of Er. Er the Pamphylian ("Everyman"), at the conclusion to the *Republic,* descends to the underworld, is revived, and brings back an account of how the dead choose their next lives in the cycle of reincarnation. Socrates, at the beginning of the *Republic,* descends from Athens into the "underworld" of the Piraeus in order to help save the souls who desire to ascend to the light.[19]

But how are we to know that myths such as that of Er are not pure fantasies? Although only God, Plato would say, can ultimately judge their value, the relative truth of such accounts—such *mythoi*—must be determined by the reader who has, following the example lived by Socrates and sketched out by him in the *Republic,* attempted to turn around, to make the ascent out of the dimly lit cave, and to ascend to the upper world illuminated by the sun itself. The sun is meant to represent that vision of ultimate reality, *to agathon,* the good. The parable of the cave is yet another example of Plato's use of myth. And once again, the defining characteristic of Plato's use of myth is his profound awareness of, on the one hand, myth's shadowy ontological status and, on the other, of its capacities for philosophical speculation. The myth or narrated tale, Plato is saying, is admittedly only a representation, but it is invaluable if it can point us in a promising direction. As Socrates says to Glaucon after he has narrated the parable of the cave, "Maybe God knows whether or not it happens to be true; but this, at any rate, is how these appearances appear to me" (517b). Plato, as I have been arguing, does not view myth or fictional representation as a mere recording of material reality. Nor does he view it as a way of inculcating a particular moral truth, for in this passage he expresses a tentativeness about myth's capacity to do just this. Indeed, as I have suggested in the first chapter, philosophy itself is a searching after rather than a possession of "truth." This is not to say that the *Republic* does not have a subject, and an apparently novel one. As Adeimantus says in the second book, what justice is "in itself,

---

19. The insight is from Eric Voegelin, *Order and History,* vol. 3, *Plato and Aristotle,* 52–62.

by its own inherent force, when it is within the soul of the possessor and escapes the eyes of both gods and men, no one has ever adequately set forth in poetry or prose"[20] [οὐδεὶς πώποτε οὔτ᾽ ἐν ποιήσει οὔτ ἐν ἰδίοις λόγοις] (367a). The prose poem known as Plato's *Republic* will answer just this need.

And this prose poem should not be interpreted as a literalist blueprint for establishing a political utopia. In the first chapter I discussed some of the "prophylactic" devices Plato uses in order to protect his work against literalist misunderstandings. An excellent example of this occurs toward the end of the *Republic.* The transmigrating soul who made the tragic mistake of impulsively choosing to be reborn as a despot is presented as having made the poor choice he did because he had spent his previous life "in a well-ordered republic" (πολιτεῖα, which is Plato's word for the city his work sketches out as well as the title by which his work came to be known) and had therefore "become virtuous from habit without pursuing philosophy"[21] (ἄνευ φιλοσοφίας, 619c), that is, without pursuing wisdom in a deliberate and self-conscious manner. Does this imply, as Derrida might suggest, that the *Republic* has no foundation, that with this passage Plato's elaborate construction of a republic comes tumbling down? Is the *Republic,* in other words, undoing itself, since Plato is perhaps suggesting that if you spend your life in the ideal republic, you will thereby render yourself incapable of choosing your next incarnation wisely? I would rather give Plato the benefit of the doubt and suggest that perhaps he knew what he was doing, or undoing. Plato was interested in articulating, by counterexample, what was profoundly wrong with contemporary Athens. His construction of a paradigmatic *politeia* was, to a large extent, a metaphor through which he could sketch out the contours of the human soul. Those who wish to read the *Republic* as a literalist blueprint for constructing a utopia, therefore, will profoundly misread Plato's intentions. For if anyone were literally to inhabit such a *politeia,* this person would, by Plato's own account, paradoxically be ensuring his enslavement to the life of the tyrant in his next life. The *politeia,* therefore, is not a place in the spatiotemporal world; it is not to be understood in a literally mimetic sense, but it rather refers to the constitution of the soul. Indeed, earlier in book 10 (608), Plato specifically differentiates between an actual *politeia* and the *politeia* within each individual's soul.

20. *The Republic,* trans. Shorey, in Hamilton and Cairns, eds., *The Collected Dialogues of Plato,* 613.

21. I wish to thank Louis Orsini for pointing out to me Plato's intriguing reference to the "well-ordered republic" (*politeia*) at the very conclusion of the *Politeia.*

I mentioned that, in the myth of Er, salvation is seen to be dependent on the previous, earthly cultivation of *aretē,* or virtue. But how is one to cultivate *aretē?* For readers of the *Republic,* it is to experience the work not naturalistically, not as a mere recording of material reality. Its readers must resist the reduction of the literary work known as the *Republic* to its literal mimetic level. They must rather, through being sensitive to the work's symbolic evocations, allow it to appeal to their own souls in their search for balance (*dikē*), for true measure. They must experience the *Republic* as a classic.

CONCLUSION, IN WHICH NOTHING IS DEFINITIVELY CONCLUDED

I have patterned the title of my conclusion on the notoriously ambiguous conclusion of that classic, *Rasselas,* by that classically oriented author, Samuel Johnson. With such a title I want to stress the idea of the classic as profoundly open, as written both yesterday and tomorrow. I also want to evoke the eighteenth century, which has been a pivotal period for many of the issues that I have been discussing.

Although some of the chapters in this book are linked historically, I have not tried to weave a seamless historical argument. If the classical is truly that which, in Gadamer's words, is "something enduring, of significance that cannot be lost and is independent of all circumstances of time,"[1] then I need not, in any case, have felt compelled to have constructed such a historically delimited argument. What I have tried to do is to look at a number of works—mainly from the classical, neoclassical, and modern periods—from the perspective of a definition of the classic that accords with what is, at root, a Platonic/Aristotelian conception of literature: "a formally coherent, compelling, and rationally defensible representation that resists being reduced either to the mere recording of material reality, on the one hand, or to the bare exemplification of an abstract philosophical precept, on the other."

In Part 1 ("Classic Rationality"), I tried to articulate the significance of the meaning of "reason" that is implied in the phrase "rationally defensible" in the preceding definition of the classic. In Chapter 1, "Plato and Postmodernism," I argued that much poststructuralist theory, and most especially deconstruction, is a critique not so much of classical philosophy as represented by Plato as of rationalist epistemology from Descartes through Hegel; and that Plato may, in fact, be said to share many concerns with poststructuralist theory. Since "reason" is often so badly misunderstood in contemporary criticism, it was necessary to devote Chapters 2 and 3 to a discussion of the historical emergence of reason in Greek literature and philosophy and its relevance for understanding two more modern but classically oriented authors, Yvor Winters and Jonathan Swift. In the second chapter, "Rationalism Ancient and Modern," I made the distinction between "rationality" and "rationalism" that is crucial to understanding what I mean by the classical view of reason and thus to what I mean by the phrase "rationally defensible" in my classical definition of literature. In the third chapter, "*Animal Rationis Capax: Gulliver's Travels* and the Classical Experience of Reason," I discussed the historical emergence of reason in Plato and its relevance to Swift in his efforts at resisting the narrowing of the idea of reason in his own time. In Chapter 4, "Led by the Light of the Maeonian Star: Aristotle on Tragedy and Some Passages in the *Odyssey*," I discussed key concepts in Aristotelian critical theory and showed how Aristotle's articulation of the meaning of *katharsis* is implicit in an important scene in the *Odyssey*. I made the further point that the principles of the best literary criticism are empirically based—drawn, that is, from the literary works themselves. When Aristotle searched for the classic, he found it embodied in Homer.

Part 2 comprised five essays devoted to the limits of formalism. Within Part 2 ("The Limits of Formalism"), in chapters 5 through 7 I discussed the

---

1. *Truth and Method* (New York: Crossroad, 1986), 255.

influence and importance of Pindar. In Chapter 5, "The Pindaric Tradition and the Quest for Pure Poetry," I traced the history of the ode from Pindar through the eighteenth century and showed how the genre had become aestheticized. I argued that certain impoverished or specialized views about the nature of poetry emerged in the transformation of the Pindaric ode, which in its original form embodies a full articulation of the classical understanding of literature. In Chapter 6, "Poetry and the In-Between: Valéry's *Le Cimetière marin* and Pindar's Third Pythian Ode," I discussed how Paul Valéry's great poem—in retreating from the Mallarmean extreme of the desire for poetry to represent purity itself—shares important characteristics with Pindar's third Pythian ode, from which Valéry draws his epigraph. In Chapter 7, "'Art with Truth ally'd': Pope's *Epistle to a Lady* as Pindaric Encomium," I argued that Pope's poem—as Elroy Bundy has demonstrated with regard to the victory odes of Pindar—must be read as an encomium, in Pope's case addressed not to an athlete who had been victorious in the games, but to the exemplary Martha Blount; that Pope's poem has a rhetorical structure and is not to be understood as an "aesthetic," that is, a purely formal and autonomous, object in the Kantian sense. In Chapter 8 I treated a manifestation of eighteenth-century aestheticism in Diderot's famous dialogue *Le Neveu de Rameau* and argued that in that work Diderot is perplexed by the problem of the inherent amorality of art, a doctrine officially subscribed to by d'Alembert and Diderot in the *Discours préliminaire* of the *Encyclopédie*. In Chapter 9, "The Pastoral Tradition and the Inheritance of Alexandrian Preciosity," I discussed how formal beauty, always *one* of the qualities embodied in the classic, was a primary characteristic of the pastoral genre in Alexandrian Greece from its very inception. I went on to show how subsequent writers of the genre had always to contend with this legacy of Alexandrian preciosity.

In the chapters in Part 3 ("Resisting the Didactic Heresy") I discussed how literature resists being reduced to a didactic tool. In Chapter 10, "The Ambivalence of the *Aeneid* and the Ecumenic Age," I investigated the tension between the classic understood as politically motivated propaganda, where the work is to serve an explicitly didactic function, and the classic as that which resists such reductionism. In Chapter 11, I suggested how Apuleius may well be subverting the intention avowed in his *Metamorphoses* of converting the reader to a true belief in the religion of Isis. In Chapter 12, "Genre, Didacticism, and the Ethics of Fiction in *Moll Flanders*," I argued that *Moll Flanders* is caught between two principles of order—the allegorical/moralistic and what I call the classically ethical—that attempt to convey the work's ethical meaning. I pointed out how the allegedly un-Augustan Defoe is in fact more "classical" than has been assumed, once we recognize the close relation that exists between fiction and the concept of equity in law, a relation that is implicit in much of the best theorizing in the Aristotelian tradition. *Moll Flanders,* despite the author's avowed critical aims as expressed in his preface, resists being reduced to a moralistic tract.

Part 4 ("Resisting Mimetic Literalism") consisted of two chapters that discussed how literature, while it represents concrete experience, nonetheless resists being reduced to a flatly mimetic literalism. I discussed two treatments of the theme chosen from nearly opposite ends of the chronological spectrum. In Chapter 13 I suggested how Dryden's *Essay of Dramatic Poesy* could be seen as a working out of the competing demands of a literalist and idealist conception of imitation. In Chapter 14 I reconsidered Plato's alleged attack on poetry in the *Republic.* I argued that Plato's attack must be viewed as, in part, a critique of a flattened literalism rather than as an attack on poetry itself. In the spirit of classical ring composition, the book thus ended where it began—that is, with a chapter on Plato, whom I interpreted as being truly classical in the more fluid sense that I hope I have elucidated in the preceding pages.

Six of the fourteen chapters have dealt exclusively or primarily with late seventeenth- or eighteenth-century materials, but there is a sense in which a good deal more of this study was an attempt to consider the crucial role of the Restoration and eighteenth century—the allegedly "neoclassical" period—in the formation of contemporary critical and philosophical attitudes. In much of this book I therefore compared and contrasted Enlightenment and eighteenth-century views with their classical antecedents. In Part 1, for example, I compared the meaning of "reason" in Plato and Aristotle with some of its eighteenth-century usages to show how the word narrowed in the later period. As I suggested in the first chapter, it is not so much the reason of Plato that is the real target of postmodern critiques of "logocentrism," but rather the rationalist tradition from Descartes through Hegel.

Another legacy of the eighteenth century is the aestheticism, paradigmatically stated by Kant in the *Critique of Judgment,* against which much contemporary literary criticism sets itself in opposition. In Chapters 5 and 8 I dealt specifically with what I considered to be the limitations of our eighteenth-century inheritance of aestheticism. Although Paul Valéry's *Le Cimetière marin* is hardly an eighteenth-century work, I emphasized in my interpretation of the poem how it can be viewed as a meditation on the subject-object problem that is so crucial to seventeenth- and eighteenth-century philosophy and which the German idealist tradition attempted to resolve. Although Valéry criticizes the extremes of the doctrine of pure poetry, *Le Cimetière marin* is, nevertheless, an example of a kind of pure poetry, and it is pure poetry that attempts to overcome the narrow intentionalism of eighteenth-century (e.g. Lockean) views of language. At the same time, Valéry's stylistic influences are deeply classical and neoclassical. As Gustave Cohen has remarked of Valéry's verse, the poet was "si pétri de civilisation méditerranéenne et de culture classique, qu'on a quelquefois l'impression, comme chez Ronsard, qu'il pense en latin et en grec"[2] [so molded by Mediterranean civilization and by classical culture, that one sometimes has the impression, as with Ronsard, that he thinks in Latin and in Greek]. He was greatly impressed by and tried to emulate the formal precision of the verse of Racine, and for him the purest music—good verse, for the symbolists, should aspire to the condition of music—was that of the eighteenth-century master, J. S. Bach.[3] Chapter 9 ("The Pastoral Tradition and the Cult of Alexandrian Preciosity") culminated in a reading of a J. V. Cunningham poem that I viewed as an antipastoral very much in the spirit of Samuel Johnson's critique of *Lycidas,* a critique that I attempted to place within the context of the eighteenth-century's skeptical view of allegorical poetry. Cunningham is himself, moreover, a poet who often writes in the neoclassical mode and whose style appears at times to be modeled on Swift's tetrameter couplets.

The didacticism that is recommended by some eighteenth-century critical theory was the subject of Part 3. Didacticism is sometimes the result of a positivist view of language that attempts to assert an uncomplicated relation between signifier and signified. In Chapter 10, I discussed how the didacticism of Dryden's version of the *Aeneid,* despite its greatness as a translation, sometimes removed the ambiguities present in the original Latin. In Chapter 12 I considered how the antididactic Aristotelian tradition survives in the self-avowedly didactic "novel" *Moll Flanders.*

Much of eighteenth-century literature and criticism brought to a culmination the emphasis on historical verisimilitude associated with the neo-Aristotelian tradition of the Renaissance. In Chapter 13 I discussed how this emphasis on "realism" made itself felt in one of the most important critical documents of the period, Dryden's *Essay of Dramatic Poesy.*

---

2. *Essai d'Explication du Cimetière marin* (Paris: Gallimard, 1958), 94.

3. In "Fragments des Mémoires d'un Poème," Valéry speaks of "Une oeuvre de musique absolument pure, une composition de Sébastien Bach," from *Oeuvres de Paul Valéry,* 2 vols. (Paris: Gallimard, 1957), 1:1473.

The works I have discussed fall largely into the three chronological categories of the ancient, the early modern (specifically, the seventeenth and eighteenth centuries), and the modern. If there is merit to the definition of the classic that I have been examining, however, then such a conception should be applicable to other periods, past and future, and to traditions beyond the Western orbit. And such a conception of the classic should go beyond the classist philological origins, which I discussed in the preface, of the very word "classic."

Today we are rightly interested in a plurality of cultures and traditions. The historical field is being immeasurably enriched by the inclusion of new works by a variety of women and men. Some literary works will survive beyond the present moment and will be of continuing interest, and others will not. Their survival will depend upon many factors, including social relevance and their relationship to political and economic power structures, as well as on pure chance. But if particular works do survive, if they become recognized as classics, perhaps it will be because, at least in part, they possessed some of the qualities that I have tried to describe in this book.

APPENDIX: THE TEXT OF PINDAR'S *PYTHIAN* 3

PYTHIA III
ΙΕΡΩΝΙ ΣΥΡΑΚΟΣΙΩΙ ΚΕΛΗΤΙ

στρ. α΄   Ἤθελον Χίρωνά κε Φιλυρίδαν,
        εἰ χρεὼν τοῦθ᾽ ἁμετέρας ἀπὸ γλώσσας
           κοινὸν εὔξασθαι ἔπος,
        ζώειν τὸν ἀποιχόμενον,
        Οὐρανίδα γόνον εὐρυμέδοντα Κρόνου, βάσ-
           σαισί τ᾽ ἄρχειν Παλίου θῆρ᾽ ἀγρότερον
    5   νόον ἔχοντ᾽ ἀνδρῶν φίλον· οἷος ἐὼν θρέψεν ποτὲ
        τέκτονα νωδυνίας ἄμερον γυι-
           αρκέος Ἀσκλαπιόν,
        ἥροα παντοδαπᾶν ἀλκτῆρα νούσων.

ἀντ. α΄   τὸν μὲν εὐίππου Φλεγύα θυγάτηρ
        πρὶν τελέσσαι ματροπόλῳ σὺν Ἐλειθυί-
           ᾳ, δαμεῖσα χρυσέοις
   10   τόξοισιν ὑπ᾽ Ἀρτέμιδος
        εἰς Ἀΐδα δόμον ἐν θαλάμῳ κατέβα, τέ-
           χναις Ἀπόλλωνος. χόλος δ᾽ οὐκ ἀλίθιος
        γίνεται παίδων Διός. ἁ δ᾽ἀποφλαυρίξαισά νιν
        ἀμπλακίαισι φρενῶν, ἄλλον αἴνησεν γάμον κρύβδαν
           πατρός,
        πρόσθεν ἀκερσεκόμα μειχθεῖσα Φοίβῳ

ἐπ. α′   καὶ φέροισα σπέρμα θεοῦ καθαρόν·
16   οὐκ ἔμειν᾽ ἐλθεῖν τράπεζαν νυμφίαν,
    οὐδὲ παμφώνων ἰαχὰν ὑμεναίων, ἅλικες
    οἷα παρθένοι φιλέοισιν ἑταῖραι
    ἑσπερίαις ὑποκουρίζεσθ᾽ ἀοιδαῖς· ἀλλά τοι
20   ἤρατο τῶν ἀπεόντων· οἷα καὶ πολλοὶ πάθον.
    ἔστι δὲ φῦλον ἐν ἀνθρώποισι ματαιότατον,
    ὅστις αἰσχύνων ἐπιχώρια παπταίνει τὰ πόρσω,
    μεταμώνια θηρεύων ἀκράντοις ἐλπίσιν.

στρ. β′   ἔσχε τοι ταύταν μεγάλαν ἀυάταν
25   καλλιπέπλου λῆμα Κορωνίδος. ἐλθόν-
       τος γὰρ εὐνάσθη ξένου
    λέκτροισιν ἀπ᾽ Ἀρκαδίας.
    οὐδ᾽ ἔλαθε σκοπόν· ἐν δ᾽ ἄρα μηλοδόκῳ Πυ-
       θῶνι τόσσαις ἄϊεν ναοῦ βασιλεὺς
    Λοξίας, κοινᾶνι παρ᾽ εὐθυτάτῳ γνώμαν πιθών,
    πάντα ἴσαντι νόῳ· ψευδέων δ᾽ οὐχ
       ἅπτεται, κλέπτει τέ νιν
30   οὐ θεὸς οὐ βροτὸς ἔργοις οὔτε βουλαῖς.

ἀντ. β′   καὶ τότε γνοὺς Ἴσχυος Εἰλατίδα
    ξεινίαν κοίταν ἄθεμίν τε δόλον, πέμ-
       ψεν κασιγνήταν μένει
    θυίοισαν ἀμαιμακέτῳ
    ἐς Λακέρειαν, ἐπεὶ παρὰ Βοιβιάδος κρη-
       μνοῖσιν ᾤκει παρθένος· δαίμων δ᾽ ἕτερος
35   ἐς κακὸν τρέψαις ἐδαμάσσατό νιν, καὶ γειτόνων
    πολλοὶ ἐπαῦρον, ἅμα δ᾽ ἔφθαρεν· πολ-
       λὰν δ᾽ ὄρει πῦρ ἐξ ἑνὸς
    σπέρματος ἐνθορὸν ἀΐστωσεν ὕλαν.
ἐπ. β′   ἀλλ᾽ ἐπεὶ τείχει θέσαν ἐν ξυλίνῳ
    σύγγονοι κούραν, σέλας δ᾽ ἀμφέδραμεν
40   λάβρον Ἀφαίστου, τότ᾽ ἔειπεν Ἀπόλλων· "Οὐκέτι
    τλάσομαι ψυχᾷ γένος ἁμὸν ὀλέσσαι
    οἰκτροτάτῳ θανάτῳ ματρὸς βαρείᾳ σὺν πάθᾳ."
    ὣς φάτο· βάματι δ᾽ ἐν πρώτῳ κιχὼν παῖδ᾽ ἐκ νεκροῦ
    ἅρπασε· καιομένα δ᾽ αὐτῷ διέφαινε πυρά.
45   καί ῥά νιν Μάγνητι φέρων πόρε Κενταύρῳ διδάξαι
    πολυπήμονας ἀνθρώποισιν ἰᾶσθαι νόσους.

στρ. γ´   τοὺς μὲν ὦν, ὅσσοι μόλον αὐτοφύτων
   ἑλκέων ξυνάονες, ἢ πολιῷ χαλ-
    κῷ μέλη τετρωμένοι
   ἢ χερμάδι τηλεβόλῳ,
 50 ἢ θερινῷ πυρὶ περθόμενοι δέμας ἢ χει-
    μῶνι, λύσαις ἄλλον ἀλλοίων ἀχέων
   ἔξαγεν, τοὺς μὲν μαλακαῖς ἐπαοιδαῖς ἀμφέπων,
   τοὺς δὲ προσανέα πίνοντας, ἢ γυί-
    οις περάπτων πάντοθεν
   φάρμακα, τοὺς δὲ τομαῖς ἔστασεν ὀρθούς·

ἀντ. γ´   ἀλλὰ κέρδει καὶ σοφίᾳ δέδεται.
 55 ἔτραπεν καὶ κεῖνον ἀγάνορι μισθῷ
    χρυσὸς ἐν χερσὶν φανεὶς
   ἄνδρ᾿ ἐκ θανάτου κομίσαι
   ἤδη ἁλωκότα· χερσὶ δ᾿ ἄρα Κρονίων ῥί-
    ψαις δι᾿ ἀμφοῖν ἀμπνοὰν στέρνων κάθελεν
   ὠκέως, αἴθων δὲ κεραυνὸς ἐνέσκιμψεν μόρον.
   χρὴ τὰ ἐοικότα πὰρ δαιμόνων μα-
    στευέμεν θναταῖς φρασὶν
 60 γνόντα τὸ πὰρ ποδός, οἵας εἰμὲν αἴσας.

ἐπ. γ´   μή, φίλα ψυχά, βίον ἀθάνατον
   σπεῦδε, τὰν δ᾿ ἔμπρακτον ἄντλει μαχανάν.
   εἰ δὲ σώφρων ἄντρον ἔναι᾿ ἔτι Χίρων, καί τί οἱ
   φίλτρον ἐν θυμῷ μελιγάρυες ὕμνοι
 65 ἁμέτεροι τίθεν, ἰατῆρά τοί κέν νιν πίθον
   καί νυν ἐσλοῖσι παρασχεῖν ἀνδράσιν θερμᾶν νόσων
   ἤ τινα Λατοΐδα κεκλημένον ἢ πατέρος.
   καί κεν ἐν ναυσὶν μόλον Ἰονίαν τάμνων θάλασσαν
   Ἀρέθοισαν ἐπὶ κράναν παρ᾿ Αἰτναῖον ξένον.

στρ. δ´   ὅς Συρακόσσαισι νέμει βασιλεύς,
 71 πραῢς ἀστοῖς, οὐ φθονέων ἀγαθοῖς, ξεί-
    νοις δὲ θαυμαστὸς πατήρ.
   τῷ μὲν διδύμας χάριτας
   εἰ κατέβαν ὑγίειαν ἄγων χρυσέαν κῶ-
    μόν τ᾿ ἀέθλων Πυθίων αἴγλαν στεφάνοις,
   τοὺς ἀριστεύων Φερένικος ἕλεν Κίρρᾳ ποτέ,
 75 ἀστέρος οὐρανίου φαμὶ τηλαυ-
    γέστερον κείνῳ φάος
   ἐξικόμαν κε βαθὺν πόντον περάσαις.

ἀντ. δ´   ἀλλ᾽ ἐπεύξασθαι μὲν ἐγὼν ἐθέλω
      Ματρί, τὰν κοῦραι παρ᾽ ἐμὸν πρόθυρον σὺν
        Πανὶ μέλπονται θαμὰ
      σεμνὰν θεὸν ἐννύχιαι,
  80 εἰ δὲ λόγων συνέμεν κορυφάν, Ἱέρων, ὀρ-
        θὰν ἐπίστᾳ, μανθάνων οἶσθα προτέρων·
      ἓν παρ᾽ ἐσλὸν πήματα σύνδυο δαίονται βροτοῖς
      ἀθάνατοι. τὰ μὲν ὦν οὐ δύνανται
        νήπιοι κόσμῳ φέρειν,
      ἀλλ᾽ ἀγαθοί, τὰ καλὰ τρέψαντες ἔξω.

ἐπ. δ´   τὶν δὲ μοῖρ᾽ εὐδαιμονίας ἕπεται.
  85 λαγέταν γάρ τοι τύραννον δέρκεται,
      εἴ τιν᾽ ἀνθρώπων, ὁ μέγας πότμος. αἰὼν δ᾽ ἀσφαλὴς
      οὐκ ἔγεντ᾽ οὔτ᾽ Αἰακίδᾳ παρὰ Πηλεῖ
      οὔτε παρ᾽ ἀντιθέῳ Κάδμῳ· λέγονται μὰν βροτῶν
      ὄλβον ὑπέρτατον οἳ σχεῖν, οἵτε καὶ χρυσαμπύκων
  90 μελπομενᾶν ἐν ὄρει Μοισᾶν καὶ ἐν ἑπταπύλοις
      ἄϊον Θήβαις, ὁπόθ᾽ Ἁρμονίαν γᾶμεν βοῶπιν,
      ὁ δὲ Νηρέος εὐβούλου Θέτιν παῖδα κλυτάν.

στρ. ε´   καὶ θεοὶ δαίσαντο παρ᾽ ἀμφοτέροις
      καὶ Κρόνου παῖδας βασιλῆας ἴδον χρυ-
        σέαις ἐν ἕδραις, ἔδνα τε
  95 δέξαντο· Διὸς δὲ χάριν
      ἐκ προτέρων μεταμειψάμενοι καμάτων ἔ-
        στασαν ὀρθὰν καρδίαν. ἐν δ᾽ αὖτε χρόνῳ
      τὸν μὲν ὀξείαισι θύγατρες ἐρήμωσαν πάθαις
      εὐφροσύνας μέρος αἱ τρεῖς· ἀτὰρ λευκ-
        ωλένῳ γε Ζεὺς πατὴρ
      ἤλυθεν ἐς λέχος ἱμερτὸν Θυώνᾳ.

ἀντ. ε´   τοῦ δὲ παῖς, ὅνπερ μόνον ἀθανάτα
  101 τίκτεν ἐν Φθίᾳ Θέτις, ἐν πολέμῳ τό-
        ξοις ἀπὸ ψυχὰν λιπὼν
      ὦρσεν πυρὶ καιόμενος
      ἐκ Δαναῶν γόον. εἰ δὲ νόῳ τις ἔχει θνα-
        τῶν ἀλαθείας ὁδόν, χρὴ πρὸς μακάρων
      τυγχάνοντ᾽ εὖ πασχέμεν. ἄλλοτε δ᾽ ἀλλοῖαι πνοαὶ
  105 ὑψιπετᾶν ἀνέμων. ὄλβος οὐκ ἐς
        μακρὸν ἀνδρῶν ἔρχεται
      σῶς, πολὺς εὖτ᾽ ἂν ἐπιβρίσαις ἕπηται.

ἐπ. ε′   σμικρὸς ἐν σμικροῖς, μέγας ἐν μεγάλοις
         ἔσσομαι. τὸν δ᾽ ἀμφέποντ᾽ αἰεὶ φρασὶν
         δαίμον᾽ ἀσκήσω κατ᾽ ἐμὰν θεραπεύων μαχανάν.
110   εἰ δέ μοι πλοῦτον θεὸς ἁβρὸν ὀρέξαι,
         ἐλπίδ᾽ ἔχω κλέος εὑρέσθαι κεν ὑψηλὸν πρόσω.
         Νέστορα καὶ Λύκιον Σαρπαδόν᾽, ἀνθρώπων φάτις,
         ἐξ ἐπέων κελαδεννῶν, τέκτονες οἷα σοφοὶ
         ἅρμοσαν, γινώσκομεν· ἁ δ᾽ ἀρετὰ κλειναῖς ἀοιδαῖς
115   χρονία τελέθει· παύροις δὲ πράξασθ᾽ εὐμαρές.

INDEX

Abrams, M. H., 6, 122n.59
Apuleius, 247–62
    Apology, 255–56
    Metamorphoses, 248–62
    Metamorphoses, compared to *Odyssey*,
      250–51
    relation to Platonism, 254–58
Aristotle, 284
    Metaphysics, 14, 14–15n.18, 30n.49,
      52, 53
    Nicomachean Ethics, 53, 171–72, 271;
      equity in, 272; moral virtue, Aristotle
      defines in, 72–73; pity and fear in, 73
    Poetics, 63–77; astonishing incidents in
      epic and drama, 289–90; *katharsis*
      in, 71–76, 306; "rationalism" of, 64;
      tragedy defined in, 64–75
    reason (*nous*), 51–54
    relativism, critique of, 14
    Rhetoric, fear and pity in, 71
    stylistic appropriateness, 291
Auerbach, Erich, 248
    resolution between realism and eleva-
      tion in medieval literature, 287–88

Babbit, Irving, on Pindar as sober realist,
    88n.12
Baldry, H. C., discusses ecumenic human-
    kind, 241
Barbauld, Anna Laetitia, 104–5, 114–17
Bate, W. J., 17, 282
Batteux, Abbé, establishes modern concep-
    tion of the "fine arts," 181

Bloom, Allan, 60
Bloom, Harold, 18, 282
Bogel, Frederic V., 113n.50
Booth, Wayne, on Plato as "metaphoric"
    critic, 16n.23
Bromwich, David, discusses Derrida,
    10n.10
Bundy, Elroy L., 84, 86n.11, 99n.28, 161
Bunyan, John, *Pilgrim's Progress* com-
    pared to *Gulliver's Travels*, 56n.21
Butcher, S. H., 91n.15

Callimachus
    defends his own poetry in *Aetia*, 220–21
    influence on Virgil, 220
Casalio, G. B., on emotional effect of trag-
    edy, 75n.24
Cervantes, Miguel de, *Don Quixote* as re-
    action against mimetic literalism,
    279–80
Chrysostom, Dio, 289n.24
Cicero, on the need for rhetoric to turn
    from the particular to the universal,
    90n.15
"classic"
    author's definition of, xiii
    Chinese classic (*ching*), xi
    classicus scriptor, x
    enkrithentes, Alexandrian term for, xn.6
    political and social implications of, ix–
      xiii
Cohen, Gustav, 143–44n.34, 144
Cohen, Ralph, 28n.44

Date Due

DIS JUL 14 1995			
DIS DEC 5 1996			